FASHION ENTREPRENEURSHIP

fb

FASHION ENTREPRENEURSHIP
RETAIL BUSINESS
PLANNING SECOND EDITION

MICHELE M. GRANGER, EdD, ITAA
Missouri State University

TINA M. STERLING
President, T C Strategies

FAIRCHILD BOOKS NEW YORK

Executive Editor: Olga T. Kontzias
Assistant Acquisitions Editor: Amanda Breccia
Associate Development Editor: Lisa Vecchione
Creative Director: Carolyn Eckert
Assistant Art Director: Sarah Silberg
Production Director: Ginger Hillman
Senior Production Editor: Elizabeth Marotta
Project Manager: Monica Lugo
Copyeditor: Susan Hobbs
Ancillaries Editor: Noah Schwartzberg
Executive Director & General Manager: Michael Schluter
Associate Director of Sales: Melanie Sankel
Cover Design: Alicia Freile, Tango Media
Front cover art: Dinga/Veer; back cover art: Cultura Photography/Veer
Text Design: Sara Stemen
Page Layout: Precision Graphics
Photo Research: Jenn McKelvie

Illustrations and CD-ROM Design: Mike Miranda

First Edition, Copyright © 2003 Fairchild Publications, Inc.

Copyright © 2012 Fairchild Books, a division of Condé Nast Publications.

Library of Congress Catalog Card Number: 2011930934

ISBN: 978-1-60901-134-5

GST R 133004424

Printed in the United States of America

CH16, TP09

CONTENTS

EXTENDED CONTENTS

PREFACE

FASHION retail businesses are started every day by all kinds of people from all over the world. Some will fail, and others will succeed. The difference often lies in the quality of the planning process. We approached this joint venture with years of experience in owning businesses, consulting to entrepreneurs, and teaching fashion retail entrepreneurship to students and other future business owners. We shared a passion for the entrepreneur that led to an earnest vision of increasing the potential for success for aspiring, early-stage, and struggling entrepreneurs. This text is written for both college students and practitioners who desire to start their own retail businesses in the fashion industry. It is also developed for those fashion retailers who are already in business and who want to reexamine the direction of their companies. Although this book provides the structure for a carefully researched and well-developed business plan, it also offers the questions and the tools needed to direct an existing business toward a path of success and growth.

Entrepreneurship is a discipline like no other. It is an opportunity to act on dreams, become one's own boss, secure financial freedom, and share a passion with others. Owning a business requires an analysis of both personal and professional traits to determine if it is the right time to begin. After assessing one's self, the entrepreneur must analyze the business concept from a variety of angles, looking for its strengths, while seeking out its weaknesses with equal vigor. The challenges of business ownership are immense, but the rewards can surpass even the boldest dreams.

Although there are many textbooks on the market in both fashion and in entrepreneurship, few combine both disciplines. It became apparent to us that a book was needed to guide the reader through a sequential, step-by-step approach to starting a business, with robust and engaging business and financial planning templates that would allow for the application of knowledge to real-life goals as they relate to the business. Readers are introduced to the various components of the business, are provided with the opportunity to practice what they have learned, and are encouraged to use the business plan template and financial planning template on the CD-ROM to apply that knowledge to their individual business concepts.

We have designed this new edition to be less about presenting and explaining theory and more about assessing and applying practices and procedures. We have replaced an examination of the ideal situation for a fashion retail business with a practical, real-world approach that asks, "What happens in everyday life that impacts the success of this kind of business? What makes a fashion retail business work, and what does not?" This approach focuses on the specific tasks of the entrepreneur, such as identifying a viable target market through research, appealing to and securing customers, selecting a location, recruiting and retaining great employees, and determining how much stock to carry and how to sell it.

What makes this book distinctive is its real-world application through chapter readings, boxes connecting chapter content to the actual business plan, and discussion topics and activities. Industry terminology, recommended resources, suggested Web sites, and profiles of entrepreneurs are provided at the conclusion of each chapter. Entrepreneurs are as diverse as fashion itself; therefore, the profiles and examples within the text were selected from companies of varying sizes in diverse locations, started by entrepreneurs from an array of backgrounds.

A sample business plan is included as Appendix D. The company represented by the sample business plan, RealWomen, Inc., and its owner, Lucy Rich, are presented in the plan's Introduction. Throughout the text, RealWomen, Inc., is used as an example to illustrate such concepts as determining a business concept, selecting a location, and developing a merchandise assortment. As each chapter is read, the student/reader is encouraged to examine the corresponding section of the RealWomen, Inc., sample business plan; these sections are specified in the Business Plan Connection at the conclusion of each chapter. Seeing how the owner of RealWomen, Inc., completed that specific component of the business plan provides a model for completing one's individual business plan sequentially as the content of the text is read and applied.

The accompanying CD-ROM is the place for the individual business plan to be constructed. Each chapter in the text contains a Business Plan Connection that directs the reader to the parts of the business plan template that relate directly to the chapter. The CD-ROM contains both a blank business plan template and a financial planning template to be used for each section of the individual business plan. The business plan template on the CD-ROM (also available in Appendix E in this text) provides sections for the writer—the prospective entrepreneur—to provide an in-depth analysis of the potential retail business, from defining the target

market, to clarifying the product assortment, to selecting a location, to solidifying operational issues related to merchandising, personnel, and control. Throughout the process, the business concept is continually weighed against the target market to ensure that it has the potential to capture a large enough segment to make a profit. The financial planning template on the CD-ROM provides an Excel spreadsheet embedded with the formulas needed to enter and evaluate the start-up costs, monthly expenses, planned sales and inventory, markdowns and markups on stock, and general profitability of the potential business. The financial planning template enables flexibility in the planning stage. The entrepreneur may compare, for example, monthly lease prices before actually selecting a location. The final, completed financial plan will be submitted as part of the final business plan.

The content of this text is rooted in the real world and has been refined in the classroom. As it aims to generate skills and foster awareness, and build knowledge, the content is presented sequentially as it relates to building a business. Chapter 1 investigates the personal and professional characteristics of the entrepreneur as well as timing and opportunity. Chapter 2 describes developing a road map for success through an effective business plan. Chapter 3 focuses on developing the business concept by asking the questions, "What will the business be?" and "How will it be differentiated from others?" In Chapter 3, researching the industry, the market, and competition is explored. In Chapter 4 the product and the business concept are examined in terms of product terminology, product levels, the product life cycle, branding, and licensing.

Creating an environment in which to sell the selected product to the defined target market is outlined in seven chapters. Chapter 5 explores planning a strategy to open a business, including the choice of starting a new business from the ground up, purchasing a franchise operation, or acquiring an existing business. Chapter 6 focuses on finding the right location for the business, whether building a new facility or buying or leasing an existing space. The business location is examined from the outside in through discussion of exterior and interior options and accompanying decisions to be made. In Chapter 7, building a business using the Web is discussed, from a brick-and-mortar retail operation having a Web presence to a full e-commerce business. Chapter 8 examines market penetration, determining the most effective ways to reach the intended customer. In Chapter 9 the entrepreneur examines his or her skills, experience, and education to identify what or who it will take to build a strong management team. Planning the merchandise assortment is the subject of Chapter 10. The role of the buyer, the functions of a resident buying office (or consulting service), internal and external sources from which the merchandiser can collect buying information, and merchandising calculations used in fashion buying are presented. Chapter 11 focuses on the financial aspects of the business. Students learn the implications of buying, hiring, and how to manage the money. Chapter 12 offers guidance for developing operating and control systems for the business, from space allocation and inventory control to employee development and business security.

The world is ever changing. Markets shift, consumer buying behaviors change, technology advances, and the best way to do business is always a topic on the table. We approached this second edition challenged and invigorated with the goals of bringing forth tried and true expertise, the most current information, and new tools to simplify the business and financial planning needs. The challenges and opportunities in the global economy, and how we do business based on social media and the Web, have changed the face of entrepreneurship. Change is integral in building a business. We support and applaud the bold and the brave, the entrepreneurs. Victor Kiam describes them well: "Entrepreneurs are risk takers, willing to roll the dice with their money or reputation on the line in support of an idea or enterprise. They willingly assume responsibility for the success or failure of a venture and are answerable for all its facets."[1] For those who are entrepreneurs still seeking their openings, Richard Branson, the founder of Virgin Enterprises, offers encouragement: "Business opportunities are like buses. There's always another one coming."[2]

ACKNOWLEDGMENTS

WRITING a book can be a lonely process. Being an entrepreneur means striking out on your own, communicating your vision, and selling the idea. Fashion and business are often perceived as direct opposites, when, in fact, they are not.

This project found the best in all of these assumptions. Writing was not solitary, thanks to a partnership and the encouragement of family and friends. The entrepreneurial spirit was shining as we created this business called a book. Fashion merged with business in a fascinating, pragmatic, and unique manner.

MICHELE:

I am most grateful to my daughter, Annie, for supporting one more book. She is all I dreamt she would be. I wish for her the independence, true satisfaction, and excitement that an entrepreneurial life can bring. I would also like to express special thanks to the wonderful women of The Cool Girl Club—Carolyn, Debbie, Karla, Marci, LeAnn, LaRaine, Linda, Patty, and Randee—for their love and support. At Missouri State University I am fortunate to work with students who share my enthusiasm for the fashion industry and who inspire me to do and be my best. I thank my parents for nurturing an entrepreneurial

spirit, one that can be found in all three of their children and the work they have chosen. To my coauthor, Tina, I have learned to appreciate friendship, patience, and perspective—rewards of true collaboration.

TINA:

As an entrepreneur, you recognize that no project or entrepreneur works in isolation; it is friends, family, and colleagues who provide you with the insight, knowledge, and support to continue to move forward and strive for greatness.

I wish to thank my wonderful daughter, Sierra, for her ongoing love and encouragement. I couldn't be more proud of the person she's grown to be—compassionate, kind, giving, and resilient. I wish for her a lifetime of happiness. To my mom, my late father, my sister (who, by the way, wants a copy of the book, but laughingly says she'll never read it), and my brother, I thank them for their love and support. I thank Alan for his love, friendship, and support—for being by my side through the highs and the sometime challenges of the process. I want to thank Ron for his friendship and for pushing me forward when I needed an extra push; and Peter, whose long-time encouragement gave me the courage to pursue entrepreneurship many years ago, to fulfill my dreams.

And thanks to my many brilliant and devoted friends—Paula Amanda, Cheryl DeAngelo, Donna Duffey, Cheryl Gracie, Jami Henry, Jeff Horvath, Kelly and David Kuhn, Kim March, Kay Saunders, Leslee Terpay, Nancie Thomas, and Stefanie Weaver—who approach life with an entrepreneurial spirit and character that have had a significant impact not just on my life, but also on the quality of life for others.

To my coauthor, Michele, thank you for your friendship, understanding, and patience as we pursued this wonderful venture.

Michele and Tina also wish to thank Ron Mueller, of the Small Business Development Center, in St. Charles, Missouri, and Donna Duffey, of Johnson County Community College, for their knowledge, input, and review. Both are instrumental in the development of the accompanying financial plan template. We wish to thank the reviewers of the first edition: Leo Archembault, Mount Ida College; Rebecca Green, Stephen Austin State University; Mary Mhango, Marshall University; Karen Robinette, California State University–Northridge; and Lucy Simpson, the University of Tennessee. We thank Jenn McKelvie for her excellent work in sourcing the visuals that have made the text come to life. We thank Travis Reed for his contributions to Chapter 7. We thank all the brave entrepreneurs who have shared their stories, insights, and experience throughout this text. Finally, to our executive editor, Olga Kontzias, our deep appreciation for keeping the entrepreneurial spirit alive through the books and the authors that she supports and grows.

HOW TO USE THE CD-ROM

FASHION *Entrepreneurship: Retail Business Planning,* Second Edition, includes a CD-ROM, which can be found on the inside front cover of this book. The "Templates" folder on the CD-ROM includes the following important documents: business plan template instructions, a blank business plan template, and a financial planning template. The CD-ROM also includes electronic files for the assignments that appear at the end of each chapter. These files were developed for direct application to the chapters in the text, with the goal of creating a complete and financially stable business plan. (See also the Table of Contents on the CD-ROM where you have the option of linking to Word files or pdfs).

BUSINESS PLAN TEMPLATE OVERVIEW

The business plan is a reflection of the research, analysis, and objectivity the entrepreneur has committed to the proposed concept. The value of the business plan lies (1) in the process behind it—the commitment to evaluate the probability of success objectively and (2) the ability to communicate that knowledge to others. It provides headings and subheadings to guide the reader to the content of each stage of the plan. A description of the content is included under each heading and subheading. The descriptions are designed to ensure that key issues are addressed—those that have significant impact on the success or failure of a new business venture. (Please also refer to Appendix D in this book for a sample of a completed business plan. Appendix E is the hard copy version of the blank business plan template that appers on the CD-ROM.)

The content of the chapters in *Fashion Entrepreneurship* provide the tools to complete the blank business plan and financial planning templates. At the end of each chapter is a section titled Business Plan Connection. The assignments within this feature, indicated by a CD-ROM icon, direct the reader to the appropriate sections of the business plan or financial planning template. Later chapters may direct the reader back to sections of the plan templates addressed in earlier chapters—for example, part of the marketing plan is completed after reading Chapter 3. The remainder of the marketing plan is completed after reading Chapter 8.

Please use the business plan template instructions as a guide for completing your business plan. It may be necessary to include additional headings or delete others, depending on the nature of the business concept. Before you begin, please do the following:

1. Go to the "Templates" folder on the CD-ROM and save the business plan template instructions and

the blank business plan template to your desktop. Please note that you cannot save changes to this CD-ROM.

2. Before you create your business plan, open and carefully read the business plan template instructions.

3. After reading the instructions, open the blank business plan template. You will use this document to create your own business plan. This template also relates directly to the Business Plan Connection assignments in this book.

4. As you read each chapter, go to your saved business plan template file and click on the appropriate part of the plan, as directed by the assignment.

5. Save your work frequently to avoid losing hours of hard work.

6. Turn in your statement, as directed by your instructor.

Please also refer to Table I.1 in the "How-to-Use the CD-ROM" folder on the CD-ROM. This table describes the components of the business plan and related chapters in this book.

FINANCIAL PLANNING TEMPLATE OVERVIEW

The financial planning template is provided to eliminate hours of time in preparing the financial statements to support the business and to help ensure accuracy in calculating the financials. The template begins with a series of worksheets and ends with a set of financial statements. The financial statements will accompany your business plan.

If you are instructed to complete more than one year's financial statements, you must save the financial plan template for each year you are instructed to complete. The template is designed to prepare financials for only one year at a time.

The worksheets are presented in a required sequence and must be completed in the order in which they are presented. The template allows you to go back to the various worksheets and make changes later if necessary.

As each worksheet is completed, the numbers are carried through to the appropriate financial statement—the monthly income statement, the monthly cash flow statement, the income statement, and the balance sheet.

Each worksheet begins with a "how to" to assist you in completing that particular worksheet. Be sure to read each of these sections carefully before beginning.

Important: The financial planning template is not designed to add or remove columns or rows. Doing so may corrupt the calculations throughout the template. Enter only positive numbers without commas.

To use the financial planning template:

1. Go to the "Templates" folder on the CD-ROM and open the financial planning template.

2. Save the financial planning template to your computer. You will use this document to develop your financial plan.

3. Go to the saved file and click on the appropriate worksheet, as directed by the assignment.

4. Finish the assignment and save the file.

5. Turn in your statement, as directed by your instructor.

INTRODUCTION
CASE STUDY: REALWOMEN, INC.

YOU may know someone like Lucy Rich, or you may have something in common with her. From a professional perspective, Lucy is a college graduate and an eight-year veteran of the fashion industry, having worked in sales, management, and buying in such positions as a buyer for Saks Fifth Avenue, an assistant manager for Lane Bryant, and a public relations assistant for Showroom Seven. From a personal perspective, Lucy is bright, independent, and driven. She is an aspiring entrepreneur.

Lucy Rich has dreamt of owning her own business since high school, when she worked in a specialty apparel and accessories store owned by a successful entrepreneur. Throughout college and postgraduate employment, Lucy has been learning and planning, preparing to open her own business some day. She chose employment positions that would broaden her background in customer service, employee relations, promotion, and retail buying. She saved her money. She is mobile and ready to go where her business dream will have the greatest opportunity for success. Lucy is now ready—professionally, personally, and financially—to take the plunge and follow her dream by opening her own retail store.

RealWomen, Inc., is the name she has chosen for her business. She has recently finished preparing the business plan that she will present to bankers and other funders to acquire the capital she needs to open her store. After completing months of research and discarding a couple of business concepts, Lucy has determined to open a specialty store offering contemporary apparel for women sized 11/12 to 19/20 who desire fashion at affordable prices. The merchandise assortment will consist of clothing and accessories suitable for business, university, and casual activities. From a business perspective, providing large-size fashions for contemporary women makes sense. The customer base is increasing. Government reports indicate that more than 17 percent of teenagers are large size, more than three times the rate of a generation ago. The market for contemporary plus sizes (the consumer segment typically aged 18 to 35) has shown strong growth. Research indicates that six of every ten women wear a size 12 or larger and that half of all American women are size 14 or larger, with nearly a third at size 16 or above. Despite these statistics, fashion apparel stores have limited styles and selections for the larger-size woman.

Lucy has taken the same path you will follow as you read through this text. She read each chapter, reviewed the suggested resources, carried out the assignments, discussed the related topics with business associates and consultants, contemplated the Business Connection content at the end of each chapter, and completed the blank business plan and financial planning templates on the CD-ROM, step by step. The results of her extensive work in developing a top-notch business plan are included in Appendix D.

A review of some of her work on the business plan as it relates to each chapter follows:

» Chapter 1, "Becoming a Fashion Retail Entrepreneur," does not have an actual place in the business plan; it does, however, provide background through discussion of the successful entrepreneur, trends in entrepreneurship, and self-assessment for the prospective entrepreneur and the business concept. Lucy carefully read this chapter with notebook in hand. She listed her strengths and weaknesses and noted those areas in which she would need assistance. She also checked her résumé against the content of the chapter in order to emphasize the skills and experiences that bankers or other funders would be seeking.

» Chapter 2, "Developing a Road Map for Success," examines the reasons for developing a business plan and how the plan is structured. Lucy used the information in this chapter to organize working files for each part of the business plan.

» Chapter 3, "Analyzing the Industry and Finding Customers," focuses on market research. Although, she had completed much work in the area of market research, Lucy located additional resources to add national statistical data to her market research materials.

» Chapter 4, "Identifying the Product and the Business Concept," explores types of products, the product life cycle, and branding to help communicate the business concept clearly. At this point in her reading, Lucy began to visualize her business concept from a product perspective and focused on locating branded merchandise lines that would meet her customers' need in terms of fashion and

price, while projecting the image she desired for her store.

» Chapter 5, "Planning a Strategy to Open a Business," presents the three main entry strategies for opening a fashion retail business: starting a new business, buying an existing one, and opening a franchise. Lucy analyzed her business concept and determined that starting a new business was the only option for her, as franchise and existing store operations matching her concept were nearly nonexistent.

» Chapter 6, "Finding the Right Location for the Business," examines location variables and costs, from region to site, inside and out. After studying the chapter content, Lucy found a home for her business—a college town.

» Chapter 7, "Building a Business Using the Web," discusses e-business models and methods of integrating promotional and retailing e-commerce activities into the business. Lucy's plan to introduce the business online through a Web site and social media was validated after reviewing the material on e-businesses.

» Chapter 8, "Reaching Customers and Driving Sales," investigates how to name the business and how to market it. Lucy learned that her industry experience in promotion and public relations gave her an edge as she developed a list of promotional plans for RealWomen, Inc.

» Chapter 9, "Building a Team to Drive Success," focuses on the management of the business and human resource development. At this point, Lucy decided to hire an assistant manager. To complement her work experience, and fill in the voids, she decided to search for someone with experience in the fields of marketing and advertising for a retail clothing store as well as the daily operations of a retail apparel and accessories store.

» Chapter 10, "Planning the Merchandise Assortment," discusses the role of the buyer, the resident buying or consulting office, sources for effective buying, and merchandising calculations. Lucy's previous employment as a retail buyer helped her understand the buying process and led her to developing Excel spreadsheets to track merchandise receipts and on-order, calculate open-to-buy, and maintain an updated six-month plan.

» Chapter 11, "Building the Financial Plan," presents the financial statements (cash flow statement, income statement, and balance sheet) and explains how to use the financial planning template. Lucy used the content in this chapter and the financial planning template on the CD-ROM to develop the full financial plan for her business plan.

» Chapter 12, "Developing Operating and Control Systems," provides information needed to build these systems and to construct operations, control, and employee manuals. Lucy had viewed the business from every possible perspective while working her way through the chapters, so she was ready to develop operations and control policies for the business as well as a manual for her future employees.

The following sections of Lucy Rich's business plan for RealWomen, Inc., are located in Appendix D:

» Cover Page (see page 302)

» Table of Contents (see page 304)

» Executive Summary (see pages 305)

» Management Plan (see pages 306–307)

» Merchandising/Product Plan (see pages 308–309)

» Brick-and-Mortar Location Plan (see pages 310–311)

» Web Plan Summary (see pages 312)

» Marketing Plan (see pages 313–316)

» Financial Plan (see pages 317–318)

» Retail Operations Plan (see pages 323–324)

As you read each chapter, take time to read the section of the sample business plan that corresponds with that particular chapter. It is extremely helpful to see an example, a model, of how the chapter content can be applied to an actual business plan. By the way, Lucy Rich's dream has come true. RealWomen, Inc., is off and running; it is a huge success.

CHAPTER 1
BECOMING A FASHION RETAIL ENTREPRENEUR

OBJECTIVES

» Understand the concept of entrepreneurship.

» Identify characteristics of a successful entrepreneur.

» Recognize entrepreneurial competencies within yourself.

» Establish a personal vision as a prospective entrepreneur.

» Explain the importance of the planning process in developing and opening a business.

THIS chapter begins by developing an understanding of entrepreneurship. A self-analysis is conducted of the entrepreneurial mindset and skills. Defining and knowing the traits possessed by already successful entrepreneurs increases the chances of success for new entrepreneurs. Next, timing and funding availability are examined. Timing and funding play crucial roles in the process of determining whether or not to start a business. The prospective fashion entrepreneur then begins developing the business concept. The business concept takes the idea for a business and tests it against social, political, financial, and economic realities before the actual business venture is begun. Finally, the prospective entrepreneur looks at the importance of developing a comprehensive business plan.

THE ENTREPRENEURIAL PROFILE

The fashion industry is increasingly recognizing that entrepreneurial skills are an important component of the fashion entrepreneur's portfolio of knowledge and skills. What is an **entrepreneur**? Many views exist on the definition of an entrepreneur. Some define an entrepreneur as one who creates a product on his or her own account. But this raises questions. Does just creating a product make you an entrepreneur if you never do anything with it? What if you take someone's product and make it a success? Investorwords, a set of definitions of financial terms, defines an entrepreneur as "an individual who starts his/her own business."[1] But limiting the definition to someone starting a business implies that when a business is no longer in the start-up phase, it no longer is entrepreneurial.

1

An entrepreneur can also be defined as a person who creates and manages a business venture, assuming all the risk for the sake of profit. This may suggest that the motivation for starting a business is purely profit. Although profit is at the top of the list for most entrepreneurs, businesses are started for many reasons. Some people create businesses out of necessity after they lose their job. Others start companies because they feel excitement in creating a new method of retailing for the market. Here, an entrepreneur is someone who decides to take control of his or her future and become self-employed either by creating a unique business or by working as a member of a team, as in multilevel marketing. Entrepreneurs see themselves as the driving force and believe that success or failure lies within their personal control or influence.

None of the previous definitions is wrong. As the entrepreneurial alternative becomes more prevalent, the definition will evolve. Entrepreneurship may be more clearly defined by people's traits, strengths, and weaknesses, and by comparisons of many definitions and views. Jeffrey A. Timmons, one of the pioneers in the development of entrepreneurship education and research in the United States, defines an entrepreneur and entrepreneurship in the following terms: "Entrepreneurship is a way of thinking, reasoning, and acting that is opportunity obsessed, holistic in approach, and leadership balanced."[2]

Fashion entrepreneurs recognize an opportunity. They size up its value as well as the resources necessary to make that opportunity a success. They are visionaries. They have a vision of how the business will grow, and they have the drive to make it happen. Fashion entrepreneurs are always looking for better and innovative ways to find new markets, to add to an existing product line, and to tap into larger geographic territories. They move with the times or, more often than not, before the times. They are futurists in that they anticipate and embrace change. They see different ways of doing things. E-commerce, for example, becomes a welcome challenge, not something to be feared and rejected. Fashion entrepreneurs persevere and are not easily defeated. They thrive in a challenging environment and have a tremendous need to be in

control. They will take calculated risks and welcome responsibility. They are absolutely passionate about what they do.

Polyvore, founded by the entrepreneurs Pasha Sadri, Jianing Hu, and Guangwei Yuan, is a user-generated fashion magazine filled with user-generated ads. Consumers are able to create collages featuring pictures of clothes, accessories, and models from across the Web. Readers view the collages, which the site refers to as sets, and by clicking on a dress or necklace, they are taken to the Web site that sells it. By June 2009, Polyvore was attracting more than 835,000 unique visitors per month, almost 25 percent more traffic than for Style.com or InStyle.com. Many fashion companies are promoting their collections through Polyvore.[3] FIGURE 1.1 shows a Polyvore set.

Fashion retail entrepreneurs are the key people managing the entrepreneurial process; they are the driving force. They see an opportunity, are innovative

FIGURE 1.1

Polyvore takes an innovative approach to online buying by letting fans play stylist and create their own "magazine" pages.

in their thinking, and possess the business acumen to make things happen. For the fashion entrepreneur, the fashion retail store is the "window" to the consumer. Whether a Web site or a brick-and-mortar store, the fashion entrepreneur sizes up the market and then buys, sells, and displays fashion merchandise that will entice customers to make purchases.

A TIME FOR FASHION ENTREPRENEURS: TODAY'S ENVIRONMENT

In today's economy, entrepreneurship is at the forefront of options for fashion students. It is challenging and ever changing. Each new day brings a new set of rewards and obstacles. By recognizing opportunity, fashion entrepreneurs emerge as some of the most successful business people in the world. Understanding entrepreneurship, owning a business, understanding how that business works, planning it carefully, and knowing one's personal qualities will increase the chances of success.

Entrepreneurial businesses contribute to local economies, provide jobs, pay taxes, and generate a comfortable living for their owners. Today's economic climate and lifestyle preferences, as well as education and business trends, encourage and nurture entrepreneurship. Approximately 650,000 new businesses are opened each year. Hundreds of thousands of college graduates, corporate executives, retirees, and individuals interested in career changes are striking out on their own. These businesses have been the key to survival for individuals affected by corporate downsizing, outsourcing (contracting for services), and restructuring. The age of the entrepreneur provides opportunities for individuals from every imaginable background and category: male, female; young, old; rich, poor. It provides an abundance of opportunities for the fashion retailer.

Entrepreneurship is in an upward trend both nationally and internationally. With the growth of e-commerce, the number of **virtual companies**— companies offering goods and services on the Internet—has increased the opportunity for small businesses to increase sales and tap into global markets.

Technology has made it possible for companies to accomplish more and reach more markets with fewer employees. Thanks to entrepreneurs, technology is driving much of the world's economic growth. Research has projected that small companies can respond quickly to change, thus creating a competitive advantage over larger companies. Entrepreneurs play a key role in our economy from a macroeconomic perspective, owing in large part to their role in the growth of the Internet. Companies such as Gilt Groupe, Hautelook Couture (FIGURE 1.2), Zappos, Shopbop, and Bag

FIGURE 1.2

HauteLook.com is an online retail store offering up to 75 percent off the retail price of designer brands. Each day, HauteLook notifies members of the latest sales. Membership is free, but the invitation to join creates a level of exclusivity and plays a significant role.

Borrow or Steal are increasing purchasing (or leasing) options for consumers across the globe.

To the fashion retail student, the study of entrepreneurship can play an important role in future career opportunities. Studying the field of entrepreneurship provides the chance to deal with change on a daily basis, to study all aspects of the business, and to become familiar with entrepreneurs throughout the world. Even those seeking traditional business careers will require knowledge of various aspects of business in order to be successful. Many companies are encouraging their employees to have an entrepreneurial mindset: innovative and creative and recognizing opportunity. The entrepreneurial spirit keeps the company at the leading edge of technology and diminishes bureaucracy. Many fashion retail entrepreneurs work within a fashion company, using their entrepreneurial skills, before venturing into their own fashion business.

FASHION TRENDS LEAD TO ENTREPRENEURIAL OPPORTUNITIES

What is the future of the fashion industry? What trends and issues are having an impact on the direction of entrepreneurial business in apparel and soft goods? It is important to be aware not just of trends in the fashion industry, but also with the ways in which people buy, how they think, and what is driving buying decisions.

Entrepreneur magazine reported on "10 [and 1/2] *Trends to Watch for 2010.*" Among them: the senior market. Businesses associated with aging, including the cosmeceuticals (cosmetics that have or are purported to have medical properties) industry, are growing at a rapid rate (FIGURE 1.3).

Another trend to watch is discount retail:

Everyone's eating lower on the food chain these days. Consumer spending is down more than 30 percent from this time last year, to an average of $57 a day, according to a Gallup poll. And even those who can still afford to spend are beset by "luxury shame," which means high-end retailers

are out, and discount shopping is in. Walmart's earnings increased more than 5 percent this year, whereas Neiman Marcus reported a 14.8 percent drop in sales. And the dollar store? Long the domain of low-income shoppers and random cheapskates, dollar stores are doing brisk business with the middle class. Family Dollar saw record net income in 2009. It jumped 25 percent, to $291.3 million.

Another hand-me-down from the weak economy is the resale shop. In 2009, second-hand shops increased revenue by $223.3 million, according to IbisWorld. The National Association of Resale Professionals reports that secondhand stores had an average 31 percent increase in business this year alone. Uptown Cheapskate—a fledgling fashion-centric resale exchange franchise—opened two locations this year, with four more on the way.[4]

Consumer trend watching has become as important as fashion trend watching in this industry. Casual

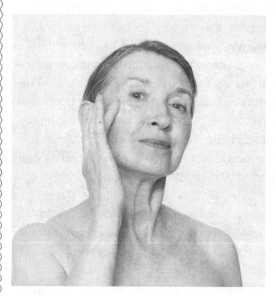

FIGURE 1.3

The increasing desire of consumers to look good, coupled with an aging population and the growing availability of high-performance cosmetics, is driving growth in the cosmeceutical industry.

dressing in the workplace, a lack of interest or knowledge of apparel quality, the resistance by manufacturers to gamble on fashion chances—these issues influence the apparel and soft goods industry. They will surely cause the death of some companies, while at the same time providing opportunities for new businesses. The successful entrepreneur identifies the trends and then translates them into business opportunities.

DO YOU HAVE WHAT IT TAKES?

Researchers and academicians continually argue whether entrepreneurs are born or made. What is important is the drive to take the entrepreneurial path. Entrepreneurs are innovative and creative. They see what others do not see and arrive at a variety of solutions to meet a need or solve a problem (FIGURE 1.4).

The retail industry requires that businesses be both people oriented and service oriented. This entails juggling both satisfied and dissatisfied customers, maintaining merchandise that sells, and keeping an eye on costs and prices. Retail success requires the effective combination of attractive layout and design, great customer service, and attention to detail. It requires a flair for selecting appealing merchandise that is priced for the right market, at the

FIGURE 1.4
Entrepreneurs are driven to fulfill the dream of owning their own business.

right time. It requires creativity and understanding of finance—that is, both left-brain and right-brain characteristics. Most important, retail success is predicated on an understanding of what customers need and want in order to create an atmosphere that will sell, sell, sell. The mindset of an entrepreneur approaches this head-on.

ADVANTAGES AND DISADVANTAGES OF OWNING YOUR OWN BUSINESS

Retailing can provide an opportunity to meet new people, develop a successful business team, travel for business, and contribute to one's community as an economic entity. Most important, it can provide the opportunity for financial success and independence from working for someone else.

There are both advantages and disadvantages to starting a fashion retail business.

Advantages:

» You can be your own boss and control the outcome of your venture.

» You have the freedom to pursue opportunities as you identify them. No one tells you what to do or when.

» You receive the recognition for the design of your store and the products it sells.

» Opportunities exist to maximize the return on your investment, whether in time or money, or both.

Disadvantages:

» Any entrepreneurial venture requires a huge time commitment, particularly in the start-up phase.

» Start-up ventures typically scramble for funds and work on tight budgets. This impacts the ability to travel to trade shows, utilize the latest technology, and bring in teams to build the business.

» Entrepreneurs are faced with juggling resources to meet deadlines and customer expectations. Problem solving is an everyday occurrence.

» Because start-up businesses often lack sufficient funds to hire a team, much of the work—often, every job—is performed by the entrepreneur. This leaves little time to focus on one particular area.

Starting a fashion retail business requires a commitment of both time and money. Those retailer entrepreneurs that have the greatest chance of success are skilled at small business management and project management. They possess a high level of interpersonal skills, such as effective communication, getting along with others, leading teams effectively, listening, and resolving conflict. Some common fatal mistakes made by retailers are given in Box 1.1.

TRAITS OF SUCCESSFUL ENTREPRENEURS

Although the need exists to understand the competitive, economic, and cultural climates in the retail industry, it is just as important to assess and understand one's personal traits, skill, and needs. Entrepreneurship requires a particular way of thinking and acting. As stated earlier, entrepreneurs, above others, are innovative and visionary and are creative in their thinking. Entrepreneurs seem to solve problems, in part, based on intuition. They are successful communicators; they develop a strong network of contacts. They have the ability to utilize resources more efficiently. Entrepreneurs are passionate, enthusiastic individuals. By observing both successful and unsuccessful entrepreneurs, you will find a wide range of personalities. Although special talent and self-discipline come naturally to some, to others, these characteristics must be learned.

Numerous studies have been conducted to analyze the differences in traits between successful and not-so-successful entrepreneurs. In the challenging world of the entrepreneur, chances of success increase dramatically if the prospective entrepreneur begins by understanding who he or she is. The following discussion covers some of the traits that research has shown are possessed by successful entrepreneurs.

Passion/Desire

Perhaps the most important of all the traits successful fashion retail entrepreneurs possess is passion. Unquestionably, the successful entrepreneur has the passion to be one. The fashion entrepreneur also relishes sharing that passion and desire with others. Entrepreneurs are driven to succeed. Many have determined that they cannot work for others; they want to be their own boss. When people are passionate about what they are doing, tasks seem relatively timeless and effortless. Launching a new venture requires long hours and many challenges.

Determination/Perseverance

Fashion entrepreneurs are determined. They want to succeed and do not give up easily, even when it may appeal to others to do so. Determination is a key factor in a winning attitude. The role of the entrepreneur requires the ability to persevere in the toughest of times. Successful entrepreneurs will figure out the path they need to take to reach their goals and challenge all obstacles blocking those paths. Establishing a successful business takes time. Most entrepreneurs acknowledge that it takes four to five years before the money starts rolling in and the hours decrease to a manageable level.

Responsibility

Many fashion retail entrepreneurs say that they believe one of the keys to their success was their willingness to take responsibility for themselves, their employees, and their businesses. Owning a business provides entrepreneurs with the freedom to make decisions independently, to make things happen, and to influence and determine outcomes, but with that comes taking ownership of one's actions.

Problem Solvers

To entrepreneurs, problem solving and decision making come naturally. Entrepreneurs are innovative in their thinking because they determine the best ways to overcome a problem or obstacle. They will solicit input from their team and stakeholders and process

BOX 1.1
FIVE FATAL MISTAKES FOR SMALL BUSINESS RETAILING

In today's fast-moving and ever-changing business environment, mistakes can be fatal. Even at best, statistics show that about half of small businesses last less than two years. My twenty-plus years of successfully operating several retail stores have made me a keen observer of the retail scene, and more important, the mistakes made by many retailers that have, in many cases, caused their demise. Even though the list of potential mistakes that retailers can make is long, I have found these five to be some of the most frequent and devastating.

1. Failure to plan effectively and objectively: Many new retailers plunge into business with little more than a prayer and a lot of optimism. Take time to prepare a business plan and estimate your financial needs. Nothing kills a retail business quicker than underfunding. Planning should also include location, your market demographics, and your product line.

2. Focusing on products and not the market: I've seen stores slowly stagnate because the owner stubbornly hangs on to a product or product line, even though the market has passed them by. You're in business to make a profit, not to sell a particular widget. Don't become married to your products. A word of caution is appropriate here: You shouldn't arbitrarily dump a product line because of seasonal or occasional setbacks. There are ways to update your product lines without ditching them entirely. For example, if you run a gift shop that carries home decor products, you need to update your product offerings regularly to stay in step with changing decorating styles.

Small retailers cannot effectively compete with big-box retailers and the Internet on many standard over-the-counter products such as small appliances and electronics and should concentrate instead on more individualized products and services. You can offer more personal service and more choices on custom-made and one-of-a-kind products, such as lamps, rugs, furniture, and locally produced merchandise.

Astute entrepreneurs plan, change with the market, and are objective in their research. Anything short of this can lead to undesired results.

3. Failure to change with the market environment: This is somewhat related to the previous point, but it's focused more on selling methods and media. Only a few years ago, movies were rented and returned at local video stores. Today, they're mostly rented online and/or by mail, or by downloading them directly to your computer. The latest trend is the $1 movie rental and return boxes at fast-food restaurants. The Internet has dramatically changed many of our shopping practices, and customers are demanding more specialized and customized products and services, as well as comfortable venues in which to shop. Selling standard products off the rack from a plain-vanilla store environment rarely works anymore.

4. Underestimating the demands of retailing: Retailing is not for sissies. The demands of operating a successful retail store are many, constant, and, frankly, all-consuming at times. Some would-be retailers mistakenly assume they can open and operate a retail store in their spare time. Retailing involves an endless cycle of buy, market, display, and sell that can be extremely tiresome and demanding, especially for some personality types. It also means lots of long days and/or nights in the store selling and in the office ordering and paying bills. Of course, with success comes an increasing quality of life if you hire more employees to provide relief, but this in itself carries its own set of problems and demands.

So if you're not prepared to commit a large portion of your life, at least in the beginning, perhaps you should consider working part time at Walmart.

5. Neglecting customer service: This may be the biggest cause of retail failure that I've observed. Some retailers think that customers are there for their convenience, not the other way around. I've seen retail businesses fail because they were located in inconvenient locations and because they didn't accommodate their business hours to customer needs. If you're targeting working people, for example, you probably won't succeed if you open at 10 AM and close at 3 PM. One store I know of was often closed during published business hours, and the owner seemed unaware that such practices alienated customers. Another retailer located a store in a building that was convenient (and cheap) for them, assuming customers would seek them out. They didn't!

The other major sin in this category is failing to treat all customers with courtesy and respect. I'm constantly amazed at the treatment customers receive from retail employees. Things as basic as not greeting customers when they enter the store, offering help in merchandise selection, and ignorance about the store policies and stock are commonplace occurrences. This ain't rocket science! Train your employees—and yourself—on the basics of customer courtesy and service.

Although avoiding these five fatal mistakes won't ensure retailing success, committing them will surely bring you closer to the brink of failure. There are so many risks and pitfalls in today's rapidly changing marketplace, it makes sense to increase your odds of success by avoiding them.

SOURCE: Bond, Ronald L. "5 Fatal Mistakes for Small Retailing." *Entrepreneur.* http://www.entrepreneur.com/article/193340 with permission of Entrepreneur Media, Inc.

information to arrive at the best decision possible (FIGURE 1.5).

Creative and Innovative Thinkers

Fashion entrepreneurs are creative thinkers. They combine imagination and ingenuity to solve a problem or create a need or want. Although not every idea is practical or can be turned into a successful venture, entrepreneurs are not discouraged and will continue to solve problems in this way.

Innovative thinkers transform an idea into a marketable product or service. They implement the idea, taking it to marketplace. Take Francis Cabot Lowell (1775–1817). He was an innovator. During a trip to England he was stunned by the number of textile mills and their machinery. He memorized the machinery, but with the goal of going further than replication. After returning to Boston in 1813, Lowell

FIGURE 1.5
Successful entrepreneurs analyze a problem from various angles.

communicated his ambition to his brother-in-law, Patrick Tracy Jackson, and to the mechanic Paul Moody. Together, they formed the Boston Manufacturing Company, organizing it into a corporation with a huge capitalization of $300,000. The mill they built together was the first to convert raw cotton into cloth by power machinery within the walls of one building. For years, entrepreneurs have started retail ventures that spin off into new products that revolutionize the way we dress and do business.

Ability to Work Independently

Employees of large corporations may have a team of assistants, accountants, marketers, researchers, and financial analysts to help them with the daily activities and overall planning of the company. When a new business is started, however, more often than not the entrepreneur is the company and all its departments. This is because in the beginning, entrepreneurs generally have little support. The funds are simply not available. Entrepreneurs start out as janitor, bookkeeper, and strategic planner. They have only themselves to rely on to do the work that may be unfamiliar or unpalatable. Recognizing the necessity to do whatever it takes to get the job done to make the business ultimately a success is crucial.

Respect for Money

It is easy to get caught up in the glamour of owning a business. Many businesses get into financial trouble because they spend far too much money on items that have very little to do with the success of the business. Successful entrepreneurs are conservative and careful with their money. They spend what is necessary and save the rest. Successful entrepreneurs do not typically judge themselves based on what they spend or can afford to buy. Satisfaction is obtained through achieving their own internal goals and objectives.

Ability to Manage Time Wisely

Getting a business started is extremely time-consuming. Because entrepreneurs are working with little or no staff and limited budgets, the ability to plan and prioritize effectively is critical. It is not uncommon for entrepreneurs to work seventy to eighty hours per week in the initial stages of a business and still leave the office with many tasks unfinished. The inability to manage time efficiently will lead to poor performance. Poor performance reflects on the company. In the initial stage of the business, entrepreneurs either are guilty of trying to perform too many tasks on their own or are doing their best with the limited funds they have. When they do employee personnel, good entrepreneurs will utilize them to their best advantage. They will learn to delegate duties and responsibilities and to enable employees to fulfill those duties by giving them the autonomy to do so.

Dependability

It is important to follow through on commitments that have been made. Storefront retail businesses need to open the doors when the sign on the front of the door says they will open. E-commerce businesses need to deliver goods within the time frame indicated. Undependability can lead to disaster for fashion retail businesses. Consumers expect excellent service.

Flexibility

Successful entrepreneurs must be able to adapt to the changing demands of customers and their businesses. The world has become a fast-paced, ever-changing place. The tastes, wants, and needs of the consumer are also ever changing. The ability of the entrepreneur to adapt to these changes will increase the opportunity for success.

TRAITS OF UNSUCCESSFUL ENTREPRENEURS

The personality traits in the following discussion have been identified as negative qualities for the entrepreneur, as they relate to success. Note that negative characteristics can be changed, but it requires effort. If the prospective entrepreneur has the determination, self-discipline, and objectivity to identify and rectify possible problem areas, the potential for entrepreneurial success increases.

Dishonesty

The fastest way to create an unsuccessful business is to be dishonest with one's customers, suppliers, funders—any of the people and businesses with whom the entrepreneur deals. People want and need to trust business associates. After that trust is broken, it is difficult to re-establish. Credibility is vital to the success of any business.

Impatience

It is true that disaster follows entrepreneurs who lack patience. Impatience may lead to hiring the wrong people, targeting the wrong market, pricing inventory too low to make a profit (just to get it sold), or opening a business at the wrong time. People who are impatient believe that the business absolutely has to be open now, or the market will disappear or go elsewhere. This does not hold true for most industries. Only after careful planning and research should a business be staffed, stocked, and opened.

Reluctance to Ask for Help

There is a misconception among potential entrepreneurs that asking questions about how to run the business suggests that they lack the skills and knowledge needed. Entrepreneurs cannot be experts in all areas of a business; all business owners need help and support. More often than not, unsuccessful entrepreneurs waited until it was too late to ask questions about issues critical to their business. There are a number of organizations across the United States with a mission to champion the entrepreneur. They provide education and resources to help small businesses succeed. A list of these support organizations is provided in Appendix A.

Lack of Interpersonal Skills

Successful fashion retailing begins with making the customer feel comfortable, welcome, and valued. If someone has a low tolerance for people, retail business ownership is not the career path to pursue. Envision trying to shop in a favorite store with the "out of control child" screaming in the background and destroying merchandise as the mother pursues her search for the perfect dress. Picture a disgruntled employee complaining to customers about the business operation. The successful entrepreneur must be able to pacify discontented customers, motivate sales associates, and negotiate with suppliers. Successful businesses provide excellent customer service. Successful entrepreneurs recognize the people skills needed to provide this service. Kay Saunders, the founder of the Human Asset Imaging Institute, which offers programs and workshops on the development of interpersonal skills, asserts, "In retail it is of enormous importance that owners and associates connect with others to influence their buying decisions. People may not remember a specific product, but they will not forget how they were treated. Being creatures of habit, people like consistency and courtesy served with conversation and commitment."[5]

ASSESSING YOURSELF: TRAITS AND SKILLS

Entrepreneurs have to know their strengths and weaknesses, both on a personal and a business level. In addition, entrepreneurs must compensate in some way for the areas in which they are not especially proficient. A business is a reflection of the person running it. By conducting a self-analysis before going into business, the prospective entrepreneur will develop an inventory of his or her personal needs in the areas of motivation, skills, and talents. Self-analysis also clarifies the entrepreneur's values in terms of money, power, fun, independence, and security. The prospective entrepreneur should compare personal qualities and preferences with those of entrepreneurs who succeed and those who have been less fortunate. The analysis should examine the following: how the prospective entrepreneur gets things done; how the entrepreneur interacts with people; and how the entrepreneur goes about making decisions. Many successful entrepreneurs constantly assess themselves and solicit feedback from friends, family, peers, and employees. The process of continual self-assessment becomes a habit for many successful business developers.

FIGURE 1.6 is a personal assessment that can be used to score and assess individuals who are considering becoming entrepreneurs. Take a moment to fill this form out and find out your rating. Assessment instruments are used in many different industries and come in many different forms. This assessment tool was developed simply to help prospective entrepreneurs identify those areas in which they are weak and those in which their strengths lie. It is recommended that the prospective entrepreneur complete it independently and then ask someone, such as a professor or colleague, to fill out an evaluation about the prospective entrepreneur. The personal assessment is most helpful when the participants are open-minded and willing to receive feedback.

The prospective entrepreneur should read each statement and enter a score in the right column, using a scale of 1 to 4. When completed, the score is calculated by adding all points in the score column.

A score of between 31 and 80 points is in the mid-to-low range. Starting a business requires a commitment by the entrepreneur to focus significant amounts of time and energy on the business. A mid-to-low score could mean that the prospective entrepreneur needs to spend more time developing confidence, skills, and abilities in certain areas before committing time and funding to a new venture.

A score between 81 and 124 points is in the mid-to-upper range. It indicates that the prospective entrepreneur possesses many of the key habits and skills needed to become successful. A high score indicates that prospective entrepreneur will welcome challenges, set goals, and implement the steps necessary in achieving those goals.

ASSESSING YOUR BUSINESS SKILLS

Many successful entrepreneurs believe that they learned much of what they know through the "school of hard knocks." Because the business climate changes much more rapidly now than it did ten or even five years ago, the school of hard knocks may not provide the education it once did. Technological, social, and economic trends have resulted in increased levels and speed of communication and product life cycles.

A PERSONAL ASSESSMENT FORM

Rating Scale (1 = strongly disagree, 2 = disagree, 3 = agree, 4 = strongly agree)

STATEMENT	RATING SCALE
I attend the organizational meetings I have scheduled.	_____
I show up for classes and other events on time.	_____
I take responsibility for my college courses and assignments.	_____
I prioritize my "list of things to do."	_____
I finish my assignments on time.	_____
I know how much time I spend on each activity and/or class per week.	_____
I manage my time well in college.	_____
I am excited when new opportunities and projects present themselves.	_____
I have the ability to make decisions quickly.	_____
I make good decisions.	_____
I like working on numerous tasks at the same time.	_____
I enjoy competition.	_____
I set goals for myself and meet those goals.	_____
I am responsible with my finances.	_____
I am happiest when I am responsible for myself and my own decisions.	_____
I prefer to work in a group setting on a class project rather than alone.	_____
I have the ability to motivate others.	_____
I volunteer to take on leadership roles. I enjoy being the one responsible for organizing a project and keeping the project on schedule.	_____
I enjoy new challenges.	_____
I am talented at finding new ways to do things.	_____
I am intuitive.	_____
I enjoy staying busy. I don't like to sit around.	_____
I am self-motivated.	_____
I enjoy public speaking and/or speaking in class.	_____
I look for ways to acquire new skills that will enable me to grow both as a person and as a student.	_____
I welcome change. I find it exciting.	_____
I can adapt easily to change.	_____
I am not timid about speaking in class and asking questions.	_____
I recognize that my health is important, and I take the steps necessary to maintain my health.	_____
I can work on projects independently.	_____
I am able to get along and work well with other students.	_____
TOTAL SCORE	

FIGURE 1.6

Globalization is part of today's business world. Entrepreneurs cannot be everywhere at once. They cannot possibly experience firsthand all the skills needed to grow a business successfully. Time and resources are limited for new companies. Entrepreneurs can, however, compensate for these limitations. How? By hiring personnel or forming an advisory team with strengths in their areas of weakness. The business failure rate is high for those who go into it without knowledge of the issues of today and tomorrow and a good support system to help them accomplish all that is needed.

Good entrepreneurs assemble a management team or advisory team to take care of areas in which they lack knowledge and experience. For example, the prospective entrepreneur may retain the services of a law firm or an accounting service, in anticipation of opening the business. It should be noted that there are businesses that have succeeded in which the owner lacked any firsthand experience in the industry but brought on a management team or advisory team that did.

On a daily basis the entrepreneur must make decisions that require a basic knowledge of business. The entrepreneur is the person responsible for the strategic planning and growth of the company. Often, he or she is the person who will develop a marketing plan for the organization, based on an evaluation of the general industry and the competition. The entrepreneur is also likely to be the person who identifies the target market, and where it is located and decides how to reach it in numbers large enough to sustain the business.

In addition to analyzing the customer, the entrepreneur will have to read and understand financial statements and know how to access money. Often because of the lack of a financial background, the entrepreneur does not initially know what the business needs in order to operate and grow. Many times, insufficient research is done to determine all the start-up capital needed. For example, retail stores in most states are required to post a **sales tax bond**, based on projected sales. A sales tax bond is essentially a deposit held by the state to offset any unpaid sales tax incurred in the business. For a business projecting large sales, the amount of the bond can be significant. Entrepreneurs may also struggle because they do not understand the impact of financials on the business. What happens when inventory does not turn over as anticipated? Should more inventory be added? How often should the inventory turn over? Good market and financial research will provide answers to these questions.

The entrepreneur will have to analyze trends and personnel requirements as well as know how to plan for growth strategically. He or she will be required to negotiate the lease agreement for securing a piece of real estate or to determine the cost of producing and distributing a catalog or the terms for developing and managing a Web site. Entrepreneurs in many areas of fashion retailing must purchase and manage stock. The entrepreneur will need to ensure that procedures are in place to turn stock the fastest way possible and to limit the amount of stock to reduce storage, stocking, and maintenance costs. Without the education and knowledge required to address these issues, the chances are high that a new business will not succeed.

Funders, such as bankers, are individuals or institutions and organizations that loan money to the business. They will always look at whether the entrepreneur has experience in the industry in which he or she wants to start the business or is associated with individual(s) with experience in the industry. Funders believe, and rightly so, that unless a person has worked in retailing, he or she will not have the knowledge and practical skills needed to run a retail operation. Many prospective entrepreneurs establish a career plan designed to enable them to gain as much experience as possible in the area or field in which they want to start a business.

An entrepreneur has to have a basic understanding of all aspects of the business. There are a number of internship programs available that provide an opportunity to work in the fashion retail industry. Small businesses are a wonderful place to learn about the world of the entrepreneur because the entrepreneurs and employees wear many hats. Business knowledge should come from academic training and texts, work experience, and networking with entrepreneurs. It is important to seek out those entrepreneurs who have been successful as well as those who have failed. Most entrepreneurs are eager to share their knowledge, as long as the prospective entrepreneur will not be in direct competition with them.

TIMING AND FUNDING AVAILABILITY

Three key factors come into play when determining the right time to start a business. The venture will demand much of the entrepreneur's time; the business may not initially provide the fashion retail entrepreneur with the lifestyle he or she had anticipated it would; and it may take more money than the entrepreneur has available or can secure.

Assessing where the entrepreneur is in his or her life is important. Careful planning, as well as articulation and revision of goals, will help the entrepreneur know when to start the new venture. It is important for the entrepreneur to address his or her life priorities. The pursuit of a higher educational degree; lack of experience in the field; need for more money more time, for a stronger support system—these are all conditions that may cause someone to postpone entrepreneurial endeavors. The ability to measure where one is and what one wants in life at a particular stage is significant to entrepreneurial success. Entrepreneurs begin by defining what is most important to them in life, for example:

»   I want to be surrounded by beautiful clothes.

»   I want to make lots of money.

»   I want to live on the East Coast.

»   My friends and family will come first in my life.

»   I want to complete a doctorate program.

After determining what is most important and most motivational, the entrepreneur will want to analyze whether the business will allow him or her to accomplish those goals, and if so, how.

Above all, life balance is critical. The burnout rate is high among entrepreneurs who do not take time for themselves, friends, and family. Numerous entrepreneurs burn out within the first two years simply because they have no other outlets in their lives. Successful entrepreneurs recognize the importance of balance.

PLANNING FOR SUCCESS

The personal traits of an entrepreneur have been examined. This section addresses issues relating directly to the proposed business. Among the top reasons for a business's failure are:

»   Lack of good initial research of the concept

»   Lack of sufficient capital for the start-up phase

»   Lack of solid business planning

»   Poor management by the entrepreneur

»   Failure to seek and identify a market niche

»   Lack of understanding of the competition

»   Lack of knowledge of the market

»   Poor customer service

A well-researched concept is critical to any entrepreneur. Furthermore, theory should be measured against reality. Successful entrepreneurs research prospective customers, product, competition, personal goals, and timing and funding availability before moving forward. Entrepreneurs who are not successful often have not taken the time to evaluate and test their concept.

Sufficient capital is a must. More often than not, entrepreneurs open their doors without sufficient capital to sustain the business through the start-up phase. Researching other fashion retail businesses will provide hard data on the approximate amount of capital needed. It is important to remember that every business will be different and that some adjustments will need to be made to the financials to fit a specific business.

In addition to sufficient capital, it is also necessary to understand the financial statements of the business. The financial statements serve as a management tool. They show the condition of the business and provide information necessary to make good financial decisions. The decisions to increase inventory, to seek additional financing, and to hire new employees rest on the financial health of the business.

A business may fail because of a lack of planning. Some prospective entrepreneurs believe that they do not have time to work on a business plan. This can be the kiss of death. The business plan provides direction, addresses both strengths and weaknesses of the proposed business, and allows the entrepreneur to look at the business as a whole, in its entirety. A good business plan will increase chances of success dramatically. How could it not? Through development of an effective business plan, the entrepreneur addresses the business from a variety of angles. The plan will confirm whether the business concept is feasible and will guide the best use of resources. It is not uncommon for entrepreneurs to produce a number of business plans for different business opportunities. The business plan is discussed in greater detail throughout this text. At this point, it is important to recognize the significant role this plan plays in the overall success of a business.

Poor management can be the greatest single cause of business failure. Management of a business encompasses planning, organizing, controlling, directing, and communicating. It is important to hire the right people, to properly train these employees, and to motivate them. Effective management requires good leadership skills. Leadership is the art of persuading, guiding, and motivating. An effective leader will encourage productivity and guide the employees through the business rather than simply dictate what tasks need to be done.

Entrepreneurs should determine how they will exit the business before the business is started. Planning can afford the entrepreneur the opportunity to create value in the company so that it can be sold sometime in the future. Closing the doors without a plan can sometimes leave unpaid obligations, employees without jobs, unsold inventory, and a broken lease. Exit strategies, further discussed in Chapter 5, involve determining what the business is worth and how this is to be calculated. It also involves knowing the time frame in which the entrepreneur plans to exit the business.

Those entrepreneurs who have succeeded generally acknowledge that perseverance is at the top of the list of success factors. They did not give up. They recognized that continually monitoring the industry and market and maintaining the willingness to change with that industry and market kept them going. Flexibility is important in their ever-changing environment. Entrepreneurs also know that to succeed in the fashion retail business, they must earn the loyalty of their customers. Good business owners will make their customers the number one priority. They will provide service beyond the expectation of the consumer. In the words of Benjamin Franklin, "I have not failed. I have found 10,000 ways that don't work." Entrepreneurs do not set out to fail. Careful planning and knowledge of the industry and markets increase the chances of finding the one way that works.

DEVELOPMENT OF THE BUSINESS CONCEPT: WHAT WILL THE COMPANY BE?

If, after careful assessment of both personal and business skills, the prospective entrepreneur determines that he or she has what it takes to open a new business or buy an existing business, then it is time to develop the business concept. A sample concept statement is included in Appendix D. The concept begins with an idea. It often arises out of a consumer need that is not currently being satisfied. The entrepreneur has thought outside of the box and created an opportunity for a new product. Although the concept is not an actual part of the written business plan, it is crucial to the planning process. To be successful, the business concept must meet four requirements:

» There must be a group of customers willing to purchase the product or product lines featured by the business at the price offered.

» The market must be large enough to support the business and generate a profit.

BOX 1.2

QUESTIONS A MISSION STATEMENT SHOULD ANSWER

>> What are the basic values of the company? What does the company stand for?

>> What principles or values guide the business?

>> Who is the business's target market?

>> What are the company's basic products and services? What customer needs and wants do they satisfy?

>> How can the company better satisfy those needs and wants?

>> Why should customers do business with this company rather than with the competition?

>> What is the personality of customer service? How can this company offer the customer better value?

>> What is the company's competitive advantage?

>> What benefits should be provided to the company's customers five years from now?

>> The entrepreneur must be able to differentiate his or her business from that of the competition.

>> The entrepreneur must be able to finance the business—either personally or through funding sources.

With these requirements taken care of, the entrepreneur is ready to contemplate business ownership.

Picture yourself totally lost. You know where you want to go. You need to know who you are and what you stand for. A **mission statement** will provide focus. It is a statement addressing the purpose of the company. Box 1.2 outlines questions that can be used to guide the development of a mission statement. A **vision statement** addresses what the owner stands for and what he or she believes.

Formulating mission and vision statements and committing those statements to writing establish a sense of direction for the company and help the entrepreneur stay on track. A sample mission statement might include, "Our mission is to provide a line

of clothing that addresses the needs of the physically challenged." The concept for the company should both agree with and help define the entrepreneur's belief system. Business goals may include creating a new Web-based fashion retail business or achieving a particular profit within a certain time period. Personal goals may include selling the business within five years, helping children who are physically challenged, or donating five outfits to a local charity each year. Box 1.3 illustrates an example of a mission and objective statement for RealWomen, Inc., the business featured in the Sample Business Plan (Appendix D).

It is essential that the mission and vision statements be communicated to employees, who, in turn, will communicate them to customers. They must become an integral part of the culture of the company. An example of a business concept that reflects a personal vision is that of Wishing Wells, a line of special clothing for special people. Although many know her as Mary Ann of *Gilligan's Island*, Dawn Wells is also an author, speaker, philanthropist, and entrepreneur.

BOX 1.3
SAMPLE MISSION AND OBJECTIVES STATEMENT

MISSION AND OBJECTIVES STATEMENT

The mission of RealWomen, Inc., is to be the premier specialty store for sized 11/12 to 19/20 contemporary women by providing affordable fashion-forward merchandise and excellent customer service. Our long-term goal is not only to achieve profit objectives, but also to be the number one fashion specialty store for our market in Diva City by targeting customers, providing value and service, promoting the company, and later expanding.

TARGET CUSTOMERS

The target customers of RealWomen, Inc., are mid-level income women who shop for fashionable, quality apparel and accessories. The customer profile is a contemporary woman between the ages of 18 to 35 who wears a size within the range of 11/12 to 19/20 and who purchases fashion apparel and accessories in a moderate price range. She believes in "fashion first" and embraces her curves. She seeks apparel and accessories for casual and work wear. She may be a college student or a working woman. This woman currently spends nearly $1,000 annually on her wardrobe, largely outside of Diva City. Twenty-five percent of Diva City's population fits this consumer description, and no retailer is focusing on her apparel preferences in this downtown location.

Within Diva City's population, 25 percent are women between the ages of 18 and 35. This age group represents one fourth of the large-size market population in this geographic area. Demographics also show a median income level of $40,500, with the vast majority being college students or working professionals. Their primary motivations for purchase are:

» desire to buy in their geographic area;

» need for quality clothing in sizes 11/12 to 19/20;

» ability to purchase fashion apparel and accessories at reasonable prices.

In a survey conducted by the local chamber of commerce and university, 300 female consumers ages 18 to 35 who indicated they were a plus size reported that they would purchase clothing in the area if the selection existed. They also indicated that they spend approximately $750 on their clothing each year.

POSITIONING

We want our target customers to perceive RealWomen, Inc., as having the most timely and competitive selections of fashionable, quality merchandise. We believe that one of the keys to our future growth is the consumer between the ages of 18 and 35 who shops for fashionable, updated merchandise in sizes 11/12 to 19/20. By positioning the company in this size range and age span, we are filling a retail void in the marketplace. Diva City has only two plus-size stores, and both carry clothing for more mature women.

MERCHANDISE

RealWomen, Inc., will present a balanced selection of fashion apparel and accessories in a variety of colors, fabrications, styles, and brands that represent current fashion trends. Our merchandise must be timely and fashion-forward, and be of the finest quality available in the moderate price range.

To create a sustainable competitive advantage, the merchandise focus will be on recognizable name brands that are not carried by the competition. Consistency and exclusivity of these lines will build brand acceptance, which will encourage repeat purchases, and, subsequently, increase profits.

VALUE AND SERVICE

Although RealWomen, Inc., wants to be a fashion leader, we also want to offer our customers the best available price on all offered goods. Through research and regular, preplanned market trips, we have the opportunity to buy top-quality merchandise in a moderate price range.

In addition we will offer the finest possible service available. Our sales staff must be courteous, caring, and knowledgeable about our merchandise and the business. Above all, our sales staff must be available to our customers and willing to help them achieve the looks they want. To accomplish this, we require a regular updating of our computerized client profile lists, and we encourage all sales associates actively to call our listed clients to advise them of new merchandise shipments that would be of interest to them.

RealWomen, Inc., will also offer services such as credit/debit card transactions, free home delivery on purchases greater than $200, low-cost alterations, and year-round gift wrapping.

PROMOTION

To reach our target customer, gain new clients, and promote our image as a fashion leader, RealWomen, Inc., will present its merchandise in a variety of formats and locations. In addition to semiannual fashion shows (fall and spring), we will sponsor several trunk shows in the store location. RealWomen, Inc., will also participate in fashion trade shows offered locally. We will actively seek cooperative advertising agreements with our vendors, and sponsor frequent television, radio, and print media ads, as well as ads on the RealWomen, Inc., Web site. Advertised quarterly sales (fall, winter, spring, and summer) and monthly one-day sales will also help gain new, value-minded customers, while keeping the inventory on the sales floor fresh and updated.

EXPANSION

It is the intention of the owner to keep the store at 2,500 square feet for at least three years. Future related merchandise lines, such as hosiery, lingerie, and shoes, may be added as the customer base grows.

RealWomen, Inc., recognizes the opportunity to create awareness of the store and to expand sales through the Internet. A Web site and social media outreach will be available upon opening of RealWomen, Inc. Because apparel goods are typically the first level of items purchased on the Web and are among the leaders in online purchases, RealWomen, Inc., will continue to monitor sales and weigh options with regard to Web sales distribution in the next two to three years.

Dawn created the company Wishing Wells, a line of apparel designed for the elderly and physically challenged. Wells believes that giving someone special clothes can make all the difference in their lives. She says, "I know what it feels like to take care of someone you love, to care for them, dress them, and even spend hours trying to rip a bathrobe down the back to make dressing easier. I know what it feels like because I had a grandmother we took care of at home."[6] Easy-on, easy-off clothing became the concept for her entrepreneurial venture (FIGURE 1.7). The market was there to support the idea.

FIGURE 1.7
Successful entrepreneurs recognize opportunities for niche markets.

After the mission and vision statements have been developed, they will become the foundation on which the business will be based and the grounds on which the direction and feasibility of the business concept will be explored. Mission statements may change as research begins. There is nothing wrong with that, as long as the mission and vision statements, as well as the business plan, complement one another. As the business concept is developed, the entrepreneur will want to look closely at what matters most to him or her. The business concept may be defined and redefined many times.

RESEARCHING THE BUSINESS CONCEPT

A significant amount of research should go into the business concept before large amounts of time, money, and energy are invested in the business. The reason for researching and developing the concept for the business is to test it against economic, financial, and political realities. This development process helps determine whether efforts should go forward and additional resources should be committed to the concept. It is important to develop a business concept and business plan from an objective perspective. The prospective entrepreneur must be willing to revise the original concept if the need arises.

It is important to identify ways in which the business will distinguish itself in the market. Some competitors may do some things well; others may not. The entrepreneur should seek new or better ways of doing things in order to offer a unique and competitive advantage over the other businesses in the marketplace. Also, the prospective entrepreneur will encounter some companies that have not changed with the industry, including e-commerce. Such businesses may provide an excellent opportunity.

It is critical for the entrepreneur to look at the economic trends, technological advances, and demographic shifts in order to assess the impact these elements will have on the fashion retail industry. For example, the ripple effect of the terrorist attack of September 11, 2001, in the United States affected small businesses in New York City and across the nation, as noted in this passage from a *New York Times* article published the following month:

> A report assessing the economic impact of September 11 that was prepared for the New York City Partnership, by KPMG and SRI International, another consulting firm, predicted that for two years, small businesses' sales would continue to fall short of what was expected before the trade center attack. Employment among small businesses will continue to fall through the first quarter of next year, the report said. On West Eighth Street in Greenwich Village, shoe salesmen stand forlornly on the sidewalk in front of [Leather & Shoes], smoking cigarettes and staring blankly into the distance, wondering where all the customers have gone.[7]

During economic downturns, sales in the better-apparel market may take a turn downward. Technological advances may provide new channels of distribution through the Internet, linked Web sites, and video catalogs. Demographic shifts in the population may indicate more disposable income for teen customers. A comprehensive survey of environmental factors often identifies trends that may offer new business niches.

For others, the concept has significant philanthropic value. TOMS Shoes is one such example (FIGURE 1.8). A 2010 article in *Fortune* magazine provides the story of TOMS Shoes. In 2002, Blake Mycoskie teamed with his sister to compete on the TV reality show, *The Amazing Race*. Although they did not win, his travels took him back to Argentina in 2006. In describing his visit he states:

> My first venture was a door-to-door laundry business for students that I started while on a partial tennis scholarship at Southern Methodist University in Dallas. I wanted to do something that didn't depend on my hands to create value.
>
> My father is a doctor, so when he's playing golf, he's losing money. When I came out of a business class and saw my trucks picking up laundry, I thought, I'm in class and making money at the same time.
>
> After we expanded EZ Laundry to four colleges, I sold my share. I moved to Nashville to start an outdoor-media company that Clear Channel scooped up three years later. In 2002 my sister and I teamed up to compete on the CBS

FIGURE 1.8

TOMS Shoes is a business with a social conscience. The company has achieved success with its humanitarian hook. Here, members of the TOMS Shoes team deliver 10,000 pairs of shoes in the first "Shoe Drop 2006" in Argentina (top) and two children wearing their new TOMS shoes share some food at the Los Piletones soup kitchen in Buenos Aires, Argentina, in 2006 (bottom).

reality show *The Amazing Race*. We didn't win, but my travels during the show led me back to Argentina in 2006. On my visit I saw lots of kids with no shoes who were suffering from injuries to their feet.

I decided a business would be the most sustainable way to help, so I founded TOMS [in Santa Monica], which is short for a "better tomorrow." For each pair of shoes sold—TOMS are based on the classic *alpargata* style worn in Argentina—we donate a pair to a child in need.[8]

In 2010, Fast Company named TOMS Shoes number six in its list of top ten most innovative retail companies:

After four years in business, 33-year-old Blake Mycoskie has proven that his socially conscious 'one for one' model is more than just a novelty project. For every pair of his signature *alpargatas* sold, one free pair is given to a child in the developing world. TOMS has expanded its line, won the 2007 People's Design Award at Cooper-Hewitt's National Design Awards, became a member of the Clinton Global Initiative, and landed shelf space in Whole Foods.[9]

What makes the TOMS Shoes concept exceptional? Creating a new market for an old product? Launching a company with a socially conscious mission? Engaging consumers in its mission? All these factors provide entrepreneurial inspiration, from the original concept to the new concepts that keep the company growing.

Researching an entrepreneurial venture involves more than a visit to the library. It encompasses seeking the advice of friends, bankers, business advisers, professors, and other entrepreneurs. As advice and information are offered, the entrepreneur must listen and keep an open mind. The entrepreneur should not expect people to simply confirm what the entrepreneur is thinking. The entrepreneur should give information sources the freedom to be honest.

Entrepreneurs should acknowledge the importance and value of the perceptions and opinions of others. The prospective entrepreneur will want to know whether a product will sell and whether financing will be available. The entrepreneur must remain objective in studying and evaluating information.

Be sure to look for the strengths of the concept, the weaknesses, any opportunities, and certainly any future threats.

WRITING THE BUSINESS CONCEPT STATEMENT

Because the business concept does not appear in the final business plan, why is it necessary to write out the **concept statement**? A concept statement is a document used to present an idea for a business. The concept is used to determine whether the business idea is potentially sound. It is also used to help the entrepreneur focus on what she or he wants the business to be and how it is going to get there. The concept should be concise and well thought out. A fully developed concept provides the entrepreneur with the opportunity to analyze potential success by addressing the target market, the financial strategy, how the market will be reached, and how the concept compares with the competition.

Note that concept statements should not be too general. A statement such as, "The business will provide good service," will mean different things to different people. Concept statements should not be too broad. "Fashion retail store" tells very little. "Fashion retail store featuring clothes designed for the physically challenged" is a more complete statement. Many concept statements are incomplete because they omit key elements that provide information about what the business is going to be and do. The test for a well-defined concept statement is to let someone such as a funder read it to see if he or she is able to understand to the business proposed. The business concept statement should not be more than one or two pages. The concept statement is the first step in developing a sound business plan (refer to the concept statement included in Appendix D).

WHY BUSINESS PLANNING IS IMPORTANT

The remainder of this text focuses on the development of the business plan itself. A **business plan** is an evolving document that outlines the focus and direction for the business. The importance of a comprehensive business plan cannot be overemphasized. A well-thought-out business plan provides direction for knowing what the company is or will be, defining what the company goals are, and determining how those goals will be reached. It reflects the commitment of the entrepreneur. The business plan is critical for obtaining outside capital. It will provide information key to managing operations and finances. It will also provide a way to measure performance; it will detail a tactical plan for carrying out strategies and accomplishing goals. The process of developing the plan gives the entrepreneur the opportunity to evaluate the entire business. In addition, the business plan will allow the entrepreneur to take a proactive, rather than reactive, approach to the business.

Business plans are not measured by size, but by content. All business plans should be organized into distinct sections.

In the content of the plan, funders look for experience in the industry, identification of a market niche, ability to generate cash flow, and whether the entrepreneur has the necessary operating and control systems in place to manage the business. The business plan is intended as a management tool to be evaluated on a regular basis.

The plan is intended to provide a means of measuring the direction the company is taking against the projected outcome. The plan will provide important information about the goals of the company, financial forecasts, the market, the industry, management strategies, and other facts needed to lead the company to success. The plan should be visited often. Fashion trends change frequently. Both the internal and external environments can affect the business. The ability to analyze and adapt to change through a well-written plan eliminates unwanted surprises.

Although there are many organizations and consultants ready and willing to assist with writing business plans, the plan should be prepared by the entrepreneur. Lenders and investors will view this as an indication that the entrepreneur understands the business. They will want to know that the entrepreneur is aware of the risks involved in creating the new venture and that measures have been taken to reduce those risks. The criteria used by lenders and investors in evaluating business plans are covered in Chapter 11.

CONCLUSION

Understanding entrepreneurship, its rewards and challenges, is the first step in considering business ownership. Entrepreneurship is a discipline like no other. It is an opportunity to act on dreams, to become one's own boss, to secure financial freedom, and to share a passion with others. Some people have the personal attributes needed to be entrepreneurs; others do what it takes to develop the skills and qualities necessary to succeed; still others never succeed in developing these skills and qualities. Developing a business requires an analysis of both personal and professional traits. It requires an examination of the characteristics that differentiate those who succeed in business from those who do not. Successful entrepreneurs persevere. They have a passion for what they want to do. They take responsibility for themselves and their businesses. They learn the skills necessary to run a business.

Planning is critical to a successful business. The entrepreneur must analyze the business from a variety of angles, looking for its strengths and weaknesses with equal vigor. The challenges of business ownership are immense, but the greatest challenge may be the objective evaluation of oneself and one's ideas.

Begin with the end in mind.

KEY TERMS

business plan

concept statement

entrepreneur

funders

mission statement

sales tax bond

virtual companies

vision statement

DISCUSSION TOPICS

1. Discuss the factors that contribute to a successful retail business.

2. Identify personal areas of weakness that may affect the success or failure of a prospective entrepreneur.

3. Conduct a self-analysis, using the areas of strength and areas of weakness discussed in topics 1 and 2.

4. Discuss the top three reasons why a business might fail. Provide examples of actual businesses that have succeeded, even though they would seemingly fit into one or more of the criteria for failure.

5. Discuss the importance of the development and evaluation of a business concept statement. Discuss the key elements.

SUGGESTED READINGS

Pink, Daniel. *A Whole New Mind.* New York: Riverhead Books, 2006.

Riso, Don Richard, and Russ Hudson. *Discovering Your Personality Type.* New York: Houghton Mifflin, 2003.

Burke, Sandra. *Fashion Entrepreneur: Starting Your Own Fashion Business.* Burke Publishing, 2008.

Harder, Frances. *Fashion for Profit.* Harder Publications.

Saunders, Kay. Interpersonal Skills Development Tools and Resources, Human Asset Imaging Institute. Bellewether, 2009.

ONLINE RESOURCES

ENTREPRENEURSHIP
http://www.entrepreneurship.org
Resource for information on entrepreneurship.

EWING MARION KAUFFMAN FOUNDATION
http://www.kauffman.org
The largest foundation in the world with entrepreneurship as its focus. Many resources available.

HUMAN ASSET IMAGING INSTITUTE
http://www.hai-institute.com
Researchs, develops, and brings to market products that increase interpersonal effectiveness.

U.S. SMALL BUSINESS ADMINISTRATION
http://www.sba.gov
Support, resources, tools for small businesses.

BUSINESS PLAN CONNECTION
THINKING LIKE AN ENTREPRENEUR

Taking the opportunity to interview an entrepreneur in the fashion industry can provide valuable information about the prospective business. You should let the entrepreneur know how much time will be needed when setting up the appointment. Knowledge gained from the interview can then be used to help in the development of the concept statement.

1. Develop a set of specific questions you want the entrepreneur to answer and the general areas about which you would like information.
2. Conduct the interview with the entrepreneur.
3. Evaluate what you have learned.
4. Write a thank-you note.

POTENTIAL QUESTIONS

Use these questions as a guide, but develop your own set of questions based on what you feel is most important to know from a practicing entrepreneur.

» What motivated you to start your own business?
» How did you start your own business?
» What inspired your business concept?
» Where did you find help for starting your own business?
» What do you like most about running your own fashion retail business?
» What do you like least about running your own fashion retail business?
» What was the biggest surprise you had?
» How do you market and sell your products?
» What advice would you give to others?

ASSIGNMENT 1.1
THE CONCEPT STATEMENT

1. Open the concept statement template in the Chapter 1 folder on the CD-ROM accompanying this text. This template will be used to write your concept statement.
2. Save the concept statement template to your computer.
3. Complete the assignment by addressing the questions contained on the concept statement template.

After completing your interview with an entrepreneur, use your saved concept statement to develop your business concept. Answer the following questions:

» Where do you need to be positioned financially to launch the business? How much money will you need to be comfortable as the business is built?
» What is your source of income as the business is launched and grows?

CONCEPT STATEMENT

» Nature of the Business
» Business Location
» Unique Aspects
» Intended Customer
» Market Penetration Strategies

PROFILE OF AN ENTREPRENEUR
PEREGRINE HONIG:
ARTIST AND FASHION RETAILER LIVES A DREAM

OPENED in 2003, Birdies is a unique lingerie store located in the Crossroads Arts District, in Kansas City, Missouri. The owner, Peregrine Honig, is a widely collected and well-known artist. She uses her artistic talents to fill a gap in the market for unique lingerie and swimwear, displayed in vintage Bitterman's candy cases. Birdies has been featured in *Elle* magazine and *Women's Wear Daily*.

What motivated you to start your own business?
I'm an artist. I've always enjoyed working hard. I like choosing my own hours and being able to design my store—to design it the way I want it to look—and being able to choose the merchandise I want to carry to meet the needs and wants of my customers. I started the business seven years ago, during the Iraq war. I know there are certain industries that do well during wars, and lingerie, in my opinion, is one of them. I was a freelancer and wanted to stop thinking about money. I wanted to create.

What training did you have that helped you start your business?
Actually, I haven't had any training in retail. But I do have an amazing eye. I was curator for a while and have always been interested in objects and how they tie into the human body.

How did you choose your company name?
I was inspired one night by reflecting on different ladies of different ages, classes, and backgrounds. I wanted a name that was sweet without sounding "young." Birdies sounds Southern, and I like that. Kansas City has a large migration of birds, so bird images come to my mind a lot. The name became the product, "I'm wearing my birdies."

How did you choose the location of your business?
Birdies is located in the Crossroads Arts District, in Kansas City. It is an area open to unique, artsy concepts. It has art galleries, boutiques, and restaurants. My retail space is owned by an independent landlord who understood there was a real-estate hopefulness in the area. The District became a story. The press and magazines were writing about what was about to happen in the Crossroads Arts District, in the Midwest. *Elle* magazine wrote a story about Birdies within six months after opening. I wanted to become part of the neighborhood.

How did you initially stock merchandise and market your store?
I started by purchasing underwear from discount stores, choosing the best I could buy at bargain prices and printing birds on them, selling them between $10 and $15 a pair in a retail location. I didn't have a wholesale license yet. We also held an underwear auction where Burlesque girls modeled the lingerie. That created awareness and was very inexpensive advertising.

We currently host the 18th Street Fashion Show. Each year, designers are selected to participate and model their current lines. This brings a lot of awareness to our store.

We have a billboard that moves around the city a couple of times each year. It typically doesn't work for us to take out ads. However, if we do, we take out a full-page ad in a local publication.

We have a Facebook page, and most find out about us by word of mouth. Customer loyalty is huge. I believe I have a strong connection with the community. Being a small, independently owned boutique, I have the ability to select charities and organizations that I feel strong about to support.

We have an online Panty of the Month Club. For $300 per year, the customer receives a pair of stunning, quality underwear each month. We act as your personal shopper. It also helps us to move our orphan underwear. It helps to move inventory. For example, if we have one pair in size small left of a certain style, it is sent to a Club member as [her] monthly pair.

We're the only independent lingerie store in Kansas City, Missouri.

What are the highlights of running your own business?

The ability to determine what I want to be surrounded with during the day. Making my own decisions. I choose the merchandise.

What contributes to your success?

I don't carry the basics. I focus on having nonbasics—unique, different lingerie—to keep the store fresh, interesting, and flirty, without becoming Shabby Chic. It's a woman's store. I understand and have educated myself about this industry. I understand why people buy what they buy, and why they don't.

I've taken it slow so I can direct my attention where it's needed.

I'm very cause and community oriented. As an independent store, I can choose what I want to support and how.

I've learned you have to know your [customers] and have the interpersonal skills to be able to direct them toward more attractive apparel for their body. If the customer is happy, she'll return. I don't push them into buying something that isn't attractive on them or I believe they won't be happy with later. That's the difference between Birdies and larger department stores.

What aspects of the business do you find particularly challenging?

While we carry a few lower price points, we're primarily higher quality and unique. It can be challenging explaining to customers why higher quality is more expensive. It's also challenging because customers don't understand that when you return lingerie it gets destroyed. So we have a policy that allows an exchange within thirty days, but the money stays in the store. No refunds. It's lingerie. It's intimate apparel.

It can be challenging to make men feel comfortable when shopping. We're a small, intimate boutique.

I also had a business partner at one time. Partners can have different values, goals, opinions. It's not always an easy business model.

Do you ever feel like giving up when the going gets hard?

Yes. Business is pleasurable when you're making money. One of the biggest challenges is being comfortable when you're not making money, when sales are slow. There is a cycle.

When I started, I built inventory with no funding. I didn't want to take out a loan. I held a party to raise money for the business. I ordered what I could afford to order and for the first three years I couldn't meet the minimum orders required so I chose another vendor. But seven years later I'm on top. I'm careful not to over order. I don't want to sit on stock. I order two smalls, two mediums, and one large of each item.

What advice do you have for someone interested in starting [his or her] own fashion retail business?

Just because you like clothes doesn't mean you should open your own store. It's a lot of time. It takes a strong commitment. I also recommend running your business as if you're going to sell it next week. Having a strong emotional attachment can present problems. It's about moving merchandise.

CHAPTER 2
DEVELOPING A ROAD MAP FOR SUCCESS

OBJECTIVES

» **Understand the significance of the business plan.**

» **Learn the key components of a business plan and why they are important to address.**

» **Learn to evaluate the business plan for completeness and clarity.**

THE basis of this text is to provide guidance and the framework necessary to grow a successful fashion retail business, with a primary outcome of developing a business plan to launch the venture. The following chapters offer detailed information concerning different sections of the plan, with a how-to approach. This chapter shows how a business plan is constructed and gives an overview of the questions used to stimulate thought processes. A sample business plan is included in Appendix D, and a blank business plan template is provided on the accompanying CD-ROM in the Templates folder.

REASONS FOR DEVELOPING A BUSINESS PLAN

To an entrepreneur in today's fast-changing environment, the business plan is critical. A business plan is a written document outlining a direction for where the business is going and how it is going to get there. If approached objectively, the business plan addresses whether the concept is feasible, whether there is enough money to start and sustain the business through the start-up phase, what makes the best use of time and money, and whether there is a market large enough for the business to be profitable. The business plan provides the entrepreneur with the opportunity to formulate a strategy for success. It is a communication tool for the entrepreneur and interested parties, such as funders and suppliers. The business plan is a living document in that it will change as the business concept is researched and developed and new information is obtained.

To funders, the plan helps ensure that funds are not being put into an unacceptable risk and that the entrepreneur has an understanding of the business, how much funding is necessary to launch and grow the business, and where the funding will be found. It gives funders a level of assurance that the entrepreneur has the ability to manage the business and overcome any hurdles.

Think of the business plan as a road map, one that guides the entrepreneur through the business. An individual would ordinarily not get into a car to travel to a new city without a map or GPS to provide direction. A business plan guides the entrepreneur's concept from an idea to reality. Finally, in terms of the prospective entrepreneur's frame of mind, the business plan forces the entrepreneur to take an objective and unemotional approach to the business.

The research needed to write a good business plan for opening a fashion retail operation affords the entrepreneur the opportunity to learn about the industry and the market. In addition, it requires the entrepreneur to "comparison shop" in terms of expenses relating to location, merchandise, operations, and personnel. A well-thought-out business plan can save the entrepreneur money. By taking time to understand the needed capital, the management team, the target market, and other factors, the entrepreneur can get off to a good start. It is easy to get caught up in the excitement of the potential new venture and want to jump in immediately. Good entrepreneurs step back and evaluate. Box 2.1 outlines common myths about business plans. Box 2.2 provides an overview of the overall purpose of the business plan.

HOW THE PLAN TAKES SHAPE: STRUCTURE OF THE PLAN

There is no one correct way to write a business plan. Various books on the market outline business plans in different ways. The order of the content should flow logically. Some issues may repeat in more than one section of the plan. FIGURE 2.1 illustrates the layout for a business plan. Following is the organization selected for this text.

BOX 2.2
OVERVIEW OF THE BUSINESS PLAN

» Defines the company, its goals, and objectives.

» Serves as a guide to help the entrepreneur stay focused on the direction of the company.

» Serves as a management tool for measuring whether the company is on target with its projections and goals.

» Provides an opportunity to understand the financial considerations of the business.

» Encourages research and the need for knowing the fashion industry and intended market thoroughly.

» Summarizes the information needed to make critical business decisions.

» Provides an opportunity to understand both the internal and external forces that can affect the business.

» Provides an opportunity to understand the competition and to position the company in relation to that competition.

» Highlights the strengths and weaknesses of the business.

» Defines a strategy for exiting the business when the time is right.

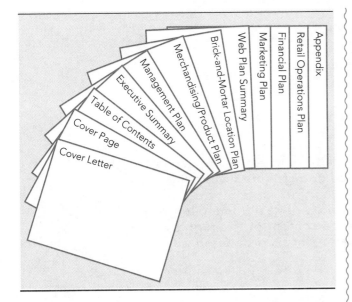

FIGURE 2.1

A business plan format.

COVER LETTER

The cover letter is the vehicle through which the entrepreneur's concept is introduced. It should state the reason the business plan is being presented and introduce the documents that are included in the package. The cover letter should be precise and to the point—no longer than one page.

COVER PAGE

The cover page identifies the document. It includes the name of the company; its address; contact information for the business (including an e-mail address, if applicable); the date; and the name, title, and address (if the address is different from that of the business) of the contact person within the company. Information on the title page may be arranged in any format deemed appropriate.

Business plans often contain confidential information that should not be distributed; for example, the finances of the entrepreneur. It is advisable to include a confidentiality statement on the cover page. FIGURE 2.2 provides a sample confidentiality statement.

Business Plan

November 15, 2011

Prepared by:

Lucy Rich, Owner and President
RealWomen, Inc.
123 Retail Avenue
Diva City, State 55512
111-555-0101
RealWomen@email.com

RealWomen, Inc. Document

FIGURE 2.2
A sample confidentiality statement.

Before reading the following sections on the specifics of the business plan and financial plan, review the tips for writing a good business plan contained in Box 2.3.

TABLE OF CONTENTS

The table of contents should list each section of the plan and the page number on which it first appears. The reader will not necessarily start at the beginning of the plan and read through it, front to back.

EXECUTIVE SUMMARY

This is the first opportunity the entrepreneur has to grab the reader's attention. The **executive summary** provides a sketch, or overview, of the business. It should contain key points relating to each section of the plan. It should include information about the business concept, the management team, the financing needed, how the entrepreneur intends to reach the market, and the prospective business's competitive advantage.

The executive summary follows the cover page in the business plan. It may be written first or last. It is not uncommon for it to be written first, to serve as a synopsis of what is to come. It can then be rewritten once the final business plan is complete, to reflect any changes. The summary should be written in narrative form, to tell the story of the business. It should not be longer than two pages. Readers will be looking for the *why* and *how* of the business as well as the factors that will contribute to the success of the venture.

The executive summary should provide the following:

1. **An overview of the business**—This section includes the products or services being offered, what is unique about them, and how these goods will get from the supplier to the customer; the type of business, such as the type of organization (a corporation or limited partnership); whether the business is retail, wholesale, or a service; and where the business will be located, such as the city and state, as well as brick-and-mortar, brick-and-click, or online only.

2. **An overview of the management team that will drive the business to success**—This section describes the key team members, their roles, and the skills they bring that will contribute to the overall success. The reader will also look for any outside support groups, such as advisors, attorneys, board members, or consultants that will be involved with the business.

3. **The critical success factors that must be met to reach the goals and objectives of the business**—Critical success factors are the essential activities that must be performed well if the business is to achieve its goals. For example, if the proposed business is a men's retail store, the critical success factors may include expanding the product line to attract more customers, sustaining a customer satisfaction rate of 98 percent, or relocating to the south side of the city where the population of men is higher.

4. **An overview of the market and the strategy for reaching that particular market**—This section includes data that supports the identification of a want of or need for the products being provided and of a market large enough to make the business profitable. This section should also include information about the benefits of the product or service to the customer as well as details about the competition, product promotion, potential sales, and branding.

5. **An overview of the market from a global perspective**—The market is looked at in terms of the industry, the customer, customer needs, product benefits, the target market, and how the market will be reached. At an industry level, the market may address trends in the fashion industry or the percentage of consumers that shop online. At a local level, the market may address the number of men, ages 24 to 38 who hold corporate jobs as well as major competitors, their strengths and weaknesses. In this section the entrepreneur identifies the companies the venture is going up against with similar product and service offerings as direct competition. Specific facts and figures are disclosed that have been obtained from the market research.

6. **An examination of finances**—Finances are examined in the following ways in this section: how much money the venture will need for start-up costs, what kind of financing will be needed, where the money will come from, and how the money will be spent.

MANAGEMENT PLAN

The **management plan** is the section of the plan that defines the management team. It must establish the credibility of the team running the business. It must reflect the team's ability to operate the business successfully and to achieve its outlined goals and objectives. If any member of the management team lacks the needed credentials or experience, the entrepreneur must explain how these deficiencies can be overcome with assistance from members of the support groups, such as the board of directors, the advisory council, consultants, attorneys, or accountants. The entrepreneur must be able to prove that he or she has access to the management expertise needed to operate the business profitably.

This section of the business plan lists the key management positions, along with a description of primary job duties and responsibilities. It should include a summary of each person's prior business experience because this explains how the person's skills will contribute to the overall performance of the business. If the person has not yet been hired, the writer must still include a brief position description that gives a list of the business skills and experience needed for the position. To develop a good management plan, the entrepreneur should address the following issues:

» **The organizational structure under which the business will operate**—The structure may be a sole proprietorship, corporation, limited liability corporation, and so on. The plan includes the percentage of the company owned by the entrepreneur and others.

» **The contribution of the management team**—The plan addresses the role of the entrepreneur (FIGURE 2.3). It also outlines the key management personnel, such as present their job descriptions

FIGURE 2.3
Successful businesses are often led by a team of people, each bringing an area of expertise that contributes to the overall success.

and prior experiences, talents, training, and any special expertise. The writer indicates that résumés are included in the appendix. Key members could include the entrepreneur, floor manager, sales manager, and buyer. Descriptions include key members' job duties, such as buying, selling, advertising, and marketing.

»   **Compensation and ownership of the management team**—The plan addresses how the owner(s) will be paid. It includes and describes the compensation package for the entrepreneur and management team. This is often listed in chart form, with salaries, benefits, bonuses, and stock options, if any.

»   **The qualifications, roles, duties, and compensation of employees**—This section addresses the amount employees will be paid and any incentive programs. Incentives may include bonuses and flex time. If an incentive plan is offered, there should be an explanation of the plan as well as of performance goals tied to projected revenues. If applicable, the plan discloses any special recognition awards and commissions. Key points are summarized, and any supporting documents placed in the appendices.

»   **The identities of the board of directors or advisory council (if applicable)**—The plan lists in table form the board of directors and advisory council members, including names, titles, addresses, and phone numbers. It is important to list members' potential contribution, salary, benefits, and any ownership in the company. The plan highlights their qualifications as they relate to the fashion retail business.

»   **Communication**—It clearly determines how the values and expectations of the business will be communicated to both internal and external stakeholders. It also explains what system will be used to ensure communication is clear.

»   **Any governmental approvals necessary to operate the business legally**—This may include the obtainment of a business license or approval by a planning and zoning commission.

The management plan is discussed in detail in Chapter 9.

It is important to recognize that key people both within and outside the company will be involved in the business. No entrepreneur works in isolation, and successful businesses require a team. FIGURE 2.4 illustrates how the fashion entrepreneur interfaces with outside sources.

MERCHANDISING/PRODUCT PLAN

The **merchandising/product plan** section of the business plan describes the products and services being offered to the customer. It states what is being delivered in broad terms, such as accessories, beauty products, menswear, or women's wear. Because the reader may not be familiar with particular designers or lines, it is a good idea to include photos or drawings of the product line in the appendix of the business plan. Many fashion entrepreneurs use storyboards to present concepts visually to funders. In addition, the competitive advantage of the product/service mix is described in terms of unique features or benefits and whether any legal protection has been or should be obtained, such as trademarks, copyrights, or patents. FIGURE 2.5 clearly shows the types of products offered by this retail store and could be included in the appendix of the business plan.

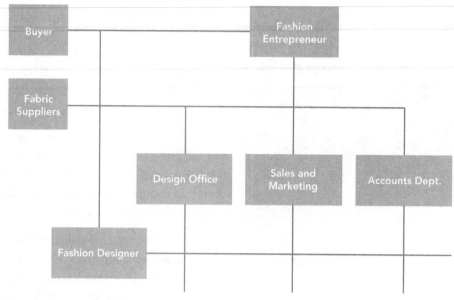

FIGURE 2.4

The organizational matrix shows how the fashion entrepreneur works with the fashion designer, design office, sales and marketing, accounts department, fabric suppliers, and buyers (customers/clients).

In the fashion retail industry it is important to know that the merchandise can be located and will be delivered. Some manufacturers will not supply their product lines to a start-up company, even if the entrepreneur stands at the door waiting with cash in hand.

FIGURE 2.5

Providing specific examples of a similar product line enables the reader of the business plan to visualize the merchandise planned for the new business.

The supplier may require the business be open one to two years before getting its merchandise to ensure that the business will be there, able to pay its bills, and that it will not be closed in six to twelve months. In addition, some lines are sold exclusively, limited to one or a few retailers in a city or region.

The merchandising/product plan section of the business plan should cover the following:

» **Description of the product**—This section describes the product and the product mix. It provides a list of the products that will be offered. The writer should consider using catalogs of merchandise with percentages of sales to describe the product mix.

» **Unique characteristics**—Anything unique about the merchandise or product, such as price, design, or quality, should be described here. The plan tells about the unique features of the store, such as store design and layout and exclusivity of the merchandise. Any available photographs or drawings of the exterior and signage and the layout of the store interior should be included in the appendices and cited in this section. Jack Rabbit is an example of a specialty retail store passionate about educating people about running and triathlon and to make sure everyone makes the best choices in gear. Jack Rabbit is illustrated in FIGURE 2.6.

» **Proposed lines**—It is important to list the various suppliers and when and how the merchandise will be delivered. The reader will want to know the process used to purchase merchandise, at what time of the year it is to be purchased, and how vendors will be paid.

» **Proprietary aspects**—If any licenses or royalty agreements will be obtained, these are clearly outlined. In the fashion industry, perhaps this will be the only retail operation to provide a certain line of clothing in this market.

» **Merchandise assortment**—Fashion retail entrepreneurs should be able to identify the assortment of merchandise and describe how that assortment will satisfy customer needs and allow the business to meet planned sales goals.

FIGURE 2.6
Jack Rabbit sets itself apart by focusing on state-of-the-art tools to help recommend running shoes, by offering the most advanced shoe fitting service, and by ensuring a highly trained staff.

» **Market trips**—This section lists the market trips planned for the year and the cost of attending each. It is helpful to list the reasons these particular trips will benefit the business and sales.

» **Markup/markdown policies**—In fashion retail, markups and markdowns are common practice. Various methods exist with regard to each of these policies. This section outlines the policies that will be implemented to markup and markdown merchandise.

Information needed to complete the merchandising/product plan is discussed in detail in Chapters 4 and 10.

BRICK-AND-MORTAR LOCATION PLAN

The **brick-and-mortar location plan** describes the business in terms of its physical location. Location plays a key role in the success of any fashion retail business. In developing the location section of the business plan, the entrepreneur must be careful to address the following topics:

» **Physical location**—This section addresses the physical location of the business, including city, state, and street address. The location of the business is disclosed in terms of the region of the country in which it will be located. It also provides information as to hours of operation.

» **Location features**—Knowing the amount of square footage available for merchandise is key to a successful fashion retail business. This section allows the entrepreneur to describe the physical location of the business in terms of square footage—allocation to selling space, office space, storage, and so on. It also addresses parking facilities and merchandise receiving access, all critical elements in selecting a location.

» **Target market considerations**—Accessibility for the target market is important. This section addresses accessibility ease for the customer—the distance of the building from major streets, highways, or interstates. It will encourage the entrepreneur to consider the ease or difficulty that customers may have in accessing the storefront.

» **Leasehold improvements**—Most buildings require some sort of leasehold improvement. The improvements enable the store to be functional and inviting. This section addresses what lease-hold improvements will be necessary to make the store attractive and functional for the customer as well as employees.

» **Other location costs**—This addresses any costs that may be incurred that do not fall under the heading of leasehold improvements; for example, the cost of inspections to ensure the building meets code.

» **Signage**—Signage is critical. Customers must be able to locate the store easily. It must be seen. This section addresses the size of the sign; its location in relation to traffic (foot, vehicular); and how easy it is to see the sign from a distance.

The location plan is discussed in detail in Chapter 6.

WEB PLAN SUMMARY

The **Web plan summary** describes the online business opportunity. These days, most brick-and-mortar retail businesses also operate an online retail store, or use the Web as a means to advertise the business. This section looks at the online portion of the business specifically. It enables the reader and the entrepreneur to know the purpose of the site (to provide information, to drive sales, to serve as a way to purchase merchandise) and how the site will be established. It also shows the entrepreneur has thought through the details of maintaining the site and providing ease of use for consumers. This section addresses the following topics:

» **Overview**—This section provides an overview of the products offered, how the site is positioned against other sites, and what will be required to launch the site.

» **Internet strategies**—This section describes the type of e-model that will be used to drive sales.

» **Online marketing strategy**—This is an opportunity for the entrepreneur to explore how he or she will drive traffic to the Web site. Methods may include e-advertising and blogging. This section addresses the online brand strategy and how this strategy will be used in relation to marketing.

» **Web development and hosting**—Web sites require development and hosting. This section addresses how the site will be developed, who will host the site, and how customers will make purchases.

» **Costs**—Some Web sites can be developed for little cost. Others require more significant funding. The entrepreneur addresses the costs incurred in developing and maintaining an online presence.

» **Buying and shipping methods**—Today's consumers expect ease of purchasing and receiving merchandise. This section discusses timing and shipping methods and how online transactions will work. It discusses the measures that ensure the site is secure, in relation to online purchases.

» **Future features**—As the business evolves, the site will evolve as well. This is an opportunity to evaluate any additional features that may be added now or in the future to attract customers.

Establishing an online presence is addressed in detail in Chapter 7.

MARKETING PLAN

The **marketing plan** describes the entrepreneur's intended actions for bringing his or her product or service to market and for persuading consumers to buy. The marketing section of the plan is divided into five parts: industry profile, market analysis, competitive analysis, pricing structure, and market penetration. The industry profile is an in-depth look at the internal and external factors that affect the fashion industry. It includes a listing of the major competitors in the industry, the demographics and psychographics of the industry's customers, and the economic trends in the fashion industry as well as factors that affect these trends. For example, the current economy has affected how consumers are buying—when and how much is being spent. This section gives the entrepreneur an opportunity to address how this recent trend may impact the proposed venture.

The marketing plan describes the target market and how that market will be penetrated. It must convince the reader that there is a large enough market to make the venture successful. It describes the promotional efforts that will be implemented to reach the customer. To develop a good marketing, plan the entrepreneur should address the following questions:

» **Industry profile**—This section provides an overview of the industry from a global perspective. It includes trends in the industry that may affect the business and any profit characteristics to be taken into consideration. It is an opportunity to address how consumer buying behaviors, technology, and online shopping impact success.

» **Market economic factors**—This section discusses the economic trends or patterns that are occurring in the specific geographic location of the business. What is happening globally may not necessarily be happening locally.

» **Market analysis summary**—This describes the primary target market, including both demographic and psychographic information. It includes the general location of the target market in relation to the physical location of the business. Questions addressed may include what percentage of the total market the target market occupies; whether a second market has been identified; and, if so, who this market is and how it will be targeted.

» **Market needs**—This section defines any gaps in the marketplace and how the business will meet the needs of that particular market.

» **Customer profile**—This section determines who the targeted customer is. The customer is described in terms of age, gender, profession, income, geographic location, and other demographics. Also included are customer psychographics—attitudes, values, belief systems, and social status. Any testimonials, results from market surveys, focus group studies, and the like should be incorporated into this section.

» **Future markets**—In this section the entrepreneur discusses any opportunities that may occur and would open the door to increase sales or change or enhance the product or service offering in the future. Although the future cannot be predicted, following trends can lend some guidance.

» **Competitive analysis**—In this section the entrepreneur should use a competitive matrix and list the main competitors to the business. The matrix includes the locations and sizes of the competing businesses, their strengths and weaknesses, merchandise or products offered, and unique features and benefits. It is important to include any direct competitor that sells similar products/services to the same target market. The sources of the information should be cited. In paragraph form, the writer will also briefly describe indirect competitors—those that offer different products or services that may fill the same need as those of the proposed business.

» **Competitive advantage**—Using a competitive analysis chart, this section summarizes how the entrepreneur's business will compete in the areas of quality, price, unique merchandise, distribution systems, marketing/advertising, and geographic location. Inclusion of the basis for the competitive position in the marketplace is important.

» **Pricing strategy**—The pricing section addresses strategy, the price list (price zones), and pricing policies. In this section the entrepreneur explains why the identified strategies have been selected and will examine the pricing strategies of competitors as well as any constraints or sensitivities that may influence pricing of the product. This section outlines purchase prices, shipping costs, and discounts and introductory offers. If pricing policies including volume pricing or packaging of products, these policies will be addressed. The entrepreneur will also want to address any strategies that impact customer service, such as warranties, guarantees, return policies, alterations, or sales on merchandise.

» **Market penetration**—This section begins by outlining the brand strategy. It identifies the avenues that will be used to reach potential customers. Today, customers are at times seeking information through social media, such as Facebook, LinkedIn, and so on. Will these venues be used to reach potential customers? Will a direct sales force be formed to sell directly to the customer? What is the sales strategy? What, if any, publicity will be used to attract customers? Will trade shows be used as a method to attract customers? How will marketing efforts be evaluated? Analyzing and addressing these questions will better ensure success at breaking through all the advertising and promotional clutter and at reaching customers.

If the business is an online store, how will the Web site be positioned for potential customers find the merchandise? Customers do not automatically flock to newly launched Web sites. Unless marketing and advertising campaigns are in place to target customers and drive traffic to the site, adding online shopping will be a waste of time. Web-based businesses are addressed further in Chapter 7.

The marketing plan is discussed in detail in Chapters 3, 7, and 8.

FINANCIAL PLAN

The **financial plan** section provides sound financial statements that reflect the potential profitability of the business. It communicates the amount of funding needed to start and grow the business and how well the business is anticipated to do in relationship to other businesses within the same industry; it will help the entrepreneur run the business on a day-to-day basis. It is absolutely critical that the entrepreneur review and analyze this section of the business plan again and again. Entrepreneurs who spend time carefully considering the impact of their decisions on the financial health of the business are much more likely to succeed.

The financial plan section should include a monthly cash flow statement, a profit and loss statement, and a balance sheet for the business. It is crucial that the numbers presented be real numbers; good funders will know if the writer is being false. Although a new company does not have historical data, it can look to similar businesses in the industry to make assumptions. This section should also include a set of assumptions for the pro forma financials that are being presented. Lack of proper research in this section can close the door before it opens. It should be noted that most funders will want three years of financial statements, from the start-up point to the projected third year of operation. For purposes of this text, the financial statements for one year are presented:

» Cash flow statement

» Assumptions

» Profit and loss statement

» Balance sheet

The financial plan is discussed in detail in Chapter 11.

RETAIL OPERATIONS PLAN

The **retail operations plan** demonstrates that the entrepreneur understands the importance of administrative policies, procedures, and controls. It is used to show that all aspects of the business, from an operation and control point of view, have been addressed. Sections may include:

» **Receiving orders**—This is an outline of the administrative policies, procedures, and controls that will be used to receive merchandise. This section explains how orders will be processed after they are received and describes the type of database that will be used to track this information.

» **Paying suppliers**—This section may outline the administrative policies, procedures, and controls that will be used for paying suppliers. It identifies procedures for controlling due dates on bills. The writer should list accounting and bookkeeping controls that will be needed to pay the suppliers.

» **Reporting to management**—For some larger retailers, entrepreneurs may address the administrative policies, procedures, and controls that will be used for reporting to management. He or she will explain the communication process that employees will follow to report incidents to management. A description of the format and schedule to be used for management meetings, who will attend, and how often meetings will be held may be included.

» **Staffing levels**—This section addresses how the business will ensure it has enough employees to cover the store during seasonal changes and promotional time periods. It addresses staffing considerations in relationship to traffic flow.

» **Inventory control**—Inventory control is critical. The plan may address the administrative policies, procedures, and controls that will be used to control inventory. It will address the frequency of taking physical inventory.

» **Handling returns and exchanges**—How will returns be documented for proper credit? How will exchanges be handled? These questions need to be addressed in this section. The entrepreneur should also identify a system for handling customer complaints. A system should be in place to obtain feedback from customers to improve customer service and potentially add new product.

» **Security systems**—What administrative policies, procedures, and controls will be used for providing security for the business?

» **Documents and paper flow**—What will be the flow of information throughout the system? What documents must be prepared for a transaction? This section identifies all things that should happen in a transaction. It includes examples of invoices, sales tickets, and charge documents, and other such forms, to be found in the appendix.

» **Planning chart: product availability**—When will the merchandise be in and ready for the store to open? List all the activities necessary to get the merchandise in the door. List the names of the persons who will be responsible for each activity as well as completion dates. Outline the timing of events by month, for a minimum of twelve months.

The operating and control systems plan is discussed in detail in Chapter 12.

APPENDICES

Appendices are any documents needed to support the plan. Appendices may include:

» Résumés of the management team and key personnel

» Any employee contracts, such as non-compete agreements or commission agreements

» Personal financial statements for the principal(s) of the business

» Copies of any contracts or documents needed by suppliers

» Samples of advertising brochures or other forms of advertising

» Copies of any logos that have been developed

» Copies of any letters of reference

» Copies of any documents needed to support data in the industry study or marketing plan

» Photographs of the preferred business location

» A map showing the location of the business

» A diagram of the layout of the store

The business plan outlines the elements of the business in detail. The entrepreneur should also be prepared with a one- to two-minute elevator pitch. Most often developed for funding or investment purposes, the elevator pitch introduces the concept in a clear and interesting manner. A description and example are shown in Box 2.4.

BOX 2.4
THE ELEVATOR PITCH

Entrepreneurs should be prepared with a one- to two-minute elevator pitch. The elevator pitch introduces the audience to the new venture and peaks its interest. It is a brief overview of the business, its products, and how it will benefit a particular market. It should be exciting to hear. Try not to get too "fluffy"; people want substance and real meaning.

Elevator pitches are important when running into a potential customer, when pitching to a friend, or when given the opportunity to introduce yourself and your business at an event. However, often they are developed for approaching investors, like on the popular TV show *Dragons' Den*.

Originating in Japan, and broadcast in the United Kingdom on the BBC, *Dragons' Den* has become a global phenomenon. The show features five multimillionaire Dragons looking to invest in Britain's business hopefuls. Entrepreneurs have three minutes to introduce their venture and peak the investors' interest—that is, to give their elevator pitch (http://www.bbc.co.uk/dragonsden/about/).

First, lay out the pain statement. What problem are you solving? Second, you must show the value proposition.

How does your business solve that problem? Be succinct and easy to understand. No tech talk. Make sure, if pitching to investors, that it is clear when and how the business will be profitable. Don't leave the audience with more questions than answers.

"Good morning. My name is José. I've just opened a retail store featuring natural clothing—vegan friendly and earth friendly. Shop our store for fabulous natural clothing, organic accessories, and more—no toxins, no animal products or byproducts in any item in the store. This is the first store of its kind in this area."

CONCLUSION

The importance of a sound business plan cannot be overemphasized. Many potentially successful businesses have failed because they lacked one, and many succeeded because of one. A well-written business plan will serve as an invaluable road map for ensuring that the company reaches its goals. It will be used as a tool for accessing capital and selling the company to potential investors and the management team.

The business plan contains the following components: the cover letter, the cover page, the table of contents, the executive summary, the management plan, the merchandising/product plan, the brick-and-mortar location plan, the Web plan summary, the marketing plan, the financial plan, the retail operations plan, and the appendices. Each section or component should objectively address both the strengths and weaknesses of the business. The business plan will become the tool for making a dream a reality.

KEY TERMS

brick-and-mortar location plan

executive summary

financial plan

management plan

marketing plan

merchandising/product plan

retail operations plan

Web plan summary

DISCUSSION TOPICS

1. Discuss the purpose of a well-researched business plan and its benefits to both the entrepreneur and parties interested in funding or working with the business.

2. Discuss the importance of including sources that support the feasibility of the concept.

3. Discuss the significance of each section of the business plan to the entrepreneur as well as an outside reader.

SUGGESTED READINGS

Abrams, Rhonda. *The Successful Business Plan: Secrets and Strategies*. UK: Capstone Publishing, 2008.

DeThomas, Arthur R., and Stephanie Derammelaere. *Writing a Convincing Business Plan*. Hauppauge, NY: Barron's Educational Series, 2008.

Harvard Business Press. *Writing a Business Plan: The Basics*. Boston: Harvard Business Press, 2004.

ONLINE RESOURCES

ABOUT.COM. SMALL BUSINESS: CANADA
http://www.sbinfocanada.about.com
Small business information

CENTRE FOR FASHION ENTERPRISE
http://www.fashion-enterprise.com
London's pioneering business incubator that supports and nurtures emerging fashion design talent

FASHION ENTREPRENEUR REPORT.
http://www.fashionentrepreneurreport.com
Trends and interviews

BUSINESS PLAN CONNECTION
THINKING LIKE AN ENTREPRENEUR

A key step in developing a business plan is to take a 30,000-foot view of the business plan as a whole. What is a business plan? What issues or questions does it address that make or break a business? Those questions have been addressed in this chapter. As you read the following chapters, the business plan components will be explained in more detail.

There are many resources for reviewing sample business plans and business plan templates. These can be found online or in college or university libraries. While investigating business plans, select a number of entrepreneurs, and ask each about his or her process for developing a plan. What sources were used, and why? How did the business plan impact the success of the entrepreneur's business?

Local nonprofit organizations, such as small business development centers, the Service Corps of Retired Executives (SCORE), universities, and community organizations can be great sources of information. Also, talk to local commercial lenders at banks, or identify investors in your area and ask what they look for in evaluating a plan and loaning or investing money.

The business plan assessment can serve not only as a guide for evaluating your business plan, but also as a tool for developing questions to ask your local entrepreneurs.

⊙ ASSIGNMENT 2.1
THE BUSINESS PLAN ASSESSMENT

1. Open the business plan assessment file in the Chapter 2 folder on the CD-ROM accompanying this text. This assessment will be used to evaluate your business plan as you develop each section.
2. Save the business plan assessment template to your computer.

Your business plan assessment template provides a checklist that may be used to critique your business plan. To become familiar with the criteria that will be used to evaluate your plan, open your saved business plan template file, and review the criteria for each section of the business plan. You will refer to this assessment as you develop each section of the plan. When appropriate, use the checklist, and place an **X** in the Yes or No checkbox to evaluate each section of the business plan. In a separate document, note specific aspects that make the plan strong. For weaknesses, explain how you could improve the plan.

PROFILE OF AN ENTREPRENEUR
ESPRIT

ESPRIT (pronounced *eh SPREE*) means a liveliness of mind, an animated intelligence or wit. It is both the image and the mission of the apparel and accessories retailer Esprit. The company was founded in 1968 in San Francisco by Susie and Doug Tompkins. The pair sold colorful hippie garments out of the back of their van. Today, Esprit has outgrown a fleet of vans. The company, after continued growth throughout the United States, turned its attention to international markets. A flagship store in the United Kingdom, a partnership with the London College of Fashion, an e-commerce push in Canada—Esprit truly went global. The Esprit Group operates more than 800 retail stores worldwide, and its lines are sold through more than 14,000 retail locations owned by other companies internationally. Now, however, the company is again turning its attention to home, with boutiques opening throughout the United States: five new stores opened recently in Manhattan, and twenty openings were planned for 2010–2011. John Gunn, the president of the Americas

for Esprit, is looking forward to the strategic plans for the future of this flourishing global brand.

Esprit is planning to reacquaint growing Gen Xers with the brand. Esprit designers provide not only the basics that have been in the line forever, but also styles that follow the trends closely. The goal is to appeal to both old and new shoppers by offering a variety of lines that appeal to different generations; in other words, to have something for everyone. To connect with the Gen X woman, Esprit has also begun to embrace the world of social media. Gunn plans to tap into sites like Facebook, MySpace, and Twitter to reach new customers and develop deeper relationships with existing ones. Esprit is ready to talk and listen to the customer with a busy life, new technology to connect with family and friends, and nostalgia for the laid-back, cool clothes of the 1970s, when all you needed was love.

SOURCE: Esprit . . . The Interview. Fashion Entrepreneur Report, February 8, 2010. http://fashionentrepreneurreport.blogspot.com/search?updated-max=2010-02-09T21%3A37%3A00-05%3A00&max-results=6

CHAPTER 3
ANALYZING THE INDUSTRY AND FINDING CUSTOMERS

OBJECTIVES

>> **Research the fashion retail industry to identify trends that will impact the success of the business.**

>> **Create a profile of the industry.**

>> **Identify the competitive advantage for the business.**

>> **Investigate and analyze the selected target market.**

THIS chapter focuses on the techniques commonly used to obtain information needed to analyze objectively the fashion industry and a potential target market. Emphasis is placed on how to analyze market data and information for the purpose of developing a comprehensive marketing plan. This section guides an exploration of the fashion industry's current trends, norms, and standards—as well as the demographics and psychographics of the intended market—in order to help the entrepreneur identify and understand opportunities to enhance the development of the retail business and position the business against the competition.

THE REASON FOR A MARKETING PLAN

The marketing plan describes the industry and the entrepreneur's specific actions intended to bring his or her products or services to market and persuade consumers to buy. Without a solid marketing plan, the business is going nowhere. Profitability rests, in large part, on not only identifying a target market, but also ensuring that there is a big enough market to make the business profitable. Researching the market and understanding that market can give the entrepreneur a better idea of the needs, wants, and habits of the customers with whom the entrepreneur will conduct business.

Market research and the analysis of that information impact decisions made throughout the business—from hiring the right sales people, to deciding the type and amount of merchandise to carry, to choosing the best location for the business.

BOX 3.1
BEAUTY IN A BOTTLE

If you want your makeup line to be the next MAC or Maybelline, heed the advice of Larry Oskin, president of Marketing Solutions, a beauty-industry marketing and consulting firm in Fairfax, Virginia.

>> **Define your niche.** Is it for teens, young professionals, or men? "Try to find a niche that no one has," says Oskin.

>> **Package well.** "Beauty care is a highly visual and emotional business," says Oskin. "You have to please the [customer's] emotions and senses." Use your packaging to please all the senses.

>> **Get press.** Try to get coverage from mainstream and trade beauty press. Familiarize yourself with beauty editors—send press kits (with samples, if possible) along with seasonal press releases.

>> **Don't be ruled by trends.** For long-term success, create a cosmetics offering that has staying power.

>> **Get good distribution channels.** Decide if you want to sell via department stores, online shops, specialty cosmetics stores or drugstores. Where does your target market shop?

>> **Plan to grow.** "You need a long-term approach to beauty care because it's rarely an overnight success story," Oskin says. Develop a three- to five-year plan of line extensions. Always have something new up your sleeve to delight the beauty-conscious consumer.

SOURCE: Torres, Nichole L. "Puttin' on the Glitz: It's a Beautiful Day," *Entrepreneur*, April 2004. http://www.entrepreneur.com/article/70024 with permission of Entrepreneur Media, Inc.

The marketing plan begins with an overview of the industry, the potential for growth, and trends that may lead to opportunities for the business. It then profiles the intended target market and how that market is going to be reached and then be influenced to buy. The plan identifies and analyzes the competition, then outlines a pricing and market penetration strategy to drive sales.

The marketing plan will answer the following questions:

>> What is happening in the industry that will impact consumer behavior, and, subsequently the prospective business?

>> Who is the target market?

>> What is the profile of the customer?

>> Who are the competitors, and how will this business be positioned against that competition?

>> What promotional efforts will be used to reach the market?

>> How will the products or services be priced?

>> What gaps exist in the immediate market, and how will this business fill those gaps?

>> How much money will the marketing efforts cost?

Box 3.1 offers advice from Larry Oskin, the president of Marketing Solutions, on marketing products in the beauty industry.

Successful entrepreneurs are those who are good at keeping an eye on the marketplace and identifying needs and gaps, then finding ways to fulfill those needs and close the gaps. Successful entrepreneurs are continually researching and reevaluating their marketing plans to determine whether there are new and better opportunities to grow their businesses.

DEFINING MARKET RESEARCH

Market research is an organized effort to find out information about an industry, the market, and its customers. Here, the term **industry** refers to all companies supplying similar or related products (which can include services). Market research identifies trends and provides answers to questions such as how consumers respond to products or services; how they buy; when they buy; and what they want, need, or believe. Market research provides the entrepreneur with information that will prevent the investment of funds and resources into a venture with insufficient customers to make the venture worthwhile. The research helps identify opportunities to turn ideas into a real business. Moreover, because markets, trends, and customers are constantly changing, market research is ongoing. The more an entrepreneur knows about a particular industry and market, the better he or she is at identifying gaps, needs, and unfulfilled wants.

Through market research, entrepreneurs can identify more effective ways of communicating with their target markets. Understanding customers' buying and spending habits, for example, can aid in the development of marketing campaigns designed to meet the specific interest and needs of the intended market. Research can also help entrepreneurs spot potential obstacles to the proposed concept, such as competition that was not readily identified and that would inhibit the ability to gain a competitive advantage, for example, a plan to develop a large shopping center with a number of retailers that would detract customers from the proposed business.

A systematic process of conducting research enables the entrepreneur to take a focused approach.

>> What are the trends in this particular industry?

>> Which markets have the greatest potential?

>> Who makes up the target market, and what are its needs?

>> What is the size of the potential target market?

The following list explains the systematic process for conducting research:

>> Step 1: Outline the scope of what you want to know.

>> Step 2: Identify sources of information.

>> Step 3: Research the industry.

>> Step 4: Identify and understand the market.

>> Step 5: Understand the customer or target market.

>> Step 6: Analyze the competition.

>> Step 7: Research supply channels and methods of distribution.

>> Step 8: Research the location.

>> Step 9: Analyze the information.

STEP 1: OUTLINE THE SCOPE OF WHAT YOU WANT TO KNOW

Entrepreneurs increase their chance of success by asking the right questions—ones that are not too open-ended or broad. This step enables entrepreneurs to step back and outline an overall scope so they can then formulate a series of questions to drive the process. As the research progresses, the scope and series of questions may change.

To aid in narrowing the focus, entrepreneurs should concentrate on finding and analyzing information that will lead to a greater understanding of these areas:

>> **Trends**—Keep your eye on trends that will have either a positive or negative impact on the proposed business concept.

>> **Who the customers are**—Knowing what the customers want will ensure the right products or services are directed at the right target market.

>> **Where the customers will make their purchase**—The products or services may be purchased online, through brick-and-mortar retailers, or through other distribution channels.

- **The price customers are willing to accept**—Learn what customers will pay for the products or services and what they perceive as value. Researching pricing strategies for the customers of other entrepreneurs in the same industry will guide the pricing strategy for the proposed business.

- **How customers receive their messages**—Various means exist to reach customers in today's market, including social networking and other Web sites; radio, television, and newspaper advertising; direct mail, and so on. However, entrepreneurs typically have limited funds during the start-up phase. Understanding the best way to reach potential customers through promotional activities will save time and money and make efforts more effective.

- **The basis of the competition**—The entrepreneur is faced with competition both directly or indirectly. Understanding how the competition will react to the proposed business is important to decisions impacting pricing, location, distribution, and so on.

- **How products or services reach the intended market**—This involves researching supply channels and methods of distribution.

STEP 2: IDENTIFY SOURCES OF INFORMATION

Numerous sources exist to discover information, from global data to local data. Research data can be divided into two categories. **Primary data** is information that is obtained through **mystery shoppers** (people who pose as normal customers; they provide detailed reports on their shopping experiences), surveys, interviews, or focus groups. Primary information is firsthand information. Box 3.2 summarizes ways of collecting primary data.

Observation

Much can be discovered by spending time with customers, observing how they buy, when they buy, what their perceived sense of value is, and how they react to customer service offerings. By visiting various stores—either brick-and-mortar or online, or both—entrepreneurs have opportunities to examine both strengths and weaknesses of retail businesses. They can analyze the visual merchandising, the ambience, how much customers will pay for an item, what attracts their attention, and what does not. The aspiring entrepreneur can become a customer for a day, for a real-life experience.

Surveys

Surveys are common and inexpensive. They provide feedback about the product or service through questions answered in person; by phone, fax, or mail; or via Internet options. Surveys can provide a nonthreatening way for consumers to give their personal and honest opinions, enabling them to be more open about their wants and needs and about their feelings toward the product or service.

Interviews

Interviews are conducted in person or by phone. Interviews can provide an advantage over surveys in that they allow the interviewer to reword questions based on the answers received for the previous questions. The ability to focus the interview can result in more in-depth responses and more relevant information.

Whether utilizing surveys or interviews, the questions should be focused on the customers' needs, perspectives, and preferences for merchandise, pricing, location, and buying behaviors, such as when, how, and what they buy.

Focus Groups

A **focus group** is a form of research in which a group of people are asked their opinions, perceptions, beliefs, and attitudes toward a product or service, advertisement, idea, or packaging. Focus groups can benefit the entrepreneur by allowing the collection of information from a larger group of people without the need to collect the information one-on-one. This helps control the cost of research. Focus groups should be large enough to represent the market, but not so large that the group can get out of control. Participants are allowed to talk freely and share ideas.

To conduct a focus group, begin by determining the overall goal. Then invite participants to attend who

BOX 3.2
KEY POINTS FOR GATHERING INFORMATION FROM PRIMARY SOURCES

» Mystery shopping or observation—Watching what people buy, counting the number of customers making purchases.

» Survey or focus group—administering a survey one-on-one or coordinating a group of people to discuss the proposed business.

» Interviews—Talking with business owners, professors, bankers, and prospective customers.

» Industry events—Attending market week, trade shows, or designer fashion shows.

Methods of gathering primary data include interviews (left) and attendance at industry events (right).

are representative of the customer the business hopes to attract. These participants can be found through networks, such as professional organizations and social media, or by approaching people shopping in stores similar to the proposed business. Next, ensure success in obtaining information that determines the feasibility of the particular business or product by:

» Developing a series of questions to ask the group to keep the process on track

» Planning the session at a time convenient for participants and in a relaxed environment

» Choosing a skilled and unbiased facilitator to lead the group

Secondary data is information that is already there for the taking, either in print or online, and provides a more inexpensive manner in which to gather information. This type of information generally focuses on industry trends, customer demographics,

BOX 3.3
LIST OF SECONDARY SOURCES

» Internet—Web site addresses listed in the appendices.

» Media agencies—Promotional agencies or media sources, such as newspapers, radio, and television.

» Census data—Available in print and online at http://www.census.gov.

» Newspapers—Determine trends by scanning articles in periodicals, such as the *Wall Street Journal* and the *New York Times*.

» Magazines—Consumer publications, such as *InStyle, People, House & Garden*, and *W*, to gain insight on trends, vendors, and retailers.

» Fashion industry trade journals—Depend upon the sector of the industry and the merchandise classifications; some are *Women's Wear Daily, STORES, Accessories, Footwear News, VMSD* (visual merchandising and store design) and *Chain Store Age*.

» Business magazines—*Inc., Entrepreneur, Bloomberg Businessweek, Money*, and *Forbes*, to name a few.

» Business publications and indexes—Standard & Poor's, Hoover's (http://www.hoovers.com).

» Competition information—Check Standard & Poor's profiles as well as Dun & Bradstreet and companies' annual reports.

» Banks—Lending institutions often provide blind data on types of businesses funded and loan amounts.

» Planning offices—Often employed by cities and counties.

» Chambers of commerce—There is often a person at the chamber of commerce assigned to small business development who will have industry data available.

» The monthly catalog of U.S. Government Publications—Call, write, or e-mail the U.S. Government Printing Office (GPO). The Catalog is a comprehensive index of available government documents. It can be accessed by subject, author, or title, and it contains a current list of publications issued by departments and bureaus of the U.S. government.

» Reports—From colleges and universities, including small business development centers.

» Databases—Some are free; some are not. Good ones include the Dow Jones News/Retrieval, Lexis/Nexis (available in many college libraries), and CompuServe.

» Real estate firms—Major real estate companies have demographic data summaries that they make available to the public.

» U.S. Small Business Administration (SBA)—Call, write, or locate at http://www.sba.gov.

» North American Industry Classification System (NAICS)—A system in which a number is assigned to almost every identifiable industry; these codes are contained in the North American Industry Classification System Manual, which is available in most libraries.

» Trade associations and organizations—Fashion Group International, Inc.; American Apparel & Footwear Association (AAFA); and International Apparel and Textile Association (ITTA).

Sources of secondary data include the Internet (left) and fashion trade publications (right).

and buying behaviors. Resources include trade journals, such as *STORES* magazine; fashion magazines, such as *W* and *InStyle*; government agencies, such as the Census Bureau, the Department of Commerce, and the Small Business Administration; financial services companies, such as Standard & Poor's and Moody's; news organizations; and trade associations. These sources can be found via the Internet or by visiting a public, college, or university library.

Other resources that can provide information for the actual business plan include display fixture companies, insurance agents, certified public accountants, attorneys, the local utility commission, and mall management. Box 3.3 provides a list of sources for collecting secondary data.

After collected, data can then be divided into **quantitative data,** information that is based on numbers (e.g., sales figures, number of retailers in a geographic area, and an individual's size), and **qualitative data**, information that is based on attitudes, beliefs, behaviors, views, or emotions.

STEP 3: RESEARCH THE INDUSTRY

It is important to recognize that no company operates in a bubble. Entrepreneurs will research an industry thoroughly to determine current trends, behaviors, and growth potential. They will identify strengths and work to anticipate future directions. By comparing the history of an industry with its current size and growth potential, the entrepreneur evaluates the industry's stability and opportunities. The fashion industry is affected by seasonal buying patterns, cyclical patterns, and the economy. Knowing this will help the entrepreneur in the planning phase of the new venture.

As stated earlier, the term *industry* refers to all companies supplying similar or related products (which can include services). It also encompasses the supply and distribution organizations supporting such companies. Types of companies representing the fashion industry include, but are not limited to, fabric and apparel manufacturers, manufacturers' representatives, trend forecasting services, fashion promotion companies, trade publications, and retail operations. A model of the types of businesses that make up the fashion industry is shown in FIGURE 3.1.

External factors, such as trends that affect the general industry, will likely affect the smaller businesses within it. The entrepreneur must be able to articulate how the prospective business will be similar to and different from those companies within the broader scope of the industry. The entrepreneur must also know where the industry is headed.

With so much information available about the fashion industry, it is important to focus on those aspects that may have an impact on the potential success of the proposed venture.

STEP 4: IDENTIFY AND UNDERSTAND THE MARKET

Because the fashion industry is dependent on economics, both nationally and internationally, it is critical to understand the economic conditions and cycles that can (and likely will) affect its businesses. Retail businesses, such as discount children's clothing stores and resale apparel shops, perform relatively better in poor economic cycles than in strong ones. Luxury products, such as special occasion wear and expensive home furnishings, have a higher success rate when the economy is on an upswing.

Entrepreneurs should identify the markets in which their businesses will most likely be well received. For example, if baby boomers are spending more time and money on beauty products, perhaps an entrepreneur's wanting to sell a new line of beauty products is a timely business concept. If people are entertaining at home more frequently than in the past, maybe a loungewear apparel retail operation with an online channel of distribution has a high chance of success. There are a number of resources that provide data on social, demographic, and political shifts in the world population. Li Edelkoort, the founder of the trend forecaster Trend Union, identifies population trends, projects outcomes for these trends, and presents findings using a number of venues. There are also a number of publications that focus on population analysis, such as *American Demographic* magazine, *Marketing Today* magazine, and *Sales and Marketing Management*. More recently, there is an emerging market for private database vendors, companies that prepare custom demographic reports for a fee.

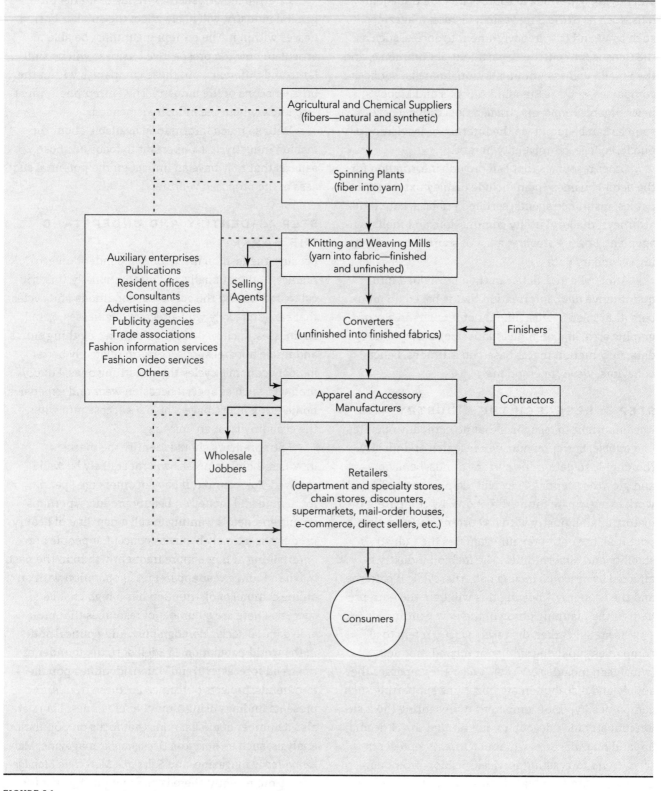

FIGURE 3.1

A fashion industry model.

STEP 5: UNDERSTAND THE CUSTOMER OR TARGET MARKET

After researching the industry and the market, the entrepreneur will home in on a specific target market. A **target market** is the specific group of customers that a business intends to capture. No business can be all things to all people. The key questions are, "Who are my potential customers?" and "Why will they buy my products?" Understanding the market at this level enables the entrepreneur to consider whether the concept will meet the needs and wants of that particular market. Through research, the customer most likely to purchase the product or service will be identified. This group then becomes the target market.

The target market or market segment is typically based on a set of characteristics identified through research and statistical analysis:

» **Demographics**—The segmentation of markets based on age, gender, education, occupation, geographic location, race, nationality, income, religion, and other commonly used census classifications. It is important that the entrepreneur identify which of these variables are relevant to the target market.

» **Psychographics**—The segmentation of markets based on the lifestyle or personality characteristics. The entrepreneur examines variables such as how consumers spend their time; their interests and activities; and their values, behaviors, and emotions.

Consumers may also be described based on how they will use the product or service. Will they become one-time purchases or repeat customers? Will they use the product in a professional or personal setting? Consumers buy based on a need or want. A consumer may be prohibited from wearing certain fashions at work, but may want to distinguish him- or herself in personal situations. FIGURE 3.2 illustrates that the market can be diverse in many ways but that "everyone" is not your target market. By asking the right kinds of questions, such as those that follow, the entrepreneur can find commonality and thereby narrow the market to a level that is reachable:

» Is the intended target market primarily male, female, or a combination of both?

» What is the age range of the potential customers?

» What is the geographic location of the customer?

» What are their most likely occupations?

» What are their general likes and dislikes?

» What makes your product more desirable to these customers than the competition's product or service?

» What does the target market do for entertainment—movies? restaurants? walks?

» What image are they trying to project with the type of clothing or accessories they wear?

» How frequently do they shop?

» What do they buy?

» Where does the target customer buy—online? retail stores? shopping malls?

» List all the ways contact could be made with the target customer.

FIGURE 3.2

The target market for your business can be both diverse and specialized.

By understanding the target market—the *who*, *what*, *where*, *when*, and *why*—the entrepreneur will better ensure merchandise is purchased that will sell and respond to market shifts more quickly. The entrepreneur will also better target marketing dollars, aiming marketing messages at those consumers most receptive to them.

Begin by thinking about the market that may be most interested in the product or service. Ask why a person might be interested in this particular merchandise. For example, this store may be the only store in the market that carries uniforms for the medical industry.

Next, create a profile of a person that might represent this particular market. Include his or her hobbies and interests, where he or she lives, an estimated income, why and where he or she currently buys, and when this person buys. Consider how this business can meet the unmet needs or wants of this particular market.

Then go where the prospective market goes. Visit Web sites that may be of interest to these consumers. Read magazines they may read. Visit stores that carry similar products that consumers may be buying as a substitute for what they really desire.

STEP 6: ANALYZE THE COMPETITION

An understanding of the competition, both direct and indirect, helps the entrepreneur develop a better business strategy and make better decisions about the prospective business. **Direct competitors** include businesses that offer essentially the same product or service. **Indirect competitors** include businesses that offer different types of products or services that may meet the same need or want of the buyer. This is particularly important in a market where consumers have access to products and services around the globe via the Internet.

By developing a competitive matrix, entrepreneurs can more easily compare their businesses with those of the competition. The matrix outlines how the prospective business compares in price range, product, quality, unique features, distribution system, marketing, location, and strengths and weaknesses. FIGURE 3.3 provides a sample competitive matrix. Use this matrix to analyze potential competitors of the proposed business.

One way to obtain this information is to conduct interviews with direct competitors outside of the target location. Talking with a competitor outside the trade area can provide a significant amount of information that local competitors are hesitant to share—information about the industry, the marketplace, and the operations of the business.

Identifying indirect competitors can be more difficult, but it is certainly not impossible. To identify indirect competitors, entrepreneurs look at the wants or needs of their customers these businesses are satisfying rather than the specific products or services. When this is accomplished, entrepreneurs then perform the same research that is conducted on the direct competition; they analyze pricing, marketing efforts, and marketing messages, and then determine whether there are ways to take advantage of the indirect competitors' weaknesses.

Understanding the competition enables the entrepreneur to find opportunities to gain a competitive advantage. A competitive advantage may be based on price, flexibility with the sales force, the speed at which the customer can access the product or service, location, or customer service. It is how the business performs better than competitors.

Some of the questions the entrepreneur should answer when compiling information regarding the competition on a geographic, national, and international level include:

» What are the major companies in the industry?

» How many new firms have entered this industry in the past five years?

» What new products have been introduced in this industry in the past five years? Why or why not?

» What is the basis for competition within the industry? Is it, for example, price, merchandise selection, or prestige?

COMPETITIVE ANALYSIS MATRIX

	Your Business	Company A	Company B	Company C	Company D
Product/Service					
Price Range					
Quality					
Unique Features					
Distribution System					
Marketing/Advertising					
Geographic Location					
Strengths					
Weaknesses					

FIGURE 3.3

» Historically, how difficult has it been for new businesses to enter the industry?

» Can you profile the intended customer based on national and international statistics?

» How is this segment of the market captured?

Answers to these questions are found using secondary sources of information. One of the ways entrepreneurs compete is by identifying a niche market. A **niche market** is defined as providing a product or service to a narrowly defined group of potential customers. For example, a niche market may be clothing for persons undergoing treatment for a major medical condition, such as cancer; high-end, or luxury, fashion for children; or accessories for motorcycle enthusiasts.

Entrepreneurs should know the personality, thought processes, and reactions of consumers to products for every significant competitor. It is important to identify the businesses that will provide the most significant competition and to anticipate what to do if a new business enters the market.

Conducting a **SWOT** (strengths, weaknesses, opportunities, and threats) **analysis** provides a way to identify the strengths, weaknesses, and opportunities of the proposed business when compared with the competition, as well as threats against it. Strengths are the attributes that give the business a competitive advantage over the competition. Weaknesses are the attributes that may limit the ability to perform as well as the competition. Opportunities are the possibilities of new or improved products that current competitors are not delivering. Threats include external conditions that can have a negative impact, such as shifts in buying behaviors and the economy. It is helpful to track this information in the form of a matrix. Using the template provided in FIGURE 3.4 conduct a SWOT analysis for the proposed business venture. Answering the following questions will be helpful:

» How do businesses within the industry compete for business? Is the competition based on price, location, promotion, or service?

» Are there changes in the economy or buying behaviors that have had an impact or that will have an impact on sales?

By understanding how each competitor is positioned in the market, the entrepreneur can position the business in the marketplace based on its competitive advantage. The entrepreneur will be able to list, prioritize, and focus on the items that are critical to the success of the venture.

STEP 7: RESEARCH SUPPLY CHANNELS AND METHODS OF DISTRIBUTION

The supply and distribution channels in an industry can greatly affect the opportunity for a business's entry into the field. In the fashion industry limited supply can create demand. For example, several years ago Ugg boots were hard-to-find items, which built demand. They were retailing for approximately $150 in the store and selling for triple that on eBay. **Supply channels** are the companies that provide materials and equipment needed to manufacture the product as well as the companies that actually produce the goods. Supply channels can dramatically influence the success or failure of a business. For example, a new fabrication may be expensive to produce and, therefore, may be available only in garments at higher prices. Limited supply can mean fewer sources, higher costs, and greater vulnerability to failure. It is important for the entrepreneur to explore the number and location of supply sources and the availability of distribution channels by, for example, investigating the apparel markets in the area and the vendors showing at these markets.

Distribution channels are the routes taken to move the product to the consumer. They can include selling directly to a manufacturer, a retail operation, wholesale businesses, or the ultimate consumer. They can also include selling through a traditional retail store, the Internet, a catalogue, or television. Analysis of the availability of distribution channels requires an examination of the different ways a business can deliver its product or service to its primary consumer. Some businesses target more than one customer

SWOT ANALYSIS

Strengths	Weaknesses
Opportunities	Threats

FIGURE 3.4

market and elect to use more than one channel of distribution. Others, particularly in the start-up stage, focus on one target market and one channel of distribution. There are advantages and disadvantages to the latter approach.

For example, a contemporary dress manufacturer based in Dallas, Texas, targeted a major department store and was contracted to produce private label dresses designed exclusively for the department store and made to its specifications. This was an advantage in that the manufacturer could focus its limited resources on one buyer. The company filled the order and shipped the dresses directly to its one client.

However, the department store had a poor selling season and did not reorder. This left the manufacturer struggling to build a larger customer base and a channel of distribution almost overnight. The dresses had been made to specifications outlined by the department store, and the manufacturer did not have another source to distribute.

STEP 8: RESEARCH THE LOCATION
Location is key for customers in a fashion retail business (FIGURE 3.5). It *can* be the single most important variable to consider. Location is covered in detail in Chapter 6. For purposes of this section, location is

FIGURE 3.5

Uniqlo, a Japan fashion retail giant, takes on Gap and H&M by strategically locating its flagship store in the center of a busy tourist and shopping district in Paris that is also home to the large French department stores Galeries Lafayette and Printemps that attract large numbers of potential customers.

addressed in relation to the customer. Whether an online or offline location, there are several factors to consider:

» What is the location's optimum level of traffic as it relates to the trade area? What generates traffic in the neighborhood—schools? businesses? hospitals? colleges?

» Will locating in close proximity to competitors create an opportunity to benefit from their marketing efforts?

» How does the cost of the location measure against the benefit of access to customers?

» Are there restrictions on signage that would prevent you from advertising the business?

Entrepreneurs can learn a great deal by talking with real estate agents, other retailers in the area, or residents of the neighborhood.

STEP 9: ANALYZE THE INFORMATION

Market research should be analyzed as objectively as possible. Frequently, entrepreneurs do not read data objectively. They see what they want to see. Only through objective analysis can an entrepreneur clearly understand the data collected and determine whether the potential business can be successful.

Market analysis is an evaluation of the conditions of a market; that is, market analysis considers all the information obtained through market research and describes the history and potential future of the market.

Market research and market analysis are processes that encompass all aspects of a company. They affect all business decisions, from hiring the best sales people to deciding which products will be sold. Internal service policies, pricing strategies, location, and promotional plans are also guided by market research and analysis.

SEASONALITY OF THE FASHION INDUSTRY

Seasonal patterns are distinct changes in activity within a calendar year. Seasonal patterns include changes in climate that influence apparel needs and holidays. These patterns affect consumer spending trends. For many types of businesses in the fashion industry, certain times of the year produce higher sales than others, thus affecting sales, cash flow, and profits. Whereas spring is the key season for prom and bridal gown manufacturers, the winter holiday months of November and December result in top revenues for many fashion retailers in other merchandise areas (FIGURE 3.6).

The geographic location of a retail operation also interrelates with the seasonality of merchandise. Retailers, for example, located in southern states with consistently warm climates will carry light-weight goods year round. Particularly in the fashion industry, these seasonal projections will drastically affect cash flow projections outlined in the financial plan.

One of the most effective ways to anticipate seasonal factors is to develop an annual chart showing each month as a percentage of sales for the total year. Table 3.1 illustrates variances between two types of retail stores and their respective monthly revenue projections. These monthly sales projections are not firm or fixed for specialty stores within these two merchandise classifications. Two location factors—climate

FIGURE 3.6

Astute retailers know the wants and needs of their customers. They are ready with what customers want, when they want it.

TABLE 3.1
MONTHLY SALES AS A PERCENTAGE OF SALES FOR THE TOTAL YEAR

	WOMEN'S SPORTSWEAR (%)	SPECIAL OCCASION FORMAL WEAR (%)
January	5	2
February	7	12
March	10	20
April	8	20
May	8	10
June	5	5
July	5	2
August	7	3
September	8	3
October	9	5
November	10	8
December	18	10
TOTAL	**100**	**100**

and community—strongly influence the seasonality of merchandise and services.

Cyclical patterns also affect the fashion retail industry. **Cyclical patterns** are those recurring swings that move the business activity—its sales, cash flow, and profits—from a downslide to an upswing or vice versa. The entrepreneur will want to compare industry cycles with those of the overall economy, using indicators such as the gross domestic product and personal disposable income. Then a determination can be made as to the extent to which industry sales and profits are sensitive to economic change.

THE IMPACT OF TECHNOLOGY

Is there an industry that is not affected by the rapid advances of technology in today's world? The raw materials from which fashion goods are produced, the methods used to manufacture the products, the speed with which they can be delivered, and the way information regarding the performance of these products is managed are some of the areas in which technology affects the fashion industry. Technology has greatly influenced when and how consumers can purchase. Online retail sites make merchandise available 24/7 and enable the consumer to comparison shop at many different locations. Although it is difficult, if not impossible, to predict the future capabilities of technology, it is important to identify the trends of the past five to ten years. In essence, entrepreneurs can create mindsets that enable them to "think future" about technological capabilities by examining recent advances in technology.

FINANCIAL PATTERNS

Financial patterns are the standards and norms used to determine pricing, evaluate merchandise performance, and specify billing terms within the fashion industry. This information is available through trade journals, academic texts, and the publications of industry trade organizations. Financial patterns vary not only by type of business, but also by merchandise classification. For example, a new business owner may expect to pay for merchandise on delivery until a positive credit rating is established. For another business owner with a good credit rating and an approved loan from the bank, the discount for merchandise payment may be an 8 percent discount if the bill is paid within thirty days of the date of the invoice. Although there are no hard and fast rules, there are general industry standards that can be determined from a number of sources. Those who are already in the industry, as well as suppliers of the product lines, are excellent resources for industry standards. What types of financial standards does the entrepreneur need to know? This information is examined in greater detail in Chapter 11.

Knowledge of financial standards within the industry is critical in helping the entrepreneur accurately develop financial plans for the business. Start-up expenses, monthly budgets for inventory payment, and profit potential are all locked onto these industry financial standards. Knowing the general industry norms allows the entrepreneur to determine specifics for the business plan. Industry information can be found in publications by Standard & Poor's and on Hoover's.

CONCLUSION

The key purpose of studying the industry and the customer is to identify strategic opportunities that exist—present and future—for a new business in the fashion industry. Study involves examination of the external and internal environments in which the business will operate. The resulting data and background information will either support or refute the business concept. In some cases, the prospective entrepreneur will scrap the plan and return to concept development when the study does not support the original idea. Scrapping the plan is better to do sooner rather than later, after resources (including blood, sweat, and tears) have been poured into the new business.

An analysis of the consumer within the region where the business will be located is of particular importance. Consumer buying behavior and product usage are among the categories examined in the regional consumer analysis. In addition to target market research, general location factors, with a focus on numbers and types of competitors, are examined. Study will further support or disprove the business concept for that particular region. The information obtained from both the industry analysis and the regional analysis is then used to create a sales forecast, a realistic set of assumptions about future sales volume. At this point, the entrepreneur decides to proceed as planned, toss out the business concept, adjust it, or investigate an alternative region in which to launch the business.

KEY TERMS

cyclical patterns

demographics

direct competitors

distribution channels

financial patterns

focus group

indirect competitors

industry

market analysis

market research

mystery shoppers

niche market

primary data

psychographics

qualitative data

quantitative data

seasonal patterns

secondary data

supply channels

SWOT analysis

target market

DISCUSSION TOPICS

1. Discuss the relevance of researching the industry.

2. Examine the process of researching the market, and prepare a list of potential sources.

3. Discuss the differences between primary and secondary data and the value, or benefit, of both.

4. Discuss the various sections of the marketing plan and their relevance to a successful strategy.

5. Discuss the various components of a SWOT analysis.

6. Discuss the impact of technology—present and future—on today's businesses as it relates to a marketing strategy.

SUGGESTED READINGS

American Demographics magazine

Entrepreneur magazine

Falk, Edgar A. *1001 Ideas to Create Retail Excitement.* New York: Prentice Hall, 2003.

Fortune Magazine

McQuarrie, Edward F. *The Market Research Toolbox: A Concise Guide for Beginners.* Thousand Oaks, California: Sage Publications, Inc., 2006.

Penn, Mark. *Microtrends.* New York: Hachette Book Group, 2007.

Kim, W. Chan, and Renée Mauborgne. *Blue Ocean Strategy: How to Create Uncontested Market Space and Make Competition Irrelevant.* Boston: Harvard Business School, 2005.

Underhill, Paco. *Why We Buy: The Science of Shopping.* New York: Simon & Schuster, 1999.

ONLINE RESOURCES

BIZSTATS
http://www.bizstats.com
Size of U.S. markets, by industry.

DUN & BRADSTREET MILLION DOLLAR DATABASE
http://www.dnbmdd.com/mddi/
Subscription database with information on more than one million U.S. public and private companies with sales greater than $1 million. Usually available in business libraries.

FASHION NET
http://www.fashion.net
General industry news, links to other sites, fashion magazines

INFOUSA
http://lp.infousa.com
Subscription database containing more than 14 million business listings, with company profiles and consumer listings. Usually available in business libraries.

WREN
http://www.thewrendesign.com
Li Edelkoort's trend forecast

BUSINESS PLAN CONNECTION
THINKING LIKE AN ENTREPRENEUR

This assignment focuses on specific sections of the marketing plan. After researching the industry, the market, the competition, and the customer, the information obtained is then written into the marketing plan section of the business plan. The specific sections are outlined as follows.

Develop a list of questions outlining information you want to collect and how you want to collect it. This information will be categorized in the marketing plan section of the overall business plan and used to determine the feasibility of the proposed business and its product offerings in relation to the intended market. Refer to the content of this chapter to guide you through the process of conducting research, analyzing that research, and determining whether the concept is feasible from a marketing perspective.

Libraries and the Web provide a significant amount of secondary information on the industry at the national and international levels. Examples include demographics for specific geographic regions, lists of national trade associations, and trends publications.

Visit a number of fashion retail stores, as well as online sites, and gather information about customers: why they buy, what they buy, when they buy, and how they buy. Prepare a matrix that enables you to capture this information and compare the various sites. Be sure to include both the demographics and psychographics of your intended market.

Compile a list of potential competitors, and identify the factors critical to their success. This allows you to compare your business with the competition and find areas in which your business is different and can compete. Be sure to complete a SWOT analysis, which identifies potential strengths, weaknesses, opportunities, and threats.

ASSIGNMENT 3.1
THE COVER LETTER, CONTACT PAGE, AND MARKETING PLAN

1. Open the blank business plan template in the Templates folder on the CD-ROM accompanying this text. Use this template to write your business plan.
2. Save this template to your computer.
3. Address the following sections of the business plan. You may also refer to the sample business plan in Appendix D.

COVER LETTER

Prepare a draft of a cover letter to accompany your business plan. Developing the letter at this stage will help you focus on the intention of the business plan.

CONTACT PAGE

Prepare the contact page of your business plan. This contains the name of your business, the address, and the date prepared.

MARKETING PLAN

Complete the following sections of the marketing plan:

- » Industry Profile
- » Market Economic Factors
- » Market Analysis Summary
- » Market Needs
- » Customer Profile
- » Future Markets
- » Competitive Analysis
- » Competitive Advantage

PROFILE OF AN ENTREPRENEUR
TONI KO: SHE UNDERSTANDS THE MARKET AND DRIVES SUCCESS

T'S more than mattes and frosts for Toni Ko, 30. This cosmetics entrepreneur worked in her family's cosmetics retail business and discovered her desire to be on the creative side of the market, not just the retail side. She saw how popular budget-line cosmetics were, and, through her own experience at the store, she knew just what customers wanted in their makeup.

Armed with that knowledge, Ko set about creating NYX, Los Angeles Inc. in 1999. It was a one-woman show early on, recalls Ko, who worked ten- to twelve-hour days, six days per week during startup.

To save money, she lived with her parents for two years while she developed and sold her line. And although she knew the retail side of the cosmetics industry, Ko had to learn all about the manufacturing and distribution side. "I was so young [25], and people actually thought I was 19 or 20," says Ko. "When I went to manufacturers, they'd look at me like 'Are you kidding?'" She actually worked this perception to her advantage, though. Ko would approach prospective suppliers and ask all the questions she could about the cosmetics business, under the caveat that she was new and needed to learn more. The industry veterans found her candor refreshing, she says, and most were willing to work with her.

She confesses she likes making the world more beautiful, but Ko doesn't particularly subscribe to trends. She creates a line of colors, which range in price from about 99 cents to $7, that she knows her customers will wear because they feel beautiful, not simply because sparkly pink is the season's hot color.

Larry Oskin, a beauty-industry specialist and president of Marketing Solutions, a beauty-industry marketing and consulting firm in Fairfax, Virginia, says this is a good way to approach the ever-changing cosmetics industry. "Don't be afraid to make a new trend or fad," he says. "But it's a pitfall if that's the whole basis of what you're doing." It's good to have a three- to five-year plan of line extensions to solidify your market share and make sure you're not just a blip on the radar.

Like all the entrepreneurs we talked to, Ko knows all too well the unglamorous side of a "glamour" business. "It's not like I'm a makeup artist [who] works backstage at a fashion show," she says. "We travel a lot for trade shows and conventions. It's usually the same city at the same time of year. It's a lot of headaches and a lot of work."

The headaches, though, have paid off. Ko saw sales hit $7.5 million in 2003. Her products are sold at specialty beauty-supply stores nationwide, along with a presence in 200 Longs Drugs stores in Northern California, and online at www.nyxcosmetics.com. Ko would like to expand her lines to include medical color cosmetics (to treat skin blemishes and wrinkles while covering them) and a higher-end beauty line under her recently acquired Doll Face brand. She's already got her fans: Ko recalls striking up a conversation with a saleswoman from the high-end Stila cosmetics line, who raved about the NYX eyeshadows she used in her beauty regime. If beauty is in the eye of the beholder, Ko's success is definitely stunning.

SOURCE: Torres, Nichole L. "Puttin' on the Glitz: It's a Beautiful Day," *Entrepreneur*, April 2004. http://www.entrepreneur.com/article/70024 with permission of Entrepreneur Media, Inc.

CHAPTER 4
IDENTIFYING THE PRODUCT AND THE BUSINESS CONCEPT

THERE are two main types of fashion retail entrepreneurs: those who create the product they sell, and those who sell an existing product. The product is often the source of inspiration for the prospective entrepreneur. It can begin with one of those lightbulb moments. A retail apparel company owner preparing for another overseas buying trip realizes that attractive, fashionable, and packable career apparel is virtually nonexistent. A lightbulb moment. While scanning fashion magazines, she notices more and more articles feature "how to pack" editorials describing new limitations on the weight and number of suitcases allowed by airlines. She finds many new travel publications available for consumer subscription. Another lightbulb moment. She talks to friends, designers, shopkeepers, and travel agents about travel wear needs. One designer shares her ideas for such a collection. The lightbulb moment strikes again. She decides that today's woman needs fashion-forward, interchangeable travel clothing, as shown in FIGURE 4.1. The product line is born, possibly before the trip is booked.

In this chapter, the product is analyzed as part of the development of the business concept. The merchandise a fashion retail store carries is often the critical factor in finding a niche, reaching the defined target market, separating the business from its competition, and assuring profitability. At this stage, entrepreneurs are envisioning the types of products they will feature in their retail operations. Later, in Chapter 10, the buying process for the selected merchandise assortment is examined. Now is the time to investigate the types of products that are available, the levels of products that may be offered, the stage in the product life cycle that these products represent, and the ways of differentiating the inventory from others, specifically through product trends such as branding and licensing.

FIGURE 4.1

The product line is born, possibly before the trip is booked.

DEFINING THE PRODUCT

What is a product? A **product** is anything offered to a market for attention, acquisition, use, or consumption. A product can satisfy a customer's want or need and may be an object, a service, a place, an organization, or an idea. A product can be a dress, a pair of shoes, an image makeover, a promotional plan, a trend forecast, a fashion show production, and more. A product can be classified as intangible or tangible. **Intangible products** include those that cannot be touched or held, such as a service or an idea. **Tangible products** are physical and touchable and are divided into two primary classifications: nondurable goods and durable goods. **Nondurable goods** are those that are normally consumed in one or a few uses, such as shampoo. **Durable goods** are those that normally survive many uses. Apparel, accessories, and fabrics are examples of durable goods. **Service products** are activities, benefits, or satisfactions that are offered for sale. Custom design work, alterations, and personal shopping are illustrations of fashion-related service products.

Another method of classifying products is through brand preference and frequency of use. **Convenience goods** are those that the customer purchases frequently and easily, usually with minimal comparison shopping and evaluating. Pantyhose and some beauty products are examples of convenience goods. **Shopping goods**, on the other hand, are those the customer shops around for and often compares on the basis of price, quality, style, and other related factors. Special occasion apparel, outerwear, and career wear are examples. **Specialty goods** are those for which a significant group of buyers is habitually willing to make a special purchase effort. This merchandise has unique characteristics or specific brand identification, or both, such as Polo Ralph Lauren sportswear and Arche shoes. Merchants work to move their products into the specialty goods arenas because this is where the devoted, repeat customer resides. FIGURE 4.2 illustrates the differences between convenience, shopping, and specialty goods in terms of price, frequency of purchase, type of shopping trip, and level of customer service.

The final category is **unsought goods**. The name says it all. Customers did not seek out the merchandise; they did not even know they needed or wanted it until it found them. Promotion is the key to selling unsought goods. An example is Snuggie, the fleece blanket with sleeves available for men, women, children, and pets in a wide variety of fashion colors and prints. Snuggie is marketed through television demonstrations, magazine advertisements, and Web sites that show the product in use. Who knew anyone needed this new form of apparel? With sales of more than $60 million in 2009, and still going strong, someone knew, and that someone is Scott Boilen, the CEO and president of Allstar Products Group, the company that makes Snuggie.

There are a number of other product terms that are commonly used in the fashion industry. **Fashion goods** refer to items that are popular for a given period of time. **Staple** or **basic goods**, in contrast, are those steadily in demand and rarely influenced by fashion changes. **Hard goods** are appliances, electronics, and home furnishings. **Soft goods** are textile and apparel products, including accessories.

Retailers also refer to merchandise in terms of pricing, with **high-end goods** being at the top of the pricing scale, and **low-end goods** representing lower or budget-priced merchandise. Types of merchandise carried by a retailer or manufacturer are also labeled in the fashion industry. A **merchandise assortment** is the

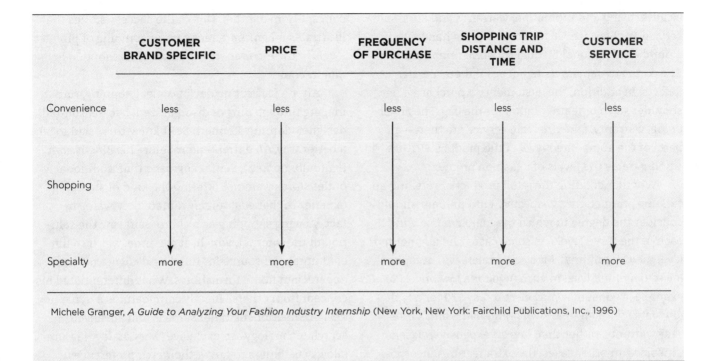

	CUSTOMER BRAND SPECIFIC	PRICE	FREQUENCY OF PURCHASE	SHOPPING TRIP DISTANCE AND TIME	CUSTOMER SERVICE
Convenience	less	less	less	less	less
Shopping					
Specialty	more	more	more	more	more

Michele Granger, *A Guide to Analyzing Your Fashion Industry Internship* (New York, New York: Fairchild Publications, Inc., 1996)

FIGURE 4.2

A comparison of convenience, shopping, and specialty goods.

selection of inventory a retailer carries or a manufacturer produces—the amount, type, size, color, and style representation. **Inventory** is the merchandise selection carried by a retailer, including fashion or basic goods and hard or soft goods, or a combination of these. **General line** refers to a wide variety of merchandise, one that has great breadth. A department store that features women's, men's, and children's apparel, as well as home furnishings and home accessories, illustrates a retail organization with a general line of merchandise. A **limited line** represents the other end of the spectrum, a particular product category with depth of selection. A limited line retail operation, for example, may feature ladies' accessories, handbags, belts, jewelry, and watches.

Why the lesson in fashion language? The entrepreneur in the fashion industry should be able to discuss the business concept in the terms of the trade when communicating with vendors, competitors, or bankers. The way entrepreneurs say what they think often adds credibility and persuasion to the message.

Another reason for understanding product terminology is to allow for the examination of product alternatives. Prospective entrepreneurs considering a fashion retail operation should explore how price lines, assortment alternatives, frequency of purchases, and amounts of fashion and basic merchandise fit within their entrepreneurial vision.

DISSECTING THE PRODUCT

One of the best ways to start analyzing a product is to divide it into parts. The three levels of all products are core, formal, and augmented. **Core** is the true product—the product's main benefit or service. If, for example, the entrepreneur intends to open a business that retails handbags, the core product is the handbag. The **formal** level includes the packaging (e.g., a fabric drawstring bag), the brand name (e.g., Coach), the quality of the product, the styling, and any other tangible features, such as the leather identification tag. The final level, **augmented**, is the product extras, such as advertising and promotion, warranty, and after-sale service. In this case, Coach advertises its handbags in a number of national fashion consumer publications. The company repairs its handbags if there are any defects. In addition, the customer can purchase a new shoulder strap or leather lotion for the bag. The advertising, warranty, and after-sale service are there—all parts of the augmented level of the product. FIGURE 4.3 illustrates the levels of a fashion product.

Whether creating the retail product or retailing an existing product, the prospective entrepreneur should consider the degree to which the merchandise will fill each of the three levels. In some cases, the augmented level may be minimal. Many customers will accept a low-augmented level in exchange for a low price. For example, a consumer may elect to pay $30 for a fashion watch with an unknown brand name and a one-year warranty, rather than buy an expensive, classic timepiece. In other cases, the extra features incorporated in the augmented level distinguish one business

FIGURE 4.3
The core product is the actual handbag; the formal level includes its brand name and the augmented level includes its after-sale warranty.

concept from another. One of the success stories that illustrates an entrepreneur's understanding of product levels in the e-commerce channel of distribution is Bluefly.com.

After a frustrating day of outlet shopping, rummaging through bins of disorganized, two-season-old designer clothing, Kenneth Seiff knew there had to be a better way. An entrepreneur before his Bluefly.com lightbulb moment, Seiff recognized that traditional outlet stores were not offering the kind of shopping experience that customers wanted; they were, in fact, viewing shopping as a chore. Seiff saw the solution in the Internet, which, at the time, was a significant untapped source for retailing designer off-price apparel and home furnishings. What differentiated his concept from others? Bluefly.com features a dynamic design, superior customer service, and advanced search technology. An exclusive "My Catalog" feature allows customers to target their own preferences in terms of brands, styles, and sizes. In essence, the customer can develop a personalized on-line catalog. The Web site also offers fashion features, such as the celebrity closet, as well as new fashion tips, competitive flat-rate shipping, and a ninety-day guarantee/return policy, as shown in FIGURE 4.4.

THE PRODUCT LIFE CYCLE

Something old, something new . . . For the entrepreneur who will develop a new product, as well as the one who will work with an existing product, an understanding of the product life cycle is essential for determining the target market, pricing and promoting the product, and selecting a channel of distribution. **The product life cycle** is a model designed to identify the maturation stage of a particular product by approximating its level of customer acceptance. To market the business concept effectively, the entrepreneur should be able to identify the product's stage in the life cycle objectively.

INTRODUCTORY STAGE

The first stage of the product life cycle is the **introductory stage,** which is the time when innovative goods that appeal to fashion leaders, or trendsetters, are first

FIGURE 4.4
Bluefly Closet Confessions.

offered. During the introductory stage the focus is on marketing the new product to potential consumers. Effective advertising and promotion is often used to educate consumers about the new product and how it will satisfy their needs. The introduction of a new product into an existing market brings with it a unique set of challenges. The cost of introducing a new product can be high, whereas profitability is often low. The entrepreneur must continually monitor the external environment for changes in economic climate, original assumptions, and reactions by the competition.

GROWTH STAGE

The next stage in the product life cycle is the growth stage. A product enters the **growth stage** when a larger number of consumers begin to accept and purchase it. The product typically generates its peak sales volume as it moves through the growth stage. Typically, profits increase as the demand for the product increases. Thus, the cash flow position of the company usually improves. In the fashion retail industry, styles change, and they change frequently. It is important to recognize that in order to continue reaping the success of a new product, consumers must believe this product is meeting their needs. Failure to do so will result in a decline in sales. Successful entrepreneurs have found a number of ways to meet the needs of consumers in the fickle fashion market. Some modify the product to make it appear new. Others find new uses for existing products. Still others develop entirely new products and use the customer's comfort level with the company as an entry into the new product category.

MATURITY STAGE

The next stage is the **maturity stage**. The product is at a peak, or plateau, in sales, and it is mass-produced and mass-marketed. During a product's maturity stage, sales generally continue to increase, but typically at a slower rate than during the growth stage. The success of the product in the marketplace brings on the challenge of increased competition. Many times, in order to compete, prices must be lowered to hold market share, thereby lowering profit margins. During the maturity stage, the entrepreneur must work diligently to differentiate the business's product from those of competitors. Often, this is the time when services are added to the product mix. The entrepreneur attempts to increase profits through competitive pricing, effective promotion, and service add-ons, such as delivery or gift wrapping. When the product enters the maturity stage, it becomes a test of marketing know-how.

DECLINE STAGE

As consumers lose interest in the product, it enters the **decline stage**, the final stage of the product life cycle. At this point, the product is often found in discount stores and on markdown racks. Some entrepreneurs take advantage of this stage of the product life cycle by selling the discounted merchandise to the consumer at clearance prices. Some retail operations, such as T.J. Maxx, Marshalls, and Gordmans, specialize in buying and reselling products in the early period of the decline stage as well as other stages when there is over-production available from manufacturers. In the decline stage, sales continue to drop until profit margins become extremely low. The product is often a dead trend unless or until someone develops a new twist, a new use, or a new image to revive its popularity. FIGURE 4.5 is a diagram of the fashion product life cycle.

PRACTICAL APPLICATION OF THE PRODUCT LIFE CYCLE

As a product moves through its life cycle, entrepreneurs can measure opportunities for growth by analyzing life cycle stages. The entrepreneur can use this information to make decisions about whether to continue selling the product and when to introduce new, follow-up products. It is important that fashion retailers recognize the life cycles of their products, as well as those of competitive products. There are a number of successful fashion companies that have survived decades of fashion changes by keeping an eye on the product life cycle.

The product life cycle must be understood in order for the entrepreneur to determine whether and when to introduce new products into the existing product lines and to revise existing ones. The time to introduce a new product into the market is during the early stages of the life cycle of the current product, when sales are strong and profit margins are high. To launch a new product successfully, the entrepreneur must be committed to the new product and be willing to adjust to changes in the environment. Adequate planning and knowledge of the market are important. The entrepreneur must understand how the different levels of the fashion industry interrelate and when new lines should be introduced. FIGURE 4.6 illustrates the timing sequence in the industry as it relates to the product life cycle for the designer, product developer, manufacturer, and retailer.

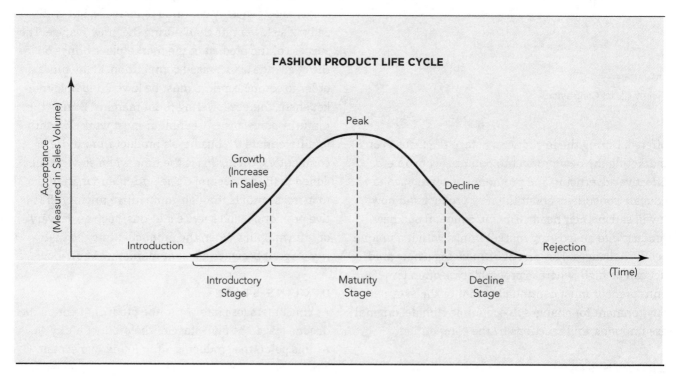

FIGURE 4.5
The fashion product life cycle.

NEW USES OR IMAGES FOR OLD PRODUCTS

Something borrowed, something blue . . . Another route for the entrepreneur is to develop new uses or images for existing products. Consider True Religion, 7 for All Mankind, and Earl jeans. Was there anything new under the sun when it came to blue jeans? Yes, and these companies found the ways. They focused on fit, used luxury denims, added updated styles, and marketed these product lines as status goods. Moreover, the influx of vintage clothing stores, as well as resale stores for sporting goods, children's apparel, and special occasion gowns, are examples of entrepreneurial ventures that put new faces on old products. Children's Orchard has grown into a national franchise that features bargain-priced, "gently used" clothes, toys, and furniture for kids. The company stays in step with today's value-conscious and environmentally concerned consumer by offering recycled merchandise at bargain prices.

AT YOUR SERVICE

For the entrepreneur whose business is a service, the examination of the product focuses on an intangible, the core service. This entrepreneur will determine how to augment the core service to make it as appealing to the consumer as possible. Examples of services as core products for businesses in the fashion industry include, among others, trend and color forecasting, image consulting, and fashion event production businesses. For the entrepreneur whose product is tangible, decisions need to be made about the types and levels of customer services the entrepreneur will offer to complement the actual product. Following is a discussion about service as both a product and a supplement to a tangible product.

WHEN THE PRODUCT IS A SERVICE

For the entrepreneur interested in a service business, plans for the types and prices of services must be carefully developed. Customer relations are at the heart of a service business. If a woman purchases a dress from a retailer and is satisfied in terms of price, styling, and quality, she may forget that the salesperson was rude or that the dressing rooms were a mess. In contrast, the customer buying a service has nothing to reflect upon except the service itself. It must be a pleasant reflection for the customer to return and to recommend the business to others.

Full-service operations within the retail fashion industry cover a wide range of businesses. For example, a designer opening a new apparel line may use a trend forecasting company, such as Trend Union, to determine color and style directions for a specific season. The designer may also visit a fiber representative, such as Cotton Inc., to gather names of fabric sources. After the line is developed, the designer may hire a public relations firm to promote it. The public relations firm may employ a special-event company to produce the fashion show debuting the designer's first collection. A glowing review in *Women's Wear Daily* and *Vogue*, and a star is born, with a range of service businesses helping launch it.

If the product of the business is a service, the entrepreneur must know how to articulate, price, and market the service. Types and levels of service need to be determined before prices can be established. The entrepreneur may decide that the business will offer a superior level of service. An illustration of high-level service is the wedding consulting firm in which the entrepreneur does everything for the bride and groom, from locating the caterer to fluffing the bride's train before she walks down the aisle. In contrast, the entrepreneur may elect to open a no-fringe service business at below-competition prices.

How does the entrepreneur of a service business set prices for the services? It is a challenging and detailed process, one that must be continually monitored and reevaluated. First, the entrepreneur should calculate the costs of materials and equipment needed to provide each service. Labor costs must then be determined. Overhead expenses, including office costs, employee wages, and promotion of the business and its services, will be calculated and divided among an estimation of the frequency of service offerings. In addition, the entrepreneur should examine the prices of services offered by competitors to learn what

	JANUARY	FEBRUARY	MARCH	APRIL	MAY	JUNE
The Designer/Product Developer	Style early fall ———————————	Shop for fall fabrics Sample, design, and construct	Duplicate sample line ———————	First of month, early fall goes into showroom		Shop and research spring and cruise seasons
		Refabricate summer promotions ———	Research late fall and holiday colors and fabrics	Style late fall and holiday	Duplicate samples	Late fall and holiday lines go into showroom late, May or early June
		Paris couture shows, spring		Paris pret-a-porter shows, fall	Interstoff, international fabric show, Germany	
The Manufacturer	Sell summer line; goes into showroom right after New Year (Introduction) ———			Sell early fall (Introduction)		Sell late fall and holiday (Introduction)
				Sell summer promotions and reorders (Growth) ———————		Order fall fabric
	Order summer stock fabric	Manufacture and ship summer goods (Growth) ———————				
		Ship and produce ——— spring clothes (reorders) (Growth)				
					Manufacture summer promotions and reorders (Decline)	
					Manufacture early fall and ship (Growth)	
The Retailer		Receive and sell ——— early spring/cruise (Introduction)	First spring mark-downs (Growth)		————————— Major spring——— mark-downs ·(Decline)	
		Rainwear important in coat department		Receive and sell early summer (Introduction)	Sell summer——— (Growth)	Major summer mark-downs (Decline)
	After-Christmas sales of holiday and late fall garments (Decline)			Easter promotions for children's wear	Wedding——— Promotions	
	Swimwear opens (Introduction)	Swimwear promotions (Growth)				Swimwear mark-downs (Decline)

(CONTINUED)

FIGURE 4.6

A timing calendar for the fashion industry.

	JULY	AUGUST	SEPTEMBER	OCTOBER	NOVEMBER	DECEMBER
The Designer/Product Developer	Style spring	Duplicate spring	Research Style Summer and trends sample fabric for summer	Early October, spring goes into showroom		Research early fall colors and fabrics / Duplicate samples
		summer colors / Refabricate and do fall promotions				
		Paris couture shows, fall		Paris pret-a-porter shows, spring	Interstoff, international fabric show, Germany	
The Manufacturer		Sell reorders and promotions	Sell spring cruise			
		Manufacture and ship late fall (Growth)				
			Order spring stock fabric	Manufacture cruise and spring. Ship in late Nov. -early Dec.		
	Order late fall and holiday fabrics			Ship holiday catalog merchandise		
		Manufacture and ship late fall and holiday				
The Retailer	Receive and sell early fall (Introduction)		Fall opens / Sell fall (Growth)		First fall mark-downs (Decline) / Children's party clothes	
		Coats important now / Furs open				
	Summer clearance (Decline)		Early fall mark-downs (Decline)		Holiday fill-ins	Holiday promotions
		Back to school for young apparel (Introduction)		Holiday merchandise arrives (Introduction)	sells (Growth)	
						Mark down glittery/dressy before or around Dec. 25th (Decline)

businesses featuring similar services charge customers for those services.

An example is an entrepreneur who wanted to establish a trend-forecasting business. Initially, she determined the types of services she would offer, deciding that she would develop four reports for each of the five fashion seasons. These reports forecast color, fabric, silhouette, and designer trends for the early fall, late fall, holiday, spring, and summer seasons. She offered consulting services as corporate or one-on-one presentations. The entrepreneur then investigated the costs of travel to Paris, London, Milan, and New York five times annually. She figured the costs of setting up an office, including technology needs, a color copier and scanner, office furniture, rent, and utilities. She calculated hourly wages for a part-time assistant. She comparison-shopped printers to produce the trend reports. She also developed a promotional plan to market the business and determined the associated costs. Armed with this stack of figures, the entrepreneur was able to estimate the cost of producing each report. Pricing intangible products can be more challenging than pricing tangible ones.

WHEN THE PRODUCT IS TANGIBLE

If the product of the business is tangible, the entrepreneur must still make customer service and pricing decisions. In most cases, the price of the product relates directly to the level and types of customer services being offered. When merchandise carries a relatively high retail price, the customer usually expects relatively high levels and forms of service. For example, high-end fashion boutiques carrying expensive designer garments will often offer a wide range of customer services, from alterations to home delivery. On the other hand, discount retail operations, such as Sam's Club, will provide fewer customer services as a means of keeping overhead and, subsequently, prices below those of its competitors. At Sam's Club, for example, the customer is not provided with dressing rooms, packaging, or delivery. Instead, the customer is provided with a focused selection of merchandise at very competitive prices.

TYPES OF SERVICE

What types of services should the entrepreneur consider for the business? Customer services can be classified in two ways: prepurchase and postpurchase. Prepurchase services include special-order availability, exclusivity, layaway, personal shopper assistance, and educational programs. Postpurchase services can include a replacement guarantee, delivery, alterations, ease of payment, gift wrap, and repeat purchase discounts. The list is ever evolving as new entrepreneurs find more and better ways to service their customers. Nike, for example, offers a personalized form of customer service through its custom shoe program, which is available online. As shown in FIGURE 4.7, the customer can select the colors, symbols, and trim, for a running shoe that is one of a kind.

LEVELS OF SERVICE

Levels of service, too, are often parallel with price. Payless Shoes, for example, offers a low level of customer service, with its racks of boxed shoes and limited number of sales associates. What is the payoff for Payless? The company retails its products in volume at below-market prices. The price element may be enough for customers to overlook service and environment. T.J.Maxx is another example of an apparel and soft-goods retailer for which low prices offset a midlevel of service.

There are a number of places in the development of a business plan in which the entrepreneur must consider types and level of customer service. How does service fit into the market niche? What are the customer service offerings of competitors? What are the target market's needs in terms of service? How much will customer services cost? Where will these costs be absorbed? How might payroll be affected? The bottom line is that the customer pays for the services offered by retailers in one of two ways: The services are either financed through higher prices or sold as entities separate from the product, through fees for such extras as gift wrapping or alterations. The entrepreneur must decide how types and level of services offered will affect the image of the company.

FIGURE 4.7

Customizing a mass-produced item.

BRANDING

Branding has become an integral part of the fashion industry. The entrepreneur thinks about branding from two different perspectives: branding of the product and branding of the business. In this chapter the focus is on the branding of the product. When prospective entrepreneurs investigate potential products or product lines for their businesses, they must consider how product brands will affect their companies' image, customer identification with the business, and profit potential.

What is a brand? A **brand** is a name, term, sign, or design, or a combination of these, that is intended to identify the goods or services of one seller or group of sellers and to differentiate them from those of competitors. **Branding** is the process of attaching a name, an image, and a reputation to a thing, person, service, or idea. Branding is used as a means of distinguishing one product or service from another; it is used to create differentiation and image.

There are brand names that immediately conjure up images in the consumer's mind. When customers think about Gucci, Calvin Klein, or Polo Ralph Lauren, they frequently envision a certain status. These brand names often conjure feelings of prestige, confidence, and success. This is exactly what the promotion departments of these companies intended with their advertising efforts. Brands such as French Connection, Kenneth Cole, and Southpole approach branding in an unconventional and spirited manner. They want to be known as the "bad boys" of fashion imagery brands, looking to rebel against traditional brand imagery. They intentionally go against the grain to create a defined image. Today's fashion customers, more than ever before, are choosing brands with which they can identify, brands that reflect their inner selves—who they believe they are or who they want to be. If customers perceive themselves to be rebels (or want the confidence to show a rebellious side), then Moschino may be the brand badge, as illustrated in FIGURE 4.8. Brands provide customers with ways to identify products as part of their personalities.

In most cases, the entrepreneur must decide whether the firm will put a name, logo, or other

FIGURE 4.8
A model on the runway at Moschino's Fall 2010 show.

INTELLECTUAL PROPERTY: BRAND NAMES, TRADEMARKS, AND COPYRIGHTS

Think about Chanel, Nike, Levi's, and Polo Ralph Lauren, and you will agree that the brand is the visual identifier of the product or business. There are a number of brands that are identifiable by the model or even the typeface used in advertisements.

An example is the cosmetic company that places a high-profile supermodel under contract to represent exclusively the product line in promotional efforts. Another example is the distinct typeface used by Calvin Klein in that company's billboards and advertisements in fashion magazines. The **brand name** is the part of the brand that can be vocalized, whereas the **brand mark** is the visual part of the brand that can be recognized but cannot be spoken.

A **trademark** is a word, logo or other symbol, or a combination of these that a company uses to identify and distinguish itself from other companies. There are a number of trademarks that have become icons in the fashion industry. The word *Nike* and the Nike "swoosh" create a powerful trademark. Trademarks may be thought of as brands. The visual components of a trademark, when combined, are referred to as **trade dress**. The unique combination of word and symbol is considered a company's trade dress, as in FIGURE 4.9. For trademark protection, trade dress must be unique

identifier on the organization's product. Branding can add value to a product. For this reason, some entrepreneurs prefer to be affiliated with established brands through franchising or to name the business so as to bring to mind a particular brand. In other cases, the entrepreneur may choose to create a brand and its related imagery. This can be extremely successful, now more than ever before, because businesses are able to reach the global masses through the Internet. Most commonly, entrepreneurs will select an assortment of brands from vendors with similar looks, price ranges, and attitudes to create an inventory that appeals to a specific target market.

FIGURE 4.9
Nike trade dress.

to a company, and another company's use of that trade dress must be likely to confuse consumers.

The exclusive rights to reproduce, publish, or sell the trademark in the form of a literary, musical, or artistic work is referred to as a **copyright**. Although the ability to copyright a brand name or brand mark is fairly cut and dried from a legal perspective, less clear is the right to protect the way an entrepreneur conducts business or the actual fashions created by a designer. These concepts are considered intellectual property—a topic of major discussion in the fashion industry. **Intellectual property** is any product, service, or retail operation that is the result of a creative process and that has commercial value. Intellectual property can be protected through the use of trademarks, patents, and copyright. Protecting intellectual property can be critical to the success of a company.

Can a dress design or a store concept be protected from copying? A.B.S. is a women's apparel and jewelry company that has generated tremendous profits from "knocking off," or copying, the gowns worn by celebrities, particularly those donned at events such as the Oscars. These special-occasion dresses are available on the racks of retailers carrying the A.B.S. line within weeks after they appear on the superstars—with one big difference. An A.B.S. knockoff sells for hundreds of dollars, compared with the several thousands of dollars a designer's original would go for (FIGURE 4.10). At this time, this practice is completely legal; however, it is a topic under scrutiny as supporters of copyrighting creative and intellectual property lobby for legislation.

Store concepts are protected from being knocked off in two different ways. The entrepreneur who develops the business concept may choose to package and

FIGURE 4.10

Kate Middleton's dress, designed by Issa, from the royal engagement announcement (left) and the instantly successful knockoffs (right).

license it as a franchise. The name, title, logo, store design, fixturing, merchandise labels, and so on are then legally protected from being copied. An example is Apricot Lane, which is discussed in Chapter 5. Also, the business concept may also be guarded from replication through its merchandise offerings and branding. Private label goods that are designed and manufactured for the store offer complete exclusivity. Examples are INC (Macy's) and Stafford (JCPenney). Private label merchandise and examples of retailers using this inventory strategy are examined in this chapter and in Chapter 10.

Should a designer or retailer have the option of copyrighting an original concept? How should "original" be defined? Should a copyright protect modification of styles? If so, where does the copyright option begin and end? Should the designer be able to copyright a collar, a sleeve, or a full garment? What if the style is today's version of a historical fashion? The dilemma is complex and lengthy. The jury is out on how the results of this debate will affect the fashion industry, but the ramifications could be tremendous.

BRAND SPONSORSHIP

The entrepreneur may need to make decisions about brand sponsorship. **Brand sponsorship** refers to the selection among three primary brand alternatives available to the fashion retailer. There is the **manufacturer's brand**, which is the most traditional type of brand sponsorship and which is often referred to as a **national brand**. Manufacturer's brands are those brand names promoted by the producers, often advertised nationally. The manufacturer targets a broad range of retailers to purchase the line and sell it to consumers. Examples of manufacturer's brands are Liz Claiborne, Donna Karan, and Adidas.

Next, there is the **private brand**, which may be referred to as the agent (intermediary) distributor or dealer brand. Usually, a distributor sells and ships merchandise purchased from a variety of manufacturers under a brand name that is developed by the distributor. This branding technique helps create consistency among the distributor's product offerings. An example of a private brand is the accessories wholesale company that purchases merchandise from an accessory manufacturer in New York and resells the goods under its name to its retail accounts.

Finally, there is the branding choice of private label. Private label represents a major trend in the fashion industry. **Private label** merchandise carries a brand name created for the retail operation. Decades ago, private label was only available to major retailers with the purchasing power to buy extremely large quantities of goods. Today, small retail operations have the opportunity to participate in private label branding because of lower minimum quantity requirements. Also, small retailers are able to secure private label goods by buying through resident buying offices or buying groups. The resident buying office collects purchase orders from several of its client stores and then consolidates the orders to meet the quantity minimum required by the manufacturer for the production of private label merchandises.

Private label goods are exclusive to the distributor. In most cases, a retailer determines the name and visual identity of a line (i.e., the private label) in a specific merchandise classification (e.g., men's tailored apparel). The apparel manufacturer attaches the label and hangtag developed by the retailer to the selected garments prior to shipping. Illustrations of private label goods are the JCPenney's Stafford line, and Material Girl at Macy's, as in FIGURE 4.11. Private label lines may also be referred to as **proprietary brands**. These lines are often represented by celebrity partners who add prestige and familiarity to the brand image. Miley Cirus and Max Azria for Walmart and Isaac Mizrahi for Target are examples of proprietary brands.

Why is there an influx of private label goods in fashion retailing? Private label merchandise allows the retailer to get involved in the development of the product or product lines. This participation allows the retailer to tailor merchandise to meet the specific needs, desires, and tastes of the clientele. The prospective entrepreneur may consider developing private labels to differentiate the merchandise assortment from that of competitive retailers. More important, however, private label adds exclusivity to the retailer's merchandise assortment. **Exclusive**

FIGURE 4.11

An example of a private label or proprietary brand is Material Girl at Macy's.

Three key concepts contribute to the message of any particular brand. Irrespective of the kind of target market or the nature of the product, most brands depend upon trust, familiarity, and difference. Brand value is the articulation of one or more of these qualities. In fashion, Diesel is an example of a manufacturer that successfully sends a message of all three values. This Italian fashion and lifestyle brand projects an image that is international, innovative, and fun. Diesel customers trust the company to bring them the newest fashions through quality clothing that allows them to express their personalities. Diesel's Web site is presented in FIGURE 4.12.

BRAND VALUE

What is brand value, and how is it established? **Brand value** is the worth of the brand in terms of customer recognition, image, and potential sales volume. The invention of a new brand overnight with subsequent rapid sales is unlikely to occur. Brands with strong images are the result of a successful nurturing of the relationship between producer and consumer. They also require economic investment, marketing, and corporate support. The most recognizable brands tend to maintain their position by establishing loyalty and ubiquity—by becoming the market standard. In some

goods are merchandise that is limited in distribution to specific retail operations. Exclusive goods aid in providing prestige and patronage motives for the consumer.

What is the downside of private label goods? The label may have little or no meaning to the customer. Worse, it may have a negative association for the customer. It often takes funding for promotion and time to create a desired image and appeal for a brand—to "teach the brand to talk." The brand that says "inexpensive and chic," for example, needs to be supported through effective sales and advertising so that it does not read to the customer as "cheap and everywhere."

FIGURE 4.12

Diesel customers trust the company to bring them the newest fashions through quality clothing that allows consumers to express their personalities.

BOX 4.1
LICENSING PARTNERSHIPS
FOR BETSEY JOHNSON LLC

Betsey Johnson apparel, shoes, footwear, handbags, belts, lingerie, leg wear, jewelry, swimwear, timepieces, outerwear, and a signature fragrance are distributed in 66 Betsey Johnson boutiques as well as more than 2,000 specialty stores. Products are also stocked in better department stores worldwide, including Bloomingdale's, Saks Fifth Avenue, Nordstrom, Macy's Vokko (Turkey), Holt Renfrew (Canada), and Galeries Lafayette (Dubai) as well as distribution in Japan. Since 2004, Betsey Johnson LLC has expanded its product offerings through more than a dozen licensing agreements. Current licenses include:

Geneva Watch Group	Watches
H. Robinson Optical Corp.	Sunglasses
Leg Resource	Hosiery
Daniel M. Freidman & Assoc.	Accessories, small leather goods
Titan Industries Inc.	Footwear
The Levy Group	Outerwear
Carol Hochman Designs	Intimate apparel
Haskell Jewels	Jewelry
Lunada Bay Corp.	Swimwear
Inter Parfums	Betsey Johnson fragrance, personal care products, cosmetics
Innova Group	Women's jeans and denim-related apparel, such as T-shirts and tops
Steve Madden	Handbags, small leather goods, belts and umbrellas, under the Betsey Johnson and Betseyville brands

cases, the brand name becomes the generic name for that product, such as Rollerblade or Levi's. The branded article, in these cases, has created a direct relationship between the consumer and the producer.

LICENSING AND ROYALTIES

Licensing can be an effective and expedient way to establish brand value. **Licensing** is the practice of buying or selling the use of a brand name from one company to another. The brand name can be that of a celebrity (e.g., Jennifer Lopez, Lauren Conrad, Jessica Simpson), a designer (e.g., Betsey Johnson, Dior, Ed Hardy, Chanel), a manufacturer (e.g., Nike, Fossil, Puma), or a company (e.g., Harley Davidson, Express, BCBG). Companies that own successful brands can expand the number of product lines carrying this name by licensing their brands to companies that make specialized products. Some companies manufacture licensed products for other companies, while licensing their names to others. For example, Fossil produces watches for Donna Karan under her label; at the same time, Fossil licenses its name to handbag and belt companies that produce the leather goods under the Fossil brand. Confusing? Possibly. Profitable? Definitely. Box 4.1 includes a list of licensing agreements for Betsey Johnson LLC.

Nautica, Ralph Lauren, Donna Karan, and Martha Stewart are masters of the licensing venture. These companies have turned names and trademarks into powerful marketing tools, ones that other companies pay large sums to use on their products. The designer (or brand house) receives a royalty for the merchandise manufactured by licensors. A **royalty** is a payment that can vary in terms of amount, usually from three to 10 percent of wholesale, often with a required minimum amount of sales.

What does this mean to the prospective entrepreneur? Licensing is a way to get into business by using an established name that has a customer following. Perhaps the entrepreneur can spot a winner before the race is run by anticipating that a product is going to be successful. If this is the case, the entrepreneur may elect to license the brand name in exchange for an established royalty. In contrast, the entrepreneur may develop a new brand, intending to build it through a long-range plan of licensing to other companies in the future. *The Licensing Book*, published monthly by Adventure Publishing Group, is a resource that provides the most current information on hot licensing properties. It has become a big business. Whether private label, national, or licensed, branding may, indeed, create the ties that bind.

CONCLUSION

Entrepreneurs have the option of creating a new product or marketing an existing product. Frequency of purchase, availability of the product, product lifespan, and product alternatives are all factors that affect entrepreneurs' choice of products for their businesses. One of the challenges in selecting merchandise for a business is determining its position in the product life cycle. To market the business concept effectively, the entrepreneur should be able to identify the product's life cycle stage.

Two factors distinguish an entrepreneur's product from that of competitors. The first is customer service. Service can actually be the product, or it can be a key tool for selling the product. The second is branding, a dominant trend in the apparel and soft goods industry. Today's consumer, more than ever before, is selecting a brand that corresponds to his or her personality and values. One of the fastest routes to branding is through licensing, the use of an established name to label and market a product. Product differentiation and company image are central to the success of entrepreneurial endeavors.

KEY TERMS

augmented product	exclusive goods	limited line	proprietary brand
brand	fashion goods	low-end goods	royalty
brand mark	formal product	manufacturer's brand	service products
brand name	general line	maturity stage	shopping goods
brand sponsorship	growth stage	merchandise assortment	soft goods
brand value	hard goods	national brand	specialty goods
branding	high-end goods	nondurable goods	staple (basic) goods
convenience goods	intangible product	private brand	tangible product
copyright	intellectual property	private label	trade dress
core product	introductory stage	product	trademark
decline stage	inventory	product life cycle	unsought goods
durable goods	licensing		

DISCUSSION TOPICS

1. Identify a fashion product that effectively represents each of the following stages of the product life cycle: introductory, growth, maturity, and decline.

2. Share examples of retailers developing new uses for old products and how companies create fresh images for their rejuvenated products.

3. Identify trends in customer service offerings by fashion retailers.

4. Examine marketing strategies that are used to generate a strong brand identity in fashion retailing.

SUGGESTED READINGS

Hancock, J. *Brand/Story: Ralph, Vera, Johnny, Billy, and Other Adventures in Fashion Branding.* New York: Fairchild Books, 2009.

Keiser, S. J., and M. B Garner. *Beyond Design: The Synergy of Apparel Product Development.* 2d ed. New York: Fairchild Books, 2008.

Kendall, G. I., *Fashion Brand Merchandising.* New York: Fairchild Books, 2009.

ONLINE RESOURCES

ABOUT.COM/ENTREPRENEURS
http://entrepreneurs.about.com/od/businessplan/a/businessconcept.htm
Features information for entrepreneurs, particularly in the area of finance.

SQUIDOO.COM
http://www.squidoo.com/newbusinessconcept
A popular publishing platform and community for users to share and gather perspectives on areas of interest.

SNUGGIE
http://www.time.com/time/nation/article/0,8599,1870762,00.html#ixzz0krujzaym
The Snuggie phenomenon is examined in this article.

BUSINESS PLAN CONNECTION
THINKING LIKE AN ENTREPRENEUR

Select the products, or product lines, that you believe have significant potential for your business. Interview a number of sources that may have helpful information about the market potential for these products or lines. Consider interviewing the owners of non-competitive retail operations and manufacturing firms, bankers, professors, business consultants, and representatives of business support organizations. Questions you may want to ask these sources include:

» What is the life cycle stage of this product?
» What is its position in terms of competitive products?
» Are supply sources currently available and affordable? In the future?
» What future opportunities exist with this particular product?

ASSIGNMENT 4.1
THE MERCHANDISING/PRODUCT PLAN

The various sections of the merchandising/product plan are addressed in both Chapters 4 and 10. Complete the sections of the merchandising/product plan section of the business plan template as follows. It may be necessary to revisit this section and revise your plan after completing Chapter 10. The business plan is an evolving document; therefore, any section may need revision prior to submitting the final plan.

1. Open your saved business plan template.
2. Address the following sections of the merchandising/product plan. You may also refer to the sample business plan contained in Appendix D.

MERCHANDISING/PRODUCT PLAN
» Merchandise/Product Description
» Unique Characteristics
» Proposed Lines
» Proprietary Aspects
» Merchandise Assortment

SPANX is no longer just for women. Now, men can hide those beer bellies and love handles thanks to the recent introduction of shapewear for guys. Spanx likes to call them "Manx," but the line was debuted as Spanx for Men during New York Fashion Week in 2010. Made of high-gauge cotton or spandex and nylon fabrics, the Spanx undershirts come in two styles—zoned performance or cotton compression—and three cuts—tank ($55), crew-neck ($58), and V-neck ($58)—in black or white.

These shaping undershirts were developed to "comfortably firm the chest, flatten the stomach, improve posture, and eliminate bulk under clothes," the company Web site indicates. "Men's undershirts have been underperforming for as long as they've been around, with stretched-out necks and bulky cuts that do nothing for the male physique," Spanx founder Sara Blakely says. Calling it "the new standard in men's underwear," Spanx's move into shapewear for men reflects the future fashion trend of body-conscious apparel for men. It will be a major shift from the oversized and boxy menswear of the past decade.

So, who is this product developer and entrepreneur, Sara Blakely, and how did she get started? The inspiration came from VPL (visible panty lines) and uncomfortable underwear alternatives. Beginning as a frustrated consumer in 2000, Sara created footless pantyhose to eliminate VPL and then funded her company with her savings. Since then, she has created more than 200 problem-solving products and recently entered the bra business. In 2006 Sara brought her shapewear know-how to more women with the national launch of Assets, a collection of shapewear and legwear, sold through Target and Dillard's, among other major retailers. In 2009 Sara launched Haute Contour by Spanx, which she calls "the dessert of shapewear."

What are Blakely's current projects? After many years of demand, Spanx brings its industry expertise

Cotton Compression Crew

SPANX
BY SARA BLAKELY®

YOU RANG?

Firms Chest & Narrows Waist Line

to the pool and the beach with swimwear. On a personal level, Sara is also pursuing her dream to build a foundation to empower women. Since launching the Sara Blakely Foundation in late 2006, she has contributed more than $1 million to causes that support women and inspire people to follow their dreams.

SOURCES:
http://www.spanx.com
http://www.stylelist.com/2010/02/04/spanx-for-men-the-wait-is-over

CHAPTER 5
PLANNING A STRATEGY TO OPEN A BUSINESS

OBJECTIVES

» Examine the three main methods of entering the market with an entrepreneurial business: starting a new business from the ground up, purchasing a franchise operation, and acquiring an existing business.

» Comprehend the letter of intent and purchase agreement as they relate to buying a business.

» Understand the business funder's interest in valuing and exiting a business.

N Chapter 3, we looked at the techniques commonly used to obtain information to analyze the industry and to determine if there is a market opportunity with a potential and profitable target market. This chapter focuses on using that information to determine the best way to enter the market. There are three methods of entering the market: starting a new business from the ground up; purchasing a franchise operation; and acquiring an existing business. Each of these entry routes is explored in this chapter. Box 5.1 provides background information to examine before getting started on the paths to starting a business.

ENTRY STRATEGIES

An **entry strategy** is the method the fashion entrepreneur chooses to begin ownership of a business. The entry strategy an entrepreneur selects affects much of what will be needed to develop the business plan. The decision to start a business through the route of franchising sets into motion one set of activities. Deciding to purchase an existing business sets another set of activities in motion. Starting a business from scratch will result in yet another set of activities. With all entry strategies, costs and benefits must be carefully weighed, and the entrepreneur's vision and goals must be supported, as illustrated by FIGURE 5.1. In the following pages, the three entry strategies will be examined in depth.

OPENING A NEW BUSINESS

Starting a new business provides entrepreneurs with the opportunity to allow their imagination, passion, and efforts to lead to financial rewards, pride of ownership, a sense of accomplishment, and control of their destinies. Owning

» Recognize your passions, expertise, and dreams. What types of fashion products do you enjoy working with, where, and in what ways?

» Gain experience by working in a fashion retail operation, preferably a business similar to the one you intend to open.

» Identify a niche or a unique specialty in the fashion retail industry.

» Ask for those you respect and who are in the know for advice and feedback on, and constructive criticism of, your plans—and listen to what they have to say.

» Investigate the different opportunities that exist for opening your business; will you start a business, find a franchise, or buy an existing business?

» Create a realistic business plan. Make sure there is enough capital available to keep you and your business going through the start-up phase.

FIGURE 5.1

Opening a business may be the personal and professional goal of many young executives working in the fashion industry today. It begins with a dream, drive, and a plan.

one's own business carries with it positive and negative sides—a sense of freedom on the one hand, and the feeling of slavery to a dream on the other. As shown in FIGURE 5.2, ideas for a new business concept can come from many places: a hobby, expansion of a part-time activity, technical expertise, a spin-off of a current job, a new invention, desperation to make more money or leave a current job, development of a home-based business, friends and family, personal

FIGURE 5.2

A new business concept may be inspired by a hobby, part-time work, a talent, or a passion.

preference, or observation of a market need. There are illustrations in the fashion industry of all of these.

An example of an entrepreneurial fashion business started as a result of observation of a market need is dELiA*s, which sells apparel, accessories, athletic gear, footwear, and home furnishings through direct-mail catalogs, Web sites, and retail outlets:

> dELiA*s was launched in 1993 from the New York apartment of Stephan Kahn, a former Wall Street analyst. . . . Kahn hatched the idea with his former Yale roommate, Christopher Edgar. . . . Kahn and Edgar noticed that the growing population of young Americans known as Generation Y was becoming a major segment of the consumer market. The partners' research revealed that these offspring of the baby boom generation were spending billions of dollars annually, much of it on apparel. More significantly, very few apparel retailers were exclusively targeting this age group, despite its obvious buying power. Kahn and Edgar saw a consumer niche with

> very little competition. . . . Kahn and Edgar hired designers and fashion consultants to create an apparel catalog for Generation Y girls. The catalog, which they called dELiA*s, combined creative layouts and editorial content with the newest fashions from more than fifty brand-name vendors. The result was more than the traditional mail-order catalog. dELiA*s marketing tool was actually a **magalog,** a hybrid catalog and fashion magazine. The publication was first distributed in 1994 through a network of on-campus college representatives, and in its first year earned $139,000 in sales. . . . A year later, Kahn and Edgar changed dELiA*s method of catalog distribution to a direct mail approach. . . . In late 1996, with more than one million names in its database, . . . and sales greater than $30 million, Kahn and Edgar took dELiA*s public.[1]

In 2003, marketing conglomerate Alloy, Inc., bought dELiA*s for $50 million.[2] FIGURE 5.3 illustrates dELiA*s e-commerce platform and a sample product.

FIGURE 5.3

*dELiA*s evolved from the concept of selling apparel and accessories to teens through peer sales representatives and catalogs, then grew into a multimillion-dollar brick-and-click corporation.*

Opening a new business from start to finish, like Edgar and Kahn did, can be a daunting and financially risky venture to many prospective entrepreneurs, some of whom believe there is an option that may reduce the planning and start-up activities while minimizing the financial risk. This route to opening a business is through a franchise operation, which is discussed next in Case Study 5.1.

PURCHASING A FRANCHISE OPERATION

What is a franchise? A **franchise** refers to the right or license an individual or a group is granted to sell products or services in a specified manner within a given territory. A franchise typically enables the entrepreneur—the investor, or the **franchisee**—to operate a business. By paying a **franchise fee**, the entrepreneur is given a format, or system, developed by the company (**franchisor**), the right to use the franchisor's name for a limited time, and assistance in business operations. For example, the franchisor may help the entrepreneur find a location for the outlet; provide initial training and an operating manual; and give advice on management, marketing, and personnel. Some franchisors offer ongoing support through such vehicles as a monthly newsletter, a toll-free telephone number for technical assistance, and periodic workshops. Although buying a franchise may reduce risk by linking the prospective entrepreneur with an established company, it can be costly. The entrepreneur also may be required to relinquish significant control over the business because of contractual obligations required by the franchisor.

The purchase of a franchise can open the door for the entrepreneur by allowing him or her to sell goods and services that have instant name recognition and a customer following. Entrepreneurs, however, must be cautious, as they would be with any investment. Purchasing a franchise is not a guarantee of success; the entrepreneur must select the right franchise. Why would a fashion entrepreneur choose a franchise operation? Many business owners have successfully entered the fashion industry by becoming a franchisee in a profitable system. There are many advantages to becoming a franchisee in a successful organization,

but the greatest advantage is that the franchisor has done most of the work for the entrepreneur. The product is proven. The franchisor has already developed the company image, positive name recognition, an appealing visual identity, training techniques, and effective ways of operating the business.

The franchisor benefits from company expansion through increased revenues, consumers, and visibility. Because it is in the franchisor's best interest for the franchisee to succeed, continued assistance as the business develops is usually provided. Much of the trial-and-error learning that comes with opening a new business has been experienced by the franchisor and is passed on to the entrepreneur so that pitfalls can be avoided. Most of the operation's "bugs" have been worked out by the parent company. Depending on the franchisor, supplies and inventory may be bought in conjunction with the parent company to save money through quantity discounts. In general, the entrepreneur may have a lower level of risk when buying a franchise operation than when starting a business from scratch. The key to success is finding a good franchise operation.

A good franchise operation should offer three primary benefits. The first and most important is experience and knowledge. The franchisor should provide the entrepreneur with the management training needed to run the business effectively. Second, the franchisor should offer a **turnkey operation**. This is a business that is completely assembled, or set up, to begin operation and is then leased or sold to an individual to manage. In most turnkey operations the franchisor will guide the new entrepreneur through the early stages of the business to make certain it is successful. It is a partnership of sorts in which the franchisor's continued reputation and profitability is dependent upon the entrepreneur's success, and vice versa. The third benefit of an effective franchise is a ready-made customer base, one that may provide a faster road to success, with consumers who know and patronize the store. Some franchisors, through strong promotional efforts and a clearly defined market niche, have created a demand for their products that will come to the entrepreneur once the business is opened.

APRICOT LANE FASHION AND GIFT BOUTIQUE FRANCHISE OPERATION

WHAT IS APRICOT LANE?

Apricot Lane is the only specialty retail franchise that combines opportunities from the gift and fashion accessory industries to offer affordable fashion jewelry, handbags, accessories and gifts in the styles and trends customers are looking for.

Apricot Lane is perfect for the fashion-conscious customer shopping for herself, or for anyone looking for a unique gift for a friend or loved one.

AN APRICOT LANE FRANCHISE OPPORTUNITY:

» Ground floor retail opportunity
» $20 billion gift industry
» $12 billion fashion accessory industry
» Prenegotiated vendor discounts
» Not just a store!
» Fashion party sales
» Business-to-business sales
» E-commerce opportunities
» Seasonal expansion opportunities
» Low investment
» Independence within a strong network
» Owner full-time management is not a requirement
» Multiple location opportunities
» Support and training
» Fifteen years of retail and franchise experience
» Proven marketing programs
» On-site training and support
» Site selection and lease negotiation

JOIN OUR TEAM!

As a member of our franchise network, you can fulfill your ambitions while creating a business of lasting value and a legacy for your family.

"Apricot Lane has a unique system that just makes sense, plus the selection and variety of what people want to shop for."

This franchise is eligible to offer expedited loan processing through the U.S. Small Business Administration (SBA).

An Apricot Lane Boutique franchise.

The key disadvantage of the franchise system relates to costs. The front-end cost, or **start-up cost,** is incurred by the entrepreneur to begin the operation of a business. It is often high and can be greater than what would be paid to open a business from the ground up. In addition, franchisees may pay a percentage of revenues to the franchisor, lowering profit margins. The franchisee may also be required to pay a monthly fee and a portion of the franchise's national advertising expenses. Some successful franchise operations require monthly payments of up to 20 percent of gross sales to cover the franchise fee, marketing, royalties, and advertising. (To avoid excessive monthly fees, the entrepreneur may elect to get in on the ground floor of new a franchise operation). Moreover, franchisees may also have to purchase supplies, fixtures, and inventory from the franchisor and may be committed to purchasing part of group inventory buys.

There are many franchise options for apparel, beauty, and accessories operations, such as Flip Flop Shops, Bijoux Terner, and Sanrio (Hello Kitty). An accessory from the Hello Kitty franchise, an international phenomenon, is illustrated in FIGURE 5.4.

The fees and assistance that franchise operations offer franchisees vary with each company and each contract. In exchange for obtaining the right to use the franchisor's name and its assistance, the entrepreneur can expect to pay some or all of the following fees:

» **Initial franchise fee and other expenses**—This fee, which may be nonrefundable, may cost several thousand to several hundred thousand dollars. Significant costs may be incurred to rent, build, and equip an outlet and to purchase initial inventory. Other costs include operating licenses and insurance. The entrepreneur may also be required to pay a grand opening fee to the franchisor for promoting the new outlet.

» **Continuing royalty payments**—Franchisor royalties may be required, based on a percentage of the weekly or monthly gross income. The entrepreneur often must pay royalties even if the outlet has not earned significant income.

» **Advertising fees**—The entrepreneur may have to make payments to an advertising fund. Some portion of the advertising fees may go for national advertising or to attract new franchise owners. The advertising is usually not directed at the entrepreneur's outlet. The entrepreneur's contribution to the advertising fund is often made without promising the entrepreneur a say in how these funds are used.

It is important to note that costs in the franchise agreement with any single company may vary from one franchisee to another. Often, franchisors offer a sliding scale of fees, based on the level of assistance the entrepreneur requires. For example, the entrepreneur who does not require assistance with personnel training, advertising, or store setup may negotiate lower monthly fees than the entrepreneur needing full assistance in every aspect of establishing and running the business. To determine the true costs of a franchise agreement, the entrepreneur should recognize the business expenses that the franchisor may cover. If the franchisor selects, purchases, labels, and distributes the inventory, the entrepreneur may be able to eliminate the costs of market trips from the operational budget. If the franchisor provides a computerized sales and inventory system, the entrepreneur may

FIGURE 5.4
Appealing to girls of many ages, Hello Kitty is one of several franchises available to fashion entrepreneurs.

be able to exclude the purchase price of this system from start-up costs. In sum, the entrepreneur should analyze costs generated and eliminated by the franchise arrangement before making a decision about the financial investment for a franchise contract. Costs, however, are not the only potential disadvantage to this entry strategy.

Another significant disadvantage to the franchise entry strategy pertains to the entrepreneur's control of the business (or lack of it). In some franchise agreements the entrepreneur is required to forfeit control of the business. In many franchise arrangements there is much less room to be creative and to vary the product. The franchisee will be required to follow the policies and procedures of the overall franchise operation. In such cases, the franchisees may feel that they are not free to manage the business as they would like. As a result, entrepreneurs may feel as though they have purchased a job, rather than a business. Franchisors, on the other hand, have a motive for developing and maintaining such controls. They are developed and implemented to ensure uniformity among outlets and to safeguard quality. The following are typical examples of such controls:

»   **Site approval**—Many franchisors require preapproval for outlet sites. This may increase the likelihood that the entrepreneur's outlet will attract customers. Franchisors may impose design or appearance standards to ensure that customers see a consistent image in every outlet. Some franchisors demand periodic renovations or seasonal design changes. Complying with these standards may increase costs. In addition, some franchisors limit the business to a specific territory. Although these territorial restrictions may ensure that other franchisees will not compete for the same customers, they could impede the entrepreneur's ability to open more outlets or move to a more profitable location.

»   **Restrictions on what is sold**—Franchisors may restrict the goods and services offered for sale. For example, the owner of an accessory store franchise may not be able to add inventory items not specified in the franchise agreement. Similarly, the franchisee may not be able to delete items noted in the agreement. From the franchisor's perspective, these limitations on goods and services can ensure that customers receive a uniform level of quality. For the entrepreneur, however, this might restrict merchandise assortment and services tailored to meet regional customers' wants and needs.

»   **Limitations on method of operation**—Franchisors may obligate the entrepreneur to operate in a particular manner. For example, the franchisor may require the entrepreneur to operate during certain hours, use only preapproved signs and advertisements, or implement certain accounting or bookkeeping procedures. These restrictions may keep the entrepreneur from operating the outlet as he or she deems best. The franchisor also may insist that the entrepreneur purchase supplies only from an approved supplier, even if supplies could be purchased elsewhere at a lower cost.

The destinies of the parent company and its franchise operations are intertwined. If the franchisor loses market share for one reason or another, such as a decline in reputation, the entrepreneur's business may experience a similar decline. If the parent company receives negative publicity, customers may view all businesses under that name in a negative light. If this occurs, and the franchisee wants to get out of the business, it may be difficult to exit the franchise agreement. Most franchise contracts specify that the business cannot be sold to just anyone. Also, most franchise contracts require a long-term commitment. Franchise agreements typically run for fifteen to twenty years; however, a three- to ten-year term of agreement is not unusual. If the parent company collapses, the individual franchise may not be able to survive. If the franchise is terminated, the entrepreneur may lose the investment. Also, if the franchisee fails to hold up things on his or her end, for example, by failing to pay royalties or abide by performance standards and sales restrictions, the franchisor can end the franchise agreement.

Franchise agreements often do not provide guarantees that the contracts will be renewed. At the expiration of the contract, the franchisor may decline to renew the contract or decide to change the original terms and conditions. The franchisor may raise the royalty payments or impose new design standards and sales restrictions. The entrepreneur's previous territory may be reduced, possibly resulting in more competition from company-owned outlets or other franchisees.

In conclusion, it is important to note that choosing a franchise is a dream for some entrepreneurs and a nightmare for others. The franchise entry strategy appeals to the following people: those who do not have the expertise or desire to build their own businesses from the bottom up; those who prefer a lower level of risk or a higher level of assistance, or both; and those who believe there is a large profit opportunity in a specific franchise system.

An example of a fashion franchise is illustrated in Case Study 5.2. Pigtails & Crewcuts is a beauty franchise that provides hairstyling services for children. The environment is one of a kind and is appealing to kids and parents alike; it is as fun as a playroom but as stylish and comfortable as a living room. In terms of services, the franchise offers a variety of theme parties for boys and girls of all ages that can be tailored to meet most budgets. In addition, Pigtails & Crewcuts salons make a child's first haircut a special experience through a keepsake card that includes a photograph and a lock of hair. The franchise also provides private label hair and body products with names like Goofy Grape, Out of This World Orange, Berries and Bows, and Wacky Wash. The company prides itself on its customer satisfaction. It reports that one happy mom stated, "The problem isn't getting my son in the door; it is getting him out the door when it is time to leave."[3]

ACQUIRING AN EXISTING BUSINESS

There can be many advantages to buying an existing business. The first may be location. Often, the only way entrepreneurs can obtain the locations they want to do business in is to buy existing businesses in those locations. The entrepreneur is buying not only a business, but also a place in which to conduct business. Also, there may be fewer start-up costs. It can take a new company three to five years to get to the point where the existing business already is financially. Buying an existing business may be a quick way to get to where the entrepreneur wants to be. The entrepreneur acquiring an existing business may also acquire a customer following, an income stream, business experience upon which to build, a well-known business name, and a positive business image and reputation.

In buying a business, the entrepreneur may find a low-cost source of financing—the seller. Sellers, in their eagerness to close the sale and possibly to sustain the businesses they have built, often give buyers in whom they have confidence highly advantageous terms of sale. The ultimate financial deal is one that allows the business to buy itself. With this arrangement the buyer pays the seller from the business's operating profits. If financing through the seller is not an option, financial institutions are more likely to fund a known entity, a business with a proven track record, rather than one without a history of success.

Price can prove to be a challenge with the entry strategy of buying an existing operation. Often, the business, with its location, fixtures, and inventory, may cost more money up front than the potential entrepreneur will have on hand. The entrepreneur may decide that with a smaller and less expensive location, a lower inventory level, and used fixtures, the business could increase in size in the future, as time and money become available. The owner of a successful business may include a charge for an intangible asset in the price of the business. This asset, called **blue sky,** is the dollar amount determined as a fee for the business's image or personality. Blue sky includes assets, such as the business's name, its customer following, and its image and reputation. In other words, through blue sky, the seller seeks compensation for building the business into a viable entity. FIGURE 5.5 illustrates blue sky for a business, its customers, and its image.

A possible disadvantage to buying an existing business is that in addition to its glory, the entrepreneur is buying its problems. It may be difficult to determine from the financial reports provided by the seller whether the business is on an upswing, maintaining, or declining. Relationships with vendors, customers, and the community will certainly affect future success, and

PIGTAILS & CREWCUTS CHILDREN'S SALON FRANCHISE

Hair care is an extremely fragmented $55 billion per year industry. Industry data has projected that hair care for children makes up approximately $5 billion of the market. According to the 2000 census, there are over fifty-two million children between the ages of zero and twelve in the United States and it's estimated that they average six haircuts per year each.

You should expect to invest approximately $150,000 per location to open a Pigtails & Crewcuts franchise. Franchise owners typically finance up to 80 percent of this amount.

The steps to open your salon include:

1. Identify retail locations
2. Negotiate a lease
3. Create the salon layout and design
4. Acquire inventory and start-up package
5. Complete owner and employee training
6. Develop a marketing plan and provide all collateral materials

Previous salon experience is not required to operate a Pigtails & Crewcuts franchise. We look for owners who are friendly, energetic, motivated, and love children. An owner from virtually any background, with these characteristics, and with the variety of support tools provided by Pigtails & Crewcuts corporate office, can be successful as a Pigtails & Crewcuts franchise owner.

In short, we look for people to operate the Pigtails & Crewcuts brand, in their hometown, as well or better than we could if we were there.

[Our] team is focused . . . on providing an exciting concept, proven business model, and the support services to give the franchise owner the greatest possible opportunity for success.

SOURCE: http://www.franchisegator.com/Pigtails-Crewcuts-franchise

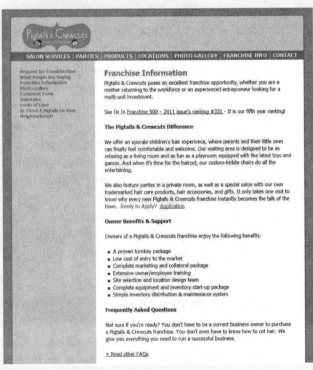

Pigtails & Crewcuts franchise information.

FIGURE 5.5

Blue sky is the value placed on the image, ambiance, reputation, and clientele established by the previous business owner.

such relationships are not spelled out in the documentation provided to assess the value of a business. When an existing business is purchased, the entrepreneur may be buying many unknowns. For example, what is the true reputation of the current owner? Did the business really make a profit, or do the financial books give a false impression of the business's actual profitability? How current and how reliable are the inventory and equipment? Planning which questions to ask may prove to be more valuable than simply sifting through information provided by the seller.

In buying an existing business, the purchase price is a major issue because it is extremely difficult to make a profit on a business if the initial price is too high. Success using this entry strategy is dependent upon how economically the entrepreneur buys the business. Buying an existing business usually requires the assistance of outside professionals. The buyer of an existing business will need to have an attorney or a licensed accountant, or both, review all legal and accounting records for the previous three to five years at a minimum. In addition, the buyer will need to arrange for a thorough inspection of the inventory, equipment, and supplies. A **letter of intent**, a letter addressed to a company stating the desire to conduct business, is typically drafted. The letter of intent usually indicates that the prospective buyer is serious and sets a timeline for negotiations. Upon agreement of

a price and other terms, the contract for sale is completed and signed, and the actual closing takes place. Throughout this process, it is important to note that attorneys, accountants, and business brokers can play key roles in the success and legal credibility of the sale.

If the buyer is purchasing real estate as part of the transaction, a title search should be conducted. A title search assures there are no recorded claims or liens against the property. Next, a **purchase agreement** will need to be drafted. The purchase agreement outlines the selling price, terms of payment, and items involved, such as fixtures, equipment, and inventory. Although protection from future liabilities may be expensive and time-consuming up front, failure to conduct a thorough investigation of the company may prove to be costly.

Typically, the best buys are businesses that are unsuccessful but for which fashion entrepreneurs believe they have solutions to the problems. If the entrepreneur determines good reasons for a turnaround, then an unsuccessful business may be advantageous from a financial perspective. A **turnaround** refers to a business that is failing but for which there are obvious changes that, when implemented, would make the business successful. A turnaround buy is also referred to as a **salvage investment**. In some cases, the entrepreneur may not have to make an actual financial investment. Management expertise and product knowledge may be enough. For example, the owner of Jellybeans, a boutique in Springfield, Missouri, that carries children's apparel, furnishings, and accessories, began by taking over a small, failing children's wear store, improving the store image, and reversing the declining sales of the store. Jellybeans has grown in size from its original 800 square feet to 4,000 square feet, with apparel, shoes, gifts, and home furnishings for infants and boys and girls to size 14.

EXIT STRATEGIES

Many fashion retailers have suffered great financial losses because they did not plan on how the business would eventually be sold or closed; they did not have an **exit strategy**. Planning allows the entrepreneur to explore the various alternatives to closing the entire business, which include direct sale, mergers, acquisitions, initial public offerings, and joint venture with another company. The decision to sell all or part of a business is one of the most complex strategic and emotional decisions an entrepreneur can make. Sooner or later, it will happen; it will be time to exit the business. The business is a result of much hard work, sweat equity, and achievement. Various factors can affect the decision to sell—some good, some bad. In many cases, selling may have been the ultimate goal all along. It other cases, selling is a reaction to changes in the market, personal circumstances, or company strategy. Retirement, health problems, relocation, or a change in career are common reasons for selling. Some owners will sell when it becomes too difficult to manage the operation or if they lack the necessary capital for expansion. Perhaps the demand for the product has lessened, thereby decreasing sales and profits. Perhaps the lease has expired and will not be renewed or can be renewed only with unfavorable terms. New competitors may be entering the marketplace, taking too great a share of the market.

On the upside, entrepreneurs often relish the excitement and risk of moving on and creating yet another new business. Selling an existing business can provide the capital necessary to begin another venture. The entrepreneur may find that by allowing an acquisition by another company, his or her personal and professional objectives may be met faster and at a lower cost. Larger companies will often have the resources, such as capital and people, to move the business forward at a faster rate and lower cost. If the entrepreneur's goal is to build the business and then to sell it at a profit, then selling it accomplishes the original goal.

FIGURE 5.6

One entrepreneur's failure to plan an exit strategy may be another's opportunity to purchase a location and fixtures at a reduced price.

Whatever the reason, the decision to sell must be given careful consideration. It is imperative to plan for the exit early, to make it the choice of the entrepreneur and not the choice of another. Selling wisely, through careful planning, can allow for greater profit and for the flexibility to pursue other opportunities. The maximum selling price will be achieved if the business is sold at some point during its growth stage. Waiting to sell until after the company shows declining sales can lead to financial disaster, as illustrated in FIGURE 5.6. Some business funders will want a plan for valuing and exiting the business before they initially provide funding for it. In Appendices B and C, exiting and valuing the business, respectively, are discussed for those prospective entrepreneurs interested in examining business planning from entry to exit.

CONCLUSION

Determining the best entry strategy is critical to the success of a new company. Entrepreneurs can enter the market in one of three ways: starting a business from scratch, purchasing a franchise operation, or buying an existing business. Each strategy sets in motion a different set of activities. With all entry strategies, costs and benefits must be carefully weighed.

KEY TERMS

blue sky

entry strategy

exit strategy

franchise

franchise fee

franchisee

franchisor

letter of intent

magalog

purchase agreement

salvage investment

start-up cost

turnaround

turnkey operation

DISCUSSION TOPICS

1. Discuss choosing to open a franchise instead of starting a business from scratch or buying an existing business. What international franchise operations are available? What services do these franchisors offer? What are the initial and ongoing costs of becoming a franchisee?

2. Consider valuing an existing business: How is the value of the business is determined? Which documents are required to validate that value? What variables can be included in the purchase of the business (e.g., hard assets, customer base, and so on)?

3. Discuss finding a business broker to locate a suitable business to purchase and to determine how the sale of a business may be structured. What affiliations, licenses, and training should a business broker have? What are the costs associated with using a business broker. Who pays the fees—the seller or the buyer? What are the advantages of working with a business broker?

SUGGESTED READINGS

Burke, R., *Entrepreneur's Toolkit*. Burke Publishing, 2006.

Burke, R., *Small Business Entrepreneur: Guide to Running a Business*. Burke Publishing, 2006.

Schroeder, C.l., *Specialty Shop Retailing: Everything You Need to Know to Run Your Own Store*, 3rd edition. Hoboken, NJ: John Wiley & Sons, Inc., 2007.

Segel, R., *Retail Business Kit for Dummies*, 2nd edition. Hoboken, NJ: Wiley Publishing, Inc., 2008.

ONLINE RESOURCES

START A FASHION BUSINESS
http://www.startafashionbusiness.co.uk
Advice and tips for new fashion business owners.

STYLECAREER.COM
http://www.stylecareer.com/fashion_designer.shtml
Publishes fashion, beauty, entertainment, arts, and business e-books.

TORONTO FASHION INCUBATOR
http://www.fashionincubator.com
Business solutions for fashion designers, entrepreneurs, professionals, and students.

BUSINESS PLAN CONNECTION
THINKING LIKE AN ENTREPRENEUR

Consider the three common methods for starting a business: starting from the ground up; purchasing a franchise operation; or acquiring an existing business. Evaluate the three opportunities in terms of your personal vision, which was discussed in Chapter 1.

ASSIGNMENT 5.1
EVALUATE METHODS OF ENTERING AND EXITING A BUSINESS

Begin by creating a matrix of the three options for entering a business, with the pros and cons of each. Approach this decision-making process with an open mind, rather than identifying with each method personally. Next, use the same process to identify how you may want to exit the business at some point in time.

This Business Plan Connection does not utilize a particular section of the business plan template. Rather, it is an opportunity to step back and consider the various methods for entering and exiting a business. It is also a topic that may be presented for discussion by potential funders who are contemplating loaning you money to open the business. The questions that follow will serve as a guide for contemplating the method that will best serve your personal wants and needs.

Using the following questions, evaluate the various methods for entering and exiting a business in terms of your personal goals, vision, needs, and desires.

1. How much money do I have to invest in the business?
2. How much control do I want to have over the business?
3. Is this a new concept or the adaptation of an existing concept?
4. How much time do I have to invest in starting a business from scratch, as opposed to buying into a franchise?
5. Is there enough value in buying into a franchise compared with the dollar amount it will cost?
6. What is the background of the franchisor?
7. What level of support will I receive from the franchisor?
8. What is the benefit of buying an existing business? Are there customers in hand?
9. What drives customers to buy currently from the existing business?
10. Do I obtain a better location by buying an existing business? Will this increase the potential of finding customers?
11. How long do I anticipate I want to stay in business?
12. Do I eventually want to sell my business?
13. Do I want to try to grow the business to a point at which it could be purchased by another company?

You will want to develop additional questions, based on your personal criteria. The answers to these questions will guide you in developing the components of the business plan.

PROFILE OF AN ENTREPRENEUR
"FASHION-FORWARD—FRUGALLY"

IN one short year, Staci Deal transitioned from student costume designer to northwest Arkansas's diva of frugal fashion. The twenty-three-year-old, who launched her first Plato's Closet franchise to lines of eager shoppers in Fayetteville in May 2008, is already gearing up to open a second store in Rogers, Arkansas. She harnesses the talents of friends and family, constantly searches for new ideas and knows just the right styles to feed the area's label-hungry fashionistas.

How did you transition from student to franchisee so quickly?

I'd been shopping in Indiana and saw a Plato's Closet, and the concept stuck with me. I just woke up one day and thought, "This would go over great in Fayetteville." It took help to get things going; this is definitely a family business. My father-in-law is a certified public accountant in Indiana and does the books. He also saw the store as an investment, so we didn't have to finance the startup; my husband, who has been in retail for years, helped me understand that aspect of the business; my brother-in-law has been doing a lot for the build-out of the second store. It's nice to have people on your team that you can trust 100 percent.

Plato's Closet.

Do you think the economy has boosted your popularity?

The economy has helped some, but we live in Fayetteville, which is a very hip college town, and Rogers is near a large community college. Kids think resale is cool anyway, so I think if the economy were good we would still do well. I mean, when we first opened, we had a huge rack of fashion denim by the door, the type of stuff that sells for $300 at boutiques. Over one hundred people lined up, and there was none of it left by the end of the day. And we're expecting way more turnout for our second opening.

Does being a young business owner cause any problems?

The toughest part is hiring people older than me. It's hard for them to say, "Hey, this girl is the boss," and a lot of times they feel like they don't have to listen. But I think everyone understands now that I'm the one running the show.

What's the advantage of running a franchise versus an independent store?

I pretty much get to do what I want with the store, and there are constant ideas coming from Plato's owner-to-owner website chat. There's useful stuff posted every day, from how to catch someone stealing to what kind of receipt paper to use. It's a real community.

What's beyond the horizon for you and your franchises?

Things are always up in the air. I'm going to school part-time to get my degree in apparel studies. I was once offered a chance to do costumes for a touring Broadway company in Japan. Broadway's always been my dream; but it's so fun being able to own my own business. Really, I think anybody can do it. You have to put your heart and soul into it, and it takes sweat and lots of work. But it can be done.

SOURCE: Daley, Jason. "Fashion-Forward—Frugally." *Entrepreneur* magazine, July, 2009. http://www.entrepreneur.com/article/202482 with permission of Entrepreneur Media, Inc.

CHAPTER 6
FINDING THE RIGHT LOCATION
FOR THE BUSINESS

EVERY entrepreneur has heard it: "The three keys to a successful business are location, location, location." Although the real key to a profitable business is likely a top-notch business plan, location certainly can play a significant role in the success of a company.

Planning to build, buy, or lease can be one of the entrepreneur's largest financial decisions in establishing the retail business. The definition and importance of a business location have changed considerably over the past decade, with the increase of e-commerce. The definition of business location is no longer confined to the geographical site of the company's headquarters or its retail outlets. **Business location** can refer to the destinations to which catalogs are mailed. It can also refer to the company's Web site or hyperlinks, or both. More traditionally, it refers to the site and facility where the business is physically situated.

Although location for today's fashion industry businesses can be interpreted in a wide variety of ways, location is always directly tied to target demographics. As defined in Chapter 3, the demographics of the target market are the homogeneous subgroups in a given population that a retail business aims to attract. These include age, income, education, and family size, among other factors. It is believed that people with similar demographic characteristics within a given region will purchase a similar range of goods and services. Consequently, the entrepreneur must define the target market before determining a location for the business—no matter if the location houses a bricks, clicks, service, or catalog operation. Target demographics are intertwined with image. Who the customer is affects how other people see the business.

FIGURE 6.1

Planning to build, buy, or lease can be one of the entrepreneur's largest financial decisions in establishing the retail business.

Whether the business is downtown or uptown, part of a regional mall or a freestanding store, the geographic location sets an image, as illustrated in FIGURE 6.1. Location as a convenience factor is also important, but ease of location alone is not the major criterion for the success of a retail business. In enclosed malls the name of the mall and the location of the business within that mall combine as image makers. In fact, shoppers often recall the name of a mall before they remember the name of the store.

Location is a multifaceted factor in business planning. It has an entirely different meaning to

e-commerce entrepreneurs. For this discussion, location factors refer to tangible buildings, brick-and-mortar stores, storefronts, or warehouses. In Chapter 7, location and visibility on the Internet are explored. In this chapter the decisions the entrepreneur must make in terms of physical location for the business are explored. These decisions involve many factors: the geographic locale of the building, the facility itself, and, finally, the design of the interior and layout of the business within the building.

In this chapter, business location is first examined in a traditional context—where to position the physical site of the company headquarters and retail outlet(s). Next, information on how to evaluate the location in terms of the specific facility from which the consumer will procure the company's product is explored. Criteria for evaluating the visual impact of the building exterior are also covered, as are the design of the building façade, logos and signing, approach, and windows. Finally, perspectives on the interior of the facility are examined, to include the size and layout of the sales area, interior display elements, lighting, fitting rooms, and the checkout area.

THE LOCATION HIERARCHY: REGION, TO STATE, TO COMMUNITY, TO SITE

The entrepreneur's ultimate objective in deciding where a business should be located is to position the business at a site that will maximize the likelihood of success. Choosing a location is a matter of selecting the place that best serves the needs of the business's target market. Sometimes, the general location for the business may be limited to the area where the entrepreneur lives. If there are no such limitations, the location selection may begin with a broad regional search that is systematically narrowed down to a state, then a city, and then a specific site. Unfortunately, many entrepreneurs never consider locations beyond the places they reside. Choosing not to look beyond one's comfort zone may prevent the entrepreneur from discovering locations that may be better suited to the business and that would improve its potential for success. Assuming that the entrepreneur is open about the location, the first step is to explore different regions. Box 6.1 is a location checklist that examines many of the decisions to be made in choosing a business location, from the region to the site.

THE REGION

The entrepreneur should begin by analyzing which regions of the country (or the world, in some cases) have the greatest number of characteristics necessary for the business to succeed. One important characteristic is the growth of a particular population segment that fits the business's target market. Rising disposable incomes and a stable economic environment are also desirable qualities. Access to suppliers and low operating costs, as well as an adequate and affordable labor pool, are additional factors to investigate. The entrepreneur should look for a low level of competition from similar businesses in the region. In some cases, climate will affect the location decision. For example, if the entrepreneur is planning to open a custom-fit swimwear business, the regional search may be limited to geographic areas with warm weather during as many months of the year as possible.

THE STATE

When the entrepreneur narrows in on a region, the next step is to select a state. Every state has a business development office that is designed to recruit new businesses to that state. Although the information provided by these offices will likely advocate for that particular state, such offices are an excellent source of facts that the entrepreneur can assess objectively. Some of the key issues to examine are state laws, regulations, and taxes and any incentives or investment credits that the state offers to businesses locating there. The entrepreneur will want to evaluate the prospective workforce by looking into the quantity and quality of the labor force, wage rates, and the union or nonunion status of the state. Proximity to suppliers, such as apparel, gift, or home furnishing market centers, as well as sales representatives for merchandise lines, may also be critical factors. Finally, the entrepreneur will want to evaluate the general business climate of the state.

THE COMMUNITY

After a state is selected, the next step is to identify a community for the location of the business. The entrepreneur will begin an assessment of a city or town as a location candidate by analyzing the city's population in terms of it psychographic and demographic characteristics. As discussed in Chapter 3, psychographic characteristics include attitudes, beliefs, and values. Demographic characteristics include population growth trends, family size, education, age breakdown, gender proportions, income levels, job categories, religion, race, nationality, and population density. **Population density** is the number of people per square mile residing in a given area. It is an important element for the success of businesses that rely on high traffic volume. For example, the customers of beauty spas will likely live or work within an eight- to ten-mile radius of the spa. If a sufficient number of residents within the target market are not within this range, it may not matter how good the spa services are. An example of a city with a growing population density is Atlanta, Georgia. Atlanta has experienced a rapid growth rate in its population of high-income, young professionals. With approximately 30 percent of its population between the ages of 20 and 39, Atlanta has seen an explosion of fashion businesses aimed at young people with rising incomes and appetites for fashion apparel.[1]

Another factor the entrepreneur will want to assess about a city is competition. One variable to consider is the number, quality, and locations of competing firms. The entrepreneur will want to examine competing companies in terms of the differences and similarities between their offerings and those of the entrepreneur's business as well as quality and pricing variances. In addition, the entrepreneur will want to look at the success and failure rates of competitors within the city. The entrepreneur may also find that the chamber of commerce, or similar city agencies, will share information on firms that will soon be opening in the city. An entrepreneur who had intended to open a home accessories business in the downtown shopping district of Boulder, Colorado, provides an illustration. She had done all her homework, thoroughly studying the competition and carefully

BOX 6.1
LOCATION CHECKLIST

Following are a number of questions the entrepreneur should ask and prioritize in order to decide on the location of the business. If the entrepreneur plans to have the company's headquarters in a location separate from other parts of the business, then the questions should be answered and weighed for each location site.

» Target market—Is this location easily accessible to the prospective company's specified target market? Does this location meet the needs and desires of the target market?

» Quality of life—Does the area fit the business's needs and the personal preferences of the entrepreneur?

» Image—Is the image of this location appropriate for the prospective business and its target market?

» Compatibility with the community—Does the business's image fit with the character of the place and the needs and wants of the residents?

» Neighbor mix—Is the assortment of neighboring businesses appropriate for the company and its target market?

» Proximity to suppliers—Are suppliers accessible, and are shipping alternatives readily available?

» Transportation networks—Are transportation alternatives available and cost-effective for the company's customers and suppliers?

» Competition—Where are direct and indirect competitors situated in relation to the location?

» Security/Safety—Is the location secure for employees, customers, inventory, and facilities?

» Labor pool—Is there an adequate number of qualified people available for employment near the business area? What are wage rates in the area? Is there a workforce of both full-time and part-time employees? The National Retail Federation reports that most part-time workers are part time by choice and that the average retail worker in 2008 cost the employer more than $16 per hour.[1]

» Restrictions—Are there any city, county, or state laws governing business locations that will affect the choice of location?

» Business climate—What is the overall attitude of customers, residents, and government officials toward this type of business? Are there any "blue laws" that prohibit business on Sundays? Are small business support programs, tax advantages, low-interest financial assistance, or incentives offered to entrepreneurs?

» Services—Are the services required for the company accessible and affordable in this location? For example, if alterations are needed by the company's customers, are alteration personnel available and affordable?

» Ownership—Is it more cost-effective to purchase or to lease in this location? Is ownership an option?

» Past tenants—Who were past tenants in this location? What types of businesses were they? Why did they leave? Where did they go?

» Space—Is the space adequate in this location? Is there room for growth?

» Physical visibility—Is the location visible to the target market? Is visibility necessary to the success of the business?

» Life cycle stage of the area—What is the maturation of the area: emerging, growing, peaking, or declining?

» Expenses—Will the total costs for this location fit within the company's budget?

REFERENCE: National Retail Federation. Retail Industry Indicators. http://www.nrf.com/modules.php?name=Pages&sp_id=702

Location can play a significant role in the success of a company.

choosing a site for her future store. By chance, she mentioned her business concept to the director of small business development at the chamber of commerce and was stunned to learn that two similar businesses were opening in her targeted area within the year. With this critical information, the entrepreneur reevaluated her plans and opened a different type of store—one that became quite successful (C. Melton, personal communication). The importance of due diligence and networking cannot be overemphasized.

Studying the size of the market for the business's products and services will help entrepreneurs determine whether they can capture a market share large enough to earn a profit. Again, U.S. Census Bureau reports (http://www.census.gov) can provide valuable demographic data. Table 6.1 illustrates the

TABLE 6.1
SAMPLE DEMOGRAPHIC REPORT

U.S. CENSUS BUREAU
STATE AND COUNTY QUICKFACTS
FULTON COUNTY, GEORGIA

PEOPLE QUICKFACTS	FULTON COUNTY	GEORGIA
Population, 2010	816,006	8,186,453
Population, percent change, 1990 to 2010	25.8%	26.4%
Persons under 5 years old, percent, 2010	7.0%	7.3%
Persons under 18 years old, percent, 2010	24.4%	26.5%
Persons 65 years old and over, percent, 2010	8.5%	9.6%
White persons, percent, 2010 (a)	48.1%	65.1%
Black or African American persons, percent, 2010 (a)	44.6%	28.7%
American Indian and Alaska Native persons, percent, 2010 (a)	0.2%	0.3%
Asian persons, percent, 2010 (a)	3.0%	2.1%
Native Hawaiian and other Pacific Islander, percent, 2010 (a)	0.0%	0.1%
Persons reporting some other race, percent, 2010 (a)	2.6%	2.4%
Persons reporting two or more races, percent, 2010	1.5%	1.4%
Female persons, percent, 2010	50.8%	50.8%
Persons of Hispanic or Latino origin, percent, 2010 (b)	5.9%	5.3%
White persons, not of Hispanic/Latino origin, percent, 2010	45.3%	62.6%
High school graduates, persons 25 years and over, 2009	323,055	2,853,605
College graduates, persons 25 years and over, 1990	131,001	777,158
Housing units, 2010	348,632	3,281,737
Homeownership rate, 2010	52.0%	67.5%
Households, 2010	321,242	3,006,369
Persons per household, 2010	2.44	2.65
Households with persons under 18, percent, 2010	32.5%	39.1%
Median household money income, 1997 model-based estimate	$39,047	$36,372
Persons below poverty, percent, 1997 model-based estimate	18.3%	14.7%
Children below poverty, percent, 1997 model-based estimate	29.8%	22.8%

(CONTINUED)

TABLE 6.1
(CONTINUED)

BUSINESS QUICKFACTS	FULTON COUNTY	GEORGIA
Private nonfarm establishments, 1999	30,590	197,759
Private nonfarm employment, 1999	726,101	3,363,797
Private nonfarm employment, percent change 1990–1999	35.6%	34.6%
Nonemployer establishments, 1998	52,085	435,338
Manufacturers shipments, 1997 ($1,000)	14,240,886	124,526,834
Retail sales, 1997 ($1,000)	9,248,184	72,212,484
Retail sales per capita, 1997	$12,779	$9,646
Minority-owned firms, percent of total, 1997	20.7%	15.6%
Women-owned firms, percent of total, 1997	27.3%	25.6%
Federal funds and grants, 2010 ($1000)	7,409,352	42,459,795
Local government employment—full-time equivalent, 1997	37,077	324,480

GEOGRAPHY QUICKFACTS	FULTON COUNTY	GEORGIA
Land area, 2010 (square miles)	529	57,906
Persons per square mile, 2010	1,542	141
Metropolitan area	Atlanta, GA	

SOURCE: U.S. Census Bureau: State and County QuickFacts. Data derived from Population Estimates, 2010 Census of Population and Housing, 1990 Census of Population and Housing, Small Area Income and Poverty Estimates, County Business Patterns, 1997 Economic Census, Minority- and Women-Owned Business, Building Permits, Consolidated Federal Funds Report, 1997 Census of Governments.

type of data the Census Bureau reports contain. After entrepreneurs complete an examination of the cities in which they are interested, they should know more about the city and its neighborhoods than do its residents. The next stage is to determine the type of area within the community in which the business will be placed.

THE SITE

There are six basic areas where businesses can be located: a central business district, first-ring suburbs, neighborhoods, shopping centers and malls, outlying areas, and even one's home. In this chapter we will examine the first four, the most common areas to open a retail business. The **central business district** is the often the historical center of a city or town, the area where downtown businesses were established early in the development of the city. **First-ring suburbs** are early-stage communities that have come about as a result of suburban sprawl. An example is Olathe, Kansas, located near Kansas City. Olathe is an area that has grown rapidly through young families' purchasing homes at lower prices, with more square footage and larger yards, outside of the metropolitan area. For fashion entrepreneurs the result of this move to the suburbs has been children's wear stores, contemporary women's apparel boutiques, beauty spas selling natural skin products, and hair salons for kids and their moms. Neighborhood locations are those in which residential areas are heavily concentrated. The city of Atlanta, Georgia, provides a good illustration of a neighborhood location. As many families, young and retired, have moved into this area, a diverse range of fashion businesses have found success through localized and congruent target markets in different areas of the same city.

Shopping centers, malls, and outlet centers provide the customers with one-stop shopping. They are classified as follows: neighborhood shopping centers, community shopping centers, regional shopping malls, and power centers. A **power center** combines the drawing potential of a large regional mall with the convenience of a neighborhood shopping center. Anchored by large specialty or department stores, these centers frequently target affluent baby boomers who desire broad selection choices and convenience. Although they still account for the majority of retail sales in apparel and soft goods, malls have declined in popularity over the past decade. Sameness and staleness are two of the adjectives used by shoppers to describe the reasons for this downslide. As a result, mall and shopping center developers are trying new formulas. Many are adding entertainment to retailing, combining an interesting environment with appealing activities and desirable merchandise. All this is developed with a specific target market in mind.

For the entrepreneur a history of the occupancy statistics for shopping centers, malls, and outlet centers is of utmost importance. An assessment of whether to lease in one of these locations should include a review of tenant turnover and leasing terms over the past one to ten years. This data may be acquired from the chamber of commerce or the leasing director of the shopping area. Another resource for information on the shopping area is the store owner renting there now as well as those who moved from there to another location. Unleased space in a shopping destination affects existing tenants in two ways—it generates a lower customer traffic base, and it creates a poor image, one that indicates the area is "off" in terms of types of stores, types of clientele, safety, and so on.

LOCATION FACTORS

Analyzing the potential location of the business, whether from a regional, state, city, or site perspective, requires an examination of many factors. Before examining actual location factors, the entrepreneur must prioritize the qualities that are most necessary to the success of the business. For example, the entrepreneur may be looking for a facility in which to locate offices and to warehouse merchandise. Entrepreneurs may intend to sell the product lines through catalogs or online. In such cases, the entrepreneur may find the factors of visibility, competition, neighbor mix, and image to be less important than if the entrepreneur were choosing a storefront location where 100 percent of the business's sales would take place.

NATIONAL RETAIL TRAFFIC INDEX

After entrepreneurs have prioritized the location characteristics for their businesses, where do they go for location information? There are a number of good sources available in print and online, such as census tracts, that can usually be found in public and university libraries. Census data range from the general to the specific. Zip code catalogs also provide general data about populations in geographic areas. In addition, city government and tourist offices, as well as chambers of commerce, often provide demographic data on neighborhood clusters. Finally, media sources may also collect and distribute demographic data that pertain to their promotional regions.

There are a number of retail business information sources that provide location data in terms of customer traffic. The **National Retail Traffic Index** (NRTI) provides information about shopper traffic and conversion trends (i.e., sales volume) for retail executives, mall developers, industry analysts, real estate consultants, and advertisers. More specifically, the NRTI evaluates department store traffic from two perspectives—the mall in which the department store is located, and the department store itself. As built-in traffic can reduce the need for advertising expenditures and increase the potential for sales, this information can be very helpful to the entrepreneur when considering a mall location. Think about the number of large, successful retail apparel chain stores that are located in malls and that do little or no advertising. Instead, they contribute to institutional advertising of the mall, or they rely on national advertising, or both. It is important for the entrepreneur to ask about the level of customer traffic in a given area, past and present.

When all the location factors are analyzed, the factor that is often most critical is cost. Locations can vary enormously in terms of price. How does the entrepreneur determine which locations are true options? An estimate of monthly income and expenses is necessary to determine a range of realistic location alternatives.

FINANCES AND LOCATION

It is possible to find the perfect location when money is no object. In the real world, however, budget limitations often create choice limitations. What if, after months of looking, the entrepreneur finds a hundred places that would be perfect for the business? What if all one hundred locations must be ruled out when costs are considered? A better approach is to begin by estimating location costs and then limiting the number of locations the entrepreneur investigates to those that fit within the budget.

ESTIMATING LOCATION COSTS

In its Retail Industry Indicators report, the National Retail Federation (NRF) compiles annual data provided by retailers from across the country. Drawing from official government data, supplemented by these industry surveys, it presents up-to-date information on a variety of topics on the industry. These include retailers' contribution to the overall U.S. economy; retail store and online sales levels and trends; employment and compensation levels and trends; and information about retail companies, including inventory shrinkage, profitability, and size of retailers.

The simplest way to determine a rough estimate of monthly sales for the business is to multiply average sales per square foot for the business type by average number of square feet in the selling space per store type. From this figure the cost of goods can be estimated and then subtracted. An example of this process follows:

» The report indicates that annual sales for a specialty store featuring ladies' sportswear are, on a national average, $150 per square foot. (Assume

that the location being considered has 2,000 square feet of selling space.)

» $150 per square foot × 2,000 square feet = $300,000, which is the sales estimate for the year.

» Using 50 percent retail markup as the industry average for apparel, the cost of goods is estimated at $150,000 (half of the $300,000 in annual sales volume).

» This leaves a balance of $150,000 for the estimated annual expenses, excluding inventory purchases. When the $150,000 is divided by 12, to find a monthly amount for expenses, the result is $12,500 per month.

Table 6.2 illustrates the distribution of monthly sales for a women's apparel store.

In the preceding scenario we see that rent above or even close to $12,500 per month will not fit within the potential business's budget. Payments for utilities, taxes, payroll, insurance, and remaining budget items must be added to the list of monthly expenses. The entrepreneur must estimate fixed and variable monthly costs and deduct these from the monthly amount for expenses before establishing a monthly location cost. For example, let us assume that the estimate for monthly expenses (not including cost of inventory and location) is $5,000 for the business. If the entrepreneur agreed to a lease of $8,000 per month, and if the business performed in alignment with similar stores, then the business would lose money every month.

Another method of estimating income and expenses for a location budget is through the Index of Retail Saturation (IRS). For retailers the number of customers in the trading area and the amount of competition are essential factors for predicting success. The **Index of Retail Saturation (IRS)** is a measure that calculates the number of customers in a specified area, customers' purchasing power, and the level of competition. It combines the average retail expenditures with the average dollar amount that each person spends for a certain type of merchandise in a given trading

TABLE 6.2
MONTHLY SALES DISTRIBUTION—SMALL CLOTHING STORES FOR WOMEN

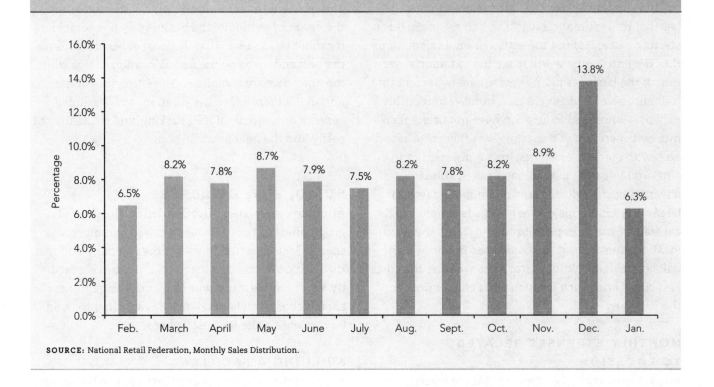

SOURCE: National Retail Federation, Monthly Sales Distribution.

area. These data can be found through the U.S. Census Bureau in two reports—County Business Patterns Economic Profile, and Economic Census. In addition, city governments and chambers of commerce often provide this type of information. When the number of customers in the trading area, the dollar retail expenditures per person in the product category, and the amount of square footage owned by competitors are determined, the IRS can be determined. It is calculated as follows:

$$\frac{\substack{\text{Number of customers in the trading area} \\ \times\ \text{Retail expenditures (per person)}}}{\substack{\text{Retail facilities (total square feet of selling space} \\ \text{allocated to the product category in the trading area)}}} = \text{IRS}$$

For example, suppose an entrepreneur is looking at two sites for an active footwear store. Through the

NRF report, the entrepreneur learns that the national average sales for shoe retail stores is $175 per square foot. Location 1 is in a geographic area that has 20,000 potential customers, each of whom spends an average of $62 on sports shoes annually. The only competitor in the trading area has an estimated 6,000 square feet of selling space. Location 2 has 25,000 potential customers who spend an average of $65 on sports shoes each year. Near this location, two competitors occupy a combined space of about 8,400 square feet.

The IRS values for these two sites are computed as follows:

IRS of Location 1 $\dfrac{20{,}000 \times \$62}{6{,}000} = \$206.67$ per square foot

IRS of Location 2 $\dfrac{25{,}000 \times \$65}{8{,}400} = \$193.45$ per square foot

At first glance, Location 2 appears to be the more productive; however, when the IRS is calculated, Location 1 proves to be better. Both IRS figures surpass the industry average of $175 per square foot.

It is imperative for the entrepreneur to remember that this estimate is just that—an estimate. It is a starting place; it is not the actual or final calculation that the entrepreneur will make in the financial section of the business plan. There are many factors that influence sales and expenses. A number of monthly expenses unrelated to location have not been taken into consideration at this point. Monthly costs associated with start-up expenses, loan repayment (principal and interest), payroll, sales taxes, shipping, advertising, markdowns, and much more have not been included in this estimate. This is simply a logical way for the entrepreneur to limit the number of location alternatives. The completed financial plan will be the determining factor as to whether the costs associated with each location will actually work for the company.

MONTHLY EXPENSES RELATED TO LOCATION

What are the monthly expenses that the entrepreneur must consider with respect to location? They vary with each location, whether a new building, a purchase, or a lease agreement, and with each contract.

Following is a list of expenses that often relate to the location of a business:

» Utilities (e.g., electricity, gas, and water)

» Maintenance

» Commons fees (e.g., charges for maintenance of areas shared by tenants, such as courtyards, plants, fountains, and so on)

» Facilities improvements

» Insurance

» Property taxes

» Advertising and other promotional costs (e.g., charges for promotional activities sponsored by the shopping center)

When examining locations that fit within your rough estimate for monthly expenses, compiling a chart of monthly costs for each and every alternative is an effective means of comparison. This allows the entrepreneur to make adjustments, if needed, when the financial section of the business plan is completed. It cannot be assumed that the least expensive alternative will end up being the actual location choice when the financials are completed. The entrepreneur may find that a more expensive location, with its added benefits of customer traffic, parking, and so on, may fit easily into the final financial plan.

BUILD, BUY, OR LEASE?

After the entrepreneur has decided on the general geographic location and has reviewed a number of specific locations that fit within the company's budget, the location decision shifts to that of a specific facility. What are the important factors the entrepreneur should consider when determining whether to build, buy, or lease a site for the business?

BUILDING A FACILITY

A critical decision for the entrepreneur is whether to build a facility. The decision to build is largely influenced by the entrepreneur's financial situation. If the entrepreneur has unlimited funds, he or she could design and build a perfect facility. Few people have this luxury; however, constructing a new facility can project a positive image to prospective customers. A new building can incorporate the most needed and efficient features, which can significantly lower operating costs and increase productivity. It allows the entrepreneur to start with a clean slate, one that he or she has helped develop, as illustrated in FIGURE 6.2.

In some areas there are few or no existing buildings to buy or lease that correspond to the entrepreneur's needs. In these situations the entrepreneur must consider the cost of constructing a building as part of the start-up capital. Constructing a building creates a high initial fixed cost that the entrepreneur must weigh against the facility's ability to generate revenue. It plays a critical role in calculating the break-even point of the business. Time is also a factor to

FIGURE 6.2

Building a location from the ground up can enable an entrepreneur to start with a clean slate and put a personal signature or brand on the retail space.

consider when assessing the build, buy, or lease alternatives. Building a facility will require more lead time than the other options. Finally, building a structure can be viewed as an investment. If the building has the potential of becoming a profitable investment because of its location, then the entrepreneur, as well as potential funders, may determine that constructing a facility is the best way to go.

BUYING A FACILITY

In some cases, there may be an appropriate building in the area where the entrepreneur wants to locate. If the building will require remodeling, buying it may be the best option. Although buying a building requires considerable financial resources, the entrepreneur will know exactly what the monthly payments will be. As with the alternative of building a facility, the entrepreneur may have significant reasons to believe that the property will actually appreciate in value. In such cases, choosing to purchase may be a wise decision. Conversely, the entrepreneur can depreciate the building each year. Both depreciation and the interest on the loan for the facility are tax-deductible business expenses.

On the downside, building or buying a facility may limit the entrepreneur's mobility. Some entrepreneurs prefer to stay out of the real estate business and focus on what they know best, running their businesses. Not all real estate appreciates in value. Surrounding properties can become run down or unsafe and consequently lower property values in the area despite the owner's efforts to keep the building in prime condition. Many downtown locations in large cities have experienced this problem. Moreover, the entrepreneur may decide that flexibility and mobility are necessary to maximize the business. If this is the case, leasing a facility offers the most flexibility, the greatest mobility, and the lowest initial cash outlay.

LEASING A FACILITY

The major advantage to leasing a facility is that leasing requires less money. This frees up funds for purchasing inventory, promoting the business, and supporting the business's operations. Monthly rental fees may be tax deductible. What are the disadvantages of leasing a structure? The property owner may decide not to renew the lease or to increase the rent drastically at the time of lease renewal. As a result, a successful business may be forced to move to a new location, which can be costly. Relocation can also result in a loss of customers.

In cases in which the building owner wants a large increase in rent when the lease is up for renewal, the landlord has the upper hand. The landlord is well aware of the tangible and intangible costs associated with moving. Another disadvantage to leasing can be the limitations to remodeling the building. For example, the building owner may believe that modifications of the facility will adversely affect the future value of the property. In this case, the landlord may likely refuse to allow remodeling or will require a long-term lease at a higher monthly rent. Also, permanent modifications of the structures, such as wallpaper, lighting, and electrical improvements, usually become the property of the building owner.

The length and terms of a lease can benefit or hinder a business. Obviously, a long-term, low-rent lease for an excellent facility in a desirable location can be viewed as a true business asset. In contrast, a short-term lease may spell trouble for a company. In addition to length of lease, there are a number of issues that need to be discussed and specified in the rental contract. Following is a list of questions that should be discussed and clarified with the facility landlord:

» What will be the terms and length of the lease?

» Will the lease be a straight rental or rent plus a percentage of gross or net profits?

» Will a sublease be permitted?

» Will there be a "due on sale" clause in the lease, stipulating that the remaining lease payments are due if the facility is sold?

» Who will pay for exterior and interior improvements?

» What restrictions will the lease contain (e.g., hours of operation, joint promotional activities)?

» Will there be any energy-efficiency requirements?

» Will electronic and computer needs be accommodated? If not, who will pay for these?

» Can the facility be expanded, if needed?

» What additions, such as walls or signage, can be made? Who will pay for these?

» How much will the deposit be for the lease, if required?

» What will be the monthly utility costs? Will these be included in the monthly rental fee?

» Will there be additional fees for janitorial, trash removal, or other facility maintenance needs?

The results of the discussion should then be specified in the lease.

Let us assume that the entrepreneur has investigated these questions and determined that leasing a specific facility is the best option. What does the entrepreneur need to know about negotiating and committing to a lease? In some instances, the building owner may require a percentage of the tenant's gross sales, in addition to the monthly rent. If this is the situation, then the entrepreneur may elect to request a long-term lease with a lid or cap that limits or prohibits monthly rental increases. Following are a number of suggestions that the entrepreneur may want to consider before signing a lease:

» Read the lease agreement thoroughly; then ask an experienced and reputable attorney to review it before signing it.

» Incorporate, or form a limited liability corporation, before signing a lease.

» Get all promises in writing.

» Be certain that insurance will cover any damage to the property.

» Verify the lease's provisions on such issues as parking spaces; improvements; repairs; maintenance; operating hours; air-conditioning and heating; and cleaning and other services, ranging from grounds keeping to promotional activities.

» Be sure that subleasing is permitted.

» If the facility is in a shopping center or mall, include a clause that guarantees that the building owner will not lease to a competing business.

» Also for shopping centers or malls, request an occupancy clause, stating that rent will be reduced or eliminated until the center reaches a specific level of occupancy.

FACTORS TO CONSIDER FOR BUILDING, BUYING, OR LEASING A SITE

4 = most preferable; 1 = least preferable

	Build				Buy				Lease			
	4	3	2	1	4	3	2	1	4	3	2	1
Building exterior												
Building interior (office and work areas, lighting, selling space, storage, traffic flow, receiving, fitting rooms, restrooms, and so on)												
Zoning												
Maintenance needs												
Insurance requirements												
Security												
Identification (signage)												
Parking												
Vehicle traffic and speed limit												
Nearby businesses												
Proximity to customers and suppliers												
Area demographics												
Population of trading area												
Economic conditions												
Property potential												

FIGURE 6.3

Funders evaluating the entrepreneur's business plan will carefully examine plans for the business's facility. They will assess initial costs relating to the structure, the value of the property, any equity that may be associated with the facility, and the potential contribution of the building to the success of the business. FIGURE 6.3 provides a list of factors and a rating system from excellent to poor for each of the three location options.

LOCATION AND THE BUSINESS PLAN

In the business plan, the entrepreneur will list the location of the company's headquarters, the primary place of business (if different), and any branch locations (if applicable). The entrepreneur will indicate whether the facility will be constructed by the entrepreneur, purchased as an existing building, or leased. In addition, the square footage, and how this square footage will be allocated for office space, warehouse, and retail, will be described. It will also be important to discuss access to parking and transportation. If visibility is a key factor to the business's success, the entrepreneur will want to discuss this in the location section of the business plan. A description of the geographical area the company will serve should also be included.

A copy of the actual unsigned lease and a letter of commitment from the building owner should be attached to the business plan. Further details about location will be provided in the business plan in the form of a blueprint and layout that denote specifics about the exterior and interior of the facility.

DESIGNING EFFECTIVE SELLING SPACE

Retail facilities must make maximum use of the space available with respect to efficiency and appearance. Both the exterior and the interior of the building should be carefully assessed by the entrepreneur. Some parts of the facility may be changed with low cost and time expenditures, such as the color of the front door or the location of the cash desk. Others, such as the store windows or parking availability, are more difficult or impossible to fix. Next, the exterior and interior of the facility are examined.

THE EXTERIOR

Customers develop opinions about a store before they enter it. They form opinions about the image, price range, quality, and exclusivity of the merchandise that are inside the store from outside. The following four factors influence the opinions that customers form before they enter the retail operation: exterior design, signs (e.g., logo, name), approach, and display windows. The exterior design of the building influences the consumer's initial opinion.

Because the expectation level of the customer is established outside the store, if the potential customer does not like the look of a retail store from the outside, he or she may never go inside to get to know the operation better. As illustrated by FIGURE 6.4, the exterior should reflect the personality of the business—similar to the way the choice of clothing expresses the personality of its wearer.

The Design of the Exterior
The architecture of shopping malls has neutralized the impact of individual store architecture. Even when successful fashion stores are clustered in spaces as beautiful as London's Burlington Arcade or as unique as Forum des Halles in Paris, few shoppers remember

FIGURE 6.4
The exterior of a building can also be the retail establishment's ultimate billboard.

the individual store's façade. A photograph of the amazing Forum des Halles shopping destination is featured in FIGURE 6.5. Downtown shops, stores in strip centers, and freestanding stores have the opportunity to use exterior design as a tool to create image and visual uniqueness. As customers approach these types of stores, effective architecture can generate a powerful first impression. The early entrepreneurs who pioneered the growth of fashion retail businesses knew this. The first department stores in New York and Chicago were, in essence, theatrical emporiums. It was the desire of these retailing leaders to create

FIGURE 6.5

Forum des Halles shopping mall and park in Paris.

a structure that would fulfill the fantasies of their clients. They made the building part of the store's total image. Today, storefronts can represent attitude, price perception, value, and target market through a combination of architecture, location, and signing. JCPenney, Urban Outfitters, Harrods, and Banana Republic are a few examples of retailers that effectively use these tools to project image.

Logos and Signs

Today, in place of eye-catching façades, the exterior image of stores in shopping centers is communicated primarily by the company name and the design of the logo. The choices of signs and designs include script, block letters, backlit, neon, pictorial, metal, wood, and plastic. The configuration of fonts, sizes, and materials for signs is unlimited. There are some interesting messages that may be communicated to customers through signage. Some designer boutiques, for example, have no significant signs, except for plaques at the entry. These prestige retailers are allowing the building itself to communicate the store's image. In addition, they are implementing the subliminal understanding that the smaller the sign, the more exclusive and higher priced the merchandise. Most department stores in downtown locations have their names on marquees or in large, illuminated letters on the façade.

FIGURE 6.6

Signs with logos have replaced the façades as the exterior signature.

Freestanding stores more often use logo or graphic and name combinations, as in FIGURE 6.6. Each variation creates a different perception of image and, subsequently, price.

Approach

As customers approach the store, even before they see the merchandise in the window, they become aware of automobiles in the parking areas, the grounds and common areas, and people moving to and from the entry. The customer quickly develops a perception of the location. The entrepreneur needs to anticipate these perceptions when selecting a location. For example, feelings of prestige may turn to concerns about safety when panhandlers are begging in an exclusive strip center. The clothing and appearance of shoppers in the area also project an image; observing other shoppers influences customers in categories such as exclusivity, price expectation, and fashion availability.

Display Windows

The last visual stimulus communicated to the customer before entry to the store is the display window. It is here that the last of the prejudged expectations is made. Because the windows are what shoppers see right before they enter the store, the appearance of

FIGURE 6.7

Because the windows are what shoppers see just before they enter the store, the appearance of the windows carries the most weight in shoppers' minds.

the windows carries the most weight in the shoppers' minds (FIGURE 6.7). Windows must have an overall consistency with the merchandise within the store. The size and number of windows should relate to the type of merchandise being sold. Bloomingdale's projects a fashion-forward and creative image through large display windows that surround the building. Compare this vision with the windows of Tiffany's. The Tiffany's exterior features small windows at eye level, tertiary windows designed to present vignettes using beautiful jewelry. On a winter afternoon the windows at Bloomingdale's may feature eye-catching coats by "hot" designers shown on gorgeous mannequins. On that same day, the Tiffany's windows may display tiny snowmen with diamond earrings as eyes and miniature pine trees wrapped with glittering bracelets and topped with star-shaped, diamond-encrusted pins. In both cases, the windows are in proportion to the featured products; they frame the merchandise and give it importance. In both cases, and as explored further in Case Study 6.1, the image of the retailer is enhanced and communicated by the exterior of the store.

THE INTERIOR

The goal shared by fashion entrepreneurs planning a retail space is a simple one—to create an environment that will entice the customer to buy. The size and layout of the store, the colors of the décor, the displays, the fixtures and mannequins, the lighting, the fitting rooms, and even the placement and look of the cash desk come together to create the visual environment that can make or break a retail business. When selecting a location, the entrepreneur will want to envision and plan how the interior space will be allocated and designed. Box 6.2 presents facts to consider when planning the interior of a retail store.

Size of the Sales Area

The amount of space within a sales area can communicate an image. When most customers see an open, spacious department, they automatically think of higher prices and exclusivity as well as excellent customer service. Bergdorf Goodman is an example of this concept. It has less merchandise per square foot

Donna Geary is the founder and executive director of Impact Visual Merchandising. For the past twenty years, Donna has consulted with clients in the retail, tourism, museum, attraction, service, wholesale, and banking sectors. Donna studied fashion design and merchandising and visual merchandising earned a master's of business administration in marketing from Concordia University, and obtained a certificate in adult education from Trent University. She was formerly a senior executive in the marketing departments of The Hudson' Bay Company and Woodward department stores. Donna is the author of *Maximizing Store Impact: A Retailer's Guide to Profitable Visual Merchandising*. She has instructed courses in marketing, visual merchandising, and business communications at Ryerson University; Seneca College; Trent University; the International Academy of Merchandising & Design; Career and Leadership Development Center, University of Pittsburgh, College of Business Administration (CLDC), in Brazil; and Fleming College, in Peterborough, Ontario, where she now resides.

1. Why is store image so important?

We've heard it again and again: "You never get a second chance to make a first impression." Even though there are many influences at work in the shopping experience, the look of a store holds the most sway in enticing us through the doors. We even tend to sum up that initial in-store encounter in visual terms: a store is exciting, clean or well organized or, at the other end of the scale, boring, messy, or overwhelming. It is not enough anymore for a store to just look good from a merchandising or display standpoint. Who can afford to spend quantum amounts of time or money on improving a store's look without being assured of a healthy return on investment? A store not only must perform by exciting and encouraging the customer to buy, but from the retailer's point of view, it must perform profitably.

Visual merchandising is composed of six components: image, layout, presentation, signing, display, and events. The component that lays the groundwork for all the other components is, simply, image. Everything you do within the store—how you develop your layout, your presentation, your signing, your displays, and your events—must fit into the image you choose to create.

2. Why start with store image?

Image can be described as the overall look of a store and the series of mental pictures and feelings it evokes within the beholder.

For the retailer, developing a powerful image provides the opportunity to embody a single message, stand out from the competition and be remembered. As a rule, image is the foundation of all retailing efforts. Store layout, presentation, signing, displays and events can all change to reflect newness and excitement from week to week, season to season, but they must always remain true to the underlying store image.

Studies indicate that a retailer has roughly *seven seconds* to capture the attention of a passing customer. Image-makers combine to form a distinctive image that not only reaches out and grabs the customer's attention, but makes a positive impression within those precious few seconds:

3. You mention "image-makers." What are they?

» An identifiable store name
» A powerful visual trademark
» An unmistakable storefront
» An inviting entrance
» A consistent and compelling store look and hook

4. What's in a name?

An effective store name sets the tone and provides a store's identification by conjuring up an image in the customer's mind.

A store name should be easy to say and remember, indicative of the images and feelings you want the customer to retain and unlikely to sound dated in a few years.

5. What do you mean by a powerful visual trademark?

An identifiable trademark adds a visual image to the memory recall of a store name, by combining words and pictures, color, shape, typeface, texture and/or style to make it stand out.

Identifiable even in the absence of the store name, a successful trademark should be unique to you, indicative of your products and services, consistent with the overall impression you want to leave customers and be professional and well-designed.

6. What are storefront traffic-stoppers?

Customers simply don't have the time to "read" into the store, so just as your store name and trademark—the title of your "book"—must provide instant recognition and recall, your exterior storefront—the cover of your "book"—must project a welcoming, clear and concise image of what's in-store. Traffic-stopping storefronts use a thoughtful combination of exterior architecture, signing and window displays to ensure a powerful first impression.

7. What does the fashion entrepreneur need to know about exterior architecture?

A store's exterior look is often referred to as the architecture, and comprises aspects such as building materials, architectural style and detail, colors and textures. A store in a Victorian brownstone building, for example, will exude images associated with the building's architectural era, such as cozy, tastefully cluttered, and comfortable. If your exterior architecture is not projecting the right image, consider painting or re-facing the storefront, adding or removing some architectural elements in keeping with your image, or consulting a designer to totally re-engineer the storefront.

8. How important is the store sign?

The store sign is a vital element of the storefront, identifying your store and beckoning the customer to take notice and stop. In realizing the value of a strong storefront sign, many retailers are employing new design techniques which include projecting or cantilevering the store sign, adding motion, or using three-dimensional lettering and unique lighting applications to add depth to the sign. If your storefront sign is losing the battle for visual dominance among neighboring stores, consider re-painting it or adding more color, making it appear bigger and bolder, incorporating your trademark, using new, more contemporary materials to create your sign, and/or adding motion or lighting.

9. What does an entrepreneur need to know about store windows in a business location?

A store's exterior windows or glass storefront provide an additional opportunity to reach out and grab the passing customer. Windows offer an opportunity to begin telling your store's unique merchandise story immediately.

Many retailers underestimate the powerful pull of an effective window, treating the area more as additional stock space than the true image-maker and magnet it can be. This prime real estate should be approached as a showcase for the newest seasonal merchandise dramatized with props and themes in keeping with your store image. Consider adding motion to your window with animated displays, turntables, fans, video screens or motorized pulleys.

10. What is "the customer's vantage point?"

This means placing yourself in the customers' shoes by considering their reverie—the speed at which they are traveling, their preoccupation levels, and the chances of getting them to stop. The more hurried and distracted customers are, the less chance there is of getting their attention. Often, plans that look good on paper fail miserably because they are developed from the retailer's vantage point, not the customer's. Many retailers plan their storefronts based on a "head-on" perspective, which entails a direct 90 degree-angle approach. But is that the customer's vantage? Not typically. Usually, the direction of customer traffic flow is influenced by the location of a parking lot, a public transportation terminal, or such. Displays slanted to that dominant direction of traffic will get more serious attention.

11. Anything else?

To increase the chances of customers noticing your store, consider the following: What direction and angle is the customer coming from? Is your exterior sign visible and legible from a distance? Is the traffic predominantly drive by or walk by? Are there any discernible traffic patterns and at what speed are customers moving at various times of the day? Are the store windows easy to read from the distance the customer will first notice them? One brilliant pet store owner made sure that dog-walkers didn't pass by his store. He placed an antique fire hydrant right beside his entrance!

12. What does the fashion entrepreneur need to think about when it comes to designing the store entrance?

The entrance to the store is the division between the outside and inside environments. Mall retailers have an easier chance of luring customers into the store with a wide, open entrance, creating a seamless entry from the mall to the store. Retailers who depend largely on impulse traffic should try to create an open storefront, either by removing storefront barriers completely or by creating an unobstructed view into the store with a glass frontage. An unobstructed and welcoming doorway combined with a great window display can provide the lure. In all types of store entrances, customers need to get the impression that they will be comfortable and welcome. Obstacle courses, visual clutter and "Do Not" signs on the doors are negative turn-offs that often result in a negative first impression and a lost customer.

13. How does the entrepreneur increase the level and number of positive impressions?

Creating a consistent positive impression is important, particularly so if you have more than one store. Even if your multiple locations differ in size, shape, design and even merchandise mix, you can create continuity of image by having common elements throughout the chain. Consider applying the same store trademark to all of your marketing, storefront and in-store applications, extending some common exterior elements to all of your stores and/or using similar props, treatments and themes in store windows.

14. Okay, so we have the customers' attention! Now what can the fashion entrepreneur do to get them in the door?

Within the first few seconds of catching their interest, the customer' s focus moves beyond the store's exterior for a visual scan of the interior while they decide whether to enter or not. Getting a customer through the door is indeed a victory. In most instances, customers are either on a mission to make a planned purchase (the Seekers), or are shopping for amusement, entertainment or ideas (the Browsers).

Seekers may plan a trip to your store to make a premeditated purchase or may decide to enter because they are comparison shopping for something specific. For Seekers, a deeper look into the store must reinforce their confidence that the store will have what they are seeking and that they can get in and out easily and quickly.

Browsers are more inclined to enter a store impulsively, drawn by the overall impression that a store may have something for them. For both Seekers and Browsers, the glance into the store and the resulting decision, to enter, or not, is often attributed to the overall store look and a compelling hook.

15. Why do you discuss a powerful visual look from the outside to the inside?

An inviting entrance is crucial in stopping the customer and establishing a positive first impression, but if the inside store messages create feelings of inconsistency or confusion, all is lost. For example, a clear and well-articulated store entrance that is followed up with a barrage of inconsistent aisle patterns, sloppy merchandising, and confusing signs signals to the customer that the exterior image will not be fulfilled on the inside. Truly impressive stores are consistent in all efforts from the storefront right through to the stockroom.

16. What is a visual hook?

A visual hook is a call to action that diverts a customer's attention to your store with a "Stop! There's something here for you!" Powerful visual hooks are created by marrying other visual merchandising components for a more memorable first impression. An exciting entrance presentation, an effectively signed promotional offering, a powerful interior display, and related in-store events all serve as magnets to draw in the customer. Well-executed hooks hold tremendous appeal for the customer, particularly the Browser.

A fashion retailer, for example, recently created a compelling promotion using the sights, sounds and smells of the Orient. Sales associates posted at the entrance offered fortune cookies containing discount coupons to customers. Large colorful posters, banners, Oriental art, and props throughout the store windows and interior carried the theme further. Even the air was filled with the subtle sounds of Oriental stringed instruments and lightest whiff of incense. Many of today's retailers are extending their store hooks into the realm of sensory appeal for a total image package. That's the beauty and future of brick-and-mortar store. You just can't get that kind of multisensory experience when you are shopping from a catalog or Web site!

SOURCE: Impact Visual Merchandising. About Donna Geary. 2007. http://www.impactvisual.com.

than any large specialty store in Manhattan; however, it reports one of the highest sales volume levels per square foot in the country. In contrast, some retailers have been able to use small spaces to their advantage, often depending upon the merchandise assortment. These retailers create the feeling of a boutique by using intimate spaces that showcase unique goods and allow for a high level of service.

SockShop of London is a perfect example of a boutique concept. The inventory is moderately priced and includes fashion and basic socks and hosiery for men, women, and children. The sales associates are approachable, friendly, and informed. The small stores are well merchandised with wall fixtures and carefully placed floor racks to create pathways or aisles. Aisle width is a feature of retail floor space. It is important to recognize that customers often equate wider aisles with higher prices. A planned balance of merchandise, display, and aisle space is necessary to project a desired image and to maximize sales.

Layout

Layout is the arrangement of the physical facilities in a business. An ideal layout contributes to efficient operations, increased productivity, and higher sales.

Retail layout refers specifically to the arrangement and method of display of merchandise in a store. A retailer's success depends, in part, on a well-designed floor plan, as illustrated by FIGURE 6.8. The retail layout in an apparel and accessories business should put customers into the store and make it easy for them to locate merchandise; compare price, quality, and features; try on the merchandise; and, ultimately, make a purchase. The floor plan should also take customers past displays of the items they may buy on impulse. An effective layout can generate sales through suggestive selling initiated by planned visual merchandising efforts. For instance, when a handbag department is located next to the footwear department, multiple sales may result, as the customer is tempted to purchase a bag to match a new pair of shoes.

Successful retailers recognize that some locations within a store are superior to others. Customers' traffic patterns give clues to the best locations for items with the greatest profit potential. The location with the highest level of customer traffic is referred to as **prime selling space**. For example, merchandise purchased on impulse and convenience goods should be placed near the front of the store, preferably adjacent to the cash desk. Customer jewelry, care products for shoes and

FIGURE 6.8

A retailer's success depends, in part, on a well-designed floor plan.

apparel, and inexpensive gift items are ideal add-on items to place in the prime selling space near the cash register. New fashion merchandise is most effectively positioned at the entrance to the store.

Some retailers generate significant increases in sales by intentionally directing **customer traffic patterns**. These retailers use the placement of a department or the design of aisles within the store to increase the customer's exposure to the merchandise assortment. The retailer may create a circular traffic pattern that requires the customer to walk around the store, from entrance to exit. Another traffic pattern designed to make the customer circulate throughout the store is formatted like a bicycle wheel, with aisles, like spokes, attached to the circle, or outer rim. In either case, the customer will pass through a number of departments before leaving the store.

Another technique used by retailers to increase sales is to locate a high-volume department in the rear of the store. Generally speaking, space values in a retail store depend on the space's relative position to the store entrance. **Space value** is the value of each square foot of space in the store with respect to generating sales revenue. Typically, the farther away an area

is from the entrance, the lower its value. Furthermore, space value typically decreases as distance from the main entry-level floor increases. Selling areas on the main level contribute a greater portion to sales than do those on the other floors because they offer greater exposure to customers than either basement or higher-level locations. Some retailers, however, work to offset lower space values through the placement of successful departments. For example, if a retail operation specializing in apparel and accessories is known for its shoe selection, the shoe department may be situated in the back of the store, on a platform level. This way, customers can see the shoe department upon entering the store, yet they must walk through the other departments to get to it. If customers come into the store for specific products and have a tendency to walk directly to those products, it may benefit the retailer to place complementary products in their path. In essence, customers are tempted to make more purchases by seeing or coming in contact with more merchandise.

Still other retailers have found success by adding entertainment facilities to their stores, known as **entertailing**. Sephora, a retailer of beauty and fragrance products, has successfully attracted customers into its Champs d'Elysée location in Paris by constructing a stage area in the front of the store where bands and singers regularly perform. It is a drawing card that pulls people in off the busy street. Similarly, the Donna Karan flagship store on Madison Avenue in Manhattan features a juice bar as well as a music and magazine department on its second floor.

This, too, pulls customers into and through the store, encouraging them to lounge for a while. More and more, retailers are including cafés, coffee shops, music areas, arcades, computer facilities, and other nonapparel entities as part of the store layout. The entertailing trend in retailing is one that has resulted from a keen understanding of the target customer's lifestyle and interests.

Effective layout in a retail store emerges from in-depth knowledge of the target customers' buying habits by the entrepreneur. Observing customers' behavior can help the entrepreneur identify the "hot spots" where merchandise sells quickly and the "cold spots" where

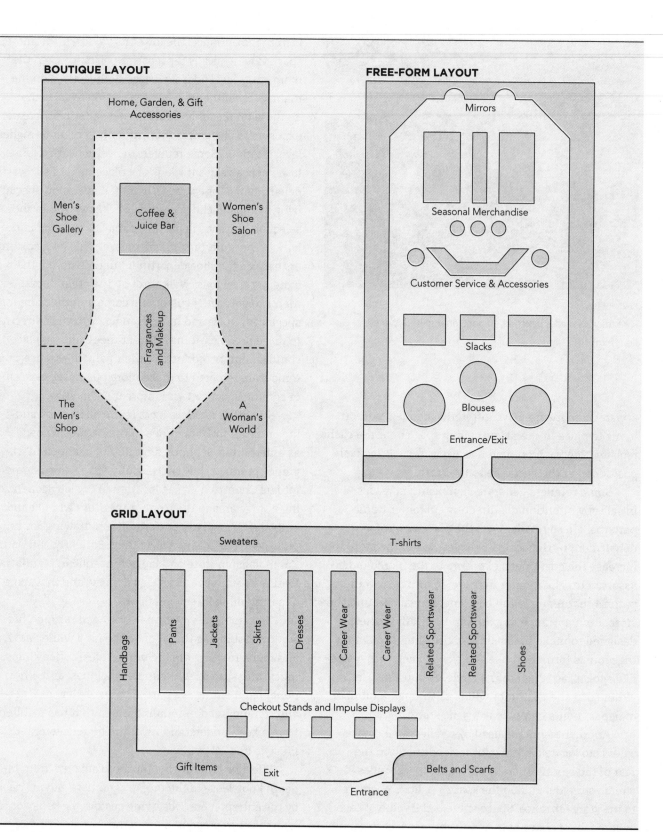

BOUTIQUE LAYOUT

Home, Garden, & Gift Accessories

Men's Shoe Gallery

Coffee & Juice Bar

Women's Shoe Salon

Fragrances and Makeup

The Men's Shop

A Woman's World

FREE-FORM LAYOUT

Mirrors

Seasonal Merchandise

Customer Service & Accessories

Slacks

Blouses

Entrance/Exit

GRID LAYOUT

Sweaters

T-shirts

Handbags

Pants

Jackets

Skirts

Dresses

Career Wear

Career Wear

Related Sportswear

Related Sportswear

Shoes

Checkout Stands and Impulse Displays

Gift Items

Exit

Entrance

Belts and Scarfs

FIGURE 6.9

Basic layout patterns for sales floors.

it may sit untouched. A plotted pattern that is created from observing the movements of random samples of shoppers in the store is called the **tracking plan**. With a tracking plan the flow of customer traffic, as well as the places where customers tend to touch merchandise, pick it up, and buy it, are indicated on a floor plan of the store. The tracking plan is used as a reference when planning the design of new spaces and when adjusting stock content by area. It is an excellent and inexpensive method that can be used to maximize the sales potential of floor space. What, however, does the entrepreneur of a new business do about layout for the opening of the business, when observation time is nonexistent?

Retailers have the following four basic layout patterns from which to choose: grid, free-form, boutique, and racetrack. FIGURE 6.9 illustrates the first three (and most common) layout patterns. In the **grid layout**, displays are arranged in a rectangular fashion, such that that aisles are parallel to one another. It is a formal layout that controls traffic in the store as it uses the available space efficiently, creates a neatly organized environment, and facilitates shopping by standardizing the location of items. Many discount stores in apparel and home furnishings use the grid layout because it is well suited to self-service operations.

In contrast, the **free-form layout** is informal, utilizing displays of varying shapes and sizes. Its primary advantage is the image it creates. This image is one of a relaxed and friendly shopping atmosphere, which encourages customers to take their time, thereby spending more time in the store, with the potential for making more purchases. In addition, the free-form layout has been shown to increase the number of impulse purchases customers make. Related merchandise can easily be placed in a common area to encourage multiple sales. For example, a circular rack of girl's dresses and a shelf unit featuring Easter hats may be placed adjacent to the children's shoe department. The major disadvantage of the free-form layout is that it can create security problems if not properly planned and staffed. It may be difficult for a small staff of sales personnel to observe customers and watch for theft in a free-form layout because of visual obstacles. Another disadvantage is that it can appear to be disorganized

and may be challenging to the consumer who wants to be directed to a specific merchandise department.

The **boutique layout** divides the store into a series of individual shopping areas, each with its own theme. As illustrated in FIGURE 6.10, it is much like building a series of specialty shops in a single store. The boutique layout is informal and can create a unique shopping environment for the customer. It also allows the retailer the freedom to create new departments, based on seasonal merchandise trends. Henri Bendel and Bloomingdale's are two examples of retailers that use the boutique layout. The look and the configuration of these retail stores may dramatically change to feature the key looks and new and prevalent designers of the season.

FIGURE 6.10

Anthropologie's interior: a boutique layout is like a series of specialty shops within a single store.

Specialty stores often use the boutique layout to project a distinctive image, one that tells the customer something new is always happening in the store.

A newer layout being used by such stores as Kohl's and Walmart is racetrack. With a **racetrack layout**, aisles, fixtures, and signing are located to guide the customer around the store in a large loop. This gives customers an outside-in view of most departments and their associated merchandise selections and conveniently directs the customers around the entire store. For these retailers impulse purchases have become much more than small items at the checkout counter. By moving around the entire store, the customer may see a pair of shoes, new bed linens, or a belt that will become an impulse purchase. It is visual stimulation, and it appears to be working.

Interior Display Elements

Customers' eyes focus on displays, as they tell the customer the type of merchandise the business sells. Merchandise displays are often referred to as silent sales associates because they market the goods and influence sales. There are a number of guidelines upon which visual merchandisers base their decisions for interior displays. For example, retailers can make it is easier for the customer to focus by creating a display, rather than by presenting simply a rack or shelf of merchandise.

Open fixtures of merchandise can surround the focal display, creating an attractive and merchandise-specific selling area. Also, retailers can boost sales by displaying together items that complement each other. For example, men's ties may be displayed near dress shirts to encourage multiple sales. Too, retailers can recognize that spacious displays provide shoppers with an increased view of the merchandise, generate an expensive image, and reduce the likelihood of shoplifting. Finally, retailers must remember to separate the selling and nonselling spaces of a store. Prime selling space should not be wasted on nonselling functions, such as storage, office, or receiving operations.

Lighting

Effective lighting has two main purposes. First, it enhances the merchandise selection, as illustrated

FIGURE 6.11

Effective lighting can be used to highlight featured merchandise.

by the footwear department featured in FIGURE 6.11. Second, it allows employees to work at maximum efficiency. A jewelry store retailer, for example, has lighting needs specific to its repair department as well as those associated with its display cases. Proper lighting is measured by what is ideal for the job to be done. New lighting systems offer greater flexibility, increased efficiency, and lower energy consumption than do older systems.

Lighting is often an inexpensive investment, considering its impact on the overall appearance and operation of the business. Just as layout and the other interior characteristics generate an image for business, so lighting, too, contributes to store image. A dimly lit business conveys an image of untrustworthiness. The effective combination of natural and artificial light can give a business an open and cheerful appearance. Lighting can have a critical influence on the attitude of the customer in a fitting room. Often, stores use a single overhead fluorescent light in the fitting room, but such lighting is unflattering to the consumer. Better choices include diffused and back lighting that create a halo effect, as in a portrait photo session.

Fitting Rooms

For an apparel store, the fitting rooms play a significant role in the sale of merchandise. Fitting rooms are usually regarded as nonselling space and, subsequently, are often pushed to small, dark corners in the back of the store. As illustrated in FIGURE 6.12, however, fitting rooms are often the place where the customers actually make their buying decisions. The effective fitting room is spacious, well lit, clean, convenient, and theft-proof. There should be adequate places for hanging the merchandise. Mirrors should provide an accurate image and be accessible to the customer. Three-way mirrors that provide a back and front view may be intentionally positioned outside, but adjacent to, the fitting rooms. This placement encourages customers to come out of the dressing room, wearing the garments in which they are interested. When customers exit the fitting room to take a look in the mirror, the salesperson has the opportunity to assist them with

suggestions for alterations, accessories, or alternative merchandise. Although the space should be comfortable, the retailer must minimize the opportunity for shoplifting in the fitting room. Furnishings, such as covered tables, cabinets, and skirted chairs, can become hiding places for the hangers of stolen merchandise. The location of a fitting room is also important. It should be situated away from exits and near the sales personnel to ensure privacy and service for the customer, without compromising store security.

Checkout Area

Placement of the checkout area, or cash-wrap desk, is very significant in a retail operation. It should be strategically located so that it is visible to the customer from all vantage points and so that the cashier or sales associate can greet and acknowledge customers entering the store, as illustrated in FIGURE 6.13. Moreover, the checkout area can serve as a security point when it is placed near the entrance or exit. The area should be clearly signed, organized, and well lit. It should be outfitted with all the equipment and materials needed to process the sale smoothly. For example, the computer terminal, cash drawer, and telephone should be installed at the checkout area, in addition to materials such as tissue paper, bags, and credit card supplies.

FIGURE 6.12

The essentials for a good fitting room include space to move around in, flattering lighting, a place to sit, and mirrors to reflect different angles.

FIGURE 6.13

The checkout area often faces the front of the store, allowing sales associates behind the counter to welcome and offer assistance to incoming customers.

CONCLUSION

The entrepreneur will have a number of decisions to make when deciding on a location for the business. Each decision affects the others. The entrepreneur may find an ideal regional location and then later identify several states appropriate for the business. After a city has been selected, the entrepreneur may learn that there are few appropriate building choices in the area. At this point, the option to build, buy, or lease becomes a key decision. When a site is selected, the entrepreneur will determine an exterior and an interior layout. Among the components of the interior layout are the size of the sales area, display elements, and lighting. Finding the right location requires research, patience, and a multitude of decisions. It is one of the most significant factors related to the success of a new business.

KEY TERMS

boutique layout

business location

central business district

customer traffic patterns

entertailing

first-ring suburbs

free-form layout

grid layout

Index of Retail Saturation (IRS)

layout

National Retail Traffic Index (NRTI)

population density

power center

prime selling space

racetrack layout

retail layout

space value

tracking plan

DISCUSSION TOPICS

1. Because people with similar demographic characteristics within a given region often purchase a similar range of goods and services, the entrepreneur must define the target market before determining a location for the business. Target demographics are intertwined with image. Who the customer is affects how other people see the business. Define demographics of the intended target market for your prospective business.

2. Predict the growth or decline over the next decade in various business locations: central business districts, neighborhoods, shopping centers and malls, outlying areas, and homes as business location alternatives. Explain your answers.

3. Review the factors for buying, building, or leasing a site listed in Figure 6.3. Which are the most important? the least important?

SUGGESTED READINGS

Gorman, G. M. *Visual Merchandising and Store Design Workbook: Merchandising, Fixturing, and Lighting Create Visual Excitement for Retail Stores.* Cincinnati, OH: ST Media Group, 2009.

Grant, J. *Budget Guide to Retail Store Planning and Design.* Rev. 2d ed. Cincinnati, OH: ST Publications, 1995.

Pegler, M. M. *Visual Merchandising and Display.* 5th ed. New York: Fairchild Books, 2006.

VMSD magazine. *Visual Merchandising 6.* Cincinnati, OH: ST Media Group International, 2009.

ONLINE RESOURCES

RETAIL DESIGN INSTITUTE
http://www.retaildesigninstitute.org
Supports the creation of attractive and functional selling environments through education, career building, and networking.

ST MEDIA GROUP
http://www.stmediagroup.com
Information for industry professionals on global visual communications markets.

VMSD
http://www.vmsd.com
Features new store designs and visual presentations, presents merchandising strategies and new products, and reports on industry news and events.

BUSINESS PLAN CONNECTION
THINKING LIKE AN ENTREPRENEUR

When investigating location options, you will have the opportunity to collect a great amount of data about the geographic location in terms of population demographics and customer psychographics. Maintain a file of all this information, as you can use it to construct other parts of the business plan.

Visit a number of existing store locations to gain a feel for size as it pertains to square footage. Most store owners and managers will share this information. Ask about the amount of square footage allocated to the sales, dressing rooms, receiving/warehousing, and office spaces. If considering a mall location, contact mall management for pricing information. Ask about lease terms, leasehold improvements, promotional fee requirements, and commons fees that may be charged for maintenance of the general mall space. In some malls you will be able to lease temporary space as a short-term arrangement, either in vacant store space or as a kiosk. This allows you to conduct a trial run in the mall, while providing the mall management with occupied space.

A commercial real estate agent can provide information about pricing and availability in shopping areas. Ask about zoning restrictions if considering a nontraditional store location, such as a residential home. The agent may also be able to give data about average costs of utilities and terms of leases. Chambers of commerce in most cities have Web sites that provide demographic data about the city. Often, the chamber of commerce has a department assigned to supporting small business growth. Some cities have a Regional Economic Development, Inc., (REDI) office that will provide demographic statistics on a specific area.

One of the key steps to preparing for the location decision is estimating sales volume for the business as a guide for the amount that can be spent on monthly location costs. Using the resources detailed in the chapter, such as those by the NRF and RMA, determine average sales per square foot for the prospective business. Use this figure to estimate the amount of sales volume needed to support the cost of each location alternative.

ASSIGNMENT 6.1
BRICK-AND-MORTAR LOCATION PLAN

1. Open your saved business plan template.
2. Address the following sections of the brick-and-mortar location plan. You may use the sample business plan in Appendix D as an additional resource.

BRICK-AND-MORTAR LOCATION

» Physical Location
» Location Features
» Target Market Considerations
» Leasehold Improvements
» Other Location Costs
» Signage

PROFILE OF AN ENTREPRENEUR
FASHION RECYCLED: LEADING
THE ECOFASHION MOVEMENT

"**Y**OU don't have to sacrifice to be both fashionable and green," says Ava DeMarco, co-founder and president of Pittsburgh-based Littlearth, a fashion accessory company that specializes in using recycled materials in its designs and was at the forefront of the ecofashion movement.

That thought was the inspiration behind Littlearth and its initial lines of accessories: purses made out of used license plates and belts made out of recycled leather and used bottle caps. DeMarco looks back on the early days nostalgically and remembers that the first designs were often determined by the materials she and her partner, Robert Brandegee, had access to at any given time. The first license-plate bags were wrapped around tuna cans on each end because, well, that's what they had. Those days are long gone. They now have specialized parts made for their bags and wine holders, and they work with different states to secure used plates.

One of the other challenges DeMarco recalls, something that seems silly for a seventeen-year-old, $6 million company that's been on *Oprah* and is about to buy its third building, was gaining credibility as a legitimate business out of a basement. There were times, however, when success seemed far off.

"We had some years we weren't sure we were going to make it," DeMarco says. What the company had going for it was a collection of skills many small companies can't assemble. Brandegee had an interest in fashion and possessed strong sales skills, which was instrumental at trade shows. DeMarco's background is in graphic design, so she designed strong marketing materials and

products. To top it all off, Brandegee's parents owned a marketing business. Early mailers were professional looking, and their trade-show booths were always among the most popular at any show, partly due to the design and partly due to Brandegee's salesmanship and musical ability. The booth was hopping.

DeMarco and Brandegee made another crucial decision in those early days: They embraced the Internet before it was a required business tool, launching a website in 1996. "I remember having to tell people, 'Type in http://www.littlearth.com,'" DeMarco says.

Looking ahead, Littlearth has growth plans, as evidenced by its building purchase. It secured a license to create and sell NFL-themed gear under its ProFANity line, and the company is now doing drop-shipping for retailers like eBay and Amazon. "It looks like it comes from them," DeMarco says, "but we pack and ship it."

SOURCE: Werling, Mike. *Fashion Recycled: Leading the Ecofashion Movement, Entrepreneur's StartUps*, March 2010. http://www.entrepreneur.com/magazine/entrepreneursstartupsmagazine/2010/march/205280.html

Littlearth recycled fashion accessories.

CHAPTER 7
BUILDING A BUSINESS USING THE WEB

E-COMMERCE, the term most people are familiar with, can be defined as the buying and selling of merchandise via the Internet. E-retailing, on the other hand, is a term that has come to represent the distinct aspects of fashion within the world of e-commerce. In the fashion industry, e-retailing, the virtual storefront, and the virtual mall are terms that are used concurrently. E-retailing is defined as the activity of direct retail shopping that provides twenty-four-hour availability, a global reach, and the ability to interact and provide custom information and ordering and multimedia prospects. The Web is a multibillion dollar source of revenue for the world's businesses. As long ago as 1999, projected e-commerce revenues for businesses were in the billions of dollars, and the stocks of companies deemed most adept at e-commerce were skyrocketing. The share of apparel sold is growing rapidly via the Internet. The figures vary, but some high estimates have put online clothing at a 35 percent share by 2018. Web retailing, whether referred to as e-commerce or e-retailing, continues to grow. Within this chapter, these terms will be used simultaneously.

SELLING ON THE INTERNET

Thousands of new e-businesses start every year. Why so many? There are numerous reasons; however, the primary ones include low start-up costs, a steady stream of new customers (often global), diverse products to sell, and a wide range of sellers specializing in varied product categories:

FIGURE 7.1

Overall, apparel retail is growing some 3 percent annually, but the share sold on the Internet is growing much more rapidly.

» **Low start-up costs**—An entrepreneur does not necessarily need millions of dollars to create an e-business. It is possible to create a successful e-business for a small cash investment (selling, for example, jewelry on the Etsy Web site), especially with the decreasing cost of technological components. It is important to recognize, though, that it is easy to spend tens of thousands of dollars as well.

» **Steady stream of new customers**—A small brick-and-mortar store will typically attract those within a close driving distance. With the power of the Internet, a business can attract customers from around the world. Through easily accessible technology, the spread of high-speed connections, and the ease of using a credit card for payment over the Internet, a potential customer base in the billions is actually possible.

» **Diverse products**—An amazing assortment of products in a wide range of prices, from diamond necklaces and designer gowns to dollar jewelry and cosmetics, are sold on the Internet. Many e-savvy customers turn to the Internet to search

for, locate, and price products before setting foot in the brick-and-mortar store.

» **Sellers specializing in varied product categories for a global consumer population**—Throughout the world, there are people who have the contacts, expertise, resources, and business experience to specialize in a product category globally. Blue Nile, with its diamonds; Shopbop, with its designer apparel (FIGURE 7.2); and Zappos, with its footwear, are examples of e-merchants specializing in specific merchandise classifications. The Internet gives entrepreneurs the opportunity to focus on product areas that they know and do well.

FIGURE 7.2

Since its 2000 launch in Madison, Wisconsin, as a modest-sized online boutique specializing in hard-to-find denim lines, Shopbop has grown to become one of the leading fashion retailers in the world in designer apparel and accessories.

E-BUSINESS MODELS

There are a number of e-business models that have opened the door to entrepreneurial success online. The most popular e-business models are the online storefront, auction site, and portal. The **online storefront** most closely resembles a traditional brick-and-mortar store. It is the most common type of e-commerce site in that it displays information about the product or service for sale and then accepts orders for those services, usually through a shopping cart. The **shopping cart** is an application that includes an order form used to process orders, with payment through credit cards or services like PayPal. Products are shipped to the customer or delivered by an immediate download, such as music and software. The most effective online storefronts offer human touches and a strong emphasis on customer service by providing recommendations of add-on-products, customer reviews, estimated arrival dates, and the option of talking to a real person if problems arise. The online storefront is the most common type of e-commerce component started by companies that already have a brick-and-mortar store, as it most closely resembles an actual store location.

Online auctions allow persons to buy or sell items through a bidding process. The seller pays a fee to the site operator for using the auction service. eBay, which was started in 1995, has become the most successful online auction on the Internet, with more than forty-five million users and fifteen million auctions going on at any time.[1] In fact, eBay now has "Boutiques" for famous designers to offer their latest collections (FIGURE 7.3). The significant difference between online auction and the storefront model is that the online auction does not manage the product; instead, it brings buyers and sellers together. The online auction allows anyone to enter into the world of e-commerce, from the individual seller to the retailer wanting to increase its target market and sales volume potential. All that is needed is a product to sell and the ability to create a listing, using the site's tools.

When most people hear the word *portal*, they think of search engines. In reality a **portal** is a Web site that offers a variety of Internet services from a

FIGURE 7.3
Narciso Rodriguez's newest collection is an example of eBay's venture into the sale of new designer apparel.

single, convenient location. The portal links online merchants with online shopping malls and auction sites, providing a wide range of shopping opportunities to both the customer and e-trepreneur. Portals aggregate information on a broad range of topics, allowing users to collect information and browse multiple independent storefronts. A popular portal is BizOffice, an online company that targets small-business owners and home-based businesses. Box 7.1 presents a chart of the wide range of e-models available to the e-trepreneur.

With the increased ease of creating an online business and of a customer's moving from one

BOX 7.1
TYPES OF E-BUSINESS MODELS

BROKERAGE MODEL

Brokers bring buyers and sellers together and facilitate transactions. Usually, a broker charges a fee or commission for each transaction. Brokerage models include:

» **Marketplace exchange**—Offers a full range of services, from market assessment to negotiation and merchandise fulfillment. Exchanges operate independently or are backed by an industry consortium.

» **Buy/sell fulfillment**—The broker takes customer orders to buy or sell a product and designates price and delivery.

» **Demand collection system**—The "name-your-price" model, in which the buyer makes a final binding bid, and the broker arranges fulfillment (such as Priceline.com).

» **Auction broker**—The broker conducts auctions for sellers (individuals or merchants) and charges the seller a listing fee and commission based on the value of the transaction (such as eBay).

» **Transaction broker**—Provides a third-party payment option for buyers and sellers to complete a transaction (such as PayPal).

» **Distributor**—A catalog operation that connects manufacturers with buyers, such as franchises. The broker facilitates business transactions.

» **Search agent**—Software used to locate the price and availability for a good or service specified by the buyer or to locate hard-to-find information.

» **Virtual marketplace**—A virtual mall for online merchants that charges setup, monthly listing, or transaction fees, or a combination of these (such as Amazon).

ADVERTISING MODEL

This model resembles the traditional media broadcast model. The Web site (i.e., broadcaster) provides content and services, such as instant messaging or a blog, mixed with banner ads. The banner ads are often the major source of revenue. The advertising model includes:

» **Portal**—Usually a search engine with a high volume of traffic makes advertising profitable. A *personalized portal* provides user customization. A *niche portal allows* access to a well-defined user demographic (such as Yahoo!).

» **Classifieds**—A listing of items for sale or wanted for purchase. Listing fees or a membership fee may be charged (such as craigslist).

» **User registration**—Content-based sites that are free to access but that require users to register and provide demographic data. Registration allows tracking of user online habits and generating of data for targeted advertising campaigns (such as Gilt Groupe).

» **Query-based paid placement**—Sells favorable link positioning (i.e., sponsored links) or advertising keyed to particular search terms in a user query (such as Google).

» **Contextual advertising/behavioral marketing**—Freeware developers who bundle adware with their products. Advertisers can provide targeted advertising, based on an individual user's surfing activity.

» **Content-targeted advertising**—Initiated by Google, it provides the ease and precision of search advertising to the entire Web. Google identifies the meaning of a Web page and then automatically delivers related advertisements when a user clicks on that page.

» **Intromercials**—Animated full-screen ads placed at the entry of a site before a user reaches the intended content.

» **Ultramercials**—Interactive online ads that require the user to respond intermittently in order to move forward through the message before reaching the intended content.

INFOMEDIARY MODEL

For a business, data about consumers and their buying habits are carefully analyzed and used to target marketing campaigns. For the consumer, data about producers and their products are provided to help with purchase decisions. Types of infomediary models include:

» **Advertising networks**—By supplying banner ads to a network of member sites, this model allows advertisers to distribute large marketing campaigns. Advertising networks collect data about Web users that can be used to analyze marketing effectiveness.

» **Audience measurement services**—Online audience market research agencies (such as Nielsen NetRatings).

» **Incentive marketing**—A customer loyalty program that provides rewards to customers, such as redeemable points or coupons for making purchases from associated retailers. Data collected about users are sold for targeted advertising (such as Talbots Red Card).

» **Metamediary**—Facilitates transactions between buyers and sellers by providing comprehensive information and services, without being involved in the actual exchange of goods or services between the parties.

MERCHANT MODEL

Sponsored by wholesalers and retailers, sales may be made based on list prices or through auction. Examples include:

>> **Virtual merchant**—A retail merchant that operates solely over the Web (such as Zappos).

>> **Catalog merchant**—A mail-order business with a Web-based catalog. Combines mail, telephone, and online ordering (such as Lands' End).

>> **Click-and-mortar (brick-and-click)**— A traditional brick-and-mortar retail establishment with a Web storefront (such as Saks Fifth Avenue and Nordstrom).

MANUFACTURER (DIRECT) MODEL

The manufacturer, or direct, model, focuses on the Internet to reach huge numbers of buyers globally. The manufacturer may use this model to sell directly to the customer to increase profits, to improve customer service, and to better understand the customer. Transactions include:

>> **Purchase**—The sale of a product, in which the right of ownership is transferred to the buyer.

>> **Lease**—In exchange for a rental fee, the buyer receives the right to use the product under a "terms of use" agreement. The product is returned to the seller upon expiration or default of the lease agreement. Another type of agreement may include a right of purchase upon expiration of the lease.

>> **License**—The sale of a product that involves only the transfer of usage rights to the buyer, in accordance with a terms of use agreement. Ownership rights remain with the manufacturer (e.g., software licensing).

>> **Brand-integrated content**—In contrast to the sponsored-content approach (i.e., the advertising model), brand-integrated content is created by the manufacturer for the sole purpose of product placement (such as Elie Tahari).

AFFILIATE MODEL

The affiliate model (such as Amazon) gives consumers the opportunity to purchase wherever they are online. It does this by offering financial incentives, through a percentage of revenue, to affiliated partner sites. The affiliates provide purchase-point click-through to the merchant. It is a pay-for-performance model. If the affiliate does not generate sales, it does not cost the merchant. Examples include:

>> **Banner exchange**—Swaps banner placement among a network of affiliated sites.

>> **Pay-per-click**—Pays affiliates for a user click-through.

>> **Revenue sharing**—Offers a percent-of-sale commission, based on a user click-through, when the user actually purchases a product.

COMMUNITY MODEL

The success of the community model is based on customer patronage. Revenue can be generated on the sale of ancillary products or voluntary contributions. Also, revenue may be tied to advertising and subscriptions for services. The success of community business models is illustrated by the growth of social networking.

>> **Open source**—Software developed by a global community of programmers. Instead of licensing code for a fee, open source relies on revenue from related services, such as product support, tutorials, and user documentation.

>> **Open content**—Openly accessible content developed collaboratively by a global community of contributors who work voluntarily (such as Polyvore).

>> **Social networking services**—Sites that allow people to connect to others via a common interest (professional, hobby, fashion, and so on). Social networking services can afford opportunities for contextual advertising and subscriptions for premium services (these include Facebook, LinkedIn, and Twitter).

SUBSCRIPTION MODEL

Users are charged a periodic (e.g., daily, monthly, annual) fee to subscribe to a service. Many Web sites combine free content and "premium" (i.e., subscriber, or member-only) content. Examples include:

>> **Content services**—Provide text, audio, or video content to users who pay a fee to gain access to the service (such as Listen).

>> **Person-to-person networking services**—Channels for the distribution of user-submitted information, such as individuals searching for former schoolmates (such as Classmates).

>> **Internet service providers**—Offer network connectivity and related services through a subscription (such as AT&T online).

SOURCE: Adapted from Rappa, Michael. "Business Models on the Web." Managing the Digital Enterprise. http://digitalenterprise.org/models/models.html

merchant to another, a shift of power from the seller to the buyer has occurred. The seller used to control the information on the product; however, increasingly, customers can easily search the Internet to find out anything they would like to know about a particular item. Product prices, shipping fees, delivery dates, and style and color alternatives are compared for the customer with the click of a mouse.

PLANNING AN E-BUSINESS

Many successful e-business entrepreneurs stress that their success was only partially due to choosing the Internet as their channel of distribution. More significantly, they report that the emphasis that they placed on developing their concepts and crafting the business startup were key to their accomplishments. Jeff Vikari, the executive director of Clickincome.com, states:

> The biggest misconception people have is that the Internet is magic. It's the gold-rush mentality. People believe that if they invest a few thousand dollars into an online business, profits will simply start shooting out of their computers automatically. That's obviously not the case. People need to follow many of the same steps they'd take if they were to start a traditional brick-and-mortar business.[2]

How can e-business entrepreneurs decide if their ideas have sales potential?

The process of moving from the idea stage into an actual e-business involves the following three steps:

1. The idea needs to be developed to its full potential.

2. The idea must be examined and carefully evaluated using variety of methods.

3. The idea(s) that emerge from the first two steps should be further developed into a formal business plan.

Box 7.2 provides a comparison of three fashion industry success stories—Zappos.com, Luckyscent.com,

and People's Revolution. All evolved from unique ideas, and each works from a very different perspective about e-commerce and e-retailing. Kelly Cutrone, the fearless entrepreneur of People's Revolution, balances high touch and high tech when promoting her business and her clients.

NICHE MARKETING AND THE INTERNET

If a new e-trepreneur has a large, established company and a million-dollar budget, it is possible to compete with other large online businesses. For the majority of e-trepreneurs starting out, however, it is most effective to target a niche market, rather than competing head-on for a mass market against large, well-funded companies. A **niche** is a small, specialized part of a market that is not served or cost-effective for the major, well-established companies to serve. Box 7.2 also presents Luckyscents.com, a niche fragrance and bath product company that began as a Web site and grew the business through a brick-and-mortar expansion. As a first step in developing a niche market for an e-business concept, the following questions should be researched and answered:

» Do the products or services have good market potential for sale online?

» Who is the target audience for these products?

» How does the product or service address the needs, wants, and interests of potential customers?

» What type of design and content will a Web site need in order to cater to the target audience?

» What will be the best way to promote and advertise the Web site to reach the target audience?

If the entrepreneur cannot adequately answer these questions, it is unlikely that potential customers will respond to the advertisements and purchase the goods or services.

BOX 7.2
STUDIES IN FASHION E-TREPRENEURSHIP

Although nearly all entrepreneurs acknowledge that the Internet can offer unlimited opportunities for promoting and selling their products online, some of them have made very specific and different choices about how they have integrated e-commerce into their businesses. Take a look at the following three entrepreneurial companies: Zappos.com, Luckyscent.com, and People's Revolution. Each of these business's founders chose a different e-commerce strategy. After reading these abbreviated case studies, take a moment to peruse the companies' Web sites before examining the discussion topics at the conclusion of this exercise.

ZAPPOS.COM

The year was 1999, and Nick Swinmurn was walking around a mall in San Francisco looking for a pair of shoes.

One store had the right style but was not available in the right color. Another store had the right color but not the right size. Nick spent the next hour in the mall, walking from store to store, and finally went home empty-handed and frustrated.

At home, Nick tried looking for his shoes online and was . . . unsuccessful. Although there were a lot of "mom and pop" stores selling shoes online, what was interesting to Nick was that there was no major online retailer specializing in shoes.

So, because it was 1999 and anything seemed possible at the time, Nick decided to quit his day job and start an online shoe retailer . . . and Zappos.com was born!

The original idea was to create a Web site that offered the absolute best selection in shoes in terms of brands, styles, colors, sizes, and widths.

Over the past nine years, the Zappos.com brand and aspirations have evolved. In addition to offering the best selection, Zappos.com has the goal to be the company that provides the absolute best service online—not just in shoes, but in any category.

So here is the vision:

» One day, 30 percent of all retail transactions in the United States will be online.

» People will buy from the company with the best service and the best selection.

» Zappos.com will be that online store.

SOURCE: http://about.zappos.com/zappos-story/in-the-beginning-let-there-be-shoes

The Zappos fulfillment centers in Shepherdsville, Kentucky, are centrally located to reach more customers more quickly. Every day, tens of thousands of items are processed in the warehouse, which runs around the clock, seven days a week.

BOX 7.2

(CONTINUED)

LUCKYSCENT.COM

According to Jargol.com:

> The fragrance world is a much more complicated and diverse world than the department store perfume counter would have us believe. Luckily, there is Luckyscent.com and its offline counterpart, Scent Bar, in Los Angeles, to help us find those fragrances that are impossible to find elsewhere. The hundred or so brands available constitute the best small fragrance makers in the world—from tiny French perfumeries, to hip Brooklyn outposts, to a private label fragrance from a legendary Italian fashion shop. Scent Bar makes trying the perfumes easy and fun, but even at Luckyscent.com low cost samples are available.

Toward the end of 2005, the owners of Luckyscent decided that it was time to bring the Luckyscent concept to street level retail. They were excited to create a retail space that would be worthy of showcasing a fine array of fragrances and bath products. Along came a perfect space on Beverly Boulevard in West Hollywood that would soon become Scent Bar.

Much time was spent designing the space until it captured the company's aesthetic and provided a perfect space in which to sample and enjoy its rare collection of perfumes. The space offers the intimacy of a wine bar without the formality. Customers are welcome to stay as long as they like.

Scent Bar is meant to be a place to sit and spend some time while discovering some the best and rarest fragrances. Often, there are special events, such as the spring trunk show and other evening events associated with the Beverly Quarter.

Starting as an e-business, and then adding a brick-and-mortar location, Luckyscent serves as an example of the Internet as a start-up location for growing a business onto the streets of Hollywood.

SOURCE: All information obtained from http://www.luckyscent.com.

Luckyscent began as a click retailer before expanding into its current brick-and-click presence.

KELLY CUTRONE: PEOPLE'S REVOLUTION

Entrepreneur Kelly Cutrone shares a story about business negotiations and communication with and without the Internet:

Here's another true story. In 2009 two young women from different publishing houses contacted me to offer me book deals. One called me on the phone. I liked her immediately, and we soon agreed to work together. Some months later, after I'd already inked a deal with her imprint, HarperOne, I was going through my junk e-mail folder and found an e-mail from the woman at the other publishing house, offering me a similar deal. I did her the favor of picking up the phone and calling her to tell her never to rely on e-mail as her primary form of communication.

Kelly Cutrone, the founder of the successful public relations, branding, and marketing firm People's Revolution, and star of *Kell on Earth*, on Bravo, has her own ways of "doing the fashion business," including determining how the world of the Internet and e-commerce fits into her world. She believes in "using personal communication to build business relationships and to make deals." She avoids working to build her business on the Web and, instead, has deliberately chosen to limit using the Internet as a resource for recruiting clients. Take a look at her company's Web site, www.peoplesrevolution.com. It simply provides contact information for her firm's business locations and a film clip. If you are a prospective client who wants more information, you had better pick up the phone.

SOURCE: All material obtained from Cutrone, K., *If You Have to Cry Go Outside and Other Things Your Mother Never Told You*. New York: HarperOne, 2010.

Kelly Cutrone.

DISCUSSION TOPICS

» Compare and contrast the different perspectives on e-commerce of each of these business founders. How have these views been implemented in their firms?

» With which do you agree: the all, nothing, or somewhere in between philosophy of integrating e-commerce into a start-up business?

» Find examples of fashion companies representing the following: those that added a Web site after succeeding in a brick-and-mortar location, those that added a physical storefront after succeeding solely online, and those that have opted to minimize their presence online.

» How will companies expand their online activities in the future? Where will we see new businesses entering the retail world of e-commerce in the fashion industry?

PRODUCTS, INVENTORY, AND FULFILLMENT

The majority of e-businesses are built around the model of selling tangible products that are created or purchased by an e-business. These products are priced to earn a profit, warehoused, and then packed and shipped out to the customers who purchased them. When developing a list of products to sell online, an e-trepreneur should tabulate projected expenses, estimate projected sales, and carefully consider the potential market. If potential profit is not enough to cover immediate needs, adjustments should be made before startup of the business. An accurate financial analysis will reveal whether the products can provide an adequate profit. It is important that new e-businesses choose and stock their inventories correctly. An online business may design, manufacture, and sell its own goods or buy goods and resell them online.

In regard to sheer profit margin, selling goods online that you have created and produced can generate successful e-business ventures. Creative entrepreneurs can sell their own work on auction sites such as eBay or Etsy or on similar Web sites that have been set up to market particular types of products. E-trepreneurs can also create their own Web sites to sell their products directly. Although almost every type of product is sold over the Internet, there are factors that give some merchandise advantages over other:

» **Product quality**—Entrepreneurs who create their own products have complete control over product quality. This can provide a competitive advantage, as companies purchasing externally are dependent upon the quality of goods shipped by outside vendors. Design workmanship should be at a high level before any products are placed online for sale.

» **Originality**—A handmade dress, custom jewelry, or a hand-knit baby blanket are examples of products that are extremely difficult to mass-market but that can be very successful online.

» **A niche product**—A handmade product may not be completely unique but will still be sought out by a specialized group of customers, such as custom apparel for pets. Niche products are particularly successful online.

» **A built-in customer base**—A product, such as woven sari or mud cloth fabrics, may be designed to appeal to specific groups of customers. Having a clearly identifiable customer base to which the product can be marketed makes selling a product much easier.

FIGURE 7.4 features Etsy, a niche Web site selling a global assortment of merchandise that illustrate product quality and originality. Founded in 2005, Etsy describes itself as both a company and a community. The Etsy community spans the globe, with buyers and sellers coming from more than 150 countries and with its sellers numbering in the hundreds of thousands. Etsy's purpose is to enable people to make a living making things and to connect makers with buyers. Its vision is to build a new economy and present a better choice through its mission: "Buy, Sell, and Live Handmade."

BUYING AND RESELLING GOODS ONLINE

Most e-trepreneurs buy products at wholesale and then sell these products through their own site, auctions, or a third-party Web site. Selling directly online means that customers come to a business's Web site to buy an item. Marketing, filling orders, and promoting the product line are all under the entrepreneur's control. Buying **wholesale** means purchasing products at a discounted price and then reselling them at a marked-up price. When buying wholesale, the entrepreneur must purchase inventory in bulk to receive a discount. Storing and marking the inventory, shipping the products to customers, and handling returns and exchanges from customers are additional activities that follow purchasing wholesale merchandise to sell. A company that has done an excellent job at this is Zappos.com which was started in 1999 as an online shoe store. As presented in Box 7.2, the Zappos

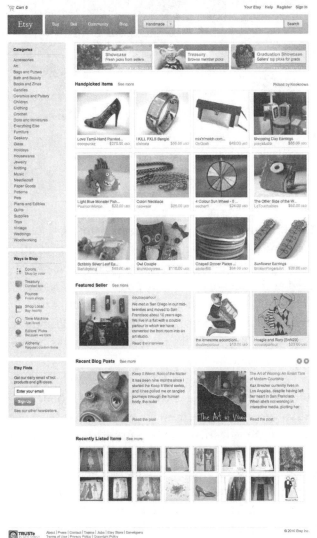

Etsy's online platform is a unique way for people to sell their specialty or niche items to buyers from around the world.

Fulfillment Centers in Shepherdsville, Kentucky, are centrally located to reach more customers as quickly as possible. Every day, tens of thousands of items are processed in the warehouse, which runs around the clock, seven days a week.

BUILDING AND MANAGING INVENTORY

It is important to offer all the products that your business's customers would like to buy. Planning a merchandise assortment that is heavy in the styles, colors, and sizes customers will order and light in those that are ordered less frequently is referred to as **inventory management**. Online customers expect to find the same availability of inventory from an online store as they would at a traditional store. If an item is not in stock at the time of purchase, most online customers will not wait a couple of days for it to arrive. Instead, they will purchase the same or a similar item from a competitor. Because it is so easy for customers to jump from site to site, customers decide quickly if a new site's inventory meets their needs. The new e-trepreneur must have a clear idea of what types of products are to be offered and in what quantities. Budget is the first factor; a small business may only be able to carry a hundred products, whereas a large business may carry thousands. The second factor is shopping cart limitations, which also depends heavily on budget. Many shopping cart software programs escalate in price based on the number of products offered. If the entrepreneur is on a tight budget, it is most economical to begin with a more narrow and targeted inventory. The third factor is the timing of product availability. The amount of time needed to manufacture goods or the lack of availability of products throughout the year may force an e-commerce business to stock a larger amount of inventory than normal during certain times of the year.

When a new entrepreneur knows what products are to be sold, how much they will be sold for, and the quantity of inventory to be stocked, marketing these products to the targeted customer is the next step.

MARKETING AN E-BUSINESS

"If you build it, they will come" is a great line from the film *Field of Dreams*, but, unfortunately, it does not ring true in the competitive world of online business. Every new e-commerce site needs a competitive marketing plan to succeed. In the early Internet years, entrepreneurs could build a Web site, be mentioned in a couple of print and online articles, and receive a large stream of new customers. The days of building a Web site and receiving instant customer traffic are over. Now, marketing must be used to gain customers through branding and advertising.

E-BUSINESS ADVERTISING

Billions of dollars are spent every year on online advertising. Online advertising may now be even more effective than traditional advertising because of mediums used and a captive audience, as online advertising is built right into the customer's screen. There are four main advertising options for online marketing: banner, pop-up, search engine, and classified.

Banner advertisements are similar to the traditional advertisements found in print venues. As shown in FIGURE 7.5, they are rectangular advertisements that display basic information about an e-business or its product line. They differ from print advertisements in that they are interactive, taking an interested viewer to the Web site when they are clicked. Banner ads are especially effective when they are visible for a long period of time and are placed on high-traffic Web sites. Although the most effective strategy, banner advertisements are also the most expensive. In general, Web sites charge for banner ads through three methods: cost per thousand, click-through rate, and cost per click. The charge for cost per thousand (CPM) is dependent on the number of people who visit the Web site. Click-through rate (CTR) is based on the number of click-throughs, that is, when the Web site viewer actually clicks on the advertisement that takes them to the Web site. Billing is based on the number of click-throughs that are tallied. Cost per click (CPC) is very similar to CTR, except that the advertiser pays when viewers click on the ad taking them to the Web site.

FIGURE 7.5

An example of a banner advertisement for Coach.

The difference is that all advertisers wanting to use the same banner advertisement bid against each other, with the high bidder securing the ad. Billing is calculated at the auctioned rate on a per-click basis. Keywords are very important in positioning banner ads, as the cost per click adds up. It is critical to make sure the viewer would actually be interested in purchasing the products offered.

A pop-up advertisement is a browser window that automatically opens on a user's computer whenever the viewer visits a site from which an ad has been purchased by an advertiser. As pop-ups demand immediate attention, they are quite effective—with almost twice the click-through rate of banner ads. Pop-ups are also larger and can occupy an entire screen to provide a more detailed or complex offer while portraying their full brand image to a viewer. Although the need for immediate attention can stimulate a potential customer's interest, pop-ups may also be irritating to Internet users. As such, a significant number of computer users implement pop-up blockers on their screens.

A key benefit of **search engine advertising** is that it targets consumers who have already specified their interests with keystrokes. With search engine advertisements, products or Web sites are tied to specific keywords. When a computer user types those keywords in the search box, a related advertisement is displayed. Suppose a potential customer is searching Google for a specific brand of blue jeans. If a business sells that brand of jeans, its advertisement appears next to the search results. Because the ad is targeted only to people who demonstrated an interest in those blue jeans, the rate of return is higher than a generic ad to an untargeted audience. The leader in search engine advertising is Google Adwords, which displays ads on the right side of the screen as a sponsored link when the keywords are triggered by a viewer's search. Google allows businesses to establish a maximum budget and bills on a per click basis. Those businesses that pay more per click appear higher on the sponsored list. When a business's budget is depleted, its advertisements no longer appear. A business owner can use Google Analytics to track how advertisements and keywords are working and to calculate the company's click-through rate.

A **classified advertisement** is a text-formatted promotion used in print or Internet media. Classifieds are often overlooked in online advertising, as they are often viewed as dated in that we have seen them in newspapers and magazines for years. E-business owners have discovered, however, that focused classifieds for a specific product or service can be very effective on the Internet. They provide buyers with an easy way to sort through and find what they are looking for. In addition, classified ads are inexpensive and can be managed using e-mail. Many sites, such as Craigslist, allow users to post and respond to classified advertisements for free. The advertisements are organized by city and category, making it easy for customers to find what they are looking for, exactly where they prefer it to be located. The customer can find items close to home for immediate pickup or less-expensive delivery.

INTERNET MAILING LISTS AND SPAM

Internet mailing lists are attached to promotional messages that are automatically sent to an e-mail inbox, allowing the recipient to respond to the e-mail or to access the Web site. Another type of mailing list is a one-way mailing list that is directly from the company and is in a newsletter or announcement format in which subscribers do not interact directly. Madewell provides an example of this. Every week or so the customer receives an e-mail introducing new styles, promotions, and discounts (FIGURE 7.6).

No matter which type of format a company chooses for Internet marketing, it is important that

FIGURE 7.6

An example of Madewell's mass e-mail to its registered customers.

members have requested the information and that they have a way to opt out or unsubscribe at any time. Carefully managed opt-in/opt out is customer friendly and does not create spam. **Spam** is an inexpensive promotional tool used by the multitude of companies that purchase large, mass mailing lists to send promotional e-mails out by the thousands. Spam may be used as an effective advertising strategy, but businesses should be cautious; many people have a negative image of spam and, subsequently, the companies that send these messages.

CREATIVE PROMOTIONAL ADVERTISING

There is room for creativity in e-business advertising as well as the opportunity for low-cost promotion. Newsletters, blogs, newsgroups, and podcasts are excellent formats for creative promotional advertising online.

All e-businesses want to get more traffic to their Web sites. More customers can generate more sales, which means more profit for the company. The goal is not simply to recruit new customers; repeat business is equally the objective. Studies have shown that encouraging a satisfied customer to return to a Web site is six times more effective than trying to entice a brand new customer to a site.

Existing customers often need some encouragement to return and buy from an e-business; a newsletter is one of the best ways to encourage patronage shopping. A **newsletter** is a communication tool that contains articles, specials, discounts, and other information promoting an e-business and its products. E-mailing a newsletter regularly to customers is a great way to communicate upcoming sales and promotions with customers, while sharing information about new product arrivals.

For example, a company retailing shoes could include an article on fashion trends and describe how various shoe styles coordinate with each of these trends. When customers find a newsletter useful, they build a connection in their mind that the e-business is a trusted source for future purchases.

A **blog** is an online digital diary or forum where text, photos, videos, and other material can be posted and made available to the public. Blogging began as a popular way for individuals to keep in touch with others and provide information about their daily life, but it has also become a very useful promotional tool for e-businesses. Blogs are versatile, easy to use, and growing. In 2009 there were more than 126 million blogs. An e-business can create a strong blog following by adding a number of components, including:

» **Information about the company's day-to-day operations**—This is especially useful if the company is in a colorful industry, such as a fashion show production business. Fashion retailers may discuss new merchandise receipts and the designers from whom the lines were purchased.

» **Details about products/services, including previews of new products**—A designer, for example, could preview a new line from her showroom and accept preorders on her blog.

» **Announcements about sales, promotions, and special events**—These announcements can even be tailored specifically for readers in order to entice first-time visitors to return to the blog.

» **Practical tips and strategies for using products or services**—Examples of blog topics include wardrobe suggestions on what to pack for a beach vacation or which coat to wear with the newest style of boots.

» **Answers to questions from customers**—One of the most effective way to build relationships with customers is to answer their questions in a friendly and conversational tone.

» **Feedback from customers**—Information on product lines, the best new merchandise, and favorite vendors can be shared on blogs encourage viewers to take a look at the merchandise assortment.

» **Testimonials from customers**—Quotes from the letters and comments of customers can help build a positive image and recruit new customers.

FIGURE 7.7
Free People's blog.

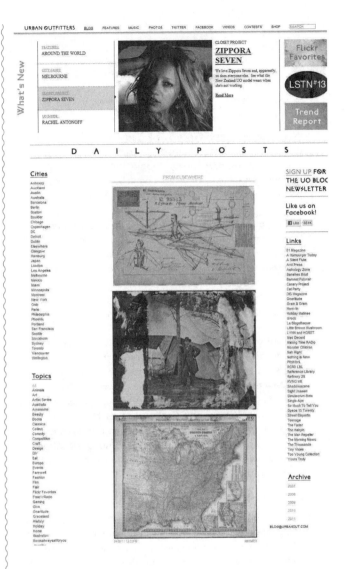

FIGURE 7.8
The Urban Outfitters blog.

Two examples of companies that developed outstanding blogs are sister companies Free People and Urban Outfitters, as shown in FIGURES 7.7 and 7.8.

Other types of creative online advertising are newsgroups and podcasting. **Newsgroups** are online communities of people. Membership is usually free; newsgroups are composed of people who are interested in a certain topic, rather than general news. Because newsgroups are similar to a public bulletin board, an e-company can post new and exciting information or offer promotions on products to a group of potential customers who fit in the e-business's target market.

Podcasting is essentially radio programming that can be produced with a standard computer, a microphone, and software, and a Web site for posting programming. The best way to understand podcasting is to imagine a merger between blogging and radio. Podcasting can be listened to with any computer connected to the Internet and able to play standard

BOX 7.3
TWELVE TIPS TO JUMP START YOUR ONLINE MARKETING STRATEGY

1. **Wiki your business.** Write a Wikipedia entry about your business or product. Wikipedia entries rank high with search engines, particularly Google. Wikipedia attracts hundreds of millions of visitors each year, making it a great place to create a presence for your business or product.

2. **Boost your blog buzz.** According to ComScore, a leading Internet marketing research firm, there are more than 346 million people around the world who read blogs. While it is essential to have your own blog, make sure you regularly read the top blogs in your industry. Post comments on those blogs that include helpful information with links back to your site.

3. **Fan out on Facebook.** With more than 200 million users worldwide, Facebook should be a key part of the e-trepreneur's marketing strategy. If you have not done it already, create a fan page for your business or product. Promote it with ads on Facebook, which are often less expensive than those available through Google Adwords. Make sure all of your Facebook friends know about your page and ask them to promote it to their friends. Be sure to distribute informative content on your page that always links back to your Web site.

4. **Stay alert.** Be certain you are signed up for alerts through Google to find out what people are saying about you, your brand, and your industry online. Find out what consumers are saying about your business in the social media realm on sites like Twitter and Facebook. You cannot effectively participate in the online conversation about your business if you do not know, in real time, what people are talking about.

5. **Stay focused.** Do not try to be all things to all consumers. It is important to keep marketing messages focused and brief. Select the thing your business does best. Choose the product or service you sell the most and stay focused on getting the word out online about those things.

6. **Take the time.** There is no magic bullet when it comes to marketing your business online. Try not to rush to implement too many strategies at once. Take your time, make a plan, and execute it logically.

7. **Master the Web.** Before you started your online business, you may not have thought of yourself as a Webmaster. Now, it is important that you do. Use the tools provided by Google Webmaster Central. Log on to the SitePro News Web sites for free Webmaster tools that can improve your site. Visit Bing Webmaster Tools as well.

8. **Become a media maven.** Make it a goal to ramp up your media relations plan. Increase your media exposure by using Google News to find articles about your industry. Then, make contact with the TV and print reporters who write those stories and offer to be a potential source for their next articles. Reach out to bloggers in your industry and do the same thing. Send out a press release at least once a month about your business or product, but make sure it is newsworthy before you do. Use services like Peter Shankman's Help a Reporter Out (HARO) or Pitchrate. com to find out about the stories reporters and editors are writing.

9. **Speak a foreign language.** Expand your reach by installing a translator plug-in on your site. This will allow users who do not speak English to translate your Web site content into different languages, exposing your business and products to foreign markets.

10. **Answer like an expert.** Demonstrate your expertise by posting and answering questions on Yahoo Answers or LinkedIn Answers. Both rank exceptionally high with search engines and will results in increased traffic to your Web site.

11. **Give the VIP treatment.** Treat your customers like royalty by soliciting their feedback, sending them special promotions via e-mail or spotlighting a Customer of the Month on your Web site.

12. **Use video to tell your story.** You can create great promotional videos for your business using simple tools like Windows Movie Maker. Google loves videos. When you make them, upload them to YouTube, Metacafe, and other video sharing sites for maximum exposure.

SOURCE: Cunningham, Tasha. "12 Tips to Jumpstart Your Online Marketing Strategy." http://www.miamiherald.com/2009/12/14/1379748/12-tips-to-jump-start-your-online.html

MP3 audio files. For example, LA Fashion District offers a free shopping tour podcast on its Web site, http://www.fashiondistrict.org. Many e-businesses are using podcasting to drum up hype for new products or to create how-to videos and educate their customers about their products.

Box 7.3 features twelve tips for marketing an e-business online.

E-BUSINESS CUSTOMER SERVICE

Making customers happy and keeping them are goals of every business; however, there are a few differences between the expectations of customers in brick-and-mortar stores and those who shop online. If entrepreneurs plan to have both a brick-and-mortar store and an e-business, it is important to remember the different expectations that online customers may have. At face value it may appear that the online shopping experience is impersonal; in reality, it is anything but that. E-businesses should use the tools provided by the Internet to offer superior customer service by providing quick and ample product information, fast responses to questions, and follow-up after purchases.

Once accidental, most online shopping is now purposeful. Customers are making conscious decisions to purchase products over the Internet because of their ability to research before buying and, subsequently, find the best prices. Consumers' reasons for shopping in brick-and-mortar stores are very different from those who shop online. Customers who patronize a physical retail operation have the following expectations:

»   **Security**—Customers may believe that paying in a retail store is more secure than giving credit card information on a Web site.

»   **Guaranteed delivery**—Sometimes, purchasing a product is a time-sensitive issue. If a customer needs an item by a certain time or date, shopping online may be an afterthought. The need-it-now mentality is true especially during a holiday rush.

»   **Instant gratification**—Sometimes, customers want an item immediately, and shopping in a store gives them that instant gratification.

»   **Loyalty**—Customers familiar with a store and its staff feel a connection. These customers are very loyal to the store. This is particularly true for older shoppers or those from small towns, where people personally know the owners.

»   **Service**—Having access to personalized service is positive for many traditional shoppers. These customers typically believe that shopping in a store is the only way to receive that level of assistance.

»   **Only option**—A few customers simply do not even consider online buying alternatives. They may believe in-store shopping is the only option because they are not comfortable or familiar with the Internet, do not have online access, or are not aware that the option to shop online exists with a particular store.

»   **Trying before buying**—Some customers need to see, touch, and try on products before making a buying decision. (However, as shown in FIGURE 7.9, e-businesses can counter this by providing an assortment of photographs, product information, customer reviews, and a good exchange or return policy.)

FIGURE 7.9

A detailed product description for men's jeans.

>> **Shipping costs**—Shipping cost is the main factor working against online shopping. Many research a product online and then shop offline simply to avoid paying additional shipping and handling fees.

At the same time, customers frequently have the following expectations from an online store:

>> **Research capabilities**—Shoppers can read product reviews to gain customer feedback, compare brands, and then make a purchase decision all in a matter of minutes, with no pressure from a sales associate. Research shows that male customers and customers making larger purchases are especially prone to do more research before they purchase online.

>> **Hard-to-find items**—An item may be out of stock in a store, or it may not be available locally at all. Shopping online provides access to products from around the world that otherwise would not be readily available.

>> **Niche/specialty items**—Customers are frequently attracted to online stores because they provide access to specialty items, including vintage goods, collector's items, designer merchandise, and other types of exclusive or niche products.

>> **Convenience**—Customers enjoy the flexibility that comes with virtual shopping and knowing the store is never closed.

>> **Value**—Although shipping cost may be a concern for a traditional retail store shopper, online shoppers may factor in such costs as gasoline and time out of their day to go to the store as offset to the delivery fee.

>> **Price**—Comparing prices and finding the best deal online are common consumer activities today. The ability to obtain prices for specific products is the main reason many customers shop online.

>> **Extended inventory**—Retail stores have limited storage space. On the other hand, a Web site can virtually host an unlimited number of products and order the products from the manufacturers when receiving customer orders. The assortment of merchandise is typically much better on a Web site than in brick-and-mortar locations. Because many Web shoppers believe that they have access to a wider product selection online, e-commerce stores are often their preferred places to shop.

Today, offering superior customer service online is relatively easy, thanks to readily available technology. E-mail is one of the easiest ways to provide customers with information about products and respond to inquiries. A customer service e-mail address should be placed on the Web site, and all inquiries should be responded to in less than twenty-four hours. It is also a good plan to have an autoresponder that automatically generates a return e-mail notifying customers that their message has been received and is being checked. In addition, all e-commerce sites should post a direct phone number for shoppers to receive immediate support. Without this, frustrated customers are likely to purchase from a competitor. To provide the support of in-store service, it is advisable to have live chat to answer questions. Live chat is done through an instant-messenger-style format and allows one person to answer several questions at once. FIGURE 7.10 shows the wide range of customer services offered by Lands' End on its Web site.

SATISFYING CUSTOMER DEMANDS

With the amount of information customers can find on the Internet about a product (e.g., prices, product descriptions, reviews), and the ease with which they can navigate from one site to another, competition is a key variable in the success of an e-trepreneur. Whereas driving to another store was a hassle for yesterday's customer, clicking a mouse requires little effort for today's and tomorrow's customer. It is now, therefore, more important than ever to satisfy customer demand.

The following list provides the most sought after and desirable product information identified by online customers:

>> **Product descriptions**—All details need to be described to customers and offered in layers. In other words, give a brief description of the product

FIGURE 7.10
Lands' End customer service online offerings.

and then give customers the option to click on a link for more details.

» **Photographs**—Because customers are not able to see the product in person and touch it physically, they need to be able to look at it from every angle. It is good idea to offer a large, pleasing overall view of the product, with the ability to click and view from different angles and distances.

» **Similar or comparison products**—Provide suggestions and links to products that support or are necessary for the operation of the selected item. Customers will appreciate being informed that a certain product will not work unless they also purchase a cable or other part that is not included.

» **Reviews**—Customer reviews became the rave after Amazon.com made them popular. Providing easy access to reviews from customers, experts, and magazines is in hot demand.

» **Delivery options**—Customers need to understand fully the method and costs of delivery, or they will be dissatisfied when their purchases do not arrive when they thought they would. Information should include the provider, the delivery options, and shipping costs. Customers also prefer having access to a shipping number with a direct link for tracking the delivery status of their purchase. This is especially true for expensive or time-sensitive purchases.

» **Return policies**—Return policies are either an afterthought in a brick-and-mortar store, or they can be explained face to face. As online purchasers have never seen the product, and do not have a place to go to return a purchase, they need to know that the product can be returned without difficulty and that they will be refunded quickly and fully. This is especially true for apparel and perishable products.

Box 7.4 features a summary of a white paper, *E-commerce: More than Just a Store*, prepared by Jesta I.S. Inc., a leading supplier of business solutions with more than forty years of expertise in supply chain management systems for such companies as Perry Ellis, Puma, Cole Haan, and Haggar. The summary examines cross-channel integration and today's sophisticated shopper.

SPECIAL DEMANDS OF ONLINE CUSTOMERS

There are many special demands customers place on e-businesses that are not expected from brick-and-mortar stores. Customers count on an online store to be open twenty-four hours a day, seven days a week. Customers expect to receive an answer to problems and questions at all hours and are displeased if a Web site is offline for routine maintenance, a server is down, or a customer service operator is not available. As no entrepreneur wants to manage a store

BOX 7.4
E-COMMERCE: MORE THAN JUST AN E-STORE

In the dawn of e-commerce, retailers were skeptical about the potential to grow sales via the Internet. Today, retailers are realizing the Internet's positive contribution to overall sales by integrating e-commerce into their business models. For many retailers, e-commerce has become the gateway into previously inaccessible markets. However, entry into this new world of opportunity comes with some strings attached: The customer is a significantly more sophisticated shopper, inventory fulfillment needs to be optimized, and existing stores must be part of the e-commerce strategy. It is not enough for retailers to be multichannel capable; retailers must be seamlessly cross-channel as well. To follow is a brief discussion of the more sophisticated consumer.

Today, customers expect to see real-time inventory availability from the Web site. Walking into a store, they expect the retailer to have stock available if the Web site indicates there is a quantity on hand. Having mobile devices capable of browsing the Web from anywhere, the customer was likely able to check inventory availability while sitting in his or her car in the parking lot of the retailer. Sophisticated retailers are integrating all their inventory positions throughout the enterprise. They are also integrating Internet customers and brick-and-mortar customers. Retailers have

retired the old batch systems and moved to real-time systems to carry them down the road of on-demand information.

Customers who shop in brick-and-mortar stores are also passing through the gates of e-commerce and are becoming better informed about the products they wish to purchase and the options available for purchasing them. According to Alterian, a leading international integrated marketing platform provider, 87 percent of online shoppers are making their purchase decisions based on professional reviews on Web sites, or advice from friends or family, or both. Only 8 percent of survey respondents indicated they believe what companies say about themselves. Although consumers appear to benefit from the competition in the market, they have also been impacted by the economic downturn. Each purchase takes on more meaning as consumers cut back on discretionary spending. They are becoming much more informed about their purchases and are willing to actively research products and the companies that sell them. In addition to researching the facts related to a product and company, today's consumer is able to take advantage of social networking tools (like Twitter, YouTube, and Facebook) to exchange opinions about products and companies. The Internet has given consumers unparalleled access to other

consumers, allowing them to share a wide variety of information and opinions. Whereas "word of mouth" used to be limited to a close circle of friends, electronic word of mouth can now be global. As consumers become more informed, they become more demanding, expecting not only a particular level of quality, but social responsibility as well.

At the end of the day, consumers call the shots. Their discretionary spending may have slowed, but their product/service expectations are on the rise; they want to be able to buy anywhere, ship anywhere, and return anywhere and still retain the ability to shop online or in-store. Although it would be reasonable to conclude that consumers' expectations for uniformity make perfect sense, the reality can be very different. Shoppers often receive inconsistent messages from their experiences of buying online and in-store. It is critical that retailers integrate e-commerce into their business models in order to assure their systems are able to identify their products, promotions, and customer base uniformly. To this end, there has been renewed interest in business intelligence tools as companies actively gather as much information as possible about their products and customers.

SOURCE: Summary of the white paper E-commerce: More Than Just an E-Store, Jesta I. S. Inc., June 2010.

---

every hour of every day, many e-business owners employ a third-party monitoring service to handle these problems.

Customers also prefer a variety of payment options in addition to credit cards. In recognition of the security concerns some customers have regarding credit card use online, it is wise for the e-trepreneur to

accept payment from third-party vendors, such as Pay-Pal. These vendors act as intermediaries in that credit card information is not required by the entrepreneur's Web site.

E-trepreneurs can turn the challenges of brick and mortar into online sales opportunities. Holiday rushes in December and before Mother's Day, for example, provide the e-trepreneur with ample opportunity to offset crowded stores with limited merchandise and long lines at the cash desk. Many e-businesses thrive during holidays or seasonal rushes by offering services such as the following:

- » **Expedited delivery**—E-business owners need to make sure they can get the items packed and out the door to meet the hectic pace.

- » **Extended delivery times**—Owners need to manage last-minute orders that arrive the day before or the day of a major holiday. Whether they can meet delivery deadlines often depends on whether they have enough employee assistance behind the scenes to fill the orders.

- » **Sufficient inventory**—The best plan is to assure that there is adequate inventory on hand and to alert suppliers to the potential increase in demand. Nothing is worse than being out of stock on a hot item and not being able to fulfill orders during a rush.

- » **Increased service rep availability**—Customers are often in a hurry and want "real people" to answer their questions.

FLEXIBILITY ONLINE AND OFF

Businesses with both a Web site and a brick-and-mortar location are in a unique predicament. The good news is that the two retail outlets complement each other and offer the opportunity for increased sales. The bad news is that customers rarely see a distinction between the two sides of the business and expect both to be accommodating of each other. For example, a customer who buys a product from the company's Web site may want to return the item to the physical store. E-businesses need to either offer this service or make clear the policy that it is not an option at the time of purchase. Similarly, customers viewing a special deal online often expect to get the same price in the physical store. REI, an outdoor sporting goods and apparel store, is an excellent example of a firm that has integrated its online site with its physical stores.

INTERNATIONAL SERVICE

Before making a big push for global customers, e-trepreneurs should realistically consider the vast cultural differences that may render Web sites effective in the United States relatively worthless in other parts of the world. An understanding and appreciation for cultural diversity is of utmost importance. For example, Web sites in Asia tend to place more emphasis on color and interactivity. A Web site that performs well in the United States by looking clean and well organized may have to be replaced with a more colorful and energetic look and options that are often found more compelling in Asian markets. In addition to the look of the Web site, the speed of Internet connections in the global market needs to be examined. As many countries have a less-developed Internet structure, a new e-business wanting to cater to these markets may want to offer a low-bandwidth version of its Web site, with fewer pictures and videos to load per page.

Language is probably the greatest barrier to overcome for e-trepreneurs entering the overseas market; however, U.S.-based companies do have the advantage that English is the most widely spoken language around the world. The best policy for handling questions from foreign customers is to provide enough basic, easy-to-follow, printed information that provides answers to questions in advance. Questions from international customers who are not fluent in English are usually best answered by e-mail unless telephone operators happen to be fluent in multiple languages.

BUILDING A WEB SITE

Although there are many steps in building and launching a successful Web site, the four main steps are as follows:

1. Choosing and registering a domain name

2. Planning and designing an effective Web site

3. Working with a professional Web designer

4. Launching the new Web site

Rather than a physical business address, e-businesses use a virtual address, or domain name. A **domain name** is the part of the URL that specifically identifies the name of the Web site. The phrase "location, location, location" is as significant in the virtual world as it is in the offline world. Before building a Web site, online entrepreneurs need to find a good location for their new businesses. The selected domain name can impact how easily customers can find a Web site or if they visit it at all. There are two common strategies for choosing a domain name. The first is to match the domain name to the company's name as closely as possible. The second is to choose a domain that clearly indicates the type of business or the customers being targeted. No matter which strategy is chosen, an effective domain name should meet these criteria:

» **Be easy to spell**—Hard-to-spell words will make it difficult for some customers to find the Web site. For example, www.RealWomenByLucyRich.com seems like a good domain name, but imagine having to spelling it out for a customer or client. Better alternatives would be www.RealWomen.com or www.Women12to20.com.

» **Be simple to remember**—A domain name does not have to be catchy or trendy to work. Simplicity goes a long way today in our crowded, busy world of information overload.

» **Be relatively short**—A shorter name is easier for customers to remember than a longer one.

» **Contain important keywords**—Using descriptive words in the domain clearly describes what an e-business does. Furthermore, using relevant words that frequently show up in search engines is beneficial to site rankings and search engine optimization.

» **Be alphabetically strategic**—Domain names that begin with a letter near the front of the alphabet are more likely to secure a spot at the top of directories and other reference lists. Relevancy still counts; it is important not to sacrifice this by adding random numbers or letters.

» **Be intuitive to customers**—Domain names should provide a vision of the products a business is selling. For highly targeted or specialized markets, an edgy or more creative name can win customers.

When a name is chosen for the new e-business, the name must be registered with a domain registrar. You may have seen the commercial for GoDaddy.com. This is an example of a domain registrar. The company completes and submits all the paperwork required to activate the new domain name. As there is a limited supply of domain names, it may be that a name will be unavailable at the time of registration. A new e-business needs to decide whether to choose a different domain name ask if the unavailable name can be placed on back order or make an offer for an already used name through a register or by contacting the owner directly.

As an example, take a look at the sample business plan and the plan for integrating e-commerce into the business of RealWomen, Inc., in Appendix D. The company will begin its Internet presence through a Web site introduction scheduled for one month before the opening of the store. The Web site will be used to introduce the business, the management team, and the sales staff; to promote new vendors; and to inform the Web site viewers about the development of the store and, later, its activities and events. Participating in social media is a strategic part of the company's marketing plan. Facebook, LinkedIn, and MySpace will be updated daily to communicate with current and potential customers about store events and new merchandise arrivals. Also, customers will be featured as models in apparel and accessories from RealWomen, Inc., and their profiles (e.g., name, occupation, interests and hobbies, favorite fashions) will be presented.

In addition, e-mail blasts will be used to inform customers who register for these communications about sales, trunk showings, new products, and events; print advertisements will be copied and sent via e-mail to the customer mass mailing list. As the company grows, Lucy Rich, the company owner, will evaluate whether to take the plunge, as Lucy describes it, and expand the inventory to sell products online. Initially, her focus is on planning and designing the company Web site, as is explored next.

PLANNING AND DESIGNING AN EFFECTIVE WEB SITE

Not long ago, owning and operating a Web site was a way for a business to differentiate itself from its competitors. As Internet companies have gained momentum, new technological options and design layouts have evolved to make e-businesses stand out. Despite these new options, customers are still drawn to a site that is simple, focused, easy to use, well organized, and functional. Although the main focus of e-business sites is to sell the company's product, the Web site will also need to provide the following information:

» What types of products will be sold? The number and organization of pages depend on the makeup and complexity of the products or services.

» How many distinct categories of products will there be? There should be a separate page for each product category. For example, an e-business may divide apparel and accessories categories into dresses, sportswear, shoes, handbags, and jewelry.

» Will customers be able to create an account? If so, there needs to be a page on which customers can log in, list and update their personal information, view their orders, and enter payment information.

» Will customers be provided with additional content? Some Web sites offer subscriptions to their customers that allow them, for a fee, to access premium content, such as special articles, interviews, video, or photo excerpts.

» How will customers pay for their orders? Web sites need to be able to accept credit card orders as well as other payment options.

» Will there be instructions for using the Web site? There should be a page of frequently asked questions (FAQs) to help customers use the site quickly and effectively.

After an e-business determines how its Web site will be used, a site map should be constructed to illustrate how the Web pages will be linked to each other, starting with the home page. Most e-commerce sites include a home page, catalog page, customer account page, order information page, FAQ page, content pages, map and direction page (if there is a retail site), checkout page, payment processing page, and "About Us" or company history page.

THREE LEVELS OF CUSTOMER-FRIENDLY WEB SITES

The customer experience should be kept in mind, first and foremost, when designing a Web site. The best Web sites make customers enjoy the experience and want to return and purchase again. There are three levels of site functionality.

The first level includes the basic functions that most Internet customers expect, as follows:

» **Quick-loading pages**—Customers expect pages to load quickly. E-commerce sites can ease the problem for customers with dial-up services by not placing too much content, including graphics and video, on one page. Sites that fail to account for varying speeds of Internet access will lose sales.

» **Easy navigation**—When customers choose to move from page to page, the site should allow them to get back to the home page, the last visited page, and the site history easily.

» **Working links**—All links, internal and external, should function properly. Having outdated links shows poor site maintenance or an outdated site.

» **Viewable images**—All images, especially product photographs, need to load quickly and correctly. Avoid grainy images or small pictures that are difficult to see.

At the second level is the site's interactive functions, designed to engage customers actively. To follow are some of these functions:

» **Site search**—A search that finds products and information within the site.

» **Downloadable documents**—Offer the option to download PDF documents of articles, product reviews, and owner's manuals.

» **Discussion boards and blogs**—Message boards, bulletin boards, discussion boards, chat rooms, and blogs are options that allow visitors to interact with an e-business and with each other.

The third level offers customers an enhanced experience on the Web site through options such as:

» **Online demonstration and tutorials**—Depending on the complexity of the product, online demonstrations can be useful, especially for new products.

» **Live or 24/7 customer support**—The Internet never sleeps. There is a customer who is always awake to purchase a product and who may need to ask questions in the middle of the night before making that purchase.

» **Second-language viewing options**—Not all online customers are fluent in English. As a result, savvy e-business owners offer customers the option to view the site in other languages.

» **New media**—Video and sound clips engage the customer, and they have moved from options to standards on most fashion Web sites.

HIRING A PROFESSIONAL WEB DESIGNER

It is important for e-business owners to know how their sites should be laid out to be effective, but if they do not have the knowledge or time to create their own site, hiring a professional Web designer is a good option. Hiring a good Web designer is similar to finding a good lawyer or accountant. The e-trepreneur should consider the following options when hiring a Web designer or developer:

» **Ask for advice**—Talk to friends, business associates, or others who have Web sites. Solicit their opinions, and look at examples of the work Web professionals have provided them.

» **Look into the work Web designers have done**—Visit Web sites that are enjoyable to use. Often, there is a link at the bottom of the home page that credits the site to a professional designer. If this is the case, follow the link back to the designer's Web site for more information.

» **Evaluate the Web designer's work**—Ask for samples of work completed for other clients, and determine if the work and style fit with the e-business's needs and goals.

CONCLUSION

The Internet will continue to evolve. It has evolved from an information exchange primarily used for research purposes to an interactive and viable platform for commerce. In essence, the Internet requires a paradigm shift in the ways in which entrepreneurs strategize, plan, develop, and implement their operations.

The Internet is impacting society in both positive and negative ways. As its full capabilities are still unknown, it is in a transition phrase. It is uncertain exactly how the Internet will affect social structures; however, it is certain to do so, as it connects the global population and offers immense opportunities for the whole world. The Internet will influence the way people do their jobs, locate and buy what they need and desire, and communicate with one another. Social networking is a growing phenomenon creating and redefining bonds and building connections.

Evolving online technologies are here to stay in some form or another. They are part of the real world and real business. A time will come soon when it is realized that the most important part of e-business is not the "e" but the actual "business," and the boundaries between the two will blur as they become fully integrated.

KEY TERMS

banner advertisements

blog

classified advertisements

click-through rate (CTR)

cost per click (CPC)

cost per thousand (CPM)

domain name

e-commerce

e-retailing

inventory management

newsgroup

newsletter

niche

online auction

online storefront

podcasting

pop-up advertisements

portal

search engine advertisements

shopping cart

spam

wholesale

DISCUSSION TOPICS

1. Compare and contrast the types of e-models. Which is most suited to grow your business concept? Why?

2. Discuss how e-trepreneurs can meet or surpass customers' expectations for online sales and services.

3. Which methods of online advertising and social networking do you believe are the most effective currently as well as in the future? Why?

4. Investigate the costs, capabilities, and opportunities associated with hiring a Web designer to develop and maintain a company Web site.

5. Examine the strategies an entrepreneur can implement to expand a business onto the Web and into e-commerce. Develop a step-by-step plan.

SUGGESTED READINGS

Jesta I. S. Inc. White paper, *E-commerce: More Than Just an E-store* June, 2010. http://www.jestais.com/en/press_room/white.php.

Holden, G., S. Belew, J. Elad, J. Rich, and Don Gulbrandsen. *E-Business*. John Wiley and Sons, 2009.

Strauss, Judy, and Raymond Frost. *E-Marketing*, 5th ed. Upper Saddle River, NJ: Prentice Hall, 2009.

ONLINE RESOURCES

BLOGTREPRENEUR.COM

http://www.blogtrepreneur.com/2008/03/10/
resources-for-online-entrepreneurs
Useful resources for online entrepreneurs.

GOOGLE

http://www.google.com/intl/en/ads/
The Internet giant's advertising program.

HOOVER WEB DESIGN

http://www.hooverwebdesign.com/articles.html
Web site design and development for professional
small businesses; large library of e-retailing articles.

REI

http://www.rei.com
A retailer of outdoor gear and clothing with more
than 100 stores and Web site sales that has made
Fortune magazine's list of the "100 Best Companies
to Work For" every year since 1998.

WEB MARKETING TODAY

http://www.wilsonweb.com
A Web site established to help business owners of
small to medium-sized companies learn how to
market their products and services more effectively
by means of the Internet.

ZAPPOS

http://about.zappos.com/zappos-story/
in-the-beginning-let-there-be-shoes
The story of an online entrepreneurial business that
is setting the bar for customer service and corporate culture.

BUSINESS PLAN CONNECTION
THINKING LIKE AN ENTREPRENEUR

For the most part, a business plan written for an e-business will follow the same format as a brick-and-mortar business plan. When developing the plan, make certain it is clear whether this business is (1) completely located on, and selling through, the Internet only; (2) selling through both a brick-and-mortar store and the Internet; or (3) using the Internet as an off-shoot for purposes of advertising the business. Indicate this in the various sections of the business plan where appropriate.

Search the Internet for both online stores and Web sites that are used primarily as venues for advertising brick-and mortar businesses. Compare and contrast the various features of each, particularly the sites that are most closely related to your business concept. It may also be helpful to conduct interviews with individuals or businesses using the Internet in the manner in which you intend to do in order to gather information for completing this particular section of the business plan.

◉ ASSIGNMENT 7.1
WEB PLAN SUMMARY

1. Open your saved business plan template.
2. Address the following sections of the Web plan summary. You may use the sample business plan in Appendix D as an additional resource.

WEB PLAN SUMMARY
- » Overview
- » Internet Strategies
- » Online Marketing Strategy
- » Web Development and Hosting
- » Costs
- » Buying and Shipping Methods
- » Future Features

MAKE YOUR WEB SITE A DAILY DESTINATION: FIVE SIMPLE STRATEGIES TO KEEP PEOPLE COMING BACK

EVERY small business loves the exposure, empathy, and sense of community that having a Web site can generate. But getting people to visit on a regular basis can be a challenge, especially if updates are infrequent or all you have to offer is the occasional monotone press release or product announcement. Thankfully, building a Web site that's "sticky" enough to keep users engaged and coming back doesn't have to require investing thousands or reinventing yourself as the next online media empire. All it takes is a little elbow grease and personal touch, as indicated by the simple strategies below, each designed to send your homepage's daily number of visitors soaring:

Connect and Communicate: Make no bones about it: Blogging should be an essential part of any modern Web site. After all, a few clicks is literally all it takes to post updates in real-time around the clock, creating a steady stream of content that promises something new and exciting with every visit. Better still, professionals at all experience levels have the capability of readily doing it, and the practice also helps put a personal face on your organization, shining the spotlight on the individuals behind it. However, to really captivate an audience enough to keep them returning, take note: You'll also need to provide content that's dynamic, unique and offers measurable informational or entertainment value, plus speak in a language that all can understand. In short, the occasional pre-approved sound bite from the HR guy or gal won't cut it. Rather, you need to address audiences like you're having a normal conversation, and provide content with meaningful substance to the reader. Making-of articles, features detailing how to get more from your products, partner profiles, project diaries, step-by-step how-to guides, interviews with notable personalities or internal stakeholders—all present compelling ways to connect with audiences while also keeping them interested and informed, providing ample incentive to keep coming back.

Emphasize Community Building: As social media insiders well know, creating a sense of community around your Web site is one of the most powerful tools for engaging and ultimately enthralling prospective fans. But doing so doesn't simply mean throwing up a sponsored message board then leaving it to stagnate, or e-mailing customers sporadic newsletter updates that regurgitate existing material easily found elsewhere. Rather, you have to not only encourage discussion and actively take part in conversations by dedicating internal time and resources, but also make customers feel as if they truly have a voice in the discussion by listening to their concerns, responding and sourcing feedback at every opportunity. Implementing programs that recognize and reward valued contributors is also vital, as is creating fan-based initiatives that allow community members to contribute and share ideas, concepts and creations of their own. Even simply giving enthusiasts the chance to submit designs for your next fundraiser's logo or arranging times where they can chat with top execs to provide input on upcoming ventures won't just engender goodwill. They'll also excite and empower a legion of amateur brand ambassadors—an essential source of free, ongoing updates and constructive conversations, which will both attract users to and keep them enamored with your site.

Design for Mass Distribution: Sharing is good—even more so if you've got a message worth spreading and it winds up in front of millions of eyeballs. As such, you should not only be updating your Web site with unique pieces of content (surveys, research reports, custom editorial clips, guides to solving common problems, unique looks behind-the-scenes, etc.) designed to grab viewers' attention, but also making everything from blog posts to pictures, photos, PDF documents and videos shareable, embeddable and ready to be commented upon or posted via social media platforms. When it comes to corporate assets, the tendency—especially among hyper-competitive start-ups—is always to tightly hold and control. But often, the more powerful strategy is to design pieces of content with the specific idea in mind of seeding them throughout the user community, as it's a great way to build brand awareness. Beyond heightened exposure and additional media mentions, using your Web site to disseminate unique, specially branded pieces of content can also lead to improved search engine optimization results through a larger number of incoming links. And, more important still, generate heightened word of mouth surrounding your homepage, letting countless potential readers know exciting things are happening there on a regular basis.

Focus on Value: Exclusive specials, contests, promotions and timed discounts can all be powerful drivers of Web site traffic, especially in these cost-conscious times. By offering direct bargains and rebate programs on both an ongoing and sporadic basis through your online headquarters, you can keep customers' interest piqued, and generate additional sales. These marketing programs become even more valuable when coupled with Facebook, Twitter, and other social marketing tools, which have the potential to help news spread like wildfire online. Just make sure that the only place such bargains can be found is on your homepage, and be consistent in terms of the pages to which you drive this traffic, to establish in shoppers' minds the importance of regularly checking

a certain destination. Similarly, establishing relationships with key bloggers and members of the media can also help reinforce the message, as can a regular series of e-mail or newsletter updates designed to inform current and prospective buyers. Customers get to save on purchases while you benefit from enhanced publicity and heightened sales, creating a win-win situation for all.

Use Targeted Demonstrations: Although special membership options, premium subscription packages, and frequent buyer programs can all prove great incentives, services that you freely give away are often just as important as those that you reserve for more exclusive clients. Whether you're looking at offering complimentary computer virus scans by having users visit your homepage, providing a suite of free continuing education resources or simply hosting an archive of complementary, corporate-branded webinars on software engineering, realize this: Providing helpful services or information at no charge that solve pressing, evergreen problems or answer important questions can all serve to generate a steady source of online traffic, and provide a ready supply of leads to upsell on premium services. Sometimes you have to give in order to get. It may seem counterintuitive, but ultimately, the practice makes a ready way to demonstrate your organization's capabilities to a potentially lucrative client base, while also giving them a taste of the benefits to be had by partnering on more advanced or long-term services.

SOURCE: Steinberg, Scott. "Make Your Web Site a Daily Destination: Five Simple Strategies to Keep People Coming Back." *Entrepreneur*, April 26, 2010. http://www.entrepreneur.com/ebusiness/expandingyouronlinepresence/article206322.html

CHAPTER 8
REACHING CUSTOMERS AND DRIVING SALES

OBJECTIVES

» **Consider effective ways to reach the market.**

» **Develop the four Ps of marketing: price, place, promotion, and product.**

» **Identify an image for the business.**

» **Develop a marketing plan for promotional activities.**

N this chapter the entrepreneur examines ways of penetrating the market. Entrepreneurs look at methods of differentiating their business from those of competitors through price, product, placement, and promotion to the right people—the target market. The life cycle of a product or service is explored, along with pricing strategies that reinforce the marketing plan. A successful fashion retail business depends, in part, on the level of customer service; this chapter explores the significance of exceptional customer service. Finally, the fashion entrepreneur examines the basics of branding and how the overall branding strategy plays a significant role in the consumer's perception.

THE ROLE OF THE MARKETING STRATEGY

Determining a successful marketing strategy is key to leading the business to success. To be successful in business, the entrepreneur must formulate and implement a plan to reach customers and to motivate those customers to buy. The marketing plan helps define and quantify user benefits, establishes the market size as well as potential customer interest, and addresses the competition (see Chapter 3). The marketing strategy serves a number of purposes. It helps the entrepreneur determine how potential customers will become aware of the product or service. It defines the message the entrepreneur wants to convey about the product, service, or company. And finally, it identifies the methods that will be used to deliver and reinforce that message and how sales will be achieved. Finally, the marketing plan addresses how the company will position itself relative to the competition.

NAMING THE BUSINESS

Naming the business is an integral part of communicating its image. Considerations in choosing a name may include the names of competitors, the message the name communicates, and how descriptive the name is of the business. Choosing a name is vitally important. It is part of the overall branding that is discussed later in this chapter.

In an article titled "8 Tips for Naming Your Business," Lahle Wolfe asks entrepreneurs to think about what they want their business name to convey. Is the intent to project a mom-and-pop feel or an image of a larger corporation? The name of the business will appear in brochures, on company letterhead, on its Web site—anywhere the name appears in print or is otherwise used to promote the business.

Wolfe asserts that the name of a business has advertising potential. If the fashion retail business specializes in a niche product or service, such as providing shoes for underserved markets, consumers may be drawn based on the name alone. When consumers are looking for a product or service (particularly online), the name may be what attracts them to one Web site instead of another. When choosing a business name, think about who the business is marketing to and not just what is being sold.

Wolfe also recommends choosing a name that consumers can remember and pronounce and that represents the type of business.

Also, consider whether the customer will attempt to create an acronym out of the name. For example, "Amazing Southern Swimwear" results in an unfavorable acronym. Finally, the entrepreneur should think about long-term growth. Select a name that will allow the introduction of new products or services and that will not be too descriptive to a particular service or product.[1]

THE MARKETING MIX: THE Ps OF MARKETING

The traditional elements needed to determine the marketing strategy include the four **Ps of marketing**: product, place, price, and promotion. A fifth P of marketing can be added—people who will be targeted as potential customers or product users. These combined market variables, or the **marketing mix**, must reinforce the image of the company's product to the potential customer. All five elements should complement one another in order to achieve the marketing objective.

The best product mix for a company is one that directs resources or dollars toward products, place, promotion, and pricing with the highest potential to increase revenue and profits.

The five Ps are the variables the entrepreneur can control within certain constraints of the external environment, such as a shift in the economy or in market behavior, or an increase in costs.

The goal is to make decisions centered on the target market to create perceived value and a positive response to the product or service being offered.

In essence, the marketing mix is used to describe the choices businesses must make within the whole process of bringing a product or service to market. It is putting the right product in the right place, at the right price, at the right time.

Case Study 8.1 tells the story of Standard Style Boutique and illustrates how the right marketing mix can mean success.

PRODUCT

A product is anything offered to a market for attention, acquisition, use, or consumption; it can be defined as any item or service that satisfies the need of a consumer. Whether the fashion retail business is providing a tangible product or an intangible service, such as convenience or comfort, consumers buy based on the ability of that product or service to satisfy a need or provide a benefit.

A series of elements combine to create the product within the mix. Among them are functionality, style, quality, packaging, warranty, accessories, and service. It is the goal of the entrepreneur to utilize the research and analysis conducted about potential customers to provide a product that meets the needs of and satisfies those customers.

STANDARD STYLE BOUTIQUE, KANSAS CITY, MISSOURI

Standard Style Boutique opened on October 16, 2003, after owners Matt and Emily Baldwin relocated from California back to their roots in the Midwest. Following their passion for people, fashion, and the Kansas City art community, they created their vision of Standard.

The first boutique opened up in Leawood, Kansas (a suburb of Kansas City) with men's and women's clothing ranging from casual classics to high-end fashion. The concept morphed to include shoes, handbags, gifts, kids, and accessories and became a premiere one-stop shopping destination for the entire family with over 150 collections. After outgrowing their first space, they expanded the boutique to 4,500 square feet during 2006 in Leawood's Town Center Plaza.

Standard Style's vision to serve clients in its hometown allowed for the opportunity for a second location in Kansas City, Missouri. With 4,300 square feet on the Country Club Plaza, Standard Style constructed another one-stop shopping destination, which opened in November 2006.

STANDARDSTYLE.COM

The next part of growing the vision was to launch an online boutique. Standardstyle.com opened up for business in January of 2005. Standardstyle.com aims at superior customer service, the hottest fashions first, and personalizing individuals' needs. Standardstyle.com

will continue to improve the online boutique experience through technology, product, and customer service. In 2009, Standardstyle.com morphed into Standardsocial. com, and they also created a full fashion magazine as a way of continuing to connect with their clients and the people of Kansas City.

OUR COMMITMENT

Standard believes in supporting its community by contributing to and being a part of multiple charity organizations locally and nationally through donations, events, and education. Standard is committed to superior customer service and staying up on the latest trends through featuring classic designers as well as supporting emerging new designers. Standard will continue to grow its concept to support and encourage individualism and creativity through fashion, art, and music as well as growing friendships.

Standard Style has been recognized in multiple publications for its products, concept, and image including: the *Wall Street Journal*, *GQ*, *Lucky*, *InStyle*, *Shop Etc.*, *Elle*, *Rolling Stone*, *US Weekly*, *People*, Daily Candy, fashion blogs (Allplaidout.com, Denimdebate.com) and multiple local publications.

SOURCE: Standard Style Boutique (press release).

Standard Style reaches customers through its mix of brick-and-mortar store, Web site, and creative magazine.

The following series of questions will help define the product as it relates to marketing:

» What does the customer want from the product/ service? What needs does it satisfy?

» What features does it have to meet these needs? Are there any features you've missed out? Are you including costly features that the customer won't actually use?

» How and where will the customer use it?

» What does it look like? How will customers experience it?

» What size(s), color(s), and so on, should it be?

» What is it to be called?

» How is it branded?

» How is it differentiated versus your competitors? What is the most it can cost to provide and still be sold at a sufficient profit?[2]

To stay competitive in the marketplace, entrepreneurs must be open to innovation and change in their current product lines. They must also be willing to explore bringing in new products, perhaps in a way the market is not accustomed to seeing. In 2007 entrepreneurs Hil Davis and Veeral Rathod launched J. Hilburn, a Dallas-based company that delivers luxurious, custom-made dress shirts in just three weeks at a relatively low cost. Hil and Veeral studied the men's luxury market and saw that no one was delivering quality custom clothing and personal service at a price competitive with off-the-rack products. They also recognized that men often find shopping a hassle and introduced a product and delivery method to ease that hassle. J. Hilburn's personal style advisors will go to a customer's chosen location, take measurements, offer suggestions for individual style, and use that information to create the ideal dress shirt. In Box 8.1, Hil Davis offers advice for developing a product line and bringing that line to market.

Every product has a life cycle (see Chapter 4). The product life cycle must be understood for the entrepreneur to determine if and when to introduce new products into the existing product line and to revise existing ones. The product life cycle for fashion goods can be short—a fad item may last as little as four to six weeks. Fashion trends can last for a season or a decade. The trick is to anticipate when to get into a fashion and when to get out. The time to introduce a new product is during the early life cycle of the current product, when sales are strong, and profit margins are higher. To launch a new product successfully, the entrepreneur must be committed to the new product and be willing to adjust to changes in the environment. Adequate planning and knowledge of the market are important. The entrepreneur must be able to differentiate the new product from existing products, usually through promotional efforts.

Remember to keep in mind the product life cycle discussed in Chapter 4. The model presented in that chapter is designed to identify the maturation stage of a particular product by approximating its level of customer acceptance: introductory, growth, maturity, or declining. In this chapter the product is discussed as an integral component of the total marketing strategy.

Successful fashion companies often use the product to build a marketing strategy and to penetrate the market. A theory propounded by Malcolm P. McNair (Harvard Business School, 1958) attempts to explain changes in retailing institutions. It represents phases retailing institutions may pass through as they move through their cycle. Retail innovators begin the growth cycle as low-status, low-margin, low-price operators. A period follows during which facilities become more elaborate, costs increase, and higher margins are required to survive. Eventually, the innovators come to resemble the conventional retailers they hoped to replace, and the cycle begins again with the next low-margin innovator.[3]

In essence, it is believed products fall within the **wheel of retailing**—a retail marketing process whereby original low-price discounters upgrade their services and gradually increase prices. As these discounters evolve into full-line department stores, a competitive opportunity develops for new low-price discounters to develop, and the process continues with the next generation.

BOX 8.1
INTERVIEW WITH HIL DAVIS, OF J. HILBURN CLOTHIER

Who are your customers? What are your most significant products or services?
Our customers are all males who buy off-the-rack apparel. We started with custom shirts and focused on that for two-and-a-half years before we launched additional products, which now include trousers, sweaters, polos, outerwear, and accessories. I think a mistake businesses make is to go too wide too fast. Develop a relevant and high-demand product, and build a loyal customer base. Then think about introducing additional product categories.

How has your market changed in the past few years? And how has your business kept pace?
The big change in our market was the recession. Prior to the recession, we found that customers had traded up to luxury items and focused on brands. Price was never a concern.

After the recession, customers still wanted luxury items, but price became a relevant factor in their decision making. So we added a ton of customers who knew our products were the same quality as their luxury brands. That allowed us to introduce a lot more product categories because the customer asked for more.

How do you market your products or services?
Through a direct sales force, like Avon, and then support the sales force with e-commerce online. This enables a customer to buy 24/7, while having customer service 24/7 through [its] sales partner.

INTERVIEW conducted by Travis Reed.

J. Hilburn founders Hil Davis and Veeral Rathod.

PLACE
In their book *The Portable MBA in Marketing*, Charles D. Schew and Alexander Hiam discuss the role of place in marketing strategy:

Place, or distribution, involves making sure that the product is available where and when it is wanted. Marketers can choose among many ways of moving products to consumers. They may choose among different types of outlets and store locations. With today's high tech, online access, entrepreneurs are turning to an online presence. Not only to promote the business, but in many cases to offer the sale of products to consumers on a much broader scale. Distribution also involves decisions such as how much inventory to hold, how to transport goods, and where to locate warehouses.[4]

Following is a series of questions that can be asked to determine whether the "place" of the product or service is in line with customer expectations:

» Where do buyers look for your product or service?

» If they look in a store, what kind? A specialist boutique or in a supermarket, or both? Or online? Or direct, via a catalog?

» How can you access the right distribution channels?

» Do you need to use a sales force? Or attend trade fairs? Or make online submissions? Or send samples to catalog companies?

» What do you competitors do, and how can you learn from that and/or differentiate?[5]

Consumers are looking for products and services that are convenient to purchase when they are wanted or needed. In selecting the **channel of distribution**—the avenue selected for moving goods from producer to consumer—careful consideration should be given to using distributors that can provide good service at a reasonable price. The primary channel of distribution for the fashion retail industry moves from manufacturer, to retailer, to consumer. Some manufacturers, however, sell directly to the consumer through catalogs, Web sites, or factory outlets. An alternative, and less often used, channel of distribution in the fashion industry is the wholesaler. In this case, the manufacturer sells merchandise to a wholesale company, one that sells the goods to the retailer for subsequent resale to the consumer. FIGURE 8.1 illustrates the position of the wholesale operation in the common channels of distribution.

PRICE

Pricing decisions impact almost every aspect of a business—the product or service's image sales, and financial projections. Pricing is a component of the marketing strategy. Although covering expenses is crucial, it is also an issue of relationship to competitors' pricing, positioning, and supply and demand—what the customer is willing to pay.

The following series of questions can aid in the establishment of a price point for the product or service being offered:

» What is the value of the product or service to the buyer?

» Are there established price points for products or services in this area?

» Is the customer price sensitive? Will a small decrease in price gain you extra market share? Or will a small increase be indiscernible, and so gain you extra profit margin?

» What discounts should be offered to trade customers, or to other specific segments of your market?

» How will your price compare with your competitors'?[6]

Pricing is not just about numbers. The price of the merchandise sends a message to customers about the product or service they are buying. It sends a message about the value of the product. Pricing has a direct impact on the following.

» **Market share**—Sometimes lower pricing can demand a higher capture of market share.

» **Company image**—Prices convey a perceived value in the minds of the consumer. Higher prices are often thought of as higher-end products, whereas lower pricing can sometimes reflect an image of lesser quality.

» **Profitability**—Pricing affects the business' gross margin and gross profit.

» **Competitive advantage**—Businesses can sometimes create a competitive advantage by pricing products against the competition.

» **Sales volume**—Higher prices can sometimes mean lower volume, whereas lower prices generally result in higher volume.

» **Sales revenue**—If prices increase, sales volume may decrease, causing a reduction in total revenue. Effectively priced products or services, however, can increase revenue and profit.

Every product or service has a price range. The **price ceiling** is the highest price a business can ask for its product or service and is often set by customers.

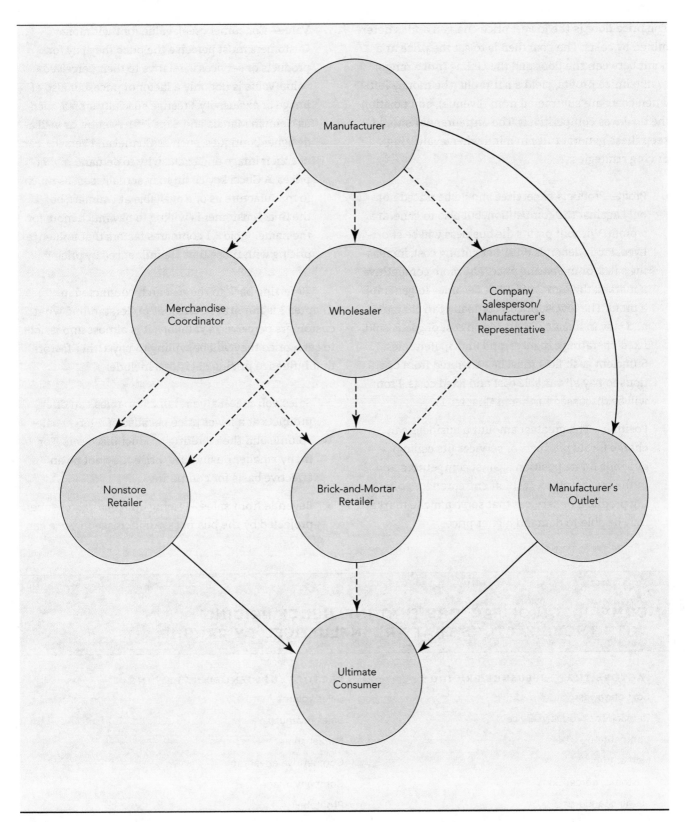

FIGURE 8.1

Channels of distribution.

The **price floor** is the lowest price charged and is determined by costs. The goal then is to set the price at a point between the floor and the ceiling (**price range**) to maximize profits, yield a net profit (the money left when costs are subtracted from revenue), and position the business competitively. The entrepreneur should keep these general rules in mind when evaluating pricing strategies:

» **Profit**—Products or services should be priced not only against the competition, but also to generate a profit. Without profits the business will be short-lived. Profit depends on either cutting cost, increasing sales, or increasing price. The more competitive a market, the more difficult it becomes to generate a profit. The lowest price a company can charge and stay in business depends on cost of goods sold, fixed operating expenses, and anticipated sales. Sufficient cash flow must be generated from operations to pay all variable cost and fixed costs. Profit will be discussed further in Chapter 11.

» **Position**—The greatest amount a business can charge for its products or services (its ceiling) depends on its position against competitors and in the marketplace. Fashion entrepreneurs offering products or services that serve a niche market may be able to demand higher prices.

» **Value**—Consumers seek value for their money. Customers must perceive the price they pay for products or services is relative to their perceived value. Value is not only a factor of price, but also of image or exclusivity. Prestige specialty stores, such as Neiman Marcus and Saks Fifth Avenue, as well as designer boutiques, such as Chanel and Versace, can use their image and exclusivity to demand higher prices. A Gucci key chain may actually cost as much to manufacture as one available at Walmart, but the Gucci customer is willing to pay much more for the name. Table 8.1 compares factors that influence pricing with those that are influenced by pricing.

Referring back to the research conducted in Chapter 3 is important. Without understanding what customers perceive as valuable, it is almost impossible to set a price they will be willing to pay. Other factors that influence pricing decisions include:

» **Sales volume**—Large retail companies can offer products at a lower price because of a larger sales volume and the resulting product discounts. For many smaller businesses, price may not be an effective basis for competing.

» **Revenue from sales**—Pricing affects total revenue projected by the business. An increase in price can

TABLE 8.1
COMPARISON OF FACTORS THAT INFLUENCE PRICING WITH THOSE FACTORS THAT ARE INFLUENCED BY PRICING

FACTORS THAT INFLUENCE PRICING	FACTORS INFLUENCED BY PRICING
Cost of goods	Sales volume
Demand for product/service	Sales revenue
Competition	Market share
Market pricing	Competitive advantage
Customer perceptions	Company image
Margin standards	Profitability

SOURCE: Ewing Marion Kauffman Foundation. FastTrac NewVenture. Kansas City, MO: 2005.

reduce volume, thereby reducing revenue. Effective pricing can increase revenue and profit.

»   **Market share**—Sometimes, lower price points enable the entrepreneur to capture higher market share. However, consideration is to be given to the position the business wants to hold against the competition—high-end, exclusive, and so on.

As shown in FIGURE 8.2, recently more and more high-end designers, such as Vera Wang, are introducing **diffusion labels** (secondary lines) to increase market share. These designers are offering less expensive labels and distributing those labels through discount stores, such as Target and Kohl's.

Various strategies may be used in establishing price. As today's consumers become more price conscious, fashion retail entrepreneurs have been forced to take a hard look at their pricing strategies. They have begun to focus on the value of their products and services. Advertising and promotion strategies have been changed to relate the value of the product or service to the consumer. Common among retailers are strategies such as the following:

»   **Markup**—The amount added to the cost of the product to establish the selling price. It may be determined by the type of merchandise sold; services provided by the retailer, such as free alterations; how often the product sells; and the amount of profit the entrepreneur wants to make. The markup can be expressed in terms of dollars and cents or as a percentage of cost or selling price. It is commonly expressed as a percentage of the retail price. Markup is discussed in detail in Chapter 10.

»   **Competitive pricing**—A strategy in which a retailer bases its prices on those of the competitors. It is important in this type of pricing to base figures on stores comparable in size and merchandise. Larger stores often buy in large volume, enabling them to have a lower cost-per-unit price. Retail prices may be set either above or below the competition.

To price below the competition often requires the business to increase its sales volume and reduce costs. As a result, inventory needs to turn over at a faster rate, making a close monitoring of the inventory essential. The entrepreneur will want to be aware that pricing below the competition can bring about price wars. Competitors can cut prices too, leaving both businesses to find alternative ways to generate profit.

Pricing above the competition is possible when considerations other than price are important to

FIGURE 8.2
Vera Wang offers SimplyVera, a low-priced diffusion line, through Kohl's department stores.

the buyer. Retailers carrying exclusive merchandise or brand names not available in other, nearby stores may be able to price above the competition. Ed Hardy, Prada, and Louis Vuitton are examples of retailers that are able to price at higher price levels because of the exclusivity and prestige of their merchandise assortments. Boutiques offering exceptional customer service can sometimes price higher than other stores as well.

» **Premium pricing**—Pricing merchandise at the top of the relevant price range. This may be viewed as the technique that can be offered by retailers selling a product that is new to the market or that is targeted to an elite group of buyers not sensitive to price. The product is marketed to be perceived as top quality and must project a prestigious image. The higher price enables high promotional costs to be recovered quickly.

» **Penetration pricing**—Pricing a product at a low price point to introduce the product to a market and promoting that product heavily, with the hope that consumers will buy the product, try it, and then purchase more of the same. Penetration pricing can be an effective pricing strategy for building sales quickly and establishing the brand.

» **Value-based pricing**—A pricing method based on the perceived worth of the good or service to the intended customer. The price is not based on the actual cost of the product, market price, historical pricing, or competitors' pricing. The goal is to align the price with the perceived value. The entrepreneur must, therefore, have an understanding of how customers measure value.

» **Price skimming**—A pricing strategy in which entrepreneurs set a relatively higher price for a product or service initially, then lower the price over time. Entrepreneurs can take advantage of early demand for a new product or the latest fashion and the lack of competition. In this situation, customers will pay anything to have the product now rather than later. As competition increases,

the price will reduce as other businesses try to achieve a competitive advantage by lowering their prices.

PROMOTION

Promotion involves the activities used to inform the potential consumer about the product. The more a business can incorporate advertising, publicity, sales promotion, and personal selling, the more likely these activities will be effective. Advertising goes only so far. Publicity, a form of promotion, can play a role in creating visibility but is not as effective if it is used as a stand-alone method. Promotions may drive customers intermittently but will require ongoing time and investment. Personal selling and sales promotion can necessitate additional resources. Each method, therefore, has its own advantages and challenges.

Technology has had an impact on the way businesses promote products and services. The Internet provides a way to reach and target a large customer base without large expense. Web sites can show the product or service, take orders using secured transaction protection, offer customer support, and deliver the product or service to the customer.

Advertising and promotions require capital. Because start-up and early-stage companies are usually working on a tight budget, entrepreneurs must be creative in the avenues they use to get the message out. Retailers use promotional efforts, such as personal selling, window displays (FIGURE 8.3), product labeling and packaging, and store signage as ways of promoting the product. At times, press releases or publicity is used to reach the market, especially during the start-up phase.

ADVERTISING

Advertising is paid, nonpersonal communication delivered through mass media. Businesses send messages in their promotional strategies and advertising campaigns. In addition to reaching and motivating targeted consumers, the advertising message positions the company relative to the competition. In other words, the

FIGURE 8.3

Entrepreneurs have a window of opportunity in which to capture consumers' attention and draw them into the store. A great window display can be an effective form of promotion.

company will emphasize particular attributes or target how the consumer feels about him- or herself.

For example, Victoria's Secret sells self-image. Print and television advertisements using supermodels dressed in sexy lingerie imply that buying Victoria's Secret lingerie will make the consumer feel sexy and look attractive.

Advertising can be expensive. Because of this, it is important to identify avenues that reach the specific target market. Advertising is most effective when considering how the target market receives its messages and where. For example, a customer seeking children's clothing will not do so in a magazine targeted to male high-end fashion consumers.

Print advertising includes newspapers, magazines, flyers, direct mail inserts, and the Internet. Other forms of advertising include television and radio. Table 8.2 outlines the various forms of media and presents both the advantages and disadvantages of each.

PUBLICITY

Publicity is "free advertising," in which the media publishes stories about the business at no cost. Publicity is a viable option for start-up businesses or for those introducing a new product or service.

To raise the potential of a story being accepted, the entrepreneur should be prepared to present an interesting angle about the uniqueness of the business. The media will seek stories that are timely and interesting to a large segment of their market. In 2006 Sara Wilson profiled Stacey Pecor, the highly successful founder of Olive and Bette's Company, Inc., for *Entrepreneur* magazine (FIGURE 8.4):

> Her father, a serial entrepreneur, taught her to think big while her mother, the owner of a small clothing store in Burlington, Vermont, exposed her to the world of fashion. "I can remember going to my first fashion boutique," recalls Pecor. "The noise and the sounds and the lights and the color and the people . . . it was very glamorous to experience something like that."
>
> In 1991 Pecor introduced her own dazzling creation: Olive and Bette's Co., Inc. . . . Pecor's goal was to bring the latest styles to fashion-starved women in Vermont. After succeeding there, she expanded Olive and Bette's to New York City's Upper West Side in 1995, becoming one of the first to bring trendy clothing to that neighborhood. To stay cutting-edge, she continually shops the market from coast to coast, securing top designers like Theory along the way. She has since opened three more locations in New York City, carefully choosing high-traffic places that attract a variety of consumers ranging from teenagers and stroller moms to Julia Roberts and Sarah Jessica Parker. Pecor, who has received mentions in *Life & Style* and *Newsweek*, plans to open more stores in the city and expand her existing website.[7]

Entrepreneurs will from time to time submit press releases to local and regional media venues. A **press release** is editorial copy that can be used by media representatives to promote an event or a newsworthy item. For example, a local fashion retailer hosts an event to raise money for a nonprofit organization

TABLE 8.2
ADVANTAGES AND DISADVANTAGES OF VARIOUS MEDIA

MEDIUM	ADVANTAGES	DISADVANTAGES
Newspapers	» Reach a large audience » Fit various budgets, depending on the size and frequency of ads » Have short deadlines that make placing or changing ads easy » Offer special feature sections and articles	» Short life span of ads » Uncertainty that the target audience will see ads placed for a specific date » Clutter of other ads
Magazines	» Reach a more specific audience based on well-defined geographic, demographic, or lifestyle variables » Have a longer life and more exposure, because readers look through them more than once » Provide superior production quality » Offer unsold spaces at deeper discounts » Provide extra services, such as reader response cards, which allow building a mailing list » Delay fee collection until ad appears in print	» Long lead time between placement and printing » Higher costs for production and placement » Fewer options for ad sizes and formatting
Television	» Reaches a large number of people in a short time » Conveys messages using visuals, language, sound, and motion » Offers the option of spot ads in one market with one station or cable television advertising	» High costs » Short exposure » Need multiple exposures to be effective » Competition from national and larger companies
Infomercials (cable television show)	» Demonstrate the product or service » Reach large population bases; high sales can result	» Up-front expenses, such as setting up a toll-free number and purchasing television time, before generating sales
Radio	» May reach a larger audience than print or television » Allows targeting of a very narrow segment of the market by advertising during a specific time block or program » Offers cheaper rates and shorter deadlines than print advertising	» No visual impact on the target market » Branding more difficult » Less time to convey messages » Repeat exposure for ads to be effective
Internet	» Can reach a global audience » Allows targeted messages to certain interest groups through search engine optimization or pay-per-click » Provides links from the ads directly to an online site for ordering; potentially minimal time lapse between message and result	» Must compete with lots of clutter » Up-front expenses for designing and placing an ad before sales are generated » Links can be ignored
Direct mail	» Reaches a targeted list of customers » Response rate can be tracked » The recipient will be focused on one advertisement	» Higher cost » Can be perceived as junk mail

SOURCE: Adapted from Ewing Marion Kauffman Foundation. FastTrac NewVenture. Kansas City, MO: 2005.

dedicated to increasing literacy among children. The retail business receives significant media coverage for the upcoming event, and customer traffic increases as a result of the press.

PROMOTIONAL STRATEGIES

Promotions offer fashion retailers an opportunity to stay in front of their customers time and time again. Common promotions include coupons, sales, and trunk shows for specific designers. The effectiveness of promotions depends on the ability to promote the products or services to the same customers over and over again. Promotions are intended to create interest or to serve as a referral source for new customers.

The following series of questions will help the entrepreneur determine the most effective means to reach the target market:

» Where and when can you get across your marketing messages to your target market?

» Will you reach your audience by advertising in the press, or on TV, or radio, or on billboards? By using direct marketing mailshot? Through PR? On the Internet?

» When is the best time to promote? Is there seasonality in the market? Are there any wider environmental issues that suggest or dictate the timing of your market launch, or the timing of subsequent promotions?

» How do your competitors do their promotions? And how does that influence your choice of promotional activity?[8]

WEB SITES

Web sites have become standard and are often expected by customers. The Web site can serve as an online retail store, a means of communicating information about the business, or the hardest working salesperson in the company. With access by the market 24/7, the Web site works to build the brand and customer list, while promoting the business. The look and feel of the Web site should be consistent with the brand image.

FIGURE 8.4

The home page for Pecor's entrepreneurial venture, Olive and Bette's, not only invites visitors to review the latest arrivals, but also provides timely info on relevant and interesting events.

Following are questions to consider when developing a Web site:

» What is the purpose of the Web site? To generate leads? Serve as a brochure? Or serve as an online retail store?

» Who is the target audience?

» How will the customer find the Web site? With more than four billion sites, it is unlikely a customer will find the site by chance. Offline strategies, such as advertising, can drive traffic, as can search engine optimization, which is typically left to someone with experience in positioning Web sites.

» What does the customer expect to find at my site? The ability to purchase? Pricing? Location?

» What can be done to cause customers to linger longer at the site?

» How does the Web site of the competition compare? Just as brick-and-mortar stores compete for customers, so do Web sites. How are they designed? What are the messages?

» How will the Web site be monitored? A good Web site will host will provide a set of statistics that disclose number of visitors, when they visited, and how they found the site.

NETWORKING

Never underestimate the power of networking. **Networking** can be defined as "the ability to connect with a broad range of contacts for the purpose of sharing useful information and resources."[9] Networking has always played a significant role in the entrepreneur's ability to build and grow a business. It costs very little and is one of the most effective avenues for penetrating a market. Business networks have always served many purposes: generating sales and leads, accruing marketing knowledge, exchanging ideas, and recruiting employees.

A network may include colleagues, buyers, suppliers, friends, family, owners of businesses, and acquaintances. Online networks can be an effective piece of the overall marketing strategy. Networking through social networks provides an opportunity to participate in discussion forums, blog, and reach hundreds of thousands of people. It may also offer a venue for testing marketing concepts or receiving feedback on the product or service. The landscape for social tools, services, and networks is rapidly evolving. With this will come the chance to be create new ways of networking and staying in touch with customers. Some would argue that staying in touch through online conversations will be critical for competing in the future.

FIGURE 8.5, created by Brian Solis and Jesse Thomas, is a graphic charting the online conversations between the people that populate communities as well as the networks that connect the social Web. This representation of social media will evolve as services and conversation channels emerge, fuse, and dissipate.

Entrepreneurs build lists of contacts. They contemplate ways in which both parties benefit from the connection. Not only do they seek input *from* others, but they also become known as a resource *to* others. They are very clear about their intent, articulating what they are looking for and how others can help.

Fashion entrepreneurs can build a network of contacts to help start and grow the business through mentors; fashion incubators; fashion clusters, such as the Garment District in New York; and the Internet.

THE ADVERTISING BUDGET

To build sales, the business must be advertised. Consumers have to know that the business exists before they can buy anything. Advertising takes money, however, and often start-up businesses have limited advertising budgets. Therefore, careful consideration should be given to how much to include in the advertising budget, where ads are placed, and how effective those ads may be in getting the word out about the business and its products. The entrepreneur should determine the type and amount of advertising necessary to get the message out. Various methods exist for determining the advertising budget. Not all methods work for

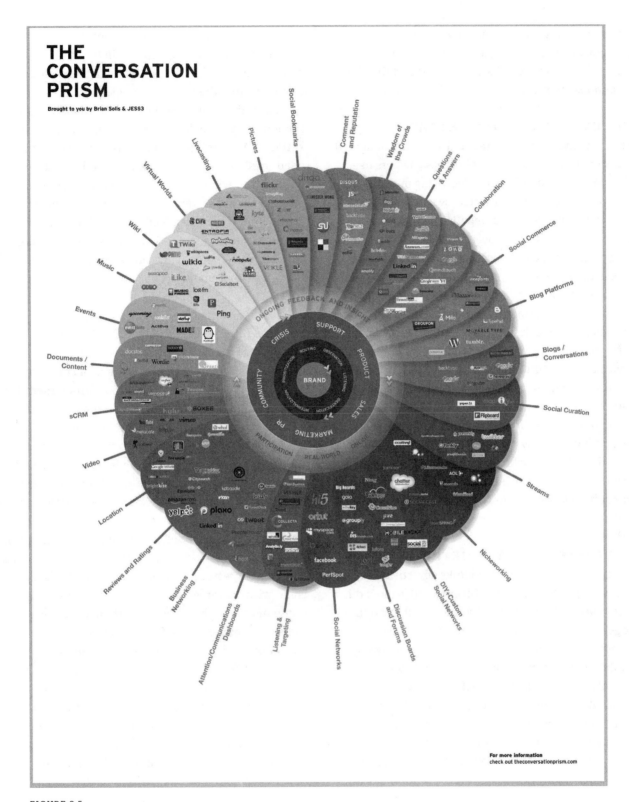

FIGURE 8.5

The conversation prism.

all businesses. Two methods are primarily used to establish advertising budgets for fashion retail businesses: the percentage of sales method and the objective and task method.

PERCENTAGE OF SALES METHOD

In the **percentage of sales method**, costs are budgeted as a percentage of sales. Most business owners use this method to establish the advertising budget. The exact percentage can be affected by competitive factors and the marketing strategy. Using the percentage of sales method avoids problems that can result from using profits as the base because sales tend to fluctuate less than profits.

Sales can be based on past sales, estimated future sales, or both. Determining the typical ratio of advertising expense to sales for a particular industry can be found through Census Bureau and Internal Revenue Service reports, Dun & Bradstreet, and the *Annual Statement Studies* by Robert Morris Associates. Industry averages are just that—averages. Because each business and market is different, it may be necessary at times to increase advertising to bring more customers in the door. Also, a fashion retail business may carry seasonal merchandise. If the business primarily offers swimsuits, a larger amount of advertising money may be allocated just before the swimwear season hits.

OBJECTIVE AND TASK METHOD

The objective and task method links advertising expenditures to specific objectives. This method is more difficult to use but is the most accurate. To establish the budget using this method, a coordinated marketing strategy based on a thorough survey of the markets and their potential must be established. Advertising expenditures are linked to specific objectives. Costs are calculated after establishing what must be done in order to meet objectives. For example, the entrepreneur of a children's wear store wants to attract mothers of small children to the new brick-and-mortar store. The entrepreneur must determine which media channels will best reach this target market. The entrepreneur will want to estimate how much it will cost to run the number and types of advertisement for each media choice

needed to generate the opening month's sales. Next, the media alternatives are compared in terms of cost and reach for the target market. The costs are totaled and calculated into the projected budget.

After the budget has been established, the entrepreneur must be able adjust to changes in the marketplace. A planning calendar will help ensure that deadlines are met and will help keep the advertising budget on track. The shorter the budget period, the more likely the entrepreneur will spot a problem early, giving him or her more flexibility to change tactics.

Regardless of method, the results must be prepared and evaluated. This can serve as useful information for further planning.

PEOPLE: EXCEPTIONAL CUSTOMER SERVICE

Promotion alone will not generate all a company's sales. Customer service is an important element for most successful retail operations. Poor customer service can put a fashion retail store out of business quickly. In this age of information, in which we communicate by e-mail, the Internet, Facebook, LinkedIn, and Twitter, face-to-face interaction is all but obsolete. It is vital that we do not lose touch with our most valuable assets: our customers. A typical business hears from only a very small percentage of its unhappy customers; most just go away and never come back. Despite this, an individual who is dissatisfied with customer service is much more likely to relate his or her dissatisfaction than a satisfied customer is to express satisfaction. Good customer service makes a difference in customer retention.

One of the ways small businesses can differentiate from each other and compete with larger companies is by providing exceptional customer service (FIGURE 8.6). Effective customer service helps smaller businesses attract and maintain a loyal customer base. Working closely with customers to build lasting relationships is important in retaining lifelong customers.

Nordstrom is committed to exceptional customer service. It implements a culture of motivated, empowered employees, each with an entrepreneurial spirit.

FIGURE 8.6

Good entrepreneurs never leave their customers hanging.

Nordstrom expects sales associates to do all they can to make sure a shopper leaves the store a satisfied customer. The Web site includes a live chat room, which allows customers to communicate online, in real time, with personal shoppers. Nordstrom has a hassle-free return policy, a postage-paid mailing envelope included with each order that allows customers to return merchandise with ease. (Returns may also be made at all Nordstrom stores.)

Successful retailers recognize the importance of providing customer service beyond customer expectations. As today's culture becomes less personal, a focus on individualized attention by the business can set it apart from the competition. Personalized attention includes calling the customer by name and providing a friendly smile. Customers sense when salespeople truly want to help them—or not. A company can improve customer satisfaction by paying attention to the following:

» **Give a good first impression**—Individuals decide within minutes of meeting someone for the first time whether they want to continue the relationship. More important, this decision usually lasts a lifetime. If customer interaction is poor, the customer will not forget it.

» **Listen to the customer**—Businesses use a variety of techniques, such as customer survey, focus groups, comment cards, and one-on-one conversations, to find out what the customer wants. Listening to each customer each time he or she visits the store is essential in building customer satisfaction. Everyone wants to be heard.

» **Hire a good sales force**—In a highly competitive market, fashion retail businesses rely on a sales team that is friendly, courteous, and customer-oriented.

» **Make service a core value**—Employees must know what is expected of them in situations related to customer service. It is the responsibility of management to embed the importance of customer service as a core value.

» **Empower employees to offer great customer service**—Has a customer ever walked into a retail operation to exchange an item, only to find that the salesperson has to ask management if she or he has the authority to do the exchange? The employee is the point of contact between the retailer and the customer. Customers will be more likely to leave satisfied and return to purchase more merchandise if the salesperson can offer superior customer service.

» **Provide a customer training program for employees**—Often, employees do not arrive on the job knowing how to handle customers. Many companies will allocate time for training on operations, but little time and money training employees to provide good customer service.

Entrepreneurs must make it a point to work on attracting, training, and retaining a sales force that will provide quality customer service. Often, when asked, customers will state they decided to buy from a particular fashion retailer because of the reputation of the company, the level of customer service and support, the manner in which the retailer responded to complaints and requests, and the relationship they have with the individual salesperson.

The value of a customer is tied to what entrepreneurs refer to as the bottom line. In other words, the value of a customer has a monetary value, in addition to other variables. Box 8.2 offers a formula to determine the lifetime value of a customer.

CREATING AND COMMUNICATING THE BRAND

Branding is the sum of all the associations, feelings, beliefs, attitudes, and perceptions customers have with a company. The American Marketing Association defines a brand as "a name, term, design, symbol, or any other feature that identifies one seller's good or service as distinct from those of other sellers."[10]

Iconic fashion names such as Louis Vuitton, Nike, and Gucci have brands that are recognizable and unmistakable. The brand is reflected in the name, logo (color, font, taglines), trademarks, trade dress, and service of a business. When a brand has been established, good or bad, it is difficult to change the way customers view the business; it is not, however, impossible. Walmart recently changed its logo and issued a statement that locations would update store logos as part of an ongoing evolution of its overall brand.

FIGURE 8.7 shows Walmart's old and new logos. "This update to the logo is simply a reflection of the refresh taking place inside our stores and our renewed sense of purpose to help people save money so they can live better."[11]

Branding is not an easy process but has significant consequences if not well thought out. Following are some tips on creating a brand:

» **Develop a vision for the brand**—What does the business aspire to be? The vision should focus on a longer-term perspective. Brands take time to become recognized in the marketplace. The more solid the brand vision, the greater the likelihood the customer will understand and relate to that vision.

» **Position the brand in relationship to the competition**—The brand should serve to differentiate the business from the competition. Brands carry

FIGURE 8.7

The old Walmart logo featured on a sign in Loveland, Colorado (left), and the new Walmart logo displayed in the Toronto suburb of Oakville, Ontario (right).

with them a number of images and associations in the minds of the consumer. Successful brands have a particular focus that separates them from their competitors.

» **Create a personality**—Each brand has a distinct personality. Some take on a more comical approach, whereas others lend themselves to a more serious product or service. For example, Chanel conveys sophistication, luxury, glamour, and beauty. The more emotion a brand can evoke, the more memorable it will be in the minds of consumers.

» **Articulate the benefits**—The brand represents a set of benefits and value to the customer, from emotion to positioning.

» **Define the values the brand represents**—The brand represents a defined set of values established by the entrepreneur. Clearly defining the business's values can create long-term customers.

When established, the message of the brand is then conveyed through its marketing materials, logo, business cards, brochures, flyers, Web site, and so on.

CONCLUSION

Developing a marketing strategy, as well as constructing and implementing a marketing plan, is key to the successful penetration of the market. Analyzing the marketing mix includes an examination of the interrelationship of product, price, placement, and promotion in a cohesive marketing plan.

Setting the price of the product or service can help define and differentiate the marketing strategy and play a crucial role in the success of the business. Regarding promotion, several media options exist for getting the message to the target market about the product or service. It is important to recognize that not all forms of media work for all businesses. Determining the target market, selecting the right medium, and identifying promotional goals will help the business reach and penetrate the market.

Effective customer service is a significant part of the marketing plan. Poor customer service will drive away customers; good customer service will keep them coming back. Finally, the brand communicates the image of the business. It is the reason consumers will choose to buy one company's product over another.

KEY TERMS

advertising

channel of distribution

competitive pricing

diffusion labels

marketing mix

markup

networking

penetration pricing

percentage of sales method

position

premium pricing

press release

price ceiling

price floor

price range

price skimming

profit

promotion

Ps of marketing (marketing mix)

publicity

value-based pricing

wheel of retailing

DISCUSSION TOPICS

1. Evaluate the five Ps of marketing and why they are important to a company's marketing strategy.

2. Discuss pricing. What does price mean to customers, and how does it impact their decision to buy or not to buy?

3. Discuss the implications of pricing a product too high or too low.

4. Outline the advantages and disadvantages of the various advertising media.

5. Discuss the importance of customer service. What constitutes good or valuable customer service?

SUGGESTED READINGS

Levinson, Jay, and Jeannie Levinson. *Startup Guide to Guerrilla Marketing: A Simple Battle Plan for First-Time Marketers*. Newburgh, NY: Entrepreneur Press, 2007.

Belch, George, and Michael Belch. *Advertising and Promotion: An Integrated Marketing Communications Perspective*. New York: McGraw-Hill, 2004.

Pink, Daniel H. *A Whole New Mind*. New York: Riverhead Books, 2006.

Niagle, Thomas T., and Reed K. Holden. *The Strategy and Tactics of Pricing: A Guide to Profitable Decision Making*. 3d ed. Upper Saddle River, NJ: Prentice-Hall, 2002.

Lindstrom, Martin. *Brand Sense*. New York: Free Press, 2005.

Sosinsky, Barrie. *Networking Bible*. Indianapolis, IN: Wiley, 2009.

ONLINE RESOURCES

ABOUT.COM
http://www.marketing.about.com
Articles related to pricing strategies, marketing strategies, and related topics.

CENTER FOR BUSINESS PLANNING
http://www.businessplans.org/Market.html
Offers a template and rationale for a market penetration strategy.

HOOVER'S
http://www.hoovers.com
Comprehensive information on companies from around the globe. Requires a subscription.

MARKETING POWER, AMERICAN MARKETING ASSOCIATION
http://www.marketingpower.com
Marketing and advertising articles, tips, and more.

BUSINESS PLAN CONNECTION
THINKING LIKE AN ENTREPRENEUR

A number of venues exist for reaching the intended market, from direct mail, to promotional activities, to social media, to advertising. What is important is knowing your budget for reaching the market; how the market receives it messages—when, where, and how; and what the message needs to convey to have the greatest impact on sales. Contact a retailer in your area, and ask about its marketing mix: product, place, promotion, and price. How did the combination of these elements help the company penetrate the market?

Collect as much information as you can on the prices of goods and services that would be considered your competition. Although the ability to compete is not based on price alone, this will tell you how the competition values its products or services. Remember, pricing is based on cost as well. The business must at least break even—that is, revenue (the amount of money the company takes in) must be exactly equal to costs—in order to survive.

Now, place yourself in the shoes of the buyer—the consumer who will consider purchasing the good or service from your business. Assume you want to purchase a line of beauty products. How do the sources of these products advertise? In what venues? What kind of promotion is used? What messages do they send to get you, the consumer, to buy? Does the company have a Web site? Use this information to draft the methods that will be used to penetrate your market. Remember to keep in mind frequency—how many times can you place the ad or offer a promotion? Consumers need to hear a message more than once.

Next, visit a number of stores, both in your area and on the Web. What is the level of customer service? How do the sales associates make you feel when you walk in the door? Are they attentive? Have they recognized that you are actually in the store? The quality of customer service can make or break a retail operation. Take note of what works well and what does not. What is happening all around you? Are there too few associates?

Use Table 8.3 to begin to identify the costs associated with marketing your business. This information will be used to build your financial plan. This activity relates to marketing the business rather than getting the merchandise ready to sell.

Be sure to include costs for promotions, such as a grand opening mailing, trade shows, and so on.

Advertising	Venue	
	Frequency (weekly, monthly, quarterly)	
	Cost	$
Promotion	Venue	
	Frequency (weekly, monthly, quarterly)	
	Cost	$
Publicity	Venue	
	Frequency (weekly, monthly, quarterly)	
	Cost	$
Web site	Venue	
	Frequency (weekly, monthly, quarterly)	
	Cost	$

ASSIGNMENT 8.1
MARKETING PLAN (PRICING AND MARKET PENETRATION)

1. Open your saved business plan template.
2. Address the following sections of the marketing plan. You may also refer to the sample business plan in Appendix D.

PRICING
» Pricing Strategy
» Price List
» Pricing Policies

MARKET PENETRATION
» Brand Strategy
» Advertising and Promotion
» Sales Strategy
» Publicity
» Promotional Efforts
» Evaluating Marketing Efforts

PROFILE OF AN ENTREPRENEUR
LAUREN LUKE'S MAKEUP TUTORIALS
LEAD TO A NEW LINE OF WORK

LAUREN Luke would often experiment with her mom's Avon products to give herself a little extra confidence. She eventually started selling makeup brushes, eye shadows and the like on eBay.

Her eBay clients had bombarded her with questions about how to use her products, and because showing is easier than telling, in 2007 she began to upload unedited, not-rehearsed, real-woman-giving-it-a-go makeup application tutorials under the name panacea81, signing off with her trademark "zoom zoom"— what it sounds like, she says, when characters in the Sims games say goodbye.

Her word-of-mouth fan base grew, and with more than five million channel views logged, she launched her own makeup line, By Lauren Luke, in April.

"She is totally funny, and she's real and riveting and so honest," explains Linda Wells, *Allure* editor in chief, of Luke's popularity, "It's that voice of every woman looking in the mirror and fantasizing what they can do with makeup. She demonstrates it step-by-step and makes you think you can do it, too."

Luke has a small-screen presence akin to Julia Child or Rachael Ray, Wells says. "Her language is hilarious. It's a real person speaking."

The demand for Luke is only increasing. She started a beauty column for the *Guardian* newspaper in January, has a book coming out and will be a beauty-advising avatar in a Nintendo DS game. And how did Anomaly and Zorbit, her makeup-line business partners, first contact her? Through Facebook.

"I was in my own bedroom having my own fun," Luke says by phone when asked about her sudden popularity. "It was when I started getting contacted by press and media. . . . It's not until people start contacting you that you realize it's a big deal."

Luke's first detailed video demonstrated how you too could get the smoky eye look with cocoa colors and sparkly eye shadow. She's also made a name for herself with interpretations of celebrity styles. Her take on singer Leona Lewis' green, heavily lined cat eyes from Lewis' "Bleeding Love" video could be considered Luke's breakthrough video, as it now has more than 2.6 million views. But her favorite, she says, is an ode to the 1980s punk scene, using what she says were "lilac purple with plummy purple and blue colors. That's when I went completely out there, crazy experimental."

In case you couldn't tell, the warm, perky Brit has a thing for color (the first makeup she bought herself was turquoise MAC eye shadow). And it shows in her makeup line. Her five palettes—with names including Vintage Glams, Sultry Blues and Luscious Greens— each have a primer, blush, black eyeliner, two lipsticks, and three eye shadows in dramatic shades.

They're available now online at Bylaurenluke.com, but Luke closed a deal to have them on Sephora.com and in Sephora's Times Square flagship.

Luke hasn't been working in a vacuum. Just as she'd respond to viewers' comments and e-mails about her videos, she involved fans in shaping the line.

"I take comments off of YouTube," she says. "When I first started this, I asked people what they would like to see in a palette. I keep taking feedback off of people. That's the good thing about it—people can tell me what they want and I'll see if it's doable." For Luke, this is a way of giving back.

"I know it sounds silly, but I really don't have many friends in real life," says Luke. "When I go on YouTube, I feel like I've got friends even though I've never met them."

We doubt that will be the case for long.

Zoom zoom.

SOURCE: Friedlander, Whitney. "Lauren Luke's Makeup Tutorials Lead to a New Line of Work." *Los Angeles Times*, May 17, 2009. http://articles.latimes.com/2009/may/17/image/ig-beauty17

CHAPTER 9
BUILDING A TEAM
TO DRIVE SUCCESS

OBJECTIVES

» Identify the key roles needed to build the management team.

» Develop a plan to hire key employees and the management team.

» Explore options for employee and management compensation.

THIS chapter focuses on the importance of the management team and the key elements needed to complete the management plan section of the business plan. Leadership styles and company structure are significant components of management. Recruiting, hiring, training, and motivating employees are key activities that play roles in business management. This chapter also examines compensation for management and employees as well as contracts that protect both the employer and employee.

THE MANAGEMENT TEAM

Managing a fashion retail business involves planning, organizing, controlling, directing, and communicating. Managers of entrepreneurial companies experience a variety of issues on a daily basis and, subsequently, need the right team to make it all happen. They set the tone for the culture of the company.

Creating a team ensures that the functions of a business, such as sales, finance, marketing, and operations, will be handled on a daily basis. It is unlikely that one person will be competent in all aspects of the business or have the time to fulfill all the daily functions. Power lies in recognizing the strengths and weaknesses of each member of the team and in bringing people on board, either as employees or an advisory team, to compensate for limitations.

It is the decision of the entrepreneur to manage the business alone or hire managers to relieve some of the day-to-day functions and help better position the business. During the start-up phase, most fashion entrepreneurs struggle to find the cash to bring in a management team. Therefore, it is helpful to identify the functions necessary to grow the business and then determine when those tasks should be completed and the persons needed to perform them.

From the funders' perspective, they would rather see an entrepreneur with a first-rate management team and a second-rate product than one with a second-rate management team and a first-rate product—the premise being that a good management team can turn the product or concept around. It is not unusual in the fashion industry for a successful CEO to be recruited by a competitor.

Establishing that the management skills are in place is critical to the business and the plan. The management section of the business plan outlines key personnel and describes the contribution each member of the team will make. In addition, it indicates where weaknesses exist and how the management team will compensate for those weaknesses. The management team section will clearly define job descriptions and include an organizational chart showing to whom each member of the team reports. It must also address any contracts between the company and its employees. The remainder of this chapter focuses on key issues related to developing an effective team.

Before determining job positions within the company and who will be hired for those positions, it is important to establish the culture of the company. **Organizational culture,** sometimes referred to as company culture, is the personality of the business—its attitudes, values, and communication style.

BUILDING AN ORGANIZATIONAL CULTURE

Organizational culture dictates the way things are done in a particular company. It is defined by its management and embodied by the employees. In it there is a system of shared characteristics that is valued within the organization. To be successful in creating an organizational culture that supports the goals of the company, entrepreneurs must establish the core values and ensure that they are carried out on a day-to-day basis. For example, Halls Kansas City values customer service above all else; it is dedicated to providing personal attention to every customer. The recent president of Halls, seeing a customer walk in the door with clothes to be altered in hand, insisted on helping the customer even though sales associates were nearby (but not at the door). Here, the president is leading by example.

Hiring and maintaining quality workers often requires creating an environment in which they want to stay. This has much to do with the culture of the organization. The fashion retail industry lends itself to offering a fun, creative, and well-liked culture. Companies, across industries, have begun to embrace such concepts as casual dress, virtual teams, and flexible work schedules. Companies that have been successful in creating an employee-friendly and relaxed culture tend to rely on certain principles, which include:

» **Balance**—Respect for a healthy balance between work and life. Companies create an environment that is fun and respectful of employees' lives away from work.

» **Direction**—A sense of purpose that makes employees feel connected to the company's mission.

» **Valuing diversity**—Companies not only accept cultural diversity, but also embrace and celebrate it. They seek out workers with different backgrounds.

» **Honesty, transparency, and integrity**—Employees pride themselves on working for a company that is ethical and socially responsible. They expect the company to communicate openly and honestly about issues that are of importance to them.

» **Participative management style**—This style encourages employees at all levels of the organization to be trusted and empowered to make decisions and to take the actions necessary to get the job done. Employee input is valued.

» **Empowerment**—Encouragement of lifelong learning among the employees.[1]

LEADERSHIP

Effective entrepreneurial managers need to be especially skillful at building teamwork and consensus, managing conflict, balancing multiple viewpoints and demands, and motivating employees. Entrepreneurs must recognize the importance of keeping up with innovation and anticipating changing environments and markets and respond quickly to these shifts. Entrepreneurial managers often thrive in a chaotic environment and enjoy the challenge of keeping their team motivated and committed. The effective entrepreneur remains calm and possesses the confidence to turn adversity into opportunity.

According to the management theorist and teacher Peter Drucker, "The only definition of a *leader* is someone who has *followers*."[2] Many definitions of leadership exist. Leadership can be defined as the ability to create an environment in which others feel empowered to work together to achieve a common goal. Entrepreneurs must learn to be effective leaders if they are to take a company forward and help it grow.

As our culture changes, the skills needed to lead will change. In an entrepreneurial culture certain leadership skills are required to elicit certain behaviors. Entrepreneurs must deal with the challenges of rapidly changing markets, innovation by technology, and starting and growing a company.

Most employees are no longer interested in simply following a set of rules and focusing on one task. Today's generation is driven by the desire to be a part of the company. Today's workforce is more skilled and knowledgeable than those in the past.

Jeffry Timmons, known as a pioneer in the area of entrepreneurship, in his book *New Venture Creation: Entrepreneurship for the 21st Century*, discusses the interpersonal/team work skills, or entrepreneurial influence skills, needed by managers/leaders. These skills involve the ability to create, through management, a climate and spirit conducive to high performance, including pressing for performance while rewarding work well done and encouraging innovation, initiative, and calculated risk taking. It is the ability to understand the relationships among tasks and between the leader and followers. And the ability to lead in those situations where it is appropriate, including a willingness to actively manage, supervise, and control activities of others through directions, suggestions, and the like.[3]

Timmons goes on to expand on these interpersonal skills:

» **Leadership/vision/influence**—These managers are skillful in creating clarity out of confusion, vagueness, and uncertainty. They are able to define who has what responsibility and authority. They do this in a way that builds motivation and commitment to cross-departmental and corporate goals, not just parochial interest. This is not perceived by other managers as an effort to jealously carve out and guard personal turf and prerogatives. Rather, it is seen as a genuine effort to clarify roles, tasks, and responsibilities, and to make sure there is accountability and appropriate approvals. This does not work unless the managers are seen as willing to relinquish their priorities and power in the interest of an overall goal. It requires skill in making sure the appropriate people are included in setting cross-functional or cross-departmental goals and in making decisions. When things do not go as smoothly as was planned, the most effective managers work them through to an agreement.

» **Helping/coaching and conflict management**—The most effective managers are very creative and skillful in handling conflicts, generating consensus decisions, and sharing their power and information. They are able to get people to open up, instead of clamming up; they get problems out on the table, and they do not become defensive when others disagree with their views. They seem to know that high-quality decisions require a rapid flow of information in all directions and that knowledge, competence, logic, and evidence need to prevail over official status or formal rank in the organization.

» **Teamwork and people management**—Another form of entrepreneurial influence has to do with encouraging creativity and innovation and with taking calculated risks. Simply stated, entrepreneurial managers build confidence by encouraging innovation and calculated risk taking, rather than by punishing or criticizing whatever is less than perfect. They breed independent, entrepreneurial thinking by expecting and encouraging others to find and correct their own errors and to solve their own problems. They are perceived by their peers and other managers as accessible and willing to help when needed, and they provide the necessary resources to enable others to do the job.

» **The capacity to generate trust**—The most effective managers are perceived as trustworthy; they behave in ways that create trust. How do they do this? For one thing, they are straightforward: They do what they say they are going to do. They are open and spontaneous, rather than guarded and cautious with each word. They are perceived as being honest and direct. These entrepreneurial managers have a reputation for getting results.[4]

Management and leadership are not the same, although they are intertwined, and both are essential to the success of the business. **Leadership** deals with guiding and motivating people (FIGURE 9.1). **Management** is concerned more about logistics and meeting requirements.

Good leaders know that real leadership is earned. They recognize that they are only as successful as their employees. The business environment has changed over the years. Effective leadership is challenging. Employees must be inspired to achieve success; telling them to succeed is not sufficient. Effective leadership is based on hiring the right employees, training those employees, building a culture that promotes teamwork, and motivating employees to achieve a higher level of performance and good communication skills.

EFFECTIVE COMMUNICATION

In the business plan the ability to communicate effectively can mean the difference between a successful business and one that struggles. **Communication** is the process of transferring information and ideas from one person to another, with consistent understanding of meaning. To make a business successful, leaders must effectively communicate the beliefs and principles of the business—its vision. They must ensure that all employees understand the mission of the company and how to carry it out. Good written and oral communication skills are essential when it comes to employees, customers, and vendors, and when presenting the business plan internally and externally to others. Body language is also important (FIGURE 9.2).

Communication may not always be effective. Often, employees fail to perform tasks or duties not

FIGURE 9.1

Effective entrepreneurial leaders build trust, encourage ideas, and are open to new and different approaches to business.

FIGURE 9.2

Communication works both ways, and body language is just as important as verbal communication.

BOX 9.1
COMPARING VERBAL COMMUNICATION WITH NONVERBAL COMMUNICATION

VERBAL CONSIDERATIONS IN COMMUNICATING WITH OTHERS:

» Tone of voice

» Words chosen

» Speed at which the message is communicated

NONVERBAL CONSIDERATIONS IN COMMUNICATING WITH OTHERS:

» Body language

» Visual appearance

» Physical touch

» The distance one stands from another

» Posture

» Gestures

» Facial expressions

---

out of lack of motivation, but out of a lack of understanding about what to do or how to do it. In these instances, the problem lies in communication between manager and employee. To perform the tasks, employees must hear and comprehend what they are being requested to do. They must also recognize that they have the authority to complete the task. They require feedback on their performance.

Barriers to communication can occur in both verbal and nonverbal communication methods. **Verbal communication** relates to what is said or written. **Nonverbal communication** relates to how one acts. It consists of gestures, expressions, body language, and tone of voice. Because messages are interpreted, they are not always received as they are intended. Both managers and employees must overcome verbal and nonverbal barriers in order to communicate effectively and leave a good impression on customers. Box 9.1 compares verbal forms of communication with non-

verbal forms. Box 9.2 provides a list of obstacles to communication.

TECHNOLOGY AND COMMUNICATION

The options for methods of communication have expanded over the years. Computers and technology, including e-mail, have revolutionized the way we exchange information. With the various forms of communication available now, one must be aware of more than just verbal and nonverbal communication. To become a more effective communicator and overcome the barriers of communication, entrepreneurs must focus on clarifying their ideas. They must consider the implications of their written communication. They must also assess the environment in which the communication occurs. Effective communicators stop and think about what is being written or said and how it may be interpreted. They also encourage feedback from communication recipients.

BOX 9.2
OBSTACLES TO COMMUNICATION

» **Insufficient knowledge of the topic**—The lack of sufficient knowledge of a topic by either sender or receiver will create a communication barrier. For example, in the business plan, the use of language or acronyms specific to the fashion industry will do the readers no good if they are not familiar with the field. If the sender knows the language, but the reader does not, a barrier in communication will result.

» **Ambiguity**—The same words can have different meanings to different people. For example, the business plan may include the following sentence: "We will carry high-end fashion merchandise." "High-end" will mean different things to different people. Instead, the business plan may include the statement, "We will carry fashions produced by Donna Karan," giving the reader a better idea of the merchandise.

» **Selective listening**—Often, people hear only what they want to hear. The receivers in the communication process selectively hear based on their experience, needs, motivations, background, and other personal characteristics.

» **Inability to be honest**—To a degree, people need to be given permission to say what they really mean and know that there will be no negative consequences for such openness. If the entrepreneur asks for honest feedback and then punishes the sender, the resulting environment will not be a culture where everyone tells the truth. The truth is important when starting a business. Managers need to know what employees and customers are feeling and thinking.

» **Distractions**—The lack of ability to concentrate on the message being sent will create a barrier to effective communication. People can be distracted in a number of ways. Someone trying to meet a deadline will not want to be interrupted to deal with another matter. By interrupting, the sender will not have the full attention of the receiver.

» **Communication via written documents, particularly e-mail**—Although effective in terms of getting the message out quickly, written communication can lead to misunderstandings. Often, people are in a hurry to get the message out and do not consider how it may be interpreted. Without the help of nonverbal communication, the message may be interpreted differently from what was intended. Written documents must be explicit to make up for the lack of nonverbal communication to reinforce the message.

» **Thought structure**—When the one conveying the message has not given sufficient thought to what he or she wants to say and how best to say it, given the audience, then miscommunication occurs. In short, if the one conveying the message has not planned questions and in some cases practiced delivery, then the *listener* is left to decipher and find meaning in what the speaker is trying to say. The speaker must first be clear in his or her own mind before sharing thoughts.

» **Timing**—All messages have the right and perfect time to be delivered. A great message can be delivered too late to be effective. Therefore, one must ask oneself, "Is the timing right to deliver this message?" Will it have its greatest impact now or a week from now?

» **One must be clear as to who needs to receive what communication**—Often, selective hearing takes place because a message is being delivered to the wrong address. Make sure messages are targeted to the correct audience for them to be received, remembered, and acted upon.

SOURCE: K. Saunders, personal communication, 2010.

MOTIVATING EMPLOYEES

To motivate employees, one must first understand what inspires or encourages them. Money is not the only motivator. In the context of the business world, **motivation** is defined as "the internal and external factors that stimulate desire and energy in people to be continually interested in and committed to a job, role, or subject, and to exert persistent effort in attaining a goal."[5] Employees often start a job highly motivated (FIGURE 9.3). Keeping them that way is difficult

FIGURE 9.3

Motivated employees become strong contributors to the business. They are productive, energetic, and filled with enthusiasm.

and challenging, but important. Motivated employees on staff reduce turnover and increase productivity. Motivated employees have positive morale that results in satisfied, well-served customers.

One of the ways in which employers can motivate employees is through empowerment. Employees are more motivated to make decisions and meet company objectives if they are given the freedom, responsibility, and authority to do so. Employees bring with them an array of skills, talents, and knowledge that they are ready to put to use. If business owners empower employees to draw on their talents and creativity, employees will feel challenged to use these attributes. To empower employees successfully, business owners must have the confidence to give their employees the authority and responsibility to grow in their jobs, be willing to step back and let the employees do the job,

trust that they can handle the empowerments, and acknowledge them for their contribution.

In addition to empowerment, employees can be motivated by other factors. Employees need feedback. Defining and then assessing measurable goals is one way of providing feedback. The entrepreneur has the performance of the company to measure as well. By linking employee performance to the overall goals of the company, the entrepreneur can measure employees' performance against the progress of the company. Two factors improve the bottom line: increasing revenue and decreasing expenses. One way to increase revenue is to increase the customer base through effective sales personnel.

One of the more common ways in which employers provide feedback to employees is through the use of performance appraisals. The **performance appraisal** measures an employee's actual performance against the performance desired. Performance appraisals should be designed to provide the employee with measurable outcomes, to link the job description to the employee's performance, and to incorporate the goals of the employee. Employees are not always motivated solely by money. Today's generation is interested in being a part of a company. If designed and used properly, a performance appraisal can give employees feedback on how well they are performing in the company, which in turn can provide a source of motivation. It also provides the business owner and employee with the opportunity to set goals and create a plan for improving performance as well as a basis for rewarding employees for good performance. It is important to review an employee's performance more than once a year. By frequently visiting the performance appraisal, the employee has the opportunity to correct and improve performance. The performance evaluation process, if done properly and often, can be a great motivational tool. A sample performance appraisal is shown in FIGURE 9.4.

ORGANIZATIONAL STRUCTURE

Organizational structure is the way in which the organization defines job tasks, how these tasks are divided

EXECUTIVE PERFORMANCE EVALUATION
BUYER/MANAGER

NAME

SPRING   FALL

○ 1 - Unacceptable   ○ 2 - Marginal   ○ 3 - Good   ○ 4 - Very Good   ○ 5 - Outstanding

MERCHANDISE RESPONSIBILITY	1	2	3	4	5
1. Initiates plans/actions to optimize sales.	○	○	○	○	○
2. Understands the importance of floor presentation by proper classification, color, or trend.	○	○	○	○	○
3. Understands the components of coordinated merchandise presentation by proper arrangement/assortment.	○	○	○	○	○
4. Understands the importance of proper stock levels relative to the business.	○	○	○	○	○
5. Sees that stock is filled in, labelled accurately as to price and size, counted per schedule, and is neat and accessible.	○	○	○	○	○
6. Department records are kept up to date correctly (turnover, etc.).	○	○	○	○	○
7. Plans actions and recommendations for assigned classification, which reflect an understanding of the department's current potential, trends, seasonal needs, and past experience.	○	○	○	○	○

MERCHANDISE KNOWLEDGE	1	2	3	4	5
1. Understands the merchandise budget.	○	○	○	○	○
2. Understands merchandising reports/information and effectively utilizes them.	○	○	○	○	○
3. Understands the flow of paperwork and related systems.	○	○	○	○	○
4. Able to project and forecast in a concise and precise manner (rates of sale, reorders, etc.).	○	○	○	○	○

LEADERSHIP RESPONSIBILITY	1	2	3	4	5
1. Constantly apprises and informs sales staff of merchandise selection and trends.	○	○	○	○	○
2. Is flexible and can adapt to the changing needs of the business within the context of the departments' goals and objectives.	○	○	○	○	○
3. Is well informed of the merchandise situations (on hand, on order, stock conditions); the action of the competition; department problems and recommended solutions.	○	○	○	○	○
4. Informs store owner about sales objectives (through communication, store visits, etc.).	○	○	○	○	○
5. Interacts well and deals effectively with store personnel.	○	○	○	○	○
6. Takes constructive criticism well and tries to correct shortcomings.	○	○	○	○	○
7. Is well motivated and a self-starter.	○	○	○	○	○
8. Maintains high standards for self and department.	○	○	○	○	○

PLANNING AND ORGANIZATION	1	2	3	4	5
1. Is well organized and apportions time constructively and wisely.	○	○	○	○	○
2. Meets deadlines and schedules.	○	○	○	○	○
3. Reacts to the changing needs of the business by taking actions which reflect a basic understanding of priorities.	○	○	○	○	○
4. Learns quickly and effectively.	○	○	○	○	○

FIGURE 9.4

ACCOMPLISHMENTS

What specific measurable results has this individual accomplished in the appraisal period (sales growth, profit):

OBJECTIVES

What specific business objectives are to be achieved by the next evaluation period:

FUTURE GROWTH AND DEVELOPMENT

What ideas and thoughts do you have for this individual's professional development:

OVERALL EVALUATION	1	2	3	4	5
Performance as a manager	○	○	○	○	○
Performance as a buyer	○	○	○	○	○
Potential for merit increase	○	○	○	○	○

DISCUSSED WITH ASSISTANT BUYER:

Signature   Date

Owner's Signature   Salary Action

SOURCE: M Granger, Case Studies in Merchandising Apparel & Soft Goods (New York, New York: Fairchild Publication, 1996), p. 261.

and grouped, and how they are coordinated. The organizational structure will determine how employees interact with one another and will influence employee attitudes toward their jobs and other employees. When structure is used to clarify what is to be done, how it is to be done, and who is to do it, attitudes and relationships among employees will improve.

The way the organization is structured often depends on its size. A one-person entrepreneurial company will have a different organizational structure from a company with twenty employees. Many fashion retail businesses operate with a manager, or assistant manager, or both, and sales associates. Each employee has a different role and is assigned different tasks, but all work together as a team.

DETERMINING KEY ROLES AND TASKS

Typically, a fashion retail business cannot be run by only one person. A single individual cannot usually fill all the roles and handle all the duties required to make the business successful. It takes a team of sales associates and management to ensure that all tasks have been completed.

Funders reviewing business plans recognize the importance of designating responsibilities. They will go over the business plan to ensure that the entrepreneur is aware of the roles employees must play and the tasks they must perform to make the company successful. FIGURE 9.5 gives an example of a divisional breakdown of job responsibilities for a retail operation.

The first step in the management planning process is to evaluate the tasks that will need to be accomplished. This is referred to as a job analysis. A **job analysis** gathers information about the duties and activities necessary to perform a job. The data obtained are used to develop a description for each position. Although job analysis is typically used in larger companies, it can be very beneficial to the small entrepreneurial company as well.

The first step in performing a job analysis is to determine the tasks required for each job. Data about the jobs or tasks needed by a start-up company may be obtained from managers, supervisors, and employees of similar operations. A number of methods may be used to collect these data. Some of the more common methods include interviews, questionnaires, observation, and diaries.

Interviews may be conducted with employees and managers to acquire information regarding the duties involved in doing the job. Questionnaires may be distributed to gather data regarding the skills, education level, level of experience, and task requirements needed to fulfill the job. Another method of obtaining information, observation, can prove very effective. It allows the job analyst to learn about the jobs by watching and recording the activities of the jobholders. With the final method of diaries, jobholders are asked to keep a journal detailing their work activities.

A job analysis defines in detail the requirements of the job. It goes beyond the specific tasks involved in the job to include a description of the conditions or environment in which the employees will work. For example, employment in the fashion retail industry requires working nights and weekends. It is not enough for the job description to state, "Must be available to work five days per week," while saying nothing about working on the weekends. Some people may not be able to work weekends. By conducting a thorough analysis, entrepreneurs can do a better job of screening potential applicants, and applicants can make more informed decisions about working for that company. FIGURE 9.6 shows a sample job analysis.

After a job analysis is completed, the entrepreneur can begin the process of creating job descriptions. The **job description** outlines the duties and responsibilities of the position, based on the job analysis. The job description will provide information needed to set skill requirements, physical demands, experience, education, knowledge, and abilities needed to perform the job. The job description also defines the working conditions of the position and whom workers report to in the organization. The job description should clearly state what is expected of the person who will fill the position.

CREATING JOB DESCRIPTIONS

The job description is beneficial to both employee and manager. With a job description, employees know

BREAKDOWN OF JOB RESPONSIBILITIES FOR A RETAIL OPERATION

DIVISION	RESPONSIBILITIES
Merchandising	• Merchandise development, selection, pricing, and selling • Controlling inventory (joint responsibility with Operations) • Sets merchandising policies: quality standards, price ranges, fashion leadership position, exclusivity The **Merchandising Division** is the only division that generates income for the store.
Control	• Payroll • Expense planning and control • Credit office • Internal auditing • Accounts payable • Inventory monitoring and reconciliation • Statistical: generates purchase journal The **Control Division** initiates and monitors all areas covering finance and general accounting within the store.
Promotion	• Advertising, copy, and layout • Catalog, radio, television • Display: interior and windows • Store design and décor • Public relations/Special events The **Promotion Division** works closely with the **Merchandising Division** to generate customer traffic and a favorable store image.

(CONTINUED)

FIGURE 9.5

DIVISION	RESPONSIBILITIES
Human Resources	• Training • Employee selection and development • Rating and reviews • Termination • Job analysis • Benefits The **Human Resources Division** *recruits, develops, evaluates, and manages the store's personnel.*
Store Operations	• Customer service—sales, service desk • Telephone and mail order • Warehouse • Restaurants • Receiving and marking • General operations activities: security, housekeeping, delivery, alterations The **Store Operations Division** *provides general support services, internally and externally, that allow the store to function.* The **Branch Store Division** *operates as a microcosm of the other divisions—solely for branch store locations.* *Within each branch are offices for* **Advertising, Operations, Personnel,** *and* **Control**. *Branch department managers perform the operational and merchandising functions.*

SOURCE: Granger, Michele M. Case Studies in Merchandising Apparel and Soft Goods. New York: Fairchild Publications, 1996.

A JOB ANALYSIS FOR A BUYER/MANAGER

	D	W	M	O
1. Plan and monitor sales, inventory, and purchase budgets.	○	○	○	○
2. Project merchandise trends that will be preferred by target market.	○	○	○	○
3. Work with vendors on merchandise selections, to include reorders, timely delivery, purchase discounts, and exclusive stock.	○	○	○	○
	○	○	○	○
4. Write purchase orders and monitors deliveries of goods on time.	○	○	○	○
5. Manage time efficiently to balance management and buying duties.	○	○	○	○
6. Educate sales staff on merchandise assortment (e.g., trends, vendors, and items).	○	○	○	○
7. Organize and process all paperwork to include payroll, merchandise receipts and sales, markdowns, and orders.	○	○	○	○
	○	○	○	○
8. Install displays of merchandise with sales associates.	○	○	○	○
9. Motivate and review sales personnel.	○	○	○	○
10. Travel to markets in Dallas and New York.	○	○	○	○
11. Process all paperwork required to order merchandise.	○	○	○	○
12. Develop schedules for personnel.	○	○	○	○
13. Oversee receiving division for timely transfer of goods to sales floor.	○	○	○	○
14. Collaborate with store owner on personnel and merchandise performance.	○	○	○	○
15. Model high standards of motivation, team work, and flexibility.	○	○	○	○
16. Work nights and weekends, as needed.	○	○	○	○
17. Must be able to handle multiple tasks.	○	○	○	○

D = Daily   W = Weekly   M = Monthly   O = Other

FIGURE 9.6

what is expected of them. They recognize what their goals are and how to achieve them. To management, job descriptions provide a basis for evaluation. If the duties of the job are not performed by the employee, management has a basis for taking corrective action. Employees know how they must perform to be considered for promotion or rewards of other kinds.

Developing job descriptions should be done before applicant interviews begin. A job description typically includes the job title, to whom the employee will report, a brief statement regarding the major job duties, and any specific skills needed to fulfill the requirements of the job. Flexibility within a job description is necessary in smaller firms, in which employees typically act as part of a team. Flexibility allows the manager to assign additional duties to employees to accomplish the goals of the company. Small companies may be too concerned with being specific in the job description and, therefore, may be limited in assigning different tasks to various employees. One way to avoid being too specific is to add a statement such as, "Other duties may be assigned."

Job descriptions should be reviewed and updated as the organization changes. No standard format exists for job descriptions. They vary in appearance and details from one company to another. FIGURE 9.7 outlines a job description that may be used for a fashion retail business.

When writing a job description for the potential employee, it is essential to use statements that can be clearly understood. Poorly written job descriptions will not provide enough guidance for the jobholder. As a

Job Title:	Retail Sales Associate
Wage Category:	Nonexempt
Supervisor:	Manager, Retail Sales

DESCRIPTION

Assists customers in the purchase of merchandise. Must be able to describe a product's features, demonstrate its use, and show various styles and colors. Must be outgoing, polite, friendly, and patient. Must be able to work under pressure.

TASKS AND DUTIES

- Displays clothing and fashion accessories
- Greets customers as they browse through clothing
- Advises customers on coordinating clothing and accessories
- Collects payment and wraps clothing purchases
- Keeps the store clean
- May handle customer complaints
- May keep account of inventory
- May help prepare the shop for special sales
- Opens and closes registers
- Is responsible for the contents of the register
- Handles exchanges of merchandise

QUALIFICATIONS

- High school diploma or an equivalent combination of education and experience from which comparable knowledge and abilities can be acquired.
- Two to three years' experience in retail sales preferable.

FIGURE 9.7

company grows, the duties of the employees typically change. Determining the tasks and roles required of the position will go a long way toward hiring the right person for the job.

Fashion retail sales associates perform many tasks. Many associates are required to complete sales checks, receive cash, process charge payments, package merchandise, install displays, and maintain sales records. They may be held responsible for the contents of their registers, the handling of merchandise returns or exchanges, and counting inventory. However, nonselling functions cannot stand in for good customer service. Consumers spend millions of dollars every day on merchandise and often evaluate a store by its employees. Entrepreneurs of fashion retail companies should look for people who enjoy working with others and have the patience to deal with difficult customers. A good associate provides excellent customer service.

CREATING THE ORGANIZATIONAL CHART

Designing the organizational structure involves designating the "power relationships" among owner, manager, and employees. The organizational structure is important to a business because the owner-manager cannot do all the tasks involved in making the business successful. Tasks, responsibility, and authority need to be articulated and delegated. The **organizational chart** defines how the business is organized and illustrates the relationships among the job positions. Management will want to assign individuals to positions that relate most directly to their skills and experience. FIGURE 9.8 is a sample organizational chart for a fashion retail business.

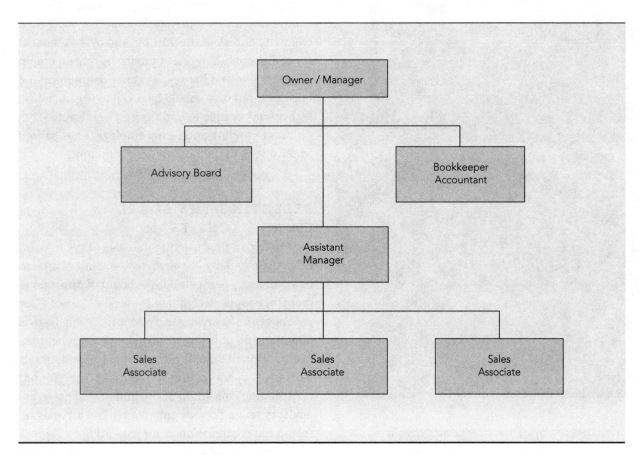

FIGURE 9.8
An organizational chart.

HIRING THE RIGHT EMPLOYEES

There are two qualifications to look for when hiring someone to join the team. The person must have the training and skills to do the job, and the person must have a track record that demonstrates his or her abilities. Good character and interpersonal skills are critical, particularly in the fashion industry (FIGURE 9.9). People are a company's most valuable asset; the quality of the personnel determines the success of the company. Entrepreneurial management means

FIGURE 9.9
Hiring the right employees means considering attitude, willingness to do a wide range of tasks, and skills and experience.

identifying the skills and knowledge needed for success in the business, recognizing what each employee does or does not know, and then compensating for shortcomings, either by hiring people to fill those voids or training or educating individuals to bring the skills and knowledge needed.

When the entrepreneur knows what to look for in an employee through the job analysis and job descriptions, the task of seeking the right person for the job can begin.

Business owners have a number of avenues available to them for hiring employees. Sources for recruitment include personal recruiting or networking, classified advertisements, employee referrals, and employment agencies. Fashion retail businesses are fortunate in that they can usually choose from a large pool of applicants. College students are always looking for part-time work; many look for an environment that promotes **intrapreneurship**, working within a company in an entrepreneurial capacity, using their creativity and skills. Recruiting employees often calls for using more than one approach. Hiring an employee requires time and money; it is an investment in the business, and care should be taken to use as many sources as possible to find the best employees. The process of finding and hiring employees has serious implications in the future of the company.

SELECTING THE BOARD OR ADVISORY TEAM

Depending on the structure or legal entity of the business, the company is overseen by a board of directors or an advisory team, or both. A **board of directors** is a group of people elected by the stockholders of a corporation who are responsible for overseeing its overall direction and policy. An individual entrepreneur will need a team of outside advisers, such as accountants, bankers, lawyers, insurance agents, and marketing consultants. This group of consultants is known as an **advisory team**. The advisory team plays an integral role in the organization, complementing entrepreneurial weaknesses. The team provides the entrepreneur with valuable input to aid in decision making, particularly in areas in which the entrepreneur has limited knowledge and expertise.

The advisers should be chosen in the early stages of the company, preferably before the business opens. They should be interviewed to determine whether they have the qualifications necessary to contribute to the success of the business. Just because someone holds a marketing degree does not necessarily mean that he or she is good at marketing. The entrepreneur may want to seek referrals from other entrepreneurs. Many professionals solicited to serve on an advisory board will do so with little or no compensation. The entrepreneur may consider providing benefits, such as in-store discounts, to replace monetary compensation for advisors' support.

Funders evaluating business plans will look for a solid advisory team to help drive the business to success. They recognize that entrepreneurs cannot do it all alone. They also recognize that most small companies do not have the capital available to hire a marketing team, a chief financial officer, and a human resources expert. Establishing an advisory team and indicating this in the business plan assure funders that a good foundation has been put in place. Advisory team members may include other entrepreneurs, Web developers, marketing specialists, and financial experts. Each would contribute to the business in a different way.

THE COMPENSATION PACKAGE

One of the challenges facing start-up and early-stage companies is the ability to hire and retain employees with a competitive compensation package. A **compensation package** is the monetary or other value an employee receives in exchange for services. Often, start-up and early-stage companies do not have the luxury of giving large bonuses or other monetary rewards to employees. Compensation packages can come in many forms. Recognition, respect, feedback, and job security are a few elements that can make up a compensation package. Entrepreneurs can be creative when it comes to rewarding employees. A resourceful entrepreneur will determine what motivates employees and what gives them a sense of reward.

Fashion retail stores often offer employees discounts on merchandise or commissions on sales to compensate for good performance. Other rewards may come in the form of tickets to a concert or dinner for two at a local restaurant. Some employees respond well to intangible rewards, such as balance between work and home life, challenges in the job, and an exciting organizational culture. Others may feel that compensation in the form of company stock is rewarding. Creative compensation packages may ensure the keeping of productive, long-term employees. Whatever the compensation package, the goal is to recognize what motivates employees and to reward them accordingly.

CONCLUSION

Management encompasses the processes of planning, organizing, controlling, directing, and communicating. Effective management is key to creating a successful venture. The business plan requires defining the management and the advisory team. Successful entrepreneurs know and admit to their weaknesses and then bring in people to compensate for their limitations in order to move the company forward.

Effective management necessitates effective leadership. Effective leaders have the ability to influence others to achieve a common goal. Effective leaders know how to create a vision for their company, build a team, respect their employees, and lead by example. They provide the tools necessary for employees to carry out their jobs and goals, and they give credit where credit is due.

The organizational culture will define the ways in which things are done within a company. With an effective company culture, employees and management share a set of values and behaviors that govern the organization. Policies such as open-book management can be explored to determine whether they fit with the organizational culture.

Effective communication is important to any organization and good leadership. In a business plan it can mean the difference between being funded or not. Effective communicators know their topic, say what they mean, listen, and give others their complete attention. Creating an intrapreneurial environment is another consideration of an organization. Intrapreneurship invites an entrepreneurial spirit among employees in an organization.

Defining the organizational structure—job tasks, how they are divided and grouped, and how they are coordinated—affects the management of the company. Knowing how to develop job descriptions and writing them before potential employees are interviewed, conducting background checks, and recruiting the right employees are invaluable to a start-up or an early-stage company. Performing a job analysis and creating job specifications help both employer and employee know what is expected of them. Hiring the right employees and motivating them is key to the success of any venture.

KEY TERMS

advisory team

board of directors

communication

compensation package

intrapreneurship

job analysis

job description

leadership

management

motivation

onverbal communication

organizational chart

organizational culture

organizational structure

participative management style

performance appraisal

verbal communication

DISCUSSION TOPICS

1. Assess the significance of the management team, and determine the key roles to drive the business to success.

2. Explain the similarities and differences between intrapreneurs and entrepreneurs.

3. Identify ways of finding the best management team candidates.

4. Discuss the importance of putting together a top-notch advisory team. Describe the *who, what, when, where,* and *how.*

5. Discuss ways of motivating employees.

SUGGESTED READINGS

Berman, Barry, and Joel R. Evans. *Retail Management: A Strategic Approach.* Upper Saddle River, NJ: Prentice Hall, 2009.

Covey, Stephen R. *Principle-Centered Leadership.* New York: Simon and Schuster, 1998.

Covey, Stephen R. *The 7 Habits of Highly Effective People.* New York: Simon and Schuster, 1998.

Perkins, P. S. *The Art and Science of Communication: Tools for Effective Communication in the Workplace.* Hoboken, NJ: John Wiley & Sons, 2008.

ONLINE RESOURCE

AMERICAN MANAGEMENT ASSOCIATION
http://www.amanet.org
Leader in management training and professional development

BUSINESS PLAN CONNECTION
THINKING LIKE AN ENTREPRENEUR

Management greatly influences the success of a business. A good management team can drive a mediocre product to success, whereas a not-so-good management team can drive a potentially good business into the ground.

Schedule an appointment with an entrepreneur who runs a business similar to the one in your business plan. Ask about his or her leadership style and what impact it has had on the company, good and bad. Be sure to ask the entrepreneur what traits and qualities he or she believes makes a great leader and contributes to successful management of a company. Maintain a file of this information. It will provide you with a list of qualities and traits that would be desirable for your particular business and help you identify roles needed to form a successful team.

Businesses comprise advisory teams made up of a number of people with varying backgrounds and experience. Ask several entrepreneurs or fashion retail managers which key people make up their team and in what ways they contribute most. Use this information to create your own list of preferred advisory team members.

Recruiting quality employees is extremely important to a fashion retail business, particularly in the start-up phase. Interview entrepreneurs to determine what methods and criteria they used to recruit quality employees.

Communication is everything, both verbal and nonverbal. Spend time at various businesses, and observe the communication styles of the employees. If possible, observe the clarity of processes, the understanding between the two parties, and the behaviors of each person involved in the "conversation." Use this information to then identify key ways in which communication is going to be critical to the success of your business and what processes might be put in place to ensure this happens.

⊙ ASSIGNMENT 9.1
THE MANAGEMENT PLAN

1. Open your saved business plan template.
2. Address the following sections of the management plan. You may use the sample business plan in Appendix D as an additional resource.

MANAGEMENT PLAN

» Business Structure
» Management Team
» Management Compensation
» Personnel Compensation
» Key Advisors/Directors
» Communication
» Governmental Approvals

PROFILE OF AN ENTREPRENEUR
CHARMING CHARLIE

FOUNDED in Houston, Texas, in 2004, Charming Charlie presents a unique retail concept that specializes in women's accessories. The stores, primarily located in malls, feature thousands of fashion jewelry pieces, a wide assortment of handbags, belts, scarves, and more—all merchandised by color, not category. The customer looking for accessories to accent a yellow dress? Visit the yellow section. And the concept must be working. Charming Charlie has nearly doubled the number of stores every year since inception and is currently the fastest growing retailer in the United States. The International Council of Shopping Centers (ICSC) named Charming Charlie the Hot Retailer of the Year in 2010.

Charlie Chanaratsopon, the CEO and founder of Charming Charlie's, received the Ernst & Young Entrepreneur of the Year 2010 Award in the retail category in Houston & Gulf Coast Area. The award recognizes outstanding entrepreneurs who are building and leading dynamic, growing businesses. Chanaratsopon, a commercial real estate professional, founded Charming Charlie in his hometown of Houston, Texas. Parlaying his graduate business school office hours into business consulting sessions, and his personal line of credit into funding, Chanaratsopon was able to manifest his retail vision into a reality when a tenant from one of his shopping centers backed out of the lease.

The concept was unique to the market, especially amid a sea of struggling apparel-based retailers. Chanaratsopon and team developed the women's accessory store concept in Houston and methodically tested different product mixes, visual merchandising schemes, and even fixtures. Chanaratsopon also found it key to listen to the consumer through customer surveys and analysis of sales trends. The end result was a combination of a fashion accessory experience,

value-oriented price points ($4.97 to $49.97), a broad selection, and a merchandising scheme based on color instead of category. Charming Charlie was positioned to be a complement to other retailers, creating a universal fit in most shopping centers and malls. In 2006 the company began its expansion across Texas; it now has stores in Alabama, Arizona, Arkansas, Florida, Georgia, Illinois, Kentucky, Louisiana, Maryland, Mississippi, Missouri, North Carolina, Ohio, Tennessee, Texas, and Virginia.

Charlie says that the key to his success has been strategically selecting his management team and keeping an open mind about improvements. Charlie aims to help customers as much as possible. Although the stores used to be organized by category, he changed them to be set up by color so that customers could easily find the right jewelry or handbag to go with a particular outfit. This created not only a unique sensory experience, but also a fun road map within the store.

The Charming Charlie store experience extends online as well, at the social Web level. The company keeps customers informed of what's happening in its stores through e-mail, Facebook, Twitter, YouTube, Flickr, and its accessories trends blog (www.charmingcharlie. com/blog), the Charm Chronicles. On a philanthropic level, Charming Charlie collaborates with Look Good . . . Feel Better, a nonprofit organization that helps women with cancer manage their treatment and recovery.

SOURCES: ICSC "Brands" Hot Retailers. Businesswire. http://www.businesswire. com/portal/site/home/permalink/?ndmViewId=news_view&newsId=2010052500 6350&newsLang=en
Charming Charlie. http://www.charmingcharlie.com
Full of Charm. Smart Business Online. http://www.sbnonline.com/Local/ Article/20119/73/0/Full_of_charm.aspx
Charming Charlie CEO and Founder Receives Ernst & Young Entrepreneur of the Year. NewsGuide.us. http://newsguide.us/index.php?path=/lifestyle/fashion/ Charming-Charlie-CEO-and-Founder-Receives-Ernst-Young-Entrepreneur-of- the-Year/

CHAPTER 10
PLANNING THE MERCHANDISE ASSORTMENT

OBJECTIVES

>> Understand the role of the merchandiser, or buyer, in the fashion retail business.

>> Identify how fashion goods differ from other product types.

>> Be aware of the functions of a resident buying office, or consulting service.

>> Recognize the internal and external sources from which the merchandiser can collect buying information.

>> Comprehend the merchandising calculations used in fashion buying.

>> Examine markup, markdown, and other pricing strategies.

>> Understand the differences in buying for store and non-store operations.

N the previous chapters the entrepreneur examined the prospective business from a company, or holistic, perspective. The market potential of the company, the product and its prospective customer, methods of entering the market niche that will service this customer, and strategies for finding a location for the company were explored in terms of the business as a whole. In this chapter the entrepreneur examines the business from an operational perspective, that of merchandising.

Merchandising is the buying and selling of goods. Merchandising is what separates a retail store with almost any product line from a fashion retail store. Fashion goods require unique policies and procedures in merchandising that other product classifications do not. The reasons for a specific focus on fashion merchandising are diverse; however, they are primarily the following: seasonality of goods, limitations and localization of resources, and diversity of product life cycles. For example, the retail fashion buyer, for the most part, purchases goods at regional apparel markets or through manufacturers' representatives. These resources determine when new goods are available through the introduction of new lines, usually in relation to seasonal changes. Often, it is the merchandise selection that generates success or failure for the fashion retail business. It is the retail buyer's responsibility to locate, secure, price, and promote the merchandise assortment. Whether the entrepreneur takes on the role of the buyer or assigns this role to someone else, it is one of the most significant jobs within the fashion business.

THE ROLE OF THE BUYER

The merchandise found in a fashion retail operation has been purchased either by the entrepreneur, a buyer who is employed by the company, or a resident buyer who represents the retailer. In large operations the buying tasks are performed by specialists who have acquired specific knowledge in preparation for the buying function. In small operations the buying function may be one of many carried out by the company's owner. Whatever the size of the business, it is the purchasing of fashion merchandise, more than any other product classification, that provides the greatest challenges. In nonfashion retail operations the goods are considered to be **staple items,** also referred to as **basic items;** this is merchandise that is in demand for extended periods of time and that is not subject to rapid style changes. In contrast, **fashion items** are frequently available in a wide range of styles and have a life expectancy that is relatively brief.

Buyers are the individuals who determine the merchandise needs of departments or sometimes entire stores and who, ultimately, make the purchases. The store buyer has a great number of responsibilities, including:

» seeking appropriate merchandise for target customers;

» purchasing and pricing the merchandise;

» assigning floor space to items or lines;

» selecting specific merchandise for visual presentation and promotion;

» managing or collaborating with personnel in various areas of the business, such as sales, receiving, accounts payable, advertising, and visual merchandising.

The most important task performed by the store buyer is selecting the right merchandise while staying within the budget. This responsibility encompasses determining which goods are needed, calculating the size of purchases, deciding from which vendors goods should be bought, recognizing when merchandise should be ordered for timely delivery, and negotiating the prices and terms of sale. From a planning perspective the buyer projects sales and inventory levels by month for each department and, subsequently, determines the amount of funding to be spent on inventory.

But even after the merchandise arrives at the store, the buyer's job is not over. For the retail operation to make a profit, buyers must determine at what prices goods should be marked. Several factors are considered before pricing decisions are made, such as the level of competition in the trading area, the speed of inventory turnover, the perishability of the merchandise, and the buyer's judgment of the value of the individual goods. In some retail organizations the manner in which merchandise is displayed on the selling floor and where it is actually placed are left to the buyer's discretion. Selecting merchandise for promotions is yet another determination that the buyer makes. In addition to determining what to promote, the buyer decides how to promote the merchandise. Decisions related to the products featured in window displays, newspaper or television advertisements, and fashion shows, as well as on the Web site, are frequently assigned to the retail buyer. Although buyers are not necessarily experts in the technical aspects of promotion, they are often considered the most knowledgeable in assessing which items should be featured to generate customer traffic.

THE RESIDENT BUYING OR CONSULTING OFFICE

Some entrepreneurs allocate funding to employ a resident buying office in order to gain support and assistance in buying and promotion. The **resident buying office,** also referred to as a **consulting service,** is a company that offers suggestions for merchandise suppliers and assists the entrepreneur or buyer, or both, by providing a significant number of services. Merchandise is generally not purchased by resident buyers, unless they have the company's authorization to do so. A resident buying office keeps the entrepreneur aware of occurrences in the marketplace, such as new vendors, fashion trends that are selling, reduced prices on merchandise, and so on. The resident buyer helps the buyer know what is going on in the market without the entrepreneur's ever having to leave the retail operation. Although these organizations provide a wide range of assistance to retail buyers, the primary function of the buying office is advisory. Some of the more typical services involve locating new resources, previewing collections, following up on orders that are to be shipped, communicating with buyers, preparing for market week visits, facilitating merchandise returns or markdown allowances, and analyzing market conditions. In the United States, buying offices are primarily located near the wholesale markets in New York City, Dallas, Los Angeles, Chicago, and Atlanta; many have branch operations abroad.

More recently, the buying office has become critically important to the fashion retailer in the area of private label merchandise. The entrepreneur of a start-up business may not be able to finance the purchase of a large quantity of goods, as required for most private label orders. Most manufacturers cannot, or simply will not, produce merchandise to specification without a substantial commitment in terms of units purchased. The buying office can be instrumental in providing this service for specialty retailers. It can develop the specifications for the merchandise, then create a label that offers exclusivity to its client fashion retailers. By combining the smaller orders of a number of these client stores, a large order can be placed with the manufacturer. This "combine and conquer" philosophy enables the entrepreneur of a specialty retail operation to have unique merchandise, exclusive to the trade area, at a reasonable cost and with acceptable profit margins.

Resident buying offices are owned and operated in a variety of ways. The majority of these companies are independent. As independents, they have no affiliation with any specific company or group of companies. Rather, they represent retailers who are willing to pay a fee for their services. Retailers contract with the independent resident buying office, guaranteeing a flat fee for its services, a percentage of the cost of the merchandise ordered by the resident buyers, or a percentage of the retailer's annual sales, or a combination of these. Another type of buying office is one that

is privately owned by the retailer. Such ownership is practical only for retailers that are very large operations and for which exclusive attention to their own needs is critical to the success of the business. Retailers such as JCPenney, Barneys, and Neiman Marcus operate their own buying offices. In addition to the assistance these offices provide to the companies' buyers, the buying office is primarily responsible for developing private label merchandise and reviewing foreign markets to secure exclusive merchandise for their own stores. In between independent and store-owned resident buying offices, the cooperative buying office represents a group of stores that operates under a corporate ownership.

One of the premiere retail consulting offices in the United States is The Doneger Group, of New York. The Doneger Group offers its retail clients a number of services, from creative to business; however, there are two directed to the merchandising division of retail stores, Henry Doneger Associates and the Consulting division. Henry Doneger Associates is a merchandising service that provides retailers with extensive advisory services, seasonal merchandising direction, and current business and market analysis in all classifications, sizes, and price levels for women's, men's, and children's apparel and accessories. The Consulting division provides its client stores with global industry expertise, including business analysis, merchandising information at retail and wholesale, trend and color forecasting, and product development direction. With this broad reference base, Doneger is able to identify growth opportunities and develop them expressly for clients' individual objectives in merchandising. Boxes 10.1 and 10.2 provide descriptions of the two types of services.

THE BUYING AND MERCHANDISE PROCESS

The buyer for a fashion retail operation seeks out information sources to help identify the wants and needs of the company's target market. Brand preferences, price ranges, sizing, and colors are among the topics the buyer will want to investigate.

BOX 10.1

THE DONEGER GROUP'S CONSULTING DIVISION SERVICES

>> **Lifestyle profiling:** Identification of lifestyle trends across categories; new concepts relating to consumer experiences; insight into style-related industries; and lateral markets.

>> **Industry analysis:** In-depth examination of specific industry segments; comprehensive retail reporting including merchandise assortment assessments; brand positioning; and growth opportunities.

>> **Custom color and trend research:** Individualized analysis of merchandise trends; color stories and delivery flow; presentation of relevant cultural influences; and consumer lifestyle profiling.

>> **Product line creation:** Development of seasonal color palettes; materials and style direction; identification of essential items and product opportunities; design and development including fabrications; and finishing details.

SOURCE: The Doneger Group, http://www.doneger.com/web/89357_102312.htm.

The entrepreneurs of fashion retail operations use a variety of sources within their own companies, in conjunction with numerous outside informational sources, to help them find key items and resources that will result in profits for their businesses. Both internal and external sources of information provide the buyer with data to purchase merchandise effectively.

INTERNAL SOURCES

Internal sources that the entrepreneur of an established business may investigate are past records, which are available most frequently through computer reports. These records may show merchandise performance by vendor, including markdowns, returns, and delivery performance. They may also illustrate unit and dollar sales by merchandise classification as well as profit margins. Retail software packages allow the entrepreneur to examine the success or failure rates of each vendor, style, color, price point, and size allocation.

For the new business, internal sources are limited. Past sales records, for example, are nonexistent.

As a result, the entrepreneur of a new operation may choose to develop questionnaires directed to potential customers, seeking information on merchandise preferences. In addition, the entrepreneur may choose to record observations. Exploring the merchandise assortments of competitive retailers and the buying patterns of customers of these retail operations can provide a great amount of insight on merchandise preferences. How many customers enter a competitor's store during a given period? How many of them exit with purchases? Which lines are carried? Which styles are featured in windows and on storefront fixtures? Which styles or vendors are heavily included on the markdown rack? Finally, the entrepreneur may decide to host meetings with employees or to implement a "want slip" program in an effort to gain information about what the customer will be looking for when the business opens and, later, when there are out-of-stock items the customer is seeking. With a want slip program the sales associate fills out a form indicating which items customers are looking for that

BOX 10.2
HENRY DONEGER ASSOCIATES MERCHANDISING SERVICES

Henry Doneger Associates (HDA) provides retailers with extensive advisory services, seasonal merchandising direction, and current business and market analysis in all classifications, sizes, and price levels for women's, men's, and children's apparel and accessories.

Our dedicated team of industry experts is fluent in all aspects of the buying and merchandising processes. Their daily market trips, extensive business networks, and up-to-the-minute knowledge of the retail and wholesale landscapes translate into actionable insight on merchandising concepts, resource information, and key-item and trend identification.

HDA market analysts target market intelligence to best serve the individual needs of each client, providing consultation throughout the season via one-on-one meetings, multimedia presentations, and frequent online updates.

A comprehensive Web presence communicates our market research and analysis to clients between markets and scheduled meetings. Clients supplement their interaction with HDA market analysts with its offering of market-by-market overviews, resource reviews, shopping recaps, and fashion direction from around the world.

Specialized divisions include the following:

» **Carol Hoffman** advises women's specialty retailers in the contemporary, better, bridge, and designer markets. The team reports on all classifications of sportswear, dresses, outerwear, suits, accessories, and intimate apparel.

» **HDA International** provides international retailers with market intelligence, merchandising consulting, sourcing, and product development opportunities from a range of U.S.-based manufacturers and importers.

» **Price Point Buying** uncovers off-price merchandise in women's, men's, and children's apparel and accessories, providing clients with outstanding buys enabling increased sales and profits.

---

are not available in stock. The sales associate then passes along these forms to the buyer, thereby communicating the customers' requests.

Employee feedback is an internal source that successful entrepreneurs often believe is of critical importance to the decision-making process for merchandise planning. Staff members can provide valuable information because of their close involvement with customers. What better resource is there than the sales associate when it comes to examining customer likes and dislikes? Although computer records can interpret the performance of merchandise that has been purchased, they fall short in terms of reporting customer requests that could not be satisfied. A particular designer line, a specific look or style, a hot color, or a significant price point are all merchandise assortment factors that may be described by sales associates and that are not reflected in a computer report. By involving the sales associate and management personnel in ways to improve sales and satisfy consumer needs, entrepreneurs and buyers accomplish two goals—they gain information that has come directly from the consumer, and they help create a team that is working on a common mission, a successful and thriving business, as illustrated in FIGURE 10.1.

EXTERNAL SOURCES

There are a number of external sources available to the entrepreneur. **External sources** are sources available outside the business, such as resident buying offices, fashion forecasters, trade publications, and reporting services on the Web and in print. These sources may be used to locate new vendors, compare merchandise performance, or identify fashion and consumer trends.

FIGURE 10.1

By involving sales associates and management personnel, the entrepreneur can build a team that is working on a common mission, satisfying the customer and creating a successful and thriving business.

FIGURE 10.2

The Worth Global Style Network.

Trend Union, Promostyl, and Worth Global Style Network (WGSN) are examples of fashion forecasters and reporting services used by fashion entrepreneurs (FIGURE 10.2).

Furthermore, the entrepreneur may study any of the many trade and consumer periodicals that focus on specific fashion industries to learn about future trends and consumer preferences. Most types of fashion merchandise are represented by a trade journal. *Women's Wear Daily*, *Accessories*, *Stores*, and *Footwear News* are some of the trade periodicals available to the entrepreneur. Consumer publications, such as *Vogue* and *Glamour*, also host seminars on seasonal trends and consumer directions for fashion retailers, as do fiber associations, such as Cotton, Inc.; The Woolmark Company; and the Mohair Council of America. Finally, the entrepreneur may seek trend and sales information from vendors, particularly during market weeks.

MARKET WEEK

There are traditional purchase periods, called **market weeks**, when buyers begin to make selections for the next season. During market weeks, buyers go to regional apparel markets to review new lines. The number of market weeks varies according to merchandise classification. Major apparel market weeks take place five to six times a year in New York City, Dallas, Chicago, Atlanta, and Los Angeles, among other major cities. Smaller regional markets are located throughout the United States, in such cities as Kansas City, St. Louis, Seattle, Boston, and Denver.

The **apparel mart** is a building or group of buildings that house showrooms in which sales representatives present apparel lines to retail buyers. Some marts are devoted entirely to apparel or gifts and home furnishings; others house showrooms for all these product types. The marts contain permanent showrooms for sales representatives and companies that elect to lease the space on a yearly basis. In addition, there are temporary booths in exhibition halls that the vendors can rent for each market week. Often, markets for men's, women's, and children's apparel are held during different weeks. The buyer can contact the market director of the apparel mart to obtain registration information, a calendar of market weeks, and a directory of vendors showing lines during the market weeks. The apparel marts also have Web sites that provide this information as well as dates of fashion shows, educational seminar schedules, and lists of special events that the buyer may want to attend. A number of these Web sites are listed under "Online Resources" at the end of this chapter.

How important are market weeks to the buyer? Market weeks allow the buyer to review a significant number of lines in a fairly short period of time. As a result, the buyer has the opportunity to comparison shop before actually ordering merchandise. The buyer can also locate new lines to purchase for the business. Moreover, by attending seminars held during market weeks, the buyer can acquire information about fashion trends, promotion and advertising, visual merchandising, and a number of other topics. Finally, the buyer can develop a network of support systems during market week. Positive working relationships with sales representatives can result in timely deliveries, advertising allowances, and merchandise adjustments. Mutual respect, trust, and cooperation between the buyer and the vendor are necessary to ensure long-term profitability for both parties.

Small, or start-up, businesses cannot overcome the edge that quantity purchasing power gives to the giants in fashion retailing (e.g., JCPenney, Macy's, Nordstrom). They can, however, improve their relative position by limiting their resources to a few key vendors and by building relationships with the sales representatives of these lines. **Key vendors** are lines carried in depth in a retail organization. These are the lines that the customer identifies with the retailer because of the broad style selection and large number of units. It is important, however, to strike a balance between developing key vendors and introducing new lines to the consumer. Herbert Seegel, the former president of R. H. Macy & Company, stated, "There is a certain synergy in having a combination of stars and rookies in a department's vendor mix."[1] Buyers can find them all during market week, new and old vendors, stars and rookies (FIGURE 10.3).

A second important network available to the buyer during market week is other buyers. Market week allows buyers to meet buyers from different geographic locations who may be purchasing for similar businesses. Because the businesses are noncompetitive, and the buyers face similar challenges, market week can be an ideal time to share successes and failures. Buyers of noncompetitive retail operations will often exchange the names of new vendors they have discovered, discuss lines with which they have had poor sales performance, and share insights on such topics as advertising, fashion trends, and travel bargains. Many of these buyers stay in touch between markets, using colleagues as sounding boards for new ideas and as sources of new information.

RESOURCE SELECTION

With a seemingly limitless number of available resources, domestic and foreign, for every merchandise classification, the buyer must evaluate those companies from which purchases were made in the past and investigate the possibility of adding other vendors to the business's list of suppliers. A **vendor analysis** that summarizes sales, markdowns, and returns for each manufacturer can guide buyers after the opening season. The buyer for a new store, however, will have to rely on his or her perception of who the target market is, what this customer will likely purchase, and which

FIGURE 10.3
Alternative Apparel at the FAME buyers' market.

lines will differentiate the business from the competition. In addition, minimum orders specified by the various vendors often determine whether the buyer can purchase a line. **Minimum orders** are the dollar or unit amount that a vendor requires before accepting an order. For example, some vendors require a minimum opening order of $1,000, or, perhaps, twenty units. Other vendors may impose a minimum order of six pieces per style, with a six-style requirement. There is no industry standard regarding minimum orders, and there are some vendors that have no minimum-order policy. The minimum order is, however, a common practice among fashion industry resources that buyers of small operations must consider.

If the minimum-order requirement does not eliminate a vendor for the buyer, then what factors should be considered in the selection of resources? Other variables include merchandise offered, distribution practices, promotional policies, shipping and inventory maintenance, cooperation, competitive pricing, and adherence to the purchase order as it was written. Primarily, a vendor is selected when the merchandise styling, brand name, level of quality, and price point blend to match the customer's preferences. A designer label or brand alone, however, does not guarantee success. Distribution practices play a significant role in merchandise desirability. **Distribution practices** are the manufacturer's policies concerning where a line is to be shipped. Few buyers want to carry the same merchandise that is found in a competitor's business.

Exclusivity, the limited availability of merchandise, is critical to specialty operations. In selecting vendors, the buyer should attempt to locate manufacturers that agree to limit sales of a particular style to a defined geographic area. Legislation makes this a difficult task, as manufacturers are not legally able to distribute merchandise at their discretion. If retailers have the appropriate credit credentials, they cannot be denied the right to purchase from a company. Vendors deal with this problem in a number of ways. They may institute a large minimum-order amount for initial seasonal purchases, thereby eliminating

retailers that are unable to meet this purchase requirement. Merchandise production may be limited so that orders are filled on a "first come, first serve" or seniority basis. Also, many vendors have initiated policies that restrict specific groups within the lines to certain retailers. These vendors will offer specific merchandise groups to retailers located in competitive trade areas. If two retailers are located in the same geographic location and target similar customers, each will have the opportunity to purchase a particular style grouping unavailable to the competition. With this option, retailers have some degree of exclusivity. The manufacturers are adhering to the law, as other merchants may still carry the line, but the retailers will not feature exactly the same style or colors.

Furthermore, manufacturers' representatives often do not call on more than one store in a locale. Unless the current account discontinues the line or reduces the amount of orders, the sales representative will not seek out competitive operations to sell the line. In other cases, the sales representative may simply let a retailer know that there is a merchant in the area already carrying the line. Many buyers will decide to pass on a line that is featured at a nearby retail operation. Finally, the sales representative may work with more than one account in a given area, with the agreement that each will carry different styles within the line.

Another factor to consider in vendor selection is the manufacturer's promotional policies. Frequently, retailers have periodic sales to entice clientele. During these sale periods, markdowns are offered in conjunction with **off-price merchandise**, goods that the buyer has been able to purchase from the manufacturer at below the wholesale price. Through combining markdown merchandise with off-price goods, the buyer is able to achieve a higher markup and, ultimately, higher profits. Similar to retailers, manufacturers need to reduce retail prices on merchandise that is slow to sell. Some manufacturers dispose of such goods through their own factory outlets or through sales to companies that deal exclusively in off-pricing retailing. Others have promotional policies that afford their regular retail accounts the opportunity to buy **closeout** merchandise, which usually includes merchandise that has been overproduced or returned by retailers, owing to a lack of sales or shipment past the cancellation dates specified on orders. Often, closeouts are available in the middle of the retailer's selling season, when the manufacturer is moving on to the next season. As a result, the buyer can bolster the inventory with fresh merchandise, and possibly generate additional sales, at lower wholesale costs. Buyers offering special sales events must make certain that a number of their vendors will provide merchandise closeouts to ensure a more profitable business.

Another facet of the manufacturer's promotional policy is the availability of **advertising allowances**, funding provided to retailers by manufacturers for advertisements featuring their products. In today's retail environment the cost of promoting the business is high. Many entrepreneurs find it extremely difficult to allocate the dollars necessary to advertise their businesses effectively. To add to the advertising budget, the buyer will negotiate with vendors for advertising allowances.

Cooperative advertising is a program in which the vendor shares the cost of advertising with the retail operations. The level of participation, dollar order requirements, and advertisement guidelines vary; however, the concept is fairly uniform among manufacturers. For example, a manufacturer may offer an advertising allowance based on five percent of the retail operation's total orders. If the buyer places orders for the year totaling $10,000 at cost, then the advertising allowance for the retail operation from this particular manufacturer is $500. According to this manufacturer's cooperative advertising plan, the retailer pays 50 percent of the cost of the advertisement, and the manufacturer pays the other half. The retailer may decide to run two newspaper advertisements at $500 each, or one at $1,000. The size of the advertisement, the media used, and the style featured are often left to the buyer's discretion. It is, however, common for the manufacturer to impose some requirements for the advertisement. These requirements vary greatly from vendor to vendor. As

an illustration, the manufacturer may state that its name and logo must be featured in the headline of the advertisement, that the advertisement will not include merchandise from another vendor, and that the cooperative advertising monies are to be used for full-price styles only, not off-price. An illustration of a cooperative advertising contract from an apparel manufacturer is shown in Box 10.3.

Other factors to consider in vendor selection are shipping and inventory maintenance. Some vendors ship merchandise in a timely manner but will only ship large orders. Others, with limited resources, have difficulty with anything but small orders, and even these may not be shipped on time. It is critical that the buyer select vendors that are eager and able to ship current orders and future reorders, both on time and as specified. The buyer will want to be certain that the merchandise will reach the retail operation on the specified delivery date, the cancellation date on the purchase order. The **cancellation date** (also referred to as the **completion date**) is the last day that the vendor is authorized to ship merchandise specified on a particular purchase order. The cancellation date is agreed upon by the buyer and the vendor at the time the order is placed. **Lead time**, the amount of time needed between placing an order and receiving the goods, is a crucial shipping factor. Speed of delivery for orders and reorders is of particular importance for fashion merchandise. The longer it takes for fashion goods to reach the retailer, the less time they will be available to the consumer during the selling period. The customer may go elsewhere to purchase the item. Speed of delivery also affects financing for the entrepreneurial company. Being able to order small shipments and then reorder more merchandise as needed reduces the risk of buying errors. In addition, speed of delivery and space limitations can go hand in hand. More and more retail operations are decreasing nonselling space to increase profits. They are eliminating excess office and storage space by changing it to selling space used to display merchandise. As a result, space is minimal for warehousing **backstock**, merchandise held off the sales floor until needed.

BOX 10.3
COOPERATIVE ADVERTISING AGREEMENT COOL GIRL ACTIVEWEAR, INC.

COOPERATIVE ADVERTISING PLAN

Because we recognize the value and importance of advertising as a mutually beneficial means of promoting increased sales of Cool Girl Activewear, Inc., we offer to all our valued customers the following cooperative advertising plan. This plan only covers first-quality branded net purchases and applies to all Cool Girl product lines. This plan is in effect until further notice for all ads run on or after May 1, 2012.

COOL GIRL AND CUSTOMER SHARES

Cool Girl will share 50 percent of the space cost in accredited media vehicles, based on a store's lowest earned rate, up to an amount not to exceed 5 percent of first-quality, branded net purchases at wholesale for each season.

CHARGES

Net cost is limited to your actual space cost only. This agreement shall not include the cost of special preparation, artwork, cuts, or any other advertising or production costs. We do not share in the cost of agency fees or special service charges. We will share in 50 percent of the cost of newspaper color change. We do not share in mechanical or production costs for color reproduction.

ENCLOSURE ADVERTISING

Each season, Cool Girl will make available print statement enclosures. Enclosures are to be ordered on the special forms provided by our advertising department. An adequate quantity of merchandise must be ordered to cover the number of enclosures requested. A fraction of the actual cost of enclosures, $16.00 per thousand, has been established, and this amount will be applied against the 5 percent Cool Girl cooperative advertising limit, as set forth in this agreement.

MEDIA

This plan covers newspaper advertising in all daily, weekly, and Sunday newspapers with recognized audited circulation and published rates. It does not cover souvenir programs, circulars, billboards, theater programs, or special editions.

We will participate in the cost of Internet, radio, and television advertising under the same terms outlined in this plan for newspaper advertising. A notarized affidavit from the advertising vehicle, itemizing specific time, location, and commercial, must accompany your invoice.

COPY REQUIREMENTS

a) The Cool Girl product logotype must appear prominently. The Cool Girl brand name must be as large as the largest type in the advertisement, exclusive of the store's own logotype. Company brand name must also appear in the heading or subheading because the use of the brand name in copy only will not meet requirements.

b) Competitive advertising cannot appear in the same advertisement with our brand. If the advertisement shows other merchandise, our portion must be separate and clearly defined. For newspaper and Internet, define the space either by a border around it or by a white space of not less than one-eighth of an inch.

PAYMENT

Claims (invoices) must be submitted within thirty (30) days of promotion's debut. An advertising credit memo will be issued for the Cool Girl share. No deductions are to be made for advertising prior to receiving our credit memo authorizing the amount deductible. Please submit bills (invoices) accompanied by tearsheets for each newspaper advertisement, and documentation of other types of advertising, to:

Cool Girl Co-op Advertising Department
Cool Girl Activewear, Inc.
640 Fifth Avenue
New York, NY 10019

We reserve the right to change or terminate this agreement at any time upon thirty (30) days' notice.

Another shipping concern that may be a determining factor in vendor selection is the vendor's adherence to the purchase order specifications. The buyer thoughtfully places a detailed purchase order that indicates style numbers, sizes, colors, delivery dates, and discount terms. The specifics of the order are based on the amount of money available for purchasing new merchandise and orders written for other manufacturers. Some vendors do not fill the order as it is written for a number of reasons. The vendor may not have the sizes or colors in stock and may substitute a different range of sizes and colors. The manufacturer may not have received delivery of the fabric that was shown in the sample garment at market, shipping an alternative fabric instead. Deviations from the original order can seriously affect retail sales. The buyer does not have to accept what was not ordered; however, the sales lost from insufficient inventory, as well as the time and expense of returning the unwanted goods, can be costly in terms of revenue and customers. Manufacturers that ship the orders as specified and in a timely manner are likely to be used again.

If a large portion of the funding available for merchandise purchases is committed to a vendor that does not ship on time, sales goals will likely be missed because the merchandise is not there to be purchased. How do buyers determine whether a vendor ships effectively? They can talk with other buyers who have made purchases from the manufacturer. More often than not, actual experience with the vendor truly tells the tale. The buyer quickly learns which vendors can be depended upon for prompt and accurate delivery as well as those that do not meet these standards. Assuming that the lines are successful at retail, those vendors that continually meet completion dates and provide the merchandise ordered should be given first consideration when a new season's orders are to be placed.

Finally, vendor cooperation is a key factor in the buyer's selection of lines. In what ways can the vendor provide the buyer with support and cooperation? Although buyers are the ultimate decision makers in style selection, they will (and should) seek the advice of the sales representative in terms of which styles are selling best and, consequently, should be ordered. The manufacturer's representative has the vantage point of seeing which styles other buyers in the sales territory are selecting. The representative also receives selling reports from across the country. It is the buyer's mission to assess the sales representative's accuracy. This assessment can usually be made only after the buyer has worked with the sales representative for a period of time.

In addition to style recommendations, the vendor may also provide financial and promotional assistance in the form of fixtures, display materials, fashion show videos, in-store appearances, educational seminars, and incentives for sales associates. Such cooperation not only enhances the retail business, but can also increase the size of the orders the buyer places with the vendor. The relationship between key vendors and the entrepreneur can become true partnerships that will positively affect profits for both.

PURCHASING IN THE MARKETPLACE

Seasoned buyers rarely commit to ordering specific merchandise the first time they view manufacturers' lines. More often, buyers take notes on the merchandise that is available at each showroom in order to evaluate each item in terms of what they saw from all the vendors. After buyers have examined everything that is available for delivery during the specific time periods that merchandise is needed, they are able to choose those styles that are best suited to their retail business. Most frequently, buyers will want to write these orders on their company's order forms, rather than on those of the vendors. The company order forms should contain all the information needed for delivery as well as company specifications regarding late deliveries and style substitutions. Using company order forms not only ensures the business of having its specifications honored, but also speeds the accounting and receiving processes by the use of a uniform document. A sample purchase order form for a fashion retail operation is provided in FIGURE 10.4.

OTHER PURCHASING PLACES

Although most buyers agree that there is no better place to view and purchase lines for a new season than at the apparel mart during market week, reviewing lines on the retailer's premises is another option. Sales representatives travel from city to city in a predetermined territory to show their lines to retailers they did not see at the market or to sell new items that have been added to the line. Buyers may welcome these sales calls, as it gives them the opportunity to purchase goods that may have been overlooked at market, that are new to the

FIGURE 10.4

line, or that they did not have the time to review. Many vendors also offer catalogs or Web sites that feature their lines. Using the catalogs or the Internet to view the lines allows buyers to shop when they have time and to solicit the opinions of sales associates and customers. The disadvantages to these selling tools are that the merchandise cannot be handled, quality is difficult to assess, and colors may not be represented correctly. Regardless of where the buyer views the line, the goal is to select the best merchandise for the customer.

MANAGING FASHION MERCHANDISE

Fashion merchandise is evaluated by the retail buyer in terms of seasons. Merchandise suppliers, or vendors, introduce new collections of styles each season for the buyer to preview and purchase.

FASHION SEASONS

What are the **fashion seasons**? Although they vary by manufacturer, most manufacturers of fashion merchandise develop five seasonal lines: fall I, fall II, holiday, spring, and summer. Some manufacturers, particularly those catering to designer customers, have an additional season—cruise or resort—that is delivered between the holiday and spring seasons. Other manufacturers, especially those with lines that do not reflect a high level of seasonal change, may present two lines a year: fall/winter and spring/summer. The two-season merchandise line presentation may be preferred by an active sportswear company or a home accessories producer. FIGURES 10.5A AND B provide examples of the British designer Gareth Pugh's seasonal fashion lines for 2010.

FIGURE 10.5A
The Gareth Pugh spring 2010 ready-to-wear collection.

FIGURE 10.5B
The Gareth Pugh fall 2010 ready-to-wear collection.

SIX-MONTH PLANNING

One of the first steps the buyer must undertake is planning dollar purchases. In most retail operations the **merchandise plan** is formulated for a six-month period and is, subsequently, referred to as the **six-month plan**. The six-month plan incorporates a number of quantitative categories for the business, designated in retail dollars for each month, as follows: planned sales, beginning-of-the-month and end-of-the-month inventory levels, markdowns, average inventory, and stock turn. A six-month plan form is shown in FIGURE 10.6.

SALES FORECASTING

One of the single most critical pieces of information contained in the six-month plan is the sales forecast. Data gathered through industry analysis and market research are used to make a realistic sales forecast. **Forecasting** is the science of estimating what is likely to happen given an assumed set of conditions. A **sales forecast** is an informed estimate, based on a given set of assumptions about the future of sales volume for a specific target market and specific merchandise classification. Sales forecasting is based on a **four-five-four calendar**—four weeks are indicated for one month, five weeks are allocated to the next month, then back to four weeks. The purpose of the four-five-four calendar, shown in FIGURE 10.7, is to compare the same days of the week against one another from year to year in order to forecast sales accurately. Almost all business planning and operating activities revolve around anticipated sales figures. For purposes of this text, sales forecasting is approached for a start-up fashion retail operation.

The accuracy of sales forecasting revolves around several factors: the stability of the market, the experience of the entrepreneur, the type of business for which the forecast is prepared, and the age of the business. All of these factors play a role in the extent to which sales can be predicted. The more stable the market, the more experienced the entrepreneur, and the more established the business, the easier it becomes to forecast sales. The sales forecast is only as good as the underlying assumptions.

To prepare the business's sales forecast, buyers begin by compiling assumptions regarding the economy, the fashion retail industry, and the market. They estimate sales potential for a particular segment of the market, a geographic target area, or a target market and then estimate the share of that total that the company can hope to capture. Using data obtained from numerous trade, business, and government publications, buyers look at what businesses in a similar market have done in the past and what potential businesses will most likely do in the future. To forecast sales for a new business, the entrepreneur will look at both **qualitative data** (informed estimates) and **quantitative data** (mathematical analyses of historical or estimated data).

PLANNING THE MERCHANDISE ASSORTMENT

Merchandise assortment is the range of the styles, colors, sizes, prices, and types of products offered to satisfy the customer's needs, allow the retail operation to meet planned sales goals, and provide an adequate amount of merchandise to support these sales goals. FIGURE 10.8 shows a merchandise assortment. Merchandise assortments are composed of merchandise classifications, or categories, which are examined next.

MERCHANDISE CLASSIFICATIONS

Merchandise classification, also referred to as **merchandise category**, is a related group of items found in an area or department of the retail operation. For example, menswear is a merchandise classification. Within menswear, there are a number of **merchandise subclassifications**, items that are part of a specific merchandise classification. In men's tailored apparel, for example, suits, sports coats, and dress trousers are subclassifications. A merchandise classification of misses' sportswear will include subclassifications of sweaters, shirts, pants, skirts, jackets, and related separates. For each of these subclassifications, the buyer will determine a detailed breakdown, based on the variables of price, color, size, and style.

A SIX-MONTH PLAN

OPEN TO BUY

DEPT. NAME				DEPT. NO.			DATE PREPARED	
CLASSIFICATION				PREPARED BY				

Month	1	2	3	4	5	6
1. On Hand						
2. On Order						
3. Other Additions						
4. Total Commitment (1+2+3)						
5. Planned Sales						
6. Planned Markdowns						
7. Other Reductions						
8. Total Reductions (5+6+7)						
9. Balance (4-8)						
10. Planned EOM Stocks						
11. Open to by + or - (10-9)						
Purchases & Returns						

Date	Transactions	$	$	$	$	$	$

Due monthly upon receipt of Perpetual Inventory to Merchandise Manager and General Merchandise Mgr.

FIGURE 10.6

A FOUR-FIVE-FOUR CALENDAR

SPRING SEASON

		2010							2011							2012						
		S	M	T	W	T	F	S	S	M	T	W	T	F	S	S	M	T	W	T	F	S
1	FEB	31	1	2	3	4	5	6	30	31	1	2	3	4	5	29	30	31	1	2	3	4
2	FEB	7	8	9	10	11	12	13	6	7	8	9	10	11	12	5	6	7	8	9	10	11
3	FEB	14	15	16	17	18	19	20	13	14	15	16	17	18	19	12	13	14	15	16	17	18
4	FEB	21	22	23	24	25	26	27	20	21	22	23	24	25	26	19	20	21	22	23	24	25
5	MARCH	28	1	2	3	4	5	6	27	28	1	2	3	4	5	26	27	28	29	1	2	3
6	MARCH	7	8	9	10	11	12	13	6	7	8	9	10	11	12	4	5	6	7	8	9	10
7	MARCH	14	15	16	17	18	19	20	13	14	15	16	17	18	19	11	12	13	14	15	16	17
8	MARCH	21	22	23	24	25	26	27	20	21	22	23	24	25	26	18	19	20	21	22	23	24
9	MARCH	28	29	30	31	1	2	3	27	28	29	30	31	1	2	25	26	27	28	29	30	31
10	APR	4	5	6	7	8	9	10	3	4	5	6	7	8	9	1	2	3	4	5	6	7
11	APR	11	12	13	14	15	16	17	10	11	12	13	14	15	16	8	9	10	11	12	13	14
12	APR	18	19	20	21	22	23	24	17	18	19	20	21	22	23	15	16	17	18	19	20	21
13	APR	25	26	27	28	29	30	1	24	25	26	27	28	29	30	22	23	24	25	26	27	28
14	MAY	2	3	4	5	6	7	8	1	2	3	4	5	6	7	29	30	1	2	3	4	5
15	MAY	9	10	11	12	13	14	15	8	9	10	11	12	13	14	6	7	8	9	10	11	12
16	MAY	16	17	18	19	20	21	22	15	16	17	18	19	20	21	13	14	15	16	17	18	19
17	MAY	23	24	25	26	27	28	29	22	23	24	25	26	27	28	20	21	22	23	24	25	26
18	JUNE	30	31	1	2	3	4	5	29	30	31	1	2	3	4	27	28	29	30	31	1	2
19	JUNE	6	7	8	9	10	11	12	5	6	7	8	9	10	11	3	4	5	6	7	8	9
20	JUNE	13	14	15	16	17	18	19	12	13	14	15	16	17	18	10	11	12	13	14	15	16
21	JUNE	20	21	22	23	24	25	26	19	20	21	22	23	24	25	17	18	19	20	21	22	23
22	JUNE	27	28	29	30	1	2	3	26	27	28	29	30	1	2	24	25	26	27	28	29	30
23	JULY	4	5	6	7	8	9	10	3	4	5	6	7	8	9	1	2	3	4	5	6	7
24	JULY	11	12	13	14	15	16	17	10	11	12	13	14	15	16	8	9	10	11	12	13	14
25	JULY	18	19	20	21	22	23	24	17	18	19	20	21	22	23	15	16	17	18	19	20	21
26	JULY	25	26	27	28	29	30	31	24	25	26	27	28	29	30	22	23	24	25	26	27	28

FIGURE 10.7

FALL SEASON

2010

AUG

S	M	T	W	T	F	S
1	2	3	4	5	6	7
8	9	10	11	12	13	14
15	16	17	18	19	20	21
22	23	24	25	26	27	28

SEPT

S	M	T	W	T	F	S
29	30	31	1	2	3	4
5	6	7	8	9	10	11
12	13	14	15	16	17	18
19	20	21	22	23	24	25
26	27	28	29	30	1	2

OCT

S	M	T	W	T	F	S
3	4	5	6	7	8	9
10	11	12	13	14	15	16
17	18	19	20	21	22	23
24	25	26	27	28	29	30

NOV

S	M	T	W	T	F	S
31	1	2	3	4	5	6
7	8	9	10	11	12	13
14	15	16	17	18	19	20
21	22	23	24	25	26	27

DEC

S	M	T	W	T	F	S
28	29	30	1	2	3	4
5	6	7	8	9	10	11
12	13	14	15	16	17	18
19	20	21	22	23	24	25
26	27	28	29	30	31	1

JAN

S	M	T	W	T	F	S
2	3	4	5	6	7	8
9	10	11	12	13	14	15
16	17	18	19	20	21	22
23	24	25	26	27	28	29

2011

AUG

S	M	T	W	T	F	S
31	1	2	3	4	5	6
7	8	9	10	11	12	13
14	15	16	17	18	19	20
21	22	23	24	25	26	27

SEPT

S	M	T	W	T	F	S
28	29	30	31	1	2	3
4	5	6	7	8	9	10
11	12	13	14	15	16	17
18	19	20	21	22	23	24
25	26	27	28	29	30	1

OCT

S	M	T	W	T	F	S
2	3	4	5	6	7	8
9	10	11	12	13	14	15
16	17	18	19	20	21	22
23	24	25	26	27	28	29

NOV

S	M	T	W	T	F	S
30	31	1	2	3	4	5
6	7	8	9	10	11	12
13	14	15	16	17	18	19
20	21	22	23	24	25	26

DEC

S	M	T	W	T	F	S
27	28	29	30	1	2	3
4	5	6	7	8	9	10
11	12	13	14	15	16	17
18	19	20	21	22	23	24
25	26	27	28	29	30	31

JAN

S	M	T	W	T	F	S
1	2	3	4	5	6	7
8	9	10	11	12	13	14
15	16	17	18	19	20	21
22	23	24	25	26	27	28

2012

AUG (weeks 27–30)

S	M	T	W	T	F	S	
29	30	31	1	2	3	4	27
5	6	7	8	9	10	11	28
12	13	14	15	16	17	18	29
19	20	21	22	23	24	25	30

SEPT (weeks 31–35)

S	M	T	W	T	F	S	
26	27	28	29	30	31	1	31
2	3	4	5	6	7	8	32
9	10	11	12	13	14	15	33
16	17	18	19	20	21	22	34
23	24	25	26	27	28	29	35

OCT (weeks 36–39)

S	M	T	W	T	F	S	
30	1	2	3	4	5	6	36
7	8	9	10	11	12	13	37
14	15	16	17	18	19	20	38
21	22	23	24	25	26	27	39

NOV (weeks 40–43)

S	M	T	W	T	F	S	
28	29	30	31	1	2	3	40
4	5	6	7	8	9	10	41
11	12	13	14	15	16	17	42
18	19	20	21	22	23	24	43

DEC (weeks 44–48)

S	M	T	W	T	F	S	
25	26	27	28	29	30	1	44
2	3	4	5	6	7	8	45
9	10	11	12	13	14	15	46
16	17	18	19	20	21	22	47
23	24	25	26	27	28	29	48

JAN (weeks 49–52)

S	M	T	W	T	F	S	
27	28	1	2	3	4	5	49
6	7	8	9	10	11	12	50
13	14	15	16	17	18	19	51
20	21	22	23	24	25	26	52
* 27	28	29	30	31	1	2	

* Fiscal Year 2012 is a 53 week year.

** Blue shaded boxes indicate a sales release date. Black shaded boxes indicate the following holidays: Valentine's Day, Presidents Day, Easter, Mother's Day, Memorial Day, Father's Day, Independence Day, Labor Day, Rosh Hashanah, Yom Kippur, Columbus Day, Halloween, Election Day, Veterans Day, Thanksgiving, Christmas, New Year's Day, and Martin Luther King Day.

Merchandise Assortment Plan:

Season _____ Class _____ Department _____ Subclass _____

Vendor | Style # | Units | Cost | Retail price | Total planned purchase (Retail)
(One line per order):

After preparing the assortment plan, the buyer prepares a range plan, as below:
Merchandise hierarchy

Menswear:

Product lines:

Classifications: (e.g., shirts, trousers, jackets):

Subclassifications (e.g., jeans, casual trousers, dress pants):

Vendors (e.g. jeans—Lee, Levi's, True Religion, and so on):

Styles:

Colors:

Size:

The objective of the merchandise assortment plan is to create a balanced range for each category of products that the retailer offers. Effective merchandise planning should accomplish the following:

1. The number of items and options available to the customer should be adequate and broad enough to help the customer make a choice—without being overwhelming.

2. The merchandise assortment planning process should ensure that overbuying and underbuying are minimized.

FIGURE 10.8

Merchandise classifications are presented in FIG-URE 10.9.

Styles are the specific looks within a subclassification. For example, in the skirt subclassification, there will be a number of style offerings that reflect the fashion trends of the season. Vendors may offer an array of fashion skirts for a particular season, such as miniskirts, knee-length pencil skirts, and long-length full skirts. The buyer must determine which styles will be presented within the inventory in the highest proportion; which will be introduced in moderate quantities; which will be purchased in small, or test, quantities; and which will not be represented. These decisions are made based on the buyer's perception of customers' taste as well as past experiences with sales and markdowns, when available.

MERCHANDISE FLOW PLANNING

The buyer's task is to select a merchandise assortment that reflects the customers' needs and wants. Color and fashion trends are prioritized, as are size selection and price points. The buyer plans staggered merchandise deliveries that maximize the sales potential of the inventory. If, for example, tuxedo pants are purchased in sizes 12 to 20, as in the sample business plan for RealWomen, Inc. (Appendix D), then the owner, Lucy Rich, should plan to have blouses and jackets to match in corresponding sizes available on the sales floor at the same time the tuxedo pants are in stock. Lucy may also plan to purchase accessories to coordinate with the tuxedo look, such as ruffled clutch handbags and pearl rope necklaces. In addition, she should plan to have a flow of related merchandise arrive at various

Changes	From	To
Size Range	Juniors 3-15	Juniors 00-15
Price Range	Designer	Very High
Price Range	Bridge	High

FIGURE 10.9
Merchandise classifications.

times of the season to encourage the customer to return to the store to see something new.

Merchandise assortment planning for the new entrepreneur illustrates the critical importance of research, the information gathered to develop the business plan. The entrepreneur must review the data collected on competition and target market demographics in order to predict consumer preferences as closely as possible. After the merchandise assortment is planned, the buyer is ready to prepare the open-to-buy in anticipation of purchasing inventory for the business.

PREPARING THE OPEN-TO-BUY

Open-to-buy (OTB) is the buyer's budget; it dictates how much money the buyer will spend in each merchandise classification for each month of business. The OTB is calculated in retail dollars; therefore, orders must be calculated at retail prices before being included in the OTB. Orders that have been placed with the vendors but that have not yet been shipped or received are referred to as the **on-order** and are logged in a purchase journal. A **purchase journal** is a spreadsheet used to keep track of all orders that have been placed. Technically, the OTB is the difference between how much the buyer needs in inventory at retail to reach sales goals less the merchandise that is currently available, referred to as **on-hand stock**. When calculating OTB, on-order is added to the on-hand stock, as the orders placed with vendors represent a contractual agreement for the merchandise. Knowing how much money at any given time can be spent on new merchandise is extremely important to the buyer. If the buyer discovers a new item and wants to purchase it for stock, there should be money in the budget to do so. Successful buyers try to keep a portion of the OTB liquid. Unspent funds that allow merchandise to be bought to update inventories and to replenish items that have sold out are referred to as the **liquid open-to-buy**. Most vendors add a few new items to their lines after the season's collections have been introduced. Often, these items are modifications of top-selling styles. As a result, a liquid OTB set aside for postmarket ordering can generate significant profits for the fashion retail operation. The formula for OTB follows:

Beginning of the month (BOM) inventory
– sales, markdowns, discounts, and returns = X

End of the month (EOM) planned inventory – X
= planned purchases

The OTB is based on the six-month plan. The difference between them is that OTB carries the calculations one step further, by subtracting the retail dollar amount of the actual ending inventory from that of the beginning inventory of the following month. This tells the buyer the number of retail dollars that must be spent to reach the inventory level planned in order to achieve sales goals for the following month. If sales are lower than anticipated, then the amount of OTB is proportionately decreased. If the sales are much lower than planned or if the buyer has purchased more than allocated, the OTB will indicate that the merchandise classification, or department, is overbought.

It is important to note that OTB is a fluctuating figure: Sales are continually being made in the department, new merchandise is arriving, markdowns are being taken, and customer returns are being credited to the inventory. As a result, it is standard practice for the buyer to update the OTB at midmonth to determine as closely as possible how much money is available for new merchandise.

MARKDOWNS

Markdown is the amount deducted from the cost of the product to determine the sale price. Most buyers find it helpful to anticipate markdowns with a plan that predetermines the dollar amount of inventory allocated to markdowns, their timing, and the percentage off retail prices. Because fashion merchandise is seasonal, markdowns are a fact of life for most apparel and accessories retailers.

REASONS FOR MARKDOWNS

Every fashion entrepreneur must face the reality of markdowns. Unlike a fine wine, fashion trends do not improve with time. Instead, as fashion merchandise ages, it becomes less desirable. Fashion items are, in essence, perishable goods. There are many reasons for reducing the prices of fashion merchandise. Some are attributable to buyer error, whereas others are caused by other factors, such as a lack of attention by the sales force and management and poor quality, or fit. The buyer may place too great an emphasis on a potential fashion trend only to find that the consumer does not share this enthusiasm. Overbuying a particular style or color may mean that markdowns must be made to entice customer purchases. Incorrectly planning the proportion of private label goods to designer labels, inaccurately timing the arrival of new merchandise, and placing too much emphasis on new and unproven vendors are other errors the buyer may make. When merchandise is not promoted properly to include visual merchandising, the result can be markdowns. If the selling prices of particular goods are not competitive, then markdowns are often necessary.

Finally, external factors affect the need for price reductions. The best merchandise can be carefully advertised, effectively displayed in the store, and presented to the consumer by knowledgeable, enthusiastic sales associates, yet markdowns may still be required to sell this merchandise. Adverse weather conditions can affect the sales of seasonal goods. Snowstorms can deter customers from leaving their homes to shop. An unusually warm winter can destroy sales in the outerwear department. A rainy and cold summer can put the damper on swimsuit sales. The economy is yet another external factor that can influence the need for markdowns. A poor or declining economy can play a significant role in the decreased sales of fashion merchandise. When the purchase of food and other essentials is affected by tough times, consumers generally make fashion-oriented items less of a priority.

TIMING OF MARKDOWNS

When a new line is purchased, retail buyers often use the time before delivery to clear out the prior season's goods through markdowns. A fashion item does not usually become unwanted because it is no longer functional; instead, it is no longer fashionable. This concept of **planned obsolescence**, in conjunction with changing seasons and fashions trends, creates the cyclical nature of fashion merchandising. FIGURE 10.10, a fashion

A BUYER'S TIMING CALENDAR

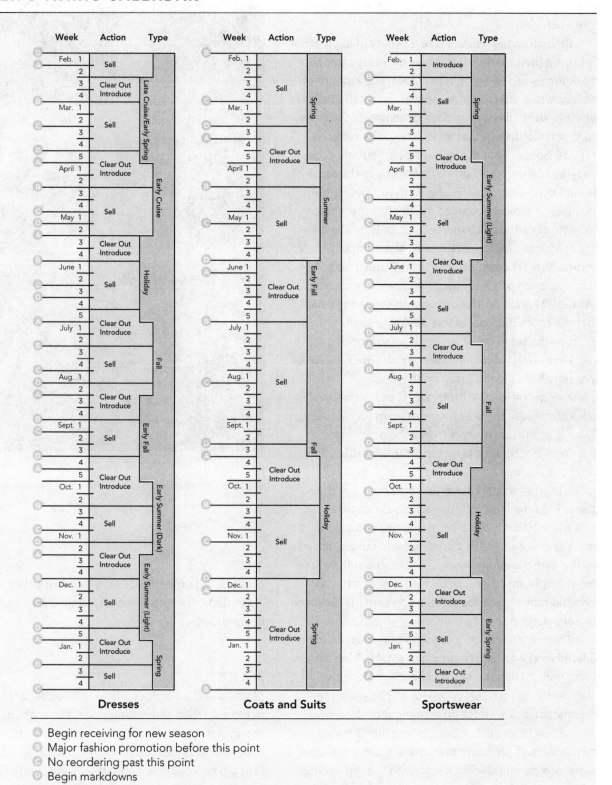

Dresses

Week		Action	Type
D A	Feb. 1	Sell	Late Cruise/Early Spring
	2		
	3	Clear Out Introduce	
B	4		
	Mar. 1	Sell	
	2		
C	3		
	4		
D	5		
A	April 1	Clear Out Introduce	Early Cruise
	2		
B	3	Sell	
	4		
	May 1		
C A	2		
	3	Clear Out Introduce	Holiday
	4		
	June 1	Sell	
C	2		
D	3		
	4		
	5	Clear Out Introduce	
A	July 1		Fall
B	2		
	3	Sell	
	4		
C D	Aug. 1		
A	2	Clear Out Introduce	
	3		
B C	4		Early Fall
	Sept. 1	Sell	
	2		
D	3		
A	4		
	5	Clear Out Introduce	Early Summer (Dark)
	Oct. 1		
B	2		
	3	Sell	
C	4		
D	Nov. 1		
A	2	Clear Out Introduce	Early Summer (Light)
	3		
B	4		
	Dec. 1	Sell	
C	2		
	3		
D	4		
A	5	Clear Out Introduce	
	Jan. 1		Spring
B	2		
	3	Sell	
C	4		

Coats and Suits

Week		Action	Type
B	Feb. 1	Sell	Spring
	2		
C	3		
	4		
	Mar. 1		
D	2		
A	3		
	4	Clear Out Introduce	
	5		
	April 1		Summer
B	2		
	3		
	4		
	May 1	Sell	
C	2		
	3		
	4		
D	June 1	Clear Out Introduce	Early Fall
A	2		
	3		
	5		
B	July 1		
	2		
	3		
	4		
C	Aug. 1	Sell	
	2		
	3		
	4		
	Sept. 1		
	2		
D	3		Fall
A	4	Clear Out Introduce	
	5		
	Oct. 1		Holiday
B	2		
	3		
	4		
C	Nov. 1	Sell	
	2		
	3		
	4		
D	Dec. 1		
A	2		Spring
	3		
	4	Clear Out Introduce	
	5		
	Jan. 1		
	2		
	3		
B	4		

Sportswear

Week		Action	Type
	Feb. 1	Introduce	Spring
	2		
B	3		
	4		
C	Mar. 1	Sell	
	2		
A	3		
	4		
	5	Clear Out Introduce	Early Summer (Light)
	April 1		
	2		
B	3		
	4		
C	May 1	Sell	
	2		
D	3		
	4		
A	June 1	Clear Out Introduce	
	2		
B	3		
	4	Sell	
	5		
D	July 1		
A	2	Clear Out Introduce	
	3		
	4		
B	Aug. 1		Fall
	2		
	3	Sell	
	4		
	Sept. 1		
	2		
D	3		
A	4	Clear Out Introduce	
	5		
B	Oct. 1		Holiday
	2		
	3		
C	4	Sell	
	Nov. 1		
	2		
	3		
D	4		
A	Dec. 1	Clear Out Introduce	Early Spring
	2		
B	3		
	4		
C	5	Sell	
	Jan. 1		
D	2		
A	3	Clear Out Introduce	
	4		

Ⓐ Begin receiving for new season
Ⓑ Major fashion promotion before this point
Ⓒ No reordering past this point
Ⓓ Begin markdowns

FIGURE 10.10

timing calendar, illustrates the impact of fashion seasons on the introduction and clearance of merchandise lines.

Fashion entrepreneurs take a variety of approaches to timing their markdowns; however, most agree that markdowns are based on rate of sale. The amount of time in which merchandise sells at full retail pricing, whether thirty days, sixty days, or longer, is the determining factor in whether goods should be reduced in price. Some fashion merchants, particularly those carrying higher-priced goods, subscribe to the semi-annual markdown philosophy. With this policy, merchandise is typically marked down after the winter holiday and after mid-June. Other retailers take different approaches to markdowns. Many implement a **perpetual markdown policy**. Through this policy, buyers reduce the prices on merchandise every month, for a variety of reasons. The primary reason is the belief that the quick disposal of less desirable goods will improve the retail operation's rate of turnover and, subsequently, enable the buyer to purchase new items that may have greater profitability.

As illustrated by FIGURE 10.11, well-promoted sales often pave the way for more room on the sales floor, or in the inventory plan, for the new season's offerings. Markdowns can help clear the selling floor. Early markdowns may also encourage the sale of goods at a lower markdown percentage; if merchandise is held too long, its sale will require more significant markdowns. With a perpetual markdown policy, buyers reduce the selling price of merchandise based on the date the goods were placed on the selling floor. For example, merchandise that is more than thirty days old may be marked down 20 percent. At the sixty-day-old stage, it may be reduced by 40 percent.

There are a number of factors that must be considered by the entrepreneur when establishing a markdown policy. First, the entrepreneur should consider that too many markdown periods might encourage the customer to wait for price reductions. Moreover, often a few pieces of the best-selling merchandise may remain. If the buyer marks down these remaining leftovers, yet reorders the style in the top-selling colors and sizes, then the new goods will be priced

FIGURE 10.11

Well-promoted clearance events often pave the way for more room on the sales floor, or in the inventory plan, for the new season's offerings.

differently. Sometimes, the markdown policy will have exceptions; the entrepreneur needs a plan that can be modified.

MARKUP

Markup is the amount added to the cost of the product to establish the selling price. The amount of the markup may be determined by the type of merchandise sold; services provided by the retailer, such as free alterations; how often the product sells; and the amount of profit the entrepreneur wants to make.

The markup can be expressed in terms of dollars and cents or as a percentage of cost or selling price. It is commonly expressed as a percentage of the retail price. A number of costs are associated with adding markup to price merchandise—**operating costs**, defined as the day-to-day expenses incurred in running a business, such as rent, utilities, and telephone, and **incidental costs**, defined as those costs that may occur sporadically, such as shipping charges and ticketing expenses.

In retailing the term *markup* may refer to one of the following three calculations: markup based on cost of goods, markup based on original selling price, or markup based on final selling price. The following example illustrates the differences. An entrepreneur who owns a retail apparel store buys dresses that cost $40 each. These garments are priced at $80 each and are placed on the selling floor. The first markup calculation on this retail price is referred to as **initial markup**. The initial markup takes the following costs into consideration: the wholesale price of the merchandise; any reductions, such as customer discounts, employee discount, markdowns, and special sales; and the amount of reasonable profit the business wants to make. Having a handle on costs will enable the entrepreneur to establish the initial markup.

Initial markup is calculated as follows. From the retail price of $80, the markup amount of $40 is deducted, leaving a remainder of $40. The $40 is then divided by the retail of $80, resulting in an initial retail markup of 50 percent. If markup is to be calculated on cost, it is figured by dividing the wholesale price of $40 by the difference between cost and retail price, $40, resulting in a markup of 100 percent. Finally, assume that the dresses did not sell at full price. They did, however, sell after being marked down to $60. The resulting markup calculation is the **maintained markup** and is determined by dividing $20, the difference between the wholesale cost and the retail price, by $60, the actual selling price. The maintained markup is 33 percent.

Markup can also be calculated from a department or business perspective, rather than an item. For example, Fabulous Fashion Retail, Inc., has decided to open an apparel shop in Smart City. It has forecasted sales of $425,000, expenses of $195,000, and $30,000 in reductions. Profits are expected to be $36,000. The markup percentage is calculated as follows:

$$\$195,000 + \$30,000 + \$36,000 = \$261,000 = 57.36\%$$

$$\$425,000 + \$30,000 = \$455,000$$

To cover costs and generate a profit, the initial markup on all merchandise would have to average 57.36 percent.

A fashion retail store carrying related products may sometimes use the technique of applying a standard markup on all its merchandise. Fashion retailers offering an array of merchandise often find it effective to use a **flexible markup policy**. This allows the entrepreneur to apply different levels of markup to varying merchandise classifications. For example, retailers carrying apparel lines frequently carry accessories as well. The initial markup on a line of belts may be different from that on a line of dresses.

PRICING STRATEGIES FOR FASHION MERCHANDISE

There are a number of pricing strategies that relate to the markdown and markup of fashion merchandise. **Introductory pricing** is a strategy often used to gain entry into a market by setting prices lower than the industry average markup. Price skimming is yet another strategy in which the retailer sets a high initial price, usually through high markup, and then gradually lowers it. **Price lining**, also referred to as **all-in-one pricing**, is the grouping of inventory into categories, setting the same price for all items in each category, resulting in a below-average markup for some items, whereas others may be at above average. Retailers use this strategy to simplify and strengthen advertising efforts while attracting clientele. With another pricing strategy, the **loss leader,** one or more items are sold at or below cost in order to attract customers. A loss leader has little or no markup. The buyer advertises loss leaders to generate customer traffic, the idea being that customers will purchase other items while in the store.

In addition to determining markup, markdown, and pricing strategies, the retailer must establish other pricing policies and general pricing guidelines. Will the business match competitors' prices? Will it use coupons or multiple-purchase discounts? Will returned merchandise be accepted at the markdown price only, if a reduction was taken after the purchase? Will employees receive discounts on the merchandise they purchase? Will the employee discount apply to clearance merchandise? There is much to consider when establishing a plan for price reductions.

THE SALES TEAM AND THE BUYER

The buyer's work is not finished when the merchandise for the retail operation is purchased. The buyer has a pivotal role in the marketing and selling of this merchandise. By conveying the reasons for merchandise selection to the sales associates, the buyer increases the probability of retail sales. The buyer thought through a number of issues when the merchandise was purchased: "Why will the customer buy it? Why is it more appealing than that of the competitors? Is the price, fit, styling, or trend unique and appealing in specific ways?" When the buyer shares these questions and answers with the sales staff, the sales personnel have the information and confidence needed to sell the merchandise to the customer.

VISUAL MERCHANDISING AND THE BUYER

Visual merchandising is an extremely important part of any retail operation's sales. Whether an employee is assigned to visual merchandising or a sales associate is responsible for this duty, the buyer can be helpful in selecting the items to be highlighted through interior displays, window displays, or signage, or a combination of these. The buyer may want to feature a particular item that will generate customer traffic or one that was purchased in quantity. Close cooperation between the buyer and the person installing the visual merchandising display can generate sales, enhance image, and encourage repeat business.

SALES PROMOTION AND THE BUYER

When buyers want to promote a key item in the inventory, they often decide to advertise the item. In some retail operations there is an advertising director to take care of the artwork, copy, and layout design needed for a print advertisement. In most start-up businesses, this responsibility belongs to the entrepreneur or buyer, often one and the same. The buyer has the product knowledge to identify key selling points and the products' benefits to potential purchasers. Working within a promotional budget, the buyer will usually work with media representatives to develop advertisements. The media outlet (newspaper, television or radio station, magazine, and so on) advertising the product will most often provide personnel to develop the ad, either for a fee or as a part of the ad cost. It is the buyer who works with these representatives to make sure that the product is shown in its best light and in a way that will make it desirable to the target customer.

SALES SUPPORTING SERVICES AND THE BUYER

The buyer will work in a variety of areas within the retail operation. With the buyer's input, orders will be entered and processed through the accounting department. Inventory counts, whether annual or more frequent, are often under the buyer's responsibilities in a new business. Merchandise will be received, ticketed, and moved to the sales floor, often with the buyer's supervision. Finally, the buyer may work with management to schedule sales personnel during holidays or special events.

THE BUYER'S GOAL: PROFIT

Selecting merchandise that sells at retail and generates a profit is the buyer's objective (FIGURE 10.12). There are a number of merchandising calculations

FIGURE 10.12

Selecting merchandise that will make a profit is the buyer's goal.

that enable buyers to monitor how successful they are at reaching this goal. Stock turn, stock-to-sales ratio, and inventory shortage all relate to the buyer's mission for profitability.

Stock turn, also referred to as **turnover**, is a statistical measurement that is formed as a simple fraction in which the numerator represents sales for a given time period, and the denominator shows the average amount of stock during that same period. Sales and stock are typically measured in retail dollars. Stock turn is a measurement of inventory performance; it guides the entrepreneur in assessing the productivity of inventory. Stock turn goals vary with the merchandise classification and the type of retail operation. A stock turn of three may be the objective for a specialty store featuring misses' sportswear, whereas a stock turn of two may be more reasonable for a bridal boutique. There are a number of sources that can be examined for national stock turn data. The most widely used reports in fashion retailing are published by the National Retail Federation.

Another measurement of sales and inventory performance is the stock-to-sales ratio, which works together with stock turn. The **stock-to-sales ratio** is a calculation in which the inventory for a given period of time is divided by the sales volume for the same period. If, for example, the inventory for the month of December is $150,000, and the sales for December are $50,000, then the stock-to-sales ratio is three to one, or 3:1. This figure indicates that the stock turn, at this particular time, is four because the stock ratio of three is divided into the twelve months of the year. A stock-to-sales ratio helps the buyer see whether the stock turn goal is within reach.

Stock turn, markup, markdowns, and inventory shortages are all critical factors in the buyer's quest for profitability. It is not enough simply to buy the merchandise and place it on the selling floor. It must be priced high enough at first to earn a profit and to offset markdowns. It must be secured adequately so that merchandise does not "walk off the floor." The buyer must have a creative eye for fashion and a quantitative mind for numbers.

BUYING FOR NONSTORE RETAIL OPERATIONS

The Internet, television shopping shows, and catalogs are three alternatives to brick-and-mortar stores that bring with them new challenges for the buyer working for businesses that sell exclusively without storefronts. **Nonstore retail operations** are those that do not have a physical environment through which the customer can see, touch, and try on the merchandise. They do not have a "home" in which the customer can get a feel for the business, its ambiance or personality, through a store visit. Because of the wide reach of many of these nonstore operations, the buyer for these businesses often serves a global clientele.

Catalogs can be distributed any place in the world; the Internet can be accessed anywhere in the world. As a result, the buyer for these businesses addresses a much broader market than do buyers employed by brick-and-mortar operations. The merchandise selection must appeal to consumers living in varying climates and willing to pay a range of prices. Value pricing and exclusivity of goods are two of the merchandise criteria upon which a number of successful nonstore operations have based their businesses.

Think about the challenges of buying for a catalog operation, as opposed to buying for a physical store.

For some fashion retailers the life span of a catalog can be quite long. JCPenney, for example, publishes major catalogs annually that must stand the test of time, as each of the vendors represented in these books must be able to provide the featured merchandise for a three- to six-month period. This retailer, as well as a host of other catalog businesses, publishes smaller catalogs between the large seasonal issues. These catalogs must be planned well in advance and also require negotiation with vendors for extended delivery periods. In addition, the buyer for a catalog operation will negotiate for exclusive styles or colors, discount pricing, and cooperative advertising allowances to offset the high cost of catalog production. For the most part, when the vendor's name appears in the catalog, cooperative advertising funds were solicited by the buyer to pay for that acknowledgment. Finally, the buyer for the catalog company works more closely with the photographer, stylist, and personnel in the promotion department than will the buyer of a brick-and-mortar operation.

As with catalog operations, the buyer for a television shopping network will serve a vast clientele, customers with few geographic or demographic limitations. The buyer for this type of retail outlet must have the skills to identify merchandise with vast market appeal and sufficient visual appeal. The buyer is challenged to locate and secure merchandise that is unavailable elsewhere and that has a high price–value relationship and broad characteristics—for example, a wide range of colors and sizes. Often, the buyer is also called upon to identify the selling points of merchandise that will convince viewers to buy.

One of the most debated issues in fashion retailing entrepreneurship is **e-retailing**, Internet-based retailing. Can an entrepreneur start and successfully establish a business on the Internet? Is it more realistic to expect that the entrepreneur has more to gain by spinning off an Internet business from the core brick-and-mortar business? Should online sales be an adjunct to a physical store or an independent operation? The buyer's role in e-commerce directly relates to the entrepreneur's answers to these fundamental questions. If e-retailing is an extension of an existing business, then the buyer must decide whether to select goods for the Web site that reflect the merchandise assortment in the store or those that are an extension of the merchandise assortment. If the Web site is the business, then the buyer has a different task. The merchandise must be evaluated in terms of its appeal to a global audience, and a competitive price must be determined at which it will retail. With price competition and exclusivity as two key sales variables on the Internet, the buyer will need to be an effective negotiator to purchase goods at the lowest possible prices.

Timing is a primary factor in buying for the nonstore operation, whether it is catalog, television shopping, or e-commerce. The buyer must determine the potential fashion life cycle for each item in the merchandise assortment and be ready and able to make adjustments to the on-order if sales decline before anticipated. Some buyers place **backup orders**, shipments planned for later deliveries, with the vendor's agreement that a specific percentage of the merchandise may be canceled if necessary. This is not a common option, however, and is not offered to buyers placing small orders. Manufacturers are often cautious about going into full-scale production and then playing a waiting game. In some cases, the buyer must commit to a full purchase upfront, warehousing the goods and shipping them to the consumer as ordered. The buyer's challenge is to locate vendors willing to share the risk or to guarantee a steady flow of goods within a specified time period.

Another challenge for the buyer of a nonstore operation relates to the item's visual presentation. The buyer may work with Web developers, photographers, or catalog copywriters on a product's images and text. They may collaborate with the scriptwriter of the television shopping operation to develop a script for the show's moderator. Through nonstore retailing, the buyer's responsibilities in marketing the product are changing. The format of a Web site, the layout of a catalog page, and the presentation of a television segment are new assignments to the buyer's realm of responsibilities. These shifts in responsibility result from a shift in retailing, a movement that has taken the buyer out of the store and into the customer's home.

CONCLUSION

Merchandising is the difference between an apparel and soft goods retailer and those retailers offering all other product classifications. The resident buying offices (consulting services), as well as internal and external sources of product information, are available to assist the buyer in determining which merchandise will best satisfy the target market's needs and desires. The resources for fashion goods primarily show new lines at apparel marts, located in market centers, during market weeks that are scheduled according to merchandise classification. Vendor selection is primarily based on the types and prices of goods and on how these goods will match with the customer's preferences. Other significant factors in selecting vendors for the retail operation include exclusivity, timely and accurate shipping, reorder availability, promotional assistance, and vendor cooperation.

After the buyer has reviewed the lines of vendors, the six-month plan and its coordinating open-to-buy are the two tools used to calculate the amount of funds to be spent on new merchandise. These planning tools are also used to guide and register the amount of markdowns that will need to be taken on slow-selling goods.

The buyer's role in the marketing and selling process of the retail store is not limited to merchandise assortment selection and pricing. The buyer is responsible for disseminating product information to management and sales personnel. In addition, the buyer shares this information with visual merchandising and sales promotion personnel and assists with sales supporting services, such as accounting, receiving, and inventory control.

The buyer's success is ultimately based on an understanding of the customer. E-commerce is bringing new challenges to buyers for catalog, e-commerce, and television shopping operations, as they are catering to a global market in the world of nonstore fashion retailing.

KEY TERMS

advertising allowances	exclusivity	liquid open-to-buy
all-in-one pricing	external sources	loss leader
apparel mart	fashion items	maintained markup
backstock	fashion seasons	markdown
backup order	flexible markup policy	market week
basic items	forecasting	markup
buyers	four-five-four calendar	merchandise classification
cancellation (completion) date	incidental costs	merchandise plan
closeout merchandise	initial markup	merchandise subclassification
consulting service	internal sources	merchandising
cooperative advertising	introductory pricing	minimum orders
distribution practices	key vendors	nonstore retail operations
e-retailing	lead time	off-price merchandise

(CONTINUED)

(CONTINUED)

on-hand stock

on-order

open-to-buy (OTB)

operating costs

perpetual markdown policy

planned obsolescence

price lining (all-in-one pricing)

purchase journal

qualitative data

quantitative data

resident buying office

sales forecast

six-month plan

staple (basic) item

stock turn (turnover)

stock-to-sales ratio

styles

turnover

vendor analysis

DISCUSSION TOPICS

1. Examine the job responsibilities of the buyer in a retail business. Which tasks could the entrepreneur delegate, and which should he or she retain?

2. Review how fashion goods differ from other product types in the areas of purchasing, delivery, promotion, and markdowns.

3. Investigate resident buying offices in major market locations, such as New York, Los Angeles, and Dallas. What services do these firms offer? What costs are associated with the different services?

4. Construct a chart of the external and internal sources from which a merchandiser can collect buying information. Indicate names and contact information for companies, publications, and Web sites.

5. Compile a list of formulas for merchandising calculations used in fashion buying, to include stock turn, stock-to-sales ratio, and markdown percentages.

SUGGESTED READINGS

Brannon, Evelyn L. *Fashion Forecasting: Research, Analysis, and Presentation*. 3rd ed. New York: Fairchild Books, 2010.

Donnellan, John. *Merchandise Buying and Management*. 3d ed. New York: Fairchild Books, 2007.

Sternquist, Brenda. *International Retailing*. 2d ed. New York: Fairchild Books, 2007.

Tepper, Bette K., *Mathematics for Retail Buying*. 6th ed. New York: Fairchild Books, 2008.

ONLINE RESOURCES

AMERICASMART
http://www.americasmart.com
This major mart in Atlanta, Georgia, hosts trade shows for apparel, gift, and home furnishings and accessories wholesale buyers.

CALIFORNIA MARKET CENTER
http://www.californiamarketcenter.com
Located in Los Angeles, this market is home to hundreds of showrooms representing thousands of brands for women, men, children, and home.

DALLAS MARKET CENTER
http://www.dallasmarketcenter.com
Attracts nearly 250,000 buyers each year to shop wholesale markets in menswear, women's wear, gifts, and home furnishings and accessories.

DENVER MERCHANDISE MART
http://www.denvermart.com
The Rocky Mountain region's wholesale market center for apparel and accessories.

THE MERCHANDISE MART
http://www.mmart.com
Located in Chicago, Illinois, the Merchandise Mart hosts more than three million visitors each year in retail shops; eleven floors of permanent showrooms for gift, residential, casual and contract furnishings; dozens of trade shows, and special educational, community, and consumer events.

BUSINESS PLAN CONNECTION
THINKING LIKE AN ENTREPRENEUR

Considerations for the merchandising/product plan include the merchandise the target market is willing to buy and the availability of this merchandise for the store or Web site. Begin by determining the merchandise that will be carried. Visit retail operations outside of your regional location, and peruse the Internet to source product lines that fit your target market's preferences. Comparison shop both direct and indirect competitors in your region carrying similar products or unique merchandise that will meet the needs of potential customers. Is there still a market for your product lines or services?

Next, assess the availability of the merchandise. Can you acquire merchandise for the business in a timely manner when customers want to buy it? Begin by analyzing which apparel marts are most feasible to attend. Visit their Web sites to locate market dates and vendors showing at these marts. Contact manufacturers' representatives of the lines you are interested in carrying to discuss line availability, minimum orders, showing dates, and delivery periods. Which vendors will you carry, and in what depth? Where and when will you attend markets to purchase lines?

⊙ ASSIGNMENT 10.1
THE MERCHANDISING/PRODUCT PLAN

1. Open your saved business plan template.
2. Address the following sections of the merchandising/product plan. You may use the sample business plan in Appendix D as an additional resource.

   Revisit the sections of the merchandising/product plan you completed in Chapter 4. Determine whether the information needs to be adjusted, based on your recent findings. If so, update the information at this time.

   » Merchandise/Product Description
   » Unique Characteristics
   » Proposed Lines
   » Proprietary Aspects
   » Merchandise Assortment

   Next, complete the remaining sections of the merchandising/product plan:

   » Market Trips
   » Markup/Markdown Policies

PROFILE OF AN ENTREPRENEUR
H&M

F merchandising is the name of the game, then Hennes & Mauritz (H&M) is the master player.

H&M was established in Västerås, Sweden, in 1947 by Erling Persson. The company now sells clothes and cosmetics in around 2,200 stores around the world. Here are some brief facts about H&M:

Karl-Johan Persson, CEO

» H&M offers fashion and quality at the best price.

» H&M's first store was opened in Sweden in 1947.

» H&M offers fashion for women, men, teenagers, and children.

» The collections are created centrally by around 100 in-house designers together with buyers and pattern makers.

» H&M also sells own-brand cosmetics, accessories, and footwear.

» The stores are refreshed daily with new fashion items.

» Online shopping is currently available in Sweden, Norway, Denmark, Finland, the Netherlands, Germany, Austria, and the UK.

» H&M does not own any factories, but instead buys its goods from around 700 independent suppliers, primarily in Asia and Europe.

» H&M has about sixteen production offices around the world, mainly in Asia and Europe.

» H&M employs about 76,000 people.

» The turnover in 2010 was Swedish krona (SEK) 126,966 million (H&M.com)

How does this merchandising master conduct its design business? A team of more than 100 designers collaborates with the store buyers in studying international runway and street wear trends. Next, they develop and design the affordable clothing that stocks H&M stores for the cost-conscious, fashion-conscious shopper. H&M's designers are driven to interpret fashion trends and create fashions that are accessible to all. The stock is kept fresh with daily deliveries of new merchandise. It is as though H&M views the year as having fifty-two fashion seasons, one for every week.

How are prices kept so low? H&M share its strategies for "cheap chic" as follows: using few middlemen; buying large volumes; having a broad, in-depth knowledge of design, fashion and textiles; buying the right products from the right market; being cost-conscious at every stage; and having efficient distribution. Quality is a central issue, from the idea stage all the way to the end customer, and includes extensive testing, as well as ensuring that the goods are produced with the least possible environmental impact, under good working conditions.

SOURCE: All information obtained from http://www.hm.com.

CHAPTER 11
BUILDING THE FINANCIAL PLAN

THIS chapter focuses on the financial concepts used by entrepreneurs to build a successful business and provides an overview of financial language, the importance of financial planning, and the purpose of each financial statement. It then breaks each key element of the financial statements into steps and guides you to specific worksheets on the financial planning template located in the Templates folder on the accompanying CD-ROM.

Key financial concepts are examined, such as understanding financial terms, developing accurate financial statements, and accessing funding. The chapter will build on the financial statements by estimating inventory and operating expenses, determining cash needs, and evaluating sources of cash. Key ratios are examined because these are the tools used to determine how well a business is doing. The chapter also explains how to calculate the break-even point for the business, how cash flow affects the business, and how to access capital.

The financial information presented in this chapter is entered into the financial planning template. A step-by-step process directs you to specific worksheets in the financial template. Each step includes estimating a key element of the financial statement, such as planned sales, markdowns, stock, start-up costs, operating expenses, and other cash expenditures. After completing each step, the financial statements are automatically generated.

Many financial scenarios exist for each business. It is beyond the scope of this text to address every scenario. Accountants should be consulted when preparing financial documents.

THE IMPORTANCE OF THE FINANCIAL PICTURE

Preparing financial statements, which include the cash flow statement, profit and loss statement, balance sheet, and a financial plan, that accurately represent the business is critical to success. Financial statements are used to gauge the financial condition of a business; they tell a story about its financial health. Almost every decision made about the business, from hiring employees and applying for a particular IRS status to merchandising and developing a Web site, has a financial impact. The financial plan helps determine the amount of financing that will be needed to make the business feasible, the type of financing needed, and when the

FIGURE 11.1

Financials tell a story. Every entrepreneur should understand the decisions that impact the financial state of the business.

financing needs to be available. It also helps determine whether the business is generating sufficient cash flow to pay all expenses.

In addition, the financial plan also serves as a management tool by helping the entrepreneur run the business on a day-to-day basis. It can affect decisions concerning the correct level of inventory, the need to hire more sales staff, or the question of changing the mix of merchandise. The financials can indicate whether pricing may be too low or too high or whether the business may be suffering from theft. The financial plan also aids in determining whether operating costs are under control and calculating the break-even point of the business.

Maintaining good financial records will help prevent catastrophes. They will provide the entrepreneur with the opportunity to stop failure before it happens. For a start-up company with limited resources, accurate financial information counts.

FINDING FINANCIAL INFORMATION

Start-up businesses have no financial history; therefore, the entrepreneur must rely on other sources to prepare reliable financial projections and assumptions. One of the first places entrepreneurs look for financial information is within the fashion retail industry itself. The fashion retail industry, through associations such as the National Retail Federation, provides information about sales and expenses that can be used to project more reliable pro forma financials. Many magazines and journals are also good resources and can be found in most libraries. Under the industry classification code, the **North American Industry Classification System (NAICS)**, information may be attained on profits, expenses, and the financials of competitors.

The NAICS is a set of standardized industry categories established for the United States, Canada, and Mexico. This system is a standard used by federal statistical agencies in classifying business establishments for the purpose of collecting, analyzing, and publishing statistical data related to the business economy. Businesses are separated into industries, by defining businesses that use similar production processes. Each category is then identified using a numbering system. Each industry has a main industry identification, and contains more specific identifiers within, such as apparel, ladies apparel, menswear, or children's wear. A fashion retail business can, therefore, determine its NAICS code and then use this code to find articles about existing businesses that may mention information about profits, expenses, sales, or other data. Using the NAICS code, entrepreneurs can compare their projected financial assumptions with those of existing businesses.

Although many entrepreneurs will not share specific information about their financial health, they may share insights into the types of costs a fashion retail business can incur. They may also share their percentage of costs in relation to sales. By conducting interviews with owners of existing fashion retail businesses, the entrepreneur can obtain valuable information.

KEY FINANCIAL TERMS

Understanding accounting terminology can seem like learning a foreign language. To communicate successfully in the business world, entrepreneurs embrace the challenge and build their knowledge base of basic financial terms that are used to describe the conditions or needs of the business. Every entrepreneur should have an understanding of the following terms:

» **Sales or revenues**—Money earned or received from providing a good or service.

» **Expenses**—The costs incurred in operating the business and providing the product or service.

» **Asset**—Any item of economic value that is owned by the business.

» **Liability**—An obligation or amount owed to others.

» **Net income**—The remaining income or revenue after all expenses have been paid.

» **Owner's equity**—Total assets minus total liability of a company; the actual dollar value of an owner's total investment in a business, plus any net profits that have been retained in the business from year to year.

» **Pro forma financial statements**—Accounting reports, including income statements, balance sheets, and cash flow statements, that represent the estimated future plans of a business.

» **Income statement**—An accounting report showing the amount of income for a specific accounting period. The income statement, also referred to as a profit and loss (P&L) statement, reflects all expenses subtracted from revenues.

» **Balance sheet**—An accounting statement that shows the financial condition of a company at a point in time. It includes assets, liabilities, and net worth.

» **Cash flow statement**—A document that shows the difference between the cash a company expects to receive and its expected cash expenditures, on a monthly basis. A historic cash flow statement identifies the changes in account balances that have affected the cash balance during the prior year.

In addition, the entrepreneur should be familiar with the following concepts:

» **Cost of goods sold or cost of product/service**—In fashion retail, the purchase price of the merchandise to be resold. In other industries this can also be the direct costs attributable to the production of the goods sold by the company.

» **Debt**—Money loaned to a company that is expected to be repaid.

» **Equity**—Money invested in a company that is not intended to be repaid, but that, rather, represents an ownership interest.

» **Stock or merchandise**—The value of existing products to be sold (as defined for accounting purposes).

» **Start-up costs**—The one-time costs involved in starting a venture. These costs include expenses such as initial marketing efforts or one-time deposits and capital expenditures.

FINANCIAL OUTCOMES

The financial plan focuses on three primary outcomes, each supported by written assumptions explaining the source and thought processes behind the numbers:

» **Financial performance**—How well is the business doing or will it do financially in comparison with other like businesses in the industry?

» **Cash flow**—What are the cash needs of the business, and can sufficient sources be obtained to meet those needs?

» **Profitability**—Will the business operate at a profit?

Planning of profitability, cash flow, and financial performance are based on the projections of start-up costs, sales projections, cost of merchandise, operating expenses, capital budget, equity, and debt. From this, financial statements are prepared that tell the story of the business:

» Monthly cash flow statement

» Year-end income statement

» Year-end balance sheet

ASSESSING PROFITABILITY

Although the entrepreneur may have enough funds to open the business, it is **profit** or profitability that sustains the business over a period of time. Profits are necessary to repay debt, purchase merchandise, and fund the growth of the business. Profits are determined by subtracting the expenses of the business from revenues generated:

Net profit or net loss = revenues – expenses

Revenue is the money earned or received from providing a product or service to the customer. Revenue equals the total number of products or services sold at the price charged:

Number of units sold × price per unit = revenue

Expenses also contribute to the net profit of the business. Expenses are made up of the **cost of goods sold** (the cost of the product or service) and operating expenses, the ongoing cost of running a business. (Businesses providing a service only will not have a cost of goods sold.) When the cost of goods is subtracted from sales, the result is **gross profit**, which is also referred to as **gross income** or **gross margin**.

Gross income = sales – cost of goods

Gross income is important because it indicates the amount of money available to cover operating expenses.

PROFITS AND CASH FLOW

Whereas profitability is the ability to generate income, cash flow is the ability to pay obligations as they become due. Cash is also necessary for future growth. Entrepreneurs use projected financial statements, the income statement and monthly cash flow statement, to forecast the ability of the business to achieve these two objectives: profit and cash flow, as illustrated in FIGURE 11.2.

THE FINANCIAL STATEMENTS

The entrepreneur preparing financial documents to open a business will develop a pro forma set of financial statements. **Pro forma**, a term commonly used in the business and accounting industry, means "projected." These pro forma financial statements will help determine the amount of funds needed to open the doors and keep them open. The three basic financial documents—cash flow, income statement, and balance sheet—correspond to one another.

THE CASH FLOW STATEMENT

The monthly **cash flow statement** is a document that reflects all cash flowing in and out of the business each month. It projects the business's ability to meet its cash obligations on a monthly basis. Businesses can operate for periods of time at a loss, but not without cash.

FIGURE 11.2

Cash is king, and profits keep the doors open. The entrepreneur must have enough money to open the business and be profitable enough to keep the business going.

The cash flow statement allows the entrepreneur and funders to understand how the business's operations are running, where the money is coming from, and how it is being spent. The cash flow statement is different from the income statement and the balance sheet in that it does not include the amount of future incoming and outgoing cash that has been recorded on credit. Therefore, cash flow is not the same as **net income**, which, on the income statement and balance sheet, includes both cash sales and sales made on credit.

THE INCOME STATEMENT

The **income statement**, sometimes referred to as a profit and loss statement, is a comparison of expenses and revenue over a certain period of time, usually one year. The income statement reflects how much money the business made or lost during a given time period. The income statement is essentially divided into two sections. The top portion of the income statement is known as the revenue section. It includes all income from the sale of merchandise throughout the year. If a fashion retail store incurred returns and provided refunds for those returns, this amount would be deducted from gross revenue to reflect net sales for the year. Similarly, any markdown taken would reduce gross revenue. The second section reflects expenses that were incurred to generate those revenues.

THE BALANCE SHEET

The **balance sheet** is a snapshot of the business at a given point in time. It reflects what the company is worth on paper (book value). It shows what the company owns (**assets**) and what it owes (**liabilities**). The balance sheet is based on the following formula:

Assets = liabilities + owner's equity

The balance sheet must balance—one side must equal the other; hence, the name. An increase or decrease on one side must be offset by an equal increase or decrease on the other side. That is, a company has to pay for all the things it has (assets) either through loans (liabilities) or shareholders' equity.

The balance sheet will let the entrepreneur know how assets, liabilities, and net worth are changing. The asset side of the balance sheets reflects accounts such as cash, inventory, and property. The liability side reflects accounts payable or long-term debt.

THE FINANCIAL PLANNING TEMPLATE

This section of the chapter focuses on completion of the financial planning template. This task entails using a set of pro-forma financial statements and ratio analysis to gauge the cash needs and profitability potential of the business. (See the financial planning template on the accompanying CD-ROM.)

FINANCIAL ASSUMPTIONS

Accompanying any good set of financial statements is a good set of assumptions. **Assumptions** provide the reader with an explanation of the sources and thought processes behind the numbers, especially in the cash flow statement; they provide an explanation of how the entrepreneur arrived at the numbers presented. The numbers are meaningless without an explanation. If the financials do indeed flow through with the rest of the business plan, the plan itself will explain the source of the numbers; however, bankers and funders will not want to sift through pages of information to reconstruct the financial plan.

For each of the worksheets on the financial planning template, be prepared with a written set of assumptions to accompany the financial statements developed through the financial planning template. The assumptions should be presented in a Word document. The sample business plan in Appendix D offers an example.

CALCULATING START-UP COSTS

The first step in preparing financial statements is to calculate start-up costs (FIGURE 11.3). **Start-up costs** are those costs that will be incurred to get the doors open. These costs may be either expenditures (generally, one-time costs) or regular expenses (ongoing costs). Assets are items purchased that retain some value over a period of time. Acquiring assets is considered a capital expenditure, an expenditure that creates a future benefit. In a fashion retail business these items may include computers, fixtures, and counters.

Items that do not retain value but are purchased to operate the business are considered *expenses*. Operating expenses may include items such as rent, payroll, office supplies, advertising, and dues and subscriptions. A list of possible expenses has been included on the start-up costs worksheet, as well as on

FIGURE 11.3

Knowing start-up costs help the entrepreneur determine the amount of money needed prior to opening the doors.

the cash flow and income statements, of the financial planning template.

It is critical that start-up costs be realistic. In other words, when estimating start-up costs, the entrepreneur should focus on what is actually needed to start the business rather than taking the amount of money on hand or accessible and making the start-up costs fit the budget.

A number of questions will guide the estimate of the amount of money needed to open the doors of the retail business:

» What kinds of deposits are required (e.g., telephone service, utilities, rent, and so on)?

» Where will the business be located?

» How many square feet will be required?

» What type of signage will be needed?

» How much merchandise will be needed to open the doors?

» How will the merchandise be paid for?

» What types of fixtures will be required?

» What types of marketing costs will be incurred before opening the business, such as advertising or mailings?

» What costs will be incurred for hiring employees?

» What types of cleaning and computer supplies will be needed?

» How much money will be invested? by the entrepreneur? by investors?

» How much money will be borrowed?

The financial planning template provides instructions for completing the start-up worksheet.

PLANNED SALES

Projecting sales for a start-up business is just that: a projection. There are no historical data on which to base the numbers; therefore, projecting sales for a start-up business is based on research. Considerations include potential market size, how much stock to have on hand, the number of square feet to be used for the sale of merchandise, and so on. Sales projections consider the sales price per item, the cost of the item, the markup and anticipated markdowns, and, at times, the average sale per customer multiplied by the number of customers expected in a year.

Entrepreneurs use three primary techniques to project sales. One method is the comparative approach. This method bases sales on the research conducted on the fashion retail industry, including competitors. Note that if these businesses have been in business for some time, their sales projections may be significantly higher than what a start-up company can anticipate. However, such research does provide a basis for making projections. The more competitors and industry numbers considered, the more accurate the projections. Consider location, experience of the owner, and other factors when using this approach.

A second method is the average sales approach. To project sales using the average sales approach, the number of sales transactions over a period of time is calculated. For example, a retail store may anticipate thirty customers per day. The entrepreneur anticipates an average sale of $150 per customer. The entrepreneur would simply multiply to determine average sales per day and then multiply for a yearly figure. In

fashion retail it is also important to remember that sales can be somewhat seasonal. Higher sales may occur during holiday seasons, whereas sales tend to decline during certain other months.

The third method is a bottom-up approach. This approach is more mathematical than intuitive. It entails estimating the annual cost of goods sold and all the expenses expected in the business. The total costs plus the amount of desired profit represent the projected annual sales. The goal is to cover costs and profit. For example, the fashion entrepreneur first estimates all the costs of goods and expenses expected in each of the first three years of the business. Then, the entrepreneur identifies the amount of profit he or she wants to make for each year. The projected sales equal the total costs of the business and the amount of profit expected. This approach offers a way to check the reasonableness of the other two methods. If the bottom-up approach determines projected sales to be much higher than those approaches, the business may not be able to achieve that level of sales and still maintain profitability.

By considering all three methods to project sales, sales projections are more likely to be reliable. A comparison of the three approaches will most likely estimate sales somewhere in the middle.

You will prepare the sales projections on the planned sales worksheet on the financial planning template.

PLANNED MARKDOWNS

Previously, we looked at approaches for determining planned markdowns (see Chapter 10). The planned markdowns worksheet of the financial planning template determines the percentage of markdown for each month of the total store stock. The planned markdowns then flow to the six-month merchandising plan.

SIX-MONTH MERCHANDISING PLAN

The six-month merchandising plan on the financial planning template focuses on ensuring that enough merchandise is in the store, whether brick-and-mortar or online, to accommodate sales projections. This plan, developed here for accounting and financial purposes, considers planned sales, planned markdowns, and planned purchases. The financial planning template on the CD-ROM will automatically generate planned sales and planned markdowns from the previous two worksheets (Planned Sales and Planned Markdowns). The goal is to utilize the six-month plan as a management tool. From a financial or accounting perspective, entrepreneurs use this document to manage the stock-to-sales ratio. The results tell the entrepreneur whether stock is too high or too low and how frequently stock turns.

OPERATING EXPENSES

Operating expenses are all the costs of operating the business. The operating expenses are necessary to support the day-to-day operations and sales and marketing of the business. To arrive at net income, the operating expenses are subtracted from the gross margin.

Sales – cost of goods = gross margin

Gross margin – operating expenses = net income

To determine operating expenses, the entrepreneur should think through the monthly costs associated with day-to-day operations. It is important to think in terms of monthly expenses for purposes of cash flow. Simply estimating annual expenses and dividing by twelve does not allow for months in which expenses may be higher because of expanding inventory or unique marketing efforts. Costs in any business will vary from month to month.

Expenses incurred in operating a business can be thought of not just in terms of "paying bills"; the entrepreneur needs to consider what expenses may be necessary to generate sales, such as employee salaries or marketing expenses, as well those expenses necessary to generate revenue.

General expenses are also taken into account. What costs are necessary to support operations not necessarily directly related to sales? These may include association dues, accounting expenses, legal fees, or subscriptions.

As stated earlier in the chapter, assumptions are critical for guiding the reader to an understanding how the numbers were obtained. The assumptions support the financial statements. For the entrepreneur they become a reality check to help ensure the numbers are as realistic as possible. If numbers vary significantly from month to month, this should be explained in the assumptions as well.

CAPITAL EXPENDITURES

Capital expenditures are assets purchased by the business that create a future benefit. In a fashion retail business these may include fixtures or computer equipment. They are typically assets that may be sold in the future to recapture cash. These expenditures are recorded as assets on the balance sheet, at the price for which they were purchased. This allows the entrepreneur to know the amount of cash that has been invested in the business. Book value, however, is not the same as market value; **market value** is the amount of money someone will pay for the asset at any given time.

The capital expenditures worksheet includes depreciation. **Depreciation** is the allocation of the cost of an asset over the term of the asset's useful life. It is simply an accounting method that is used to adjust the original value (**book value**) of the asset to reflect more accurately its current value (**depreciated value**) in the business. What is paid for an item today is not necessarily its value at a future date. The value of an asset usually declines over time; however, the book value remains the same. When the useful life of an asset is over, the item is considered fully depreciated, and the value is zero dollars. When the asset is sold or disposed of, the book value is removed from the financial statements. Depreciation is recorded on the income statement. The financial planning template will automatically calculate depreciation.

Other cash outlays may include prepayment required on items such as insurance or deposits on utilities, rent, and so on. All start-up expenses and start-up capital expenditures are reflected on the cash flow statement as pre-start-up expenses and expenditures.

Cash is required to start any business. It supports day-to-day operations and provides the money necessary to stock the retail store with merchandise.

EQUITY AND LOAN AMORTIZATION

The financial planning template contains a worksheet titled "Equity and Loan Amortization." The worksheet contains four sections that allow the entrepreneur to account for money injected into the company:

» **Section A: Equity Injections**—As stated earlier, equity is the amount of cash the entrepreneur has invested into the business. This section accounts for any investments you or others will contribute to the business in the month in which it will be received.

» **Section B: Amortizing Business Loans**—**Loan amortization** is the repayment of a loan over a period of time. This section accounts for any loans that have been received or are anticipated that will flow money into the business.

» **Section C: Line of Credit**—This section of the financial planning template allows the entrepreneur to account for money that will be used to cover shortfalls of cash. Lines of credit are explained later in this chapter.

» **Section D: Owner's Draw**—Owner's draw is the amount of money the owner withdraws from the business. Businesses operating as sole proprietorships or partnerships may issue checks at any time for compensation. Because the owner is not on a salary, when he or she makes a withdrawal, the money issued is referred to as an owner's draw. This is not an expense or an asset; it is simply a reduction in equity. For a C corporation the payout to the owner or investors is made in the form of dividends, payment to stockholders of all or part of the corporation's actual profits. The amount paid is generally based on a dollar amount tied to the amount of stock held by the owner or investor. The equity and loan amortization worksheet allows for the recording of these items.

ACCESSING CAPITAL

Accessing capital can be a challenge for a start-up company. The entrepreneur does not have the historical data to prove that the company is likely to survive. In addition, new companies typically start with few assets. Funders consider start-up companies to be higher risk. Despite these challenges, however, numerous start-up companies seek and find funding each year. To overcome the hurdles, information and knowledge is necessary. The more knowledgeable the entrepreneur, the more likely he or she is to obtain the capital needed for launching the venture (FIGURE 11.4).

Fashion retail businesses need three types of capital: seed capital (or start-up capital), working capital, and growth capital. **Seed capital** is the amount of

FIGURE 11.4

Emphasis should be placed on the amount of money needed, not the amount of money desired.

money the business needs to open the doors. It is typically money earned and saved by the entrepreneur, but it can also come from outside investors. **Working capital** is the money needed to operate the business. Working capital is typically the difference between current assets and current liabilities. Additional working capital may be needed to fund seasonality issues. **Growth capital** is money for helping a business grow and expand.

There are two types of funding: debt financing and equity financing. **Debt financing** involves securing funds by borrowing money that must be repaid (FIGURE 11.5). **Equity financing** is the personal investment of the owner, or another source of capital, such as an investor. It is important to be aware of all options available to businesses. Very few entrepreneurs have the funds in place to open a business without the need to access additional capital from some source.

Funders recognize that lending or investing money is a long-term relationship with the entrepreneur. Both debt and equity funders have criteria and considerations when investing their funds:

» **Capacity**—For funders, such as bankers, capacity is the ability of the entrepreneur to pay the loan as agreed. This is determined by reviewing the financial plan and the entrepreneur's personal finances. Bankers look to the business as the first source of repayment, turning to the entrepreneur to provide repayment should the business not meet financial projections.

» **Collateral**—Collateral represents the assets the business is willing to pledge to a bank as security for repayment of the loan. If the borrower defaults, the bank has the right to sell the collateral and apply the proceeds from the sale to satisfy the loan.

» **Credit**—The funder wants to know that the borrower has a history of not only paying back debt, but also paying debt on time. Credit reports provide information on a person's credit history. It is advisable for an entrepreneur to request a credit report from one of the three credit reporting

FIGURE 11.5

If the money borrowed is not repaid, the lender or funder can collect on the assets used to secure the loan.

agencies in the United States before approaching a bank. The report will reveal any negative information. Addressing the issue of bad credit before the bank brings it up can serve the entrepreneur well.

» **Owner risk or investment**—Funders expect the entrepreneur to have invested in the business. Generally speaking, bankers expect a 20 to 30 percent investment.

» **How funds are used**—Funders will help the entrepreneur match the term of the loan or investment with the use of funds. Shorter-term loans should be used to finance seasonal inventory and accounts receivable, whereas longer-term loans are used to finance capital expenditures and other long-lasting initiatives.

» **Return on investment**—For investors, the goal is return on investment. Investors want their money back, and then some.

Before selecting a source of funding, the entrepreneur should consider:

» the amount of money that will be required;

» the amount of time it will take to secure the money needed;

» how the money will be used;

» what it will cost to secure the funding and pay it back;

» how much control will have to be sacrificed to obtain the money.

DEBT FINANCING

Debt financing, the more common source of funding for fashion retail ventures, is found through banks, the use of credit cards, or sometimes friends and family. This type of funding leaves the entrepreneur with the most control over the business. With debt financing the entrepreneur essentially borrows money and is then required to repay the loan over a designated period of time, usually with interest, service charges, and loan origination fees.

EQUITY FINANCING

Equity financing is most often obtained through venture capitalists or angel investors. **Venture capitalists** are individuals or organizations that purchase an equity position in the company in exchange for a return of their investment. **Angel investors,** sometimes referred to as private investors, are people of wealth who decide to invest in a business in return for

FIGURE 11.6

Careful consideration should be given before using credit cards as a source of funding. Beware—the interest keeps churning!

a higher rate of return than can be obtained through other investments, a financial interest in the business, or the desire to be part of a new concept of potentially substantial business.

Equity financing is the owner's equity in the business. Equity financing can come in the form of an investment by the entrepreneur or an investment of capital from an outside source, or both. With this type of financing, outside funding is more difficult to get, for a number of reasons. As stated earlier, venture capitalists are private persons or organizations that purchase an equity position in a company in exchange for a return on their investment. This is hard to set up in a very small company. Most venture capitalists seek opportunities to invest in venture deals ranging between $3–5 million. If less than $1 million is needed, many venture capitalists will not be interested.

Angels are a more likely source of outside capital. Angels have a tendency to invest funds at the local level. They are often entrepreneurs themselves. They earn their money as the company increases in value.

SOURCES OF FUNDS

Source of funding can include family and friends, credit cards, commercial banks, microloan programs, and lines of credit.

Family and Friends

Family and friends can be an accessible source of the funding needed to start a venture. Caution should be taken to ensure that family and friends will be paid back just as a bank or outside investor would be. It is a common theme among business owners that one does not do business with friends and family; everything is fine until something goes wrong in the business, and money becomes scarce. If family and friends are going to be funding sources, it is advisable to put written agreements in place that outline the expectations of the lenders and the entrepreneur.

Credit Cards

Credit cards can be a convenient source of funding when other avenues have failed. Credit cards, however, have downsides. They carry high interest rates and are difficult to pay off.

Commercial Banks

Commercial banks represent the greatest source of funding for entrepreneurs. Entrepreneurs ready to start a new venture typically begin by visiting with their local bankers. They will often begin with the bank in which they conduct their personal banking. They may start with banks that target like businesses or banks that have been referred by their accountants, other entrepreneurs, lawyers, or consultants. Entrepreneurs will also seek banks that participate in governmental lending programs, such as the Small Business Administration.

Bankers are conservative in nature. They loan money based on the bank's deposits. In other words, they are loaning the money that is deposited by their customers. For this reason, they have an obligation to make sound lending decisions.

To assist banks in the reducing the risk taken on loans, banks often work with the U.S. Small Business Administration (SBA). The SBA does not lend money directly to consumers. Rather, it offers programs that can help start-up entrepreneurs obtain funding, through banks and other sources, that they would not have been able to get on their own. Banks receive a guarantee from the SBA that if the loan recipient is unable to repay the debt, the SBA will repay a portion of it to the bank. This reduces the risk for the lender.

Microloan Programs

Microloans are small business loans that provide funding to entrepreneurs to start or expand businesses. These loans, which range from a few hundred dollars to less than $40,000, are typically used to purchase inventory or small equipment or to cover operating expenses. The interest rates are typically higher, and repayment is required over a shorter period of time.

Lines of Credit

A **line of credit** is a short-term loan that provides cash flow for the day-to-day operations of the business. With this type of loan the bank establishes a specified amount of money that is available to the business to withdraw as needed, much like a credit card. It is expected that the line of credit will be used and paid back in a very short period of time and that the money will be there to use again. It is advantageous to the entrepreneur in that the unused portion of the line of credit does not accumulate interest. Interest is only charged on the amount outstanding.

Many types and sources of financing exist for small companies. This chapter has listed only the most common sources. Before attempting to secure any type of financing, it is important for the entrepreneur to explore all the options available. Many government agencies, such as the Department of Economic Development and Small Business Development Centers, exist in part to help locate various programs.

ANALYZING THE FINANCIALS

Financial analysis allows the entrepreneur to check the "heartbeat" of the company. Just as the instruments in the cockpit of an airplane let the pilot know how the plane is flying, the financial statements of a company let the entrepreneur know how well the business is operating. If the pilot never checked the plane's instruments, he or she would not know whether the plane was operating as it should. If the entrepreneur never checks the company's financial statements, he or she will never know how it is operating and whether adjustments need to be made (FIGURE 11.7).

Getting the business open and running is one thing. The entrepreneur then has to focus on keeping the business running profitably. Without the financial statements to guide the decision-making process, the entrepreneur is almost destined to make bad business decisions. The entrepreneur who establishes a system for analyzing the financials and for using that information to make informed decisions has a much greater chance of survival and success.

One way in which the entrepreneur and his or her accountant and banker evaluate the performance of the company is through ratio analysis. **Ratio analysis**

FIGURE 11.7

These days, entrepreneurs often seek accountants to prepare financial statements. However, it is critical to success for the entrepreneur to analyze and understand how the financial situation is influencing the business.

allows the entrepreneur to examine the relationship between one financial value and another. With ratio analysis the entrepreneur can spot trends in the business and compare its performance and condition with the average performance of similar businesses in the same industry. Through the use of ratio analysis, the entrepreneur can determine the answers to such questions as whether the business is carrying too much stock, whether operating expenses are too high, and whether enough cash is on hand to pay short-term debt if the need arises.

Key financial ratios are used to evaluate ways to run the business more efficiently and effectively. The following section focuses on the ratios that can be used to determine the heartbeat of a fashion retail store. As you read, it is important to keep in mind that all financial numbers represent one point in time. Ratio analysis, in this context, is meant to create an awareness and understanding of how the numbers in the business affect one another.

UNDERSTANDING KEY FINANCIAL RATIOS

Financial ratios are divided into four categories: liquidity, profitability, risk, and efficiency ratios. Table 11.1 provides the formulas for each category.

TABLE 11.1
KEY FINANCIAL RATIOS

RATIO TYPE	RATIO	FORMULA
Liquidity ratios	Current ratio	Current ratio = total current assets/total current liabilities
	Quick ratio	Quick ratio = (current assets – inventory)/current liabilities
Profitability ratios	Gross margin	Gross margin = gross income/net sales
	Operating margin	Operating margin = operating income/net sales
	Net margin	Net margin = net income/net sales
	Return on assets	Return on assets = net income/total assets
	Return on equity	Return on equity = net income/total equity
Risk ratios	Debt to equity	Debt to equity = total liabilities/total owner's equity (total net worth)
	Debt ratio	Debt ratio = total liabilities/total assets
Efficiency ratios	Inventory turnover	Inventory turnover = cost of goods sold/average inventory
	Investment turnover	Investment turnover = net sales/total assets

Liquidity Ratios

Liquidity ratios gauge the ability of the business to pay its current obligations as they come due. These ratios measure the amount of cash, or the investments that can be converted to cash, to pay expenses and short-term debts. The most commonly used liquidity ratios are the current ratio and the quick ratio.

CURRENT RATIO   The **current ratio** measures whether there is enough cash available to pay the bills. A rule of thumb for an effective current ratio is 2:1. This means that for every dollar in short-term obligations, the company has two dollars in current assets to pay them. Current assets include cash, accounts receivable, and inventory. Current liabilities include notes payable, accounts payable, taxes payable, and accruals. Generally speaking, the higher the company's current ratio, the stronger it is financially. However, this does not always hold true. A fashion retail business with too much nonmarketable inventory will show a good current ratio, but the business may not be able to quickly turn the inventory into cash to service its short-term obligations.

Current ratio = total current assets / total current liabilities

QUICK RATIO   The **quick ratio** shows whether the business has enough cash to cover its short-term obligations. This ratio is sometimes referred to as the acid test. A rule of thumb for the quick ratio is 1:1. This means that for each dollar the company has in short-term obligations, it has one dollar to pay those obligations. A ratio below 1:1 would indicate that the company is depending on turning its inventory and on future sales to satisfy its short-term debt. The higher the quick ratio, the more liquid the company is, and, subsequently, the more financially stable.

Quick ratio = (current assets – inventory) / current liabilities

Profitability Ratios

Profitability ratios measure how efficiently a business is being managed. Entrepreneurs use these ratios to help identify inefficient operations, expenses that are too high, and profitable margins.

GROSS MARGIN   The **gross margin ratio** measures overall profit. This is an indication of how well a business is controlling its costs. If costs are increasing faster than sales, then direct costs are out of control.

Gross margin = gross income / net sales

OPERATING MARGIN   The **operating margin ratio** indicates how well a business is managing its overhead costs. If gross margins are rising while operating margins are falling, then indirect costs are out of control.

Operating margin = operating income / net sales

NET MARGIN   The **net margin ratio** shows how many cents on each dollar of sales are profit. If the net margin is falling, costs or prices may be out of control.

Net margin = net income / net sales

RETURN ON ASSETS (ROA)   The **return on assets ratio** is used to compare the profitability of companies of different sizes. Assets remain fairly stable, so an increasing ROA indicates greater profitability, whereas a decreasing ROA indicates less profitability.

Return on assets = net income / total assets

RETURN ON EQUITY (ROE)   The **return on equity ratio** tells whether the company is a good investment. Generally, as ROE increases, the company becomes more attractive to potential investors. Improving net income will also usually improve shareholders' equity, as the profit will become retained earnings.

Return on equity = net income / total equity

Risk Ratios

Risk ratios show the extent to which the entrepreneur relies on debt, as opposed to equity capital, to finance the operations of the business.

DEBT TO EQUITY The **debt-to-equity ratio** measures the proportion of assets that are financed by creditors to assets that are contributed by the owners. It is a comparison of how much the business owes with how much it owns. This ratio helps determine whether a company has the ability to sell its assets and still have enough money to meet its obligations. The higher the debt-to-equity ratio, the less chance the business will have of obtaining financing; that is, the higher the number, the weaker the company. The acceptable debt-to-equity ratio varies from industry to industry. The fashion industry is typically a cash industry, which would allow a higher ratio.

Debt to equity = total liabilities / total owner's equity (total net worth)

DEBT RATIO The **debt ratio** measures the portion of total assets that are financed through debt. The higher the debt ratio of a company, the more debt financing the business has incurred. Creditors prefer smaller debt ratios. The smaller the number, the less likely the creditor is to lose money should the business need to be liquidated. High debt ratios are an indicator of a business with a high chance of default on the debt.

Debt ratio = total liabilities / total assets

Efficiency Ratios

Efficiency ratios measure how effectively a company utilizes its resources. The more effectively a company operates, the less it will need to access capital.

INVENTORY TURNOVER RATIO The **inventory turnover ratio** measures how many times the company's inventory is sold and replaced over a period of time. To use this formula, determining the average inventory is required. To calculate, take the average of the beginning and ending inventory figures. The average number of days it takes to sell the entire inventory one time can be calculated by dividing 360 by the inventory turnover figure. (Financial institutions treat every month as having thirty days.) Using 360 days is standard in the financial industry. Although grocery stores turn inventory very quickly, the fashion industry turns much more slowly. If the inventory is turning more slowly than the industry average, the business may have merchandise that will not sell, creating excess inventory. By the same token, if inventory turns too fast, the inventory level may not be high enough.

Inventory turnover = total sales / average stock at retail

INVESTMENT TURNOVER RATIO The **investment turnover ratio** tells how efficiently a company uses its assets. The measurement shows how quickly and often an asset (e.g., a piece of machinery, an investment) pays for itself. If an older piece of equipment works slowly but pays for itself three times in a year, whereas a newer model takes two years to pay for itself, the owner must reflect on whether the payoff is worth the greater investment.

Investment turnover ratio = net sales / total assets

Ratios are a starting point for understanding the story of the business. Ratios alone are not sufficient to evaluate the health of the business adequately. Ratios will, however, provide a set of questions to enable the entrepreneur to begin analyzing the business. Other factors, such as industry trends, changes in economic factors, and changes within the company itself, play roles in how well the business is performing.

Although performance varies among industries, it also varies within the same industry. A jewelry store will perform differently from a store that sells junior sportswear. Each entrepreneur must determine which ratios are important to understanding his or her business. It is also possible to create ratios that measure unique circumstances within an industry. A business owner can calculate ratios not only on his or her own data, but also for other businesses similar in size, geographic location, and merchandise.

THE BREAK-EVEN POINT

Entrepreneurs must be able to recognize the break-even point of the business. The **break-even point** is the point at which the company shows neither a profit nor a loss, but simply covers all its costs. It is the point at which total sales revenue equals total expenses. The break-even point lets the entrepreneur know exactly the level of business he or she will need to generate to keep the doors of the business open.

To begin to look at the point at which the business will break even, the entrepreneur must first distinguish between fixed costs and variable costs. **Fixed costs** are those costs that will be incurred whether or not a sale is made. They remain constant regardless of changes in levels of activity. For a fashion retail store, such costs include labor, rent, interest expenses, and utilities. **Variable costs** are expenses that vary in proportion to changes in the level of activity or in proportion to sales, such as of stock or merchandise.

Each time a sale is generated, the business automatically incurs a certain percentage to variable cost. Determining the difference between fixed and variable cost is not always obvious. Break-even is calculated on a yearly basis, because of the seasonality of the business.

For example, a retail store buys blouses for $15 each, marks them up, and sells them for $30. The monthly expenses (fixed costs) are $10,000. This means the break-even point would be $20,000 or 667 units.

$10,000 \div (15/30) = $20,000

$20,000 \div $30 = 667

Break-even analysis = fixed expenses / gross margin percentage

The financial planning template contains a worksheet that calculates financial ratios for your business.

CONCLUSION

The financial plan is one of the most crucial elements of the business plan. A good financial plan helps determine the amount and type of financing that will be needed to make the plan feasible. The financial plan can also serve as a valuable management tool in helping the entrepreneur run the business efficiently.

The entrepreneur can rely on three key financial documents to provide information about the business: the cash flow statement, the balance sheet, and the income statement. Together, all three provide insight into the availability of cash, the book value of the business, and where the money is going. Through a set of ratios, the entrepreneur can evaluate ways in which to run the business more efficiently and effectively. The key financial ratios and break-even analysis allow the entrepreneur to measure the performance of a business against like businesses in the industry. The entrepreneur can then begin to make adjustments as needed to ensure the success of the business.

The financial plan provides the opportunity to access capital through either debt or equity financing. A number of programs exist that provide financing to start-up and early-stage companies. It is critical that the entrepreneur know the key areas bankers and investors examine in a financial plan in order to ensure access to credit.

KEY TERMS

angel investors

assets

assumptions

balance sheet

book value

break-even point

capital expenditures

cash flow statement

cost of goods sold

current ratio

debt

debt financing

debt ratio

debt-to-equity ratio

depreciated value

depreciation

efficiency ratios

equity

equity financing

fixed costs

gross income

gross margin

gross margin ratio

gross profit

growth capital

income statement

inventory turnover ratio

investment turnover ratio

liabilities

line of credit

liquidity ratios

loan amortization

market value

net income

net margin ratio

North American Industry Classification System (NAICS)

operating expenses

operating margin ratio

owner's equity

pro forma

pro forma financial statements

profit

profitability ratios

quick ratio

ratio analysis

return on assets (ROA) ratio

return on equity (ROE) ratio

revenues

risk ratios

seed capital

start-up costs

variable costs

venture capitalists

working capital

DISCUSSION TOPICS

1. Discuss the process for determining start-up costs.

2. Explain the importance of well-prepared assumptions when completing financial statements.

3. Examine how the utilization of financial ratios can help in the analysis of the health of the business.

4. Discuss options for funding, both debt financing and equity financing. Give the both the pros and cons of each type of funding.

SUGGESTED READINGS

Berman, Karen, and Joe Knight. *Financial Intelligence for Entrepreneurs: What you Really Need to Know about the Numbers.* Boston, MA: Harvard Business Press, 2008.

Ittelson, Thomas R. *Financial Statements: A Step-by-Step Guide to Understanding and Creating Financial Reports.* Franklin Lakes, New Jersey: The Career Press, 2009.

ONLINE RESOURCES

ALLBUSINESS.COM
http://www.allbusiness.com
Offers articles on understanding financial statements.

ENTREPRENEURSHIP.ORG
http://www.entrepreneurship.org
Provides numerous articles on financial statements and entrepreneurship.

NORTH AMERICAN INDUSTRY CLASSIFICATION SYSTEM (NAICS)
http://www.naics.com
Publishes statistical data related to the business economy based on a system used by Federal statistical agencies in classifying businesses.

BUSINESS PLAN CONNECTION
THINKING LIKE AN ENTREPRENEUR

This plan focuses on the development of the financial statements for the business. Refer to your saved business plan to gather information to prepare each of the worksheets outlined on the financial planning template. This chapter's section "The Financial Planning Template" follows the series of worksheets contained in the financial template. It is suggested that you work through the template worksheets sequentially, as outlined in that section. As you complete each worksheet, the numbers are automatically incorporated into the financial statements—cash flow statement, monthly income statement, and balance sheet. You can view these statements to see how data are incorporated. As changes are made, the statements will adjust accordingly.

ASSIGNMENT 11.1
THE FINANCIAL PLANNING TEMPLATE

Refer to the financial planning template in the Templates folder on the accompanying CD-ROM.

1. Open the financial planning template. This template will be used to write your financial plan.
2. Save the financial planning template to your computer.
3. Go to the saved file, open it, and click on the first worksheet.
4. Complete the assignment by addressing the questions contained on the various worksheets.
5. Save the file.
6. Turn in your statement as directed by your instructor.

⊙ ASSIGNMENT 11.2
THE FINANCIAL PLAN

1. Open your saved financial planning template.

2. Address the following sections of the financial planning template:

   » Business Set-Up

   » Start-Up Costs

   » Planned Sales

   » Planned Markdowns

   » Six-Month Merchandising Plan

   » Operating Expenses

   » Capital Expenditures

   » Equity and Loan Amortization

   » Amortization Schedule

   The previous worksheets will flow to the:

   » Monthly Cash Flow Statement

   » Year-End Income Statement

   » Year-End Balance Sheet

   » Ratio Analysis

   Refer to the sample business plan in Appendix D.

PROFILE OF AN ENTREPRENEUR
HABITAT SHOE BOUTIQUE
KANSAS CITY, MISSOURI

JOHN and Kristen McClain had a passion and a vision. They would open a fashion-forward shoe boutique in Kansas City, Missouri, to fill an unmet need in the marketplace. Their patience, drive, and determination would build a successful business.

Tell me about Habitat.

We opened Habitat Shoes in 2005, as an S corporation to fill a niche for a fashion segment of Kansas City we felt wasn't being met. We envisioned a fashion-forward, contemporary-minded footwear boutique that would carry brands of shoes that were not currently found in Kansas City. Today, we offer brands like Chie Mihara, Coclico, and Pura Lopez. We were buying shoes when traveling to places such as Chicago and New York because the brands we wanted weren't found in Kansas City. We wanted to shop in our own city. And we thought others in the market did, too.

According to www.HabitatShoes.com, *"Habitat sells shoes. We think pretty cool shoes, actually. You won't see a gajillion brands and styles on this site. That's not the point of why we exist. We don't sell shoes based on trends or socialites. We sell the shoes we love. We also added simple apparel pieces and accessories, because some things are just meant to go together.*

Habitat is small and simple. Run by a husband and wife team with three crazy kids, we just want to add a little design and happiness to your life. Enjoy."

What motivated you to start your own business?

Even while in college I knew I wanted to open a store. I wanted to be an entrepreneur. I loved the design of product and stores and creating a space for people to shop. I wanted to create. I appreciated stores that you had an emotional response to. I have degrees in marketing and international business.

How did you choose the name Habitat?

After college I moved to London, where I lived for six months working temp jobs. The flat I rented was two blocks from a store called Habitat. The store sold modern furniture. It was a cross between Crate & Barrel and Ikea. I walked by the store every day on my way to work. There was something that struck me with the name. Our tagline is "What you live in." And we live in shoes.

How did you get into the fashion industry?

My experience didn't come from the fashion industry. I ran a coffee shop, worked for an ad agency, and handled the marketing aspects for an art gallery. I did have experience with fashion as a consumer. I knew what I wanted as a consumer and knew I had good taste for what I wanted to do.

How did you determine you wanted a small boutique?

While most people are comfortable in a big store, we wanted to offer a shopping environment that was clean and minimal and not a lot of product. We took the concept of a gourmet restaurant with a limited menu and applied the same focused, minimal offering menu to a shoe store. We wanted to focus on selecting shoes that the market wants or feels [it needs] based on current trends and not offer a larger selection that would serve as filler.

What are the highlights of running your own business?

It's ours. We get to create something every day. We get to figure it out. For us, it's like having a canvas to work with. We love determining how we will make this business work and how we will work with the product in [relation] to the market. We are excited about attending trade shows, talking with the designers to find out what styles they are most excited about, and offering those styles to our customers. We have built cool relationships with our customers. We also love that our space inspires people; not just in buying shoes, but in being creative.

What aspects of your business are particularly challenging?

Growth can be a challenge. As our business has grown, we have certainly made more money, but that means we buy more product.

Getting people into the store can be challenging. People often think that providing a store with a cool look will drive traffic into the store; however, that's not necessarily true. We work at getting people to understand our product and then making a decision to buy.

Employee management is always an issue. Employees are the most important aspect of our business—maybe even more important than the product. As an entrepreneur, you have to have patience in finding the right employees and not settling.

When financial times are tough, entrepreneurs are challenged with figuring out how to make payroll.

With all the internal challenges, you have to maintain a positive front for the customer.

What entrepreneurial traits make your business a success?
We are confident in our product, and we feel we do this well. Our personalities and commitment to the business drive us to maintain our ability to thrive in a sometimes chaotic environment.

We are also people of integrity. We are open and honest with our vendors and our customers. It impacts us in a positive way financially and with customer loyalty.

We approach our business and our customers with a commitment to excellence.

What has been the key to your success?
We have differentiated ourselves from other businesses offering shoes in our market. We have focused on ourselves rather than the competition. We are also consistent in our product and in our service.

What sets you apart from the competition?
Our product offering is designed to offer fewer choices than large retailers; however, we focus on current trends and pay close attention to our customers. Because we're a small boutique, we get to know our customers; their wants and needs. And we offer product that isn't offered in other stores in our market.

How did you determine your price point for your merchandise?
Our prices range from $110 to $600 for a pair of shoes, with an average price point between $160 and $170. Our customers appreciate quality over quantity and recognize they pay more for quality merchandise. We offer merchandise that lasts for years. We didn't want "throw away" merchandise. While we offer limited product at lower price points, it's not our primary focus.

How did you identify the financial resources available to open and grow your business?
We sought the help of our local Small Business Development Center. [Its staff was] helpful in helping us recognize the funding options we had available. At their suggestion we sought debt financing and established a relationship with our loan officer before we actually applied for the loan. The lender appreciated our proactive approach and knew we were serious business people.

When we were in a position to grow the business, we sought angel investors. We contacted friends and family that led to the successful acquisition of equity financing.

You recently relocated your business. Why did you change locations?
We needed to sell more product and knew that our prior location was limiting. The demographics of that market didn't allow us to offer the higher-end merchandise, nor did it offer us the ability to increase sales.

How has the change in location affected the business financially?
Our sales have almost doubled. We now carry product that we would not have been able to sell in the prior location. Our current location provides us with a bigger market.

What financial information do you review to make management and/or financial decisions in your business? And how frequently do you review this information?

We review our cash flow statement on a daily basis. We monitor our cash closely. We have developed systems that allow us to monitor bills and invoices daily and when merchandise will arrive. We also have financial documents in place that allow us to track when and what revenue will be received against estimated revenue. We maintain a cash buffer and know that if the numbers dip above or below our cash buffer, we need to do something. We monitor this daily.

While we use an open-to-buy, in our business a monthly open-to-buy isn't how our product or business works. At times, we find we have to order product 6 months in advance just to get the product produced by the vendor. We monitor our cash flow statement and income statement closely.

What would you say are the five key elements for running your business, from a financial perspective?

» Having firm grasp on your expenses.

» Having realistic revenue projections.

» Knowing when to receive merchandise. The delivery schedule is important. We attend trade shows and at times find that vendors want to tell you when they will ship. Some say it ships in two weeks, and we find we can't pay for the product in two weeks. We have to know how to negotiate to space out deliveries.

» Negotiating terms. As a new customer to a vendor, it's often required that you pay cash on delivery or you prepay for merchandise. We negotiate for a thirty-day term. Retailers have a say, too, particularly in this economy.

» Relationships with vendors are very important. We're honest with our vendors. If we need to delay payment on an invoice, we e-mail or call their accounts payable department and let them know immediately. We don't wait for them to call. It's made a difference in our business, from a financial perspective.

» Managing payroll. The cost of an employee is more than the dollar amount paid to [him or her] per hour. As a business owner, we pay payroll taxes, and so forth.

What is the best way to achieve long-term success, in your opinion, from a financial standpoint?

We're open to evolve, and that's made us successful. What we did three years ago we're not doing now. Don't be married to a concept. You want to surprise people.

What have you done that has helped you grow the business?

We relocated to an area that had the market we wanted to target. In our previous location, projected revenues were not where we needed them to be. To become profitable, we needed to relocate.

What advice do you have for someone starting [his or her] own business?

Be patient in the development and research process. Don't be so anxious to open your business that you sacrifice good research and the development of a strong business plan. Sometimes people think the business needs to be opened quickly to prevent someone else from opening the same type business. We didn't worry about that. We recommend taking a year to complete the planning process.

CHAPTER 12
DEVELOPING OPERATING AND CONTROL SYSTEMS

OBJECTIVES

>> Define and describe the operations and control functions of the fashion retail business.

>> Understand the operations function, from space allocation to business security.

>> Examine the inventory and its operational needs, such as receiving, marking and preparing goods for the sales floor, and calculating physical inventory for financial analysis.

>> Explore operational policies and procedures as they pertain to the merchandise and the vendors that provide it, the employees who work for the company, and the customers who sustain the business.

>> Consider the importance of research and development as it relates to the operations of the business.

PERATIONS encompass the procedures and policies that an organization must develop and implement for its merchandising and management functions. The operations part of a business is often referred to as operations and control.

Simply defined, operations are the procedures put in place to actually run the business. Control, in contrast, is the process through which results are compared with the goals and objectives. Operations are concerned with how to do things. Control is concerned with how to do things better and what obstacles to quality performance should be removed.

An operations and control plan regulates the day-to-day functions of a business, from the receiving of new merchandise to following up on the customer's purchase. A good operations and control plan facilitates a number of goals for the organization: It communicates and coordinates the activities within the business. It acts as a monitoring tool by providing continuity and assessing quality. It summarizes information about the organization's infrastructure.

How does the entrepreneur begin to develop an operational plan for the new business? Reviewing the operations and procedures manuals of existing businesses can give the entrepreneur a head start in recognizing the operations and control plans that will be needed. Envisioning the daily, weekly, and monthly tasks that must be completed to run the business smoothly and profitably is yet another way to design an operational plan for the organization (FIGURE 12.1). In this chapter, operations and control systems are examined as they relate to the facility, the merchandise, the employees, and the customers.

FIGURE 12.1

Store maintenance is one of many daily tasks to plan for in the entrepreneurial retail business.

OPERATIONS AND THE FACILITY

In operations the facility is examined from an internal perspective, beginning with the actual space—whether brick-and-mortar or an Internet click site. There are a number of operational issues that relate directly to the actual location of the business. These include space allocation, staff efficiency, customer mobility, hours of operation, leasehold improvements, utilities and maintenance needs, and business security.

SPACE ALLOCATION

The area within a brick-and-mortar retail operation can be divided into four types of space: the sales floor, the customer service area, the merchandise warehousing and handling zone, and the staff or personnel areas. The sales floor is the space that holds merchandise the customer can purchase. Customer service areas include dressing rooms, lounges, restrooms, coffee and juice bars, restaurants, checkout stations, credit departments, and merchandise return stations. The merchandise warehousing and handling zone may include receiving areas, space that holds merchandise off the sales floor (e.g., back stock and layaway), and alteration departments. Staff members may utilize space in the forms of offices, lounges, lunchrooms, conference rooms, and training areas.

Not every business needs every kind of space allocation. One of the managerial tasks of the retail entrepreneur is to determine, first, which business operations actually need space and, second, how much space to allocate for these operations. The amount of square footage to be allotted for displaying and housing merchandise to be sold is referred to as **selling space**. The remaining areas are called **nonselling space**.

Determining how much selling and nonselling space to allocate is a major decision for the entrepreneur. This decision will affect the estimated sales per square foot of the business, as this calculation is generated solely by the amount of square footage given to selling space. The more selling space a business has, the greater the opportunity to generate sales volume. Typically, a store dedicates from 65 percent to 85 percent of its space to the actual selling of merchandise.

STAFF EFFICIENCY

Staff efficiency works hand in hand with the business layout. For example, if the dressing rooms are located far from the selling floor, the sales associate has run a marathon by the time the workday is over. If the merchandise is so congested on the selling floor that sales associates cannot monitor the inventory, then missed sales and merchandise losses from theft may be high. If the telephone is located in the office, then the sales associate will have to leave the floor to answer it. A primary goal in designing the facility layout is to accommodate the duties of the staff in order to make the operation run more smoothly.

CUSTOMER MOBILITY

Like staff efficiency, the layout of a facility can affect customer mobility. **Customer mobility** is the ability of customers to enter the establishment, move about the business, and find the merchandise they are seeking. It is also about accessibility for clientele with physical limitations. Entrepreneurs need to ask themselves if a customer with physical restrictions can move through the aisles, comfortably use a dressing room or restroom, and write a check or provide a debit card at the cash desk.

HOURS OF OPERATION

In certain locations the hours of operation are predetermined for the business. In most strip centers or malls, for example, the lease agreement includes designated hours of operation by which the businesses must abide. If the entrepreneur has located the business in a facility that does not require specific hours of operation, there are several factors that may influence which hours are chosen. The entrepreneur should examine what neighboring businesses are doing in terms of opening and closing times. Also, the entrepreneur should explore the times that the organization's customer will most likely prefer to do business. For example, if a fashion retail operation appeals to a target market dominated by college students, it is unlikely that an 8:00 AM opening will elicit much customer traffic. Finally, the entrepreneur should consider external factors, such as safety, parking, and transportation options for the business's location.

LEASEHOLD IMPROVEMENTS

Operational concerns related to the leasing of the facility include the length and terms of the lease, particularly whether it is a straight lease or rent plus a percentage of sales. These issues, as well as improvements and additions (e.g., signs, wall fixtures, and utility hookups) must be considered within operational and financial plans. Will the entrepreneur pay these costs directly, split them with the landlord, or make payments to the landlord for these investments? In most cases permanent improvements, such as paint, wallpaper, and track lighting, become the property of the landlord once the lease is terminated. The rule of thumb is that if it will require repairs after it is removed, it is likely that it must remain. The important guideline for the entrepreneur is to check the lease and double-check with the landlord before assuming who pays for what and who owns what.

UTILITIES AND MAINTENANCE NEEDS

The costs of gas, water, and electricity may be covered as part of the lease; more commonly, however, the entrepreneur will be required to pay them directly to utility providers. An objective of the entrepreneur should be to estimate and anticipate these operational costs for the financial section of the business plan. In addition, the entrepreneur will want to identify energy-efficient measures to control these expenses. Light and temperature controls set to turn off when the business is closed, for example, can reduce the cost of utilities. Other facility expenses may be optional, such as janitorial assistance or trash removal. Ongoing and required facility maintenance expenses must be incorporated into the monthly financial plan if they are not part of the monthly lease payment.

SECURITY

Protecting the facility may include a security system, or a security guard, depending on the business location and type. The cost of installing a security system, if one is not in place, may be negotiated as part of the lease agreement. If there is a security system in place, the entrepreneur will likely have monthly costs associated with operating the system. These costs should be included in the financial plan. Furthermore, procedures for operating the security system need to be developed for personnel who open and close the business.

OPERATIONS AND THE MERCHANDISE

Operational procedures need to be established for receiving, marking, and preparing goods for the sales floor (e.g., steaming, hanging, and tagging merchandise). The accuracy and timeliness of paying vendors, pricing merchandise, and keeping records are dependent upon these processes. Cost, accuracy, and time efficiency are significant goals for the entrepreneur when addressing receiving and ticketing of merchandise. For example, if a handbag style that sells out is ticketed with an incorrect style number, the entrepreneur may reorder the wrong handbag; if it takes seven days to receive, ticket, and steam a shipment of dresses for the sales floor, there is a lost week of sales on this order.

RECEIVING GOODS

The purchase order is a contract that designates when merchandise is shipped too late to mandate receipt by the entrepreneur. As examined in Chapter 10, the completion date is the last day that the buyer has authorized the vendor to ship the merchandise. It is the buyer's decision whether to accept or return goods shipped past the cancellation date. In some cases, the buyer will contact the vendor to negotiate a reduced price on merchandise shipped late. In other cases, the goods will be returned to the vendor.

If the completion date is acceptable, the invoice is checked against the purchase order, and the correct style, color, size, number of units, and price are checked. The **invoice** is the vendor's detailed shipment listing with prices. Next, the **packing slip**, the vendor's listing of merchandise in a particular carton or container, is checked against the invoice. Some orders may be shipped in a series of cartons, each with an individual packing slip and with one invoice for the total shipment. When the paperwork provided by the vendor has been reconciled with the purchase order, the merchandise can be checked into inventory. Any discrepancies, such as shortages or overages, are noted on the purchase order for adjustments by the employee responsible for accounting. FIGURE 12.2 illustrates the entrepreneur using the computer to add merchandise receipts into the inventory before preparing the merchandise for the sales floor.

MARKING GOODS

After the merchandise is checked in, tickets with the necessary information are prepared and attached

FIGURE 12.2

Receiving merchandise requires financial accuracy and preparation of inventory for the sales floor.

to the goods. Some entrepreneurs use a specialized ticket-making machine; others use computer software to generate tickets; and a few prepare the tickets by hand. The entrepreneur will want to predetermine the data that will be included on the ticket.

Commonly, a department number indicating merchandise classification number, vendor identification number, style number, size, color or color number, and retail price are included. Moreover, some operations include the date the merchandise will be ticketed. Often, a code is used for the ticketing date so that this is not obvious to the customer. For example, the month of the year may be indicated by letters of the alphabet (e.g., A for January, B for February, C for March, and so on), whereas the actual day of the month is indicated by the corresponding number. In this case, February 26 would be represented by B26. Dating merchandise is extremely helpful in locating merchandise when it is time to take markdowns. Examples of merchandise tickets are illustrated in FIGURE 12.3.

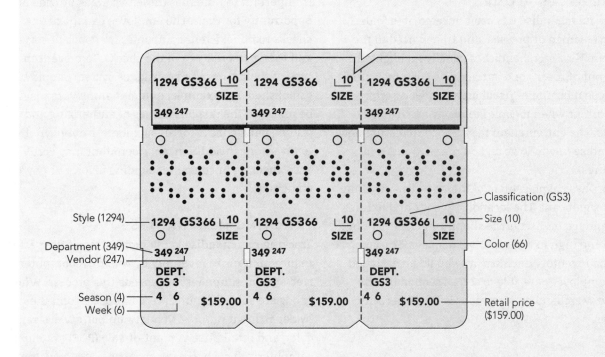

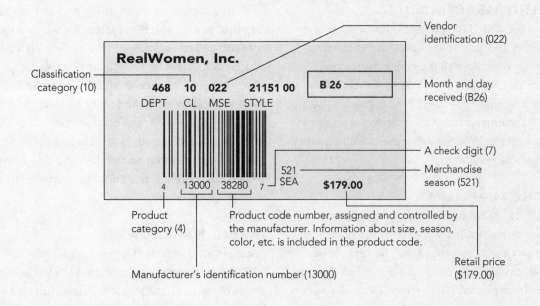

FIGURE 12.3

Examples of merchandise tickets.

PLACING MERCHANDISE ON THE SALES FLOOR

After the merchandise has been ticketed, it is folded or hung, steamed or pressed, and transported to the sales floor. New merchandise is usually highlighted at the front of the store to attract new customers and entice repeat clientele. Visual merchandising efforts are important when it comes to newly arrived merchandise. The entrepreneur may decide to feature new merchandise in windows and on mannequins and key fixtures.

The physical placement of merchandise in selling space is significant. The location of goods and fixtures can encourage or discourage shoplifting. Thieves can hide behind high fixtures and tall displays. The layout of the inventory and displays should be designed so that employees are able to see all sections of the business. Merchandise placement is key to security and sales.

OPERATIONS AND THE VENDORS PROVIDING MERCHANDISE

Another area for which the entrepreneur will want to develop policies and procedures pertains to the merchandise and the vendors that provide these goods. Strategies for paying vendors, tracking merchandise sales, taking markdowns, and returning goods to suppliers enable the entrepreneur to maintain a positive credit rating and monitor the sales volume and quality of performance of vendors.

PAYING THE SUPPLIERS

When the merchandise has been received, the purchase order, invoice, and packing slip(s) are filed together for payment. In most cases, the retailer has thirty days to pay the bill. When the buyer has a solid business relationship with the vendor, he or she may attempt to negotiate **dating**, an additional amount of time in which to pay the vendor. Dating usually means another thirty days before payment is due, or sixty days in total. This is noted on the purchase order as "30X." When the bill is paid, the check number and date of mailing are noted on the invoice.

If an employee pays bills and handles checks, it is important to note that these two areas provide an opportunity for theft. The employee can make out checks to nonexistent companies for goods or services and then personally cash the checks. To prevent this type of theft, a check-and-balance system should be established. For example, different employees may be assigned the responsibilities of authorizing and issuing bank checks for all payments, from payroll to inventory. In addition, an accountant may verify each check against a corresponding invoice or payroll statement.

TRACKING MERCHANDISE

Tracking merchandise is the monitoring of the performance of items in inventory by vendor. A computerized system simplifies and speeds this process. When goods are sold, they are entered into the computer by department number, vendor number, style, size, color, and retail price. A **point-of-sale (POS)** system is a computerized cash register that generates a customer receipt while adjusting the retail dollar inventory level. In addition to maintaining a record of merchandise that is sold, the POS system tracks items that are returned or exchanged. The system also records which items are sold or returned by vendor, providing a "scoresheet" for each supplier. The result is a complete analysis of sales and stock by unit and vendor. By analyzing these data, the entrepreneur, or buyer, can determine which vendors should be carried again the next season, which merchandise should be reordered, and which merchandise should be reduced in price to encourage sales.

TAKING MARKDOWNS

Taking markdowns is the process of designating, marking, and recording reductions in the selling prices of items that are not selling at full retail price. Markdowns are a fact of life in fashion retailing. The entrepreneur will want to establish a policy and procedure for taking markdowns. The policy may include what to markdown (e.g., merchandise that is more than thirty days old) and when to take the markdown (e.g., the first of every month). The policy should also indicate how to take markdowns. For example, entrepreneurs may determine that the first markdown will be a reduction of 30 percent off the initial price. They may decide that this price change will be noted on the merchandise ticket in red pen and that all markdowns will be processed in the computer system, according to department and vendor. Precise records of markdown amounts are necessary in order to generate an accurate inventory result (FIGURE 12.4). A detailed record of markdowns also enables the buyer to determine which vendors provided the best sales and profit performance and which vendors should be eliminated from the inventory.

FIGURE 12.4
Precise markdown amounts are necessary to generate an accurate inventory amount.

RETURNING GOODS TO THE VENDOR
When does the retailer find it necessary to return merchandise to a vendor? There are a number of reasons for an **RTM (return to the manufacturer)**, also referred to as an **RTV (return to the vendor)**. Goods shipped past the cancellation date may be designated by the buyer as returns. Also, defective merchandise may need to be returned to the vendor. Or the buyer may negotiate with the manufacturer's representative to return styles that did not sell for an exchange for other styles or a merchandise credit toward future purchases. In any case, the retailer cannot simply ship the merchandise back to the manufacturer. Instead, the buyer must request a **return authorization label** from the vendor. This label, which is attached to the carton containing the return, ensures that the shipment will be accepted at the receiving dock of the manufacturer. It is important for the entrepreneur to calculate returns as a reduction in inventory by deducting the cost and retail price of the RTM from the stock figure. If this is not done, the amount of the RTM will appear to be a shortage that may be interpreted as a loss from theft.

OPERATIONS AND THE EMPLOYEES
The number of employees the business will require is dependent upon a number of factors, including the size of the facility, the need for merchandise security, the number of customers in the store, the level of assistance these customers will require, and the amount of funding that will be allocated for payroll. When funding for payroll has been calculated, the next step is determining the number of employees as well as the hours each employee will work.

Although there is no fail-safe system for hiring perfect employees, the entrepreneur can improve the probability of finding and keeping good employees by following a few simple procedures, such as adhering to job descriptions when determining training strategies. From an operations perspective the entrepreneur will want to have established policies and procedures for motivating, managing, and maintaining effective employees.

TRAINING EMPLOYEES

There are three key pieces of advice for entrepreneurs when it comes to hiring effective employees, while minimizing the level of training they will likely require. The entrepreneur should look for actual accomplishments, or outcomes, by carefully interviewing candidates and reviewing job applications, résumés, and references. The entrepreneur should also look for the personal attributes that will benefit the position. Finally, the entrepreneur should look for people with good contacts. The entrepreneur needs employees who can hit the floor running and, subsequently, produce revenue quickly. If the position is, for example, that of sales associate, then the applicant who has an established clientele at a similar organization nearby will be a preferred candidate, assuming that all other factors are positive. Because the entrepreneur will be in a race to reach the break-even point, there is often not enough time to develop a sales force from square one. In addition, employees with work experience in receiving, purchasing, and promotion not only provide expertise in these areas, but also bring with them contacts. These contacts can prove helpful in pricing and shipping of supplies and merchandise.

As entrepreneurs prepare a training plan for employees, they will assess the job candidates in terms of how they will get along with each other. The entrepreneur will also want to evaluate which tasks will require training for all employees, whether staff members will be able to function cooperatively and interdependently, and whether differences in personalities and job descriptions require several types of training programs.

Even if the new employees the entrepreneur hires have previous work experience in a similar retail operation, they will need to be trained on the methods of the particular business. Whether the job is assisting a customer, processing shipments, arranging merchandise, or operating the computer, there should be a procedure to follow. Many entrepreneurs compile an **employee procedures manual** that lists business policies and procedures. Some entrepreneurs prefer to work individually with each employee. Others believe in a more informal approach to employee training.

Many leaders in entrepreneurship encourage interaction by asking employees for input on how to do things in a better way. Some do not believe in detailed procedures manuals. Instead, they teach employees the principles and give them plenty of room to develop—from the store managers to the employee who tickets merchandise for the sales floor. If employees are properly taught, they feel responsibility, understand what needs to be done, and have the freedom and confidence to offer suggestions on how to do things better.

In teaching employees how the business operates, there is a six-step training technique that many employers have found to be effective in formal and informal training situations:

1. The employer describes the task and explains how it should be accomplished.

2. The employer demonstrates the task.

3. The employee is asked to explain how the task should be done.

4. The employee actually does the task.

5. The employer provides feedback when the employee finishes the task, offering both praise and suggestions in areas which the employee could improve.

6. The employer confirms that the job is being accomplished in the appropriate manner.

The objective in coaching employees is to guide them fairly, consistently, and tactfully (FIGURE 12.5). Employees need to know what is expected and how they are doing. Regular employee reviews help communicate this information.

COMPENSATION AND INCENTIVES

Most employees need compensation and incentive programs to provide the consistent motivation needed to keep them pushing forward. **Compensation** is the employee's payment for services rendered. The most common form of compensation is **fixed-rate compensation**, payment that is not tied exclusively to performance. This type of compensation is set at a specific

FIGURE 12.5

Training employees to use products for sale enables them to sell the items to customers more effectively.

level for a specified time period, such as an hourly wage or a monthly salary. In the fashion industry there are variations on fixed-rate compensation that may motivate employees to work harder and to remain employed with the organization. These compensation methods are referred to as **variable-rate**, or **merit**, **compensation** programs, because they tie pay directly to the performance of the individual or group (i.e., department, area, organization, or a combination of these).

One method of variable-rate compensation that is common in fashion entrepreneurial organizations is **sales commission**. There are a number of types of commission plans. The simplest form is **straight commission**. Through this plan, sales associates are paid a percentage of their sales volume. In most situations, returns are deducted from future commission payments. Another commission alternative is **quota plus commission**. Here, the sales person is assigned a sales goal (e.g., hourly, weekly, or monthly sales volume performance) by management. The sales person receives a specified percentage of commission on sales generated above the quota. Yet another commission alternative is **hourly plus commission**, also referred to as **base plus commission**. With this arrangement, sales associates earn a set amount for each hour, week, or month worked as well as a percentage of their individual sales volume.

A word of warning is necessary regarding compensation plans that include a form of commission, particularly straight commission. The sales person receiving commission may go to extremes to make a sale. The result can be pushy salespeople who see little return business and much fighting among sales associates. Moreover, customers who do not appear to be making a purchase (in the view of the commissioned sales person) may not be serviced at all (Box 12.1).

The chief emeritus of a high-end department store told the story of a woman who was not being waited on by the sales associates in one of his stores. She did not resemble the usual, well-heeled customer. The executive proceeded to assist this customer himself. It turned out that oil had recently been discovered on her family's land. The customer had the desire and the money to purchase everything needed to furnish a new mansion and several walk-in closets. Also, the "sell or starve" aspect of commission is not appealing to some highly capable salespeople. There is not an easy answer to motivating sales personnel.

The entrepreneur should keep in mind, however, that exceptional customer service separates the retail business from its competitors and provides a foundation for success (FIGURE 12.6). Commission can be

FIGURE 12.6

Exceptional customer service can separate the entrepreneurial business from its sea of competitors and should be recognized in employee compensation.

counterproductive if improperly designed and managed but, if managed effectively, can add to the profitability of the business.

Finally, the employer may offer compensation packages unique to that particular business. A share of the profits of the business, or stock options, may be offered by the entrepreneur as compensation and incentive rolled into one. The possibility of increased future earnings and the opportunity to own a piece of a thriving business may attract exceptional employees when highly competitive salaries are difficult to offer in the start-up business.

It is important for the entrepreneur to identify a number of incentives in order to keep employees motivated. **Incentives** are methods developed to generate high performances by employees. Successful retail entrepreneurs agree that the more immediate the reward, the more effective it is. Some will offer a cash prize, a special merchandise discount, or an item from stock as a reward for top sales on a given day. But incentives are not restricted to cash prizes; they can vary from preferred days off to recognition awards. **Merchandise discounts** are another form of incentive that many fashion retailers use to recruit and reward employees. Merchandise discounts are mutually beneficial because they encourage the sales person to purchase and wear merchandise carried by the business. Salespeople are, in essence, walking advertisements for the company.

A **bonus**, a lump sum payment on performance over an extended period of time, can also provide motivation for employees. For example, the entrepreneur may offer employees a percentage of the sales volume achieved exceeding the annual sales goal, to be divided according to hours worked. As an example, the founder of a major mass merchandising chain offered company employees a bonus for keeping losses generated from shoplifting, employee pilferage, and clerical error under control. As a result, the company's shortage percentage was at an all-time low while employees gained a sense of pride, ownership, and responsibility. An attractive compensation and incentive program is needed to attract and maintain the best employees possible. This includes offering a competitive salary, with the possibility of future increased earnings, in a thriving work environment where expectations are known, and accomplishing these expectations is achievable.

REPRIMANDS AND TERMINATIONS

Negative aspects of being an entrepreneur include reprimanding employees who are not doing their jobs well and, even worse, terminating employees who are not effective. Selection procedures are not perfect. Sooner or later, someone who seemed right for the job will not work out. The need to terminate an employee may be very clear, as in cases such as theft or excessive absences. Sometimes, however, the reason to fire an employee may be less clear-cut. Before an employee is fired, the entrepreneur will want to be certain that everything possible has been done to help him or her succeed at the job. The entrepreneur will need to articulate the problems clearly, suggest ways to improve, and provide a time limit for improvements to be seen. Along the way, the entrepreneur will want to document efforts to help the employee succeed. The entrepreneur should compile a written record of the dates of reprimands and related discussions, the desired outcomes, the deadline for improvements, and the consequences of no improvement. If, after a final warning, there has been no improvement, then the entrepreneur has a responsibility to the business and the rest of the staff to terminate the employee.

COMMUNICATION WITH EMPLOYEES

Communicative supervision is the key to a satisfied staff and a profitable business. Staff meetings, memos, and meetings between an employee and the entrepreneur represent important communication efforts. The entrepreneur or supervisor should be available to answer questions, discuss problems, and suggest solutions when the employee needs assistance and direction.

OPERATIONS AND THE CUSTOMER

Operational plans must be designed for the business to interact effectively with its customer. Procedures may be established for approaching and assisting the customer, ringing up a sale, processing a return, following up on a purchase, and dealing with customer complaints. What are the advantages to developing operational plans for customer interaction? Such

strategies help ensure that the customer will receive consistent and efficient service. In addition, these efforts aid in building the confidence of sales associates and in generating repeat business.

APPROACHING AND ASSISTING THE CUSTOMER

There is a selling strategy that has been passed on from salesperson to salesperson for generations. There are variations of this actual plan. In some, the steps are in a different order. In others, two steps may be condensed into one. In all the variations, however, the techniques for selling are basically the same. According to most, the ten steps to a successful sales transaction are as follows:

1. Approach the customer, and gain his or her attention.

2. Establish rapport with the customer.

3. Find out what the customer's needs are through active listening.

4. Explain how the product will fill those needs by emphasizing its benefits.

5. Deal with customer concerns.

6. Gain commitment, and close the sale.

7. Try suggestive selling to make the "extra sale" of an accessory or an additional service.

8. Ring up the sale, and package the merchandise.

9. Reinforce the purchase decision, and thank the customer.

10. Walk the customer to the door, invite him or her to return soon, and follow up on the sale.

How do these steps influence the operational plan of a business? For many of the steps, procedures need to be developed and implemented to enable sales associates to do their job and to ensure that the business runs smoothly. What if, for example, the sales associate closes the sale but does not know how to ring it up? In many cases, the customer

At Topshop, service is paramount, with the experience of shopping being as important as the garment you pick up.

STYLE ADVISOR

In 2001, Topshop launched its hugely successful and complimentary Style Advisor service. Tailor-made to help

customers find anything from the perfect pair of jeans to the ultimate capsule wardrobe, this service is available by appointment at eighteen stores across the UK. As part of the exceptionally popular service, customers also get to use the VIP fitting rooms, browse through style magazines and books, enjoy refreshments, and even queue jump at the end.

TOPSHOP TO GO

Following the success of Style Advisor, Topshop launched Topshop To Go, a mobile style service aiming to provide the ultimate in home shopping. Wherever a customer is, Topshop Style Advisors will come armed with all the latest temptations that the store has to offer, from premium ranges and accessories to shoes.

TOPSHOP EXPRESS

This is the ultimate solution for fashion emergencies. Send a text of what you need to our Style Advisors; they'll endeavor to find the perfect thing for you. They'll even courier it to you within the same day. This service is currently available from the Oxford Circus flagship store to customers within the Greater London area.

MEMBERSHIP CARD

April 2008 saw the launch of the fabulous new premium Style Advisor membership card, inviting those serious about their style to collect loyalty rewards when spending with the Style Advisor service.

SOURCE: http://www.topman.com/careers/about_brands/ts_services.html.

would be headed for the door, empty-handed, before the sales associate could figure out how to process the sale.

Some businesses develop customer shopping programs to generate repeat business and build a clientele. These programs may include personal shopping assistance, complimentary alterations and purchase deliveries, and invitations to exclusive fashion events. Employees need to be informed about the policies and procedures of these activities and know how to promote them. Case Study 12.1 features Topshop and its lineup of customer incentive programs.

WRITING UP THE SALE— THE TRANSACTION FLOW

Most businesses operate on a computerized system. A customer **transaction** is a cash or credit sale, an exchange, or a return (FIGURE 12.7). Some businesses also offer a **layaway** plan, in which the customer has merchandise held by putting down a deposit and then making weekly or monthly payments on the merchandise until it is paid off. Layaway has become less prevalent in recent years because of the increasing speed of fashion cycles, which generate quicker markdowns. Frequently, the customer who places an item in layaway will find it at a reduced price by the time the payments are made in full. The customer will then want to receive the clearance price on the layaway merchandise. As a result of this problem, as well as limited warehousing space, a number of fashion retailers have eliminated the layaway option.

Cash and credit transactions require different procedures and policies, all of which need to be designed before the company actually opens for business. Cash transactions are the simplest. The customer's purchase is entered in the computer, or cash register, and a customer receipt is generated. The merchandise **stockkeeping unit (SKU)** is the identification number used to tag each item. The SKU and corresponding retail price should be processed for inventory reconciliation,

FIGURE 12.7

Transaction flow tracks the sale of an item as it is removed from the physical inventory, and the vendor is credited for its sale.

whether cash, debit, or credit. The process for accepting bank checks must also be clarified. Will out-of-state checks be accepted? Which types of identification will be required? Are second-party checks acceptable? Company checks? Will the business use a service such as TeleCheck to approve customer checks? If the business accepts major credit cards, the procedure can be explained by a representative of the bank providing this service to the business. The appropriate forms and telephone contact numbers and an employer identification number are tools the sales associate must have to make this transaction run smoothly.

HANDLING RETURNS

The entrepreneur must decide who will be authorized to accept returns and under what circumstances returned merchandise will be accepted. Return policies often identify a time limit (e.g., up to thirty days after purchase), whether a receipt will be required, whether the item must have the ticket attached, and whether the item is redeemable for cash or a company credit. Retailers are finding that liberal return policies are expected by most customers. As accommodating customers with returns is viewed as a component of good customer service, a number of entrepreneurs are embracing a philosophy of "the customer is always right" and developing ways to deal with returns without losing clientele or profits. For example, a customer brings a child's dress she purchased back to the retail store because the neckline frayed when the garment was washed. Rather than immediately refunding the customer's money, the storeowner might offer to have the garment repaired by an alteration service. The repair would cost about as much as the shipping fee to return the garment to the manufacturer.

FOLLOWING UP ON SALES

It takes just a moment to thank a customer, yet the memory of the thank-you lingers far longer. If an entrepreneur truly contemplates how many places the customer can purchase similar goods, it would be quite a long list. Direct competitors, indirect competitors, catalogs, Web sites, and discount retailers are all enticing the customer to buy from them.

Employees should be trained to consistently and sincerely thank their clientele. A spoken word, a thank-you note, or a follow-up call can help generate repeat business and encourage word-of-mouth promotion. Again, the employees should be provided with the tools to do this job successfully. One entrepreneur provided employees with stamped postcards to use as thank-you notes. She rewarded those employees who faithfully sent these cards to customers with a merchandise gift certificate.

Another method of following up on the sale is maintaining a **client file**. Employees are asked to complete customer profile forms that contain information about the customer, contact information, size, brand preferences, past purchases, and personal information. An example of a customer profile form is shown in FIGURE 12.8. Such forms enable the sales associate to preselect newly arrived merchandise for the customer and to contact him or her for an early look at the items. In essence, this method encourages the sales associate to be a personal shopper for the customers.

DEALING WITH CUSTOMER COMPLAINTS

Some people avoid conflict. Others take it personally. Still others resolve the problem and use the experience to improve and grow. Employees need to be educated on how to handle complaints. The entrepreneur should clarify how employees are to handle disgruntled customers. Futhermore, the entrepreneur should let employees know when and to whom they should refer complaints they feel they cannot resolve themselves. Personnel, merchandise, and general business complaints need to be communicated to the supervisor by the staff in order to resolve problems effectively. The entrepreneur may also want to implement procedures to allow employees to make suggestions or voice concerns. It is better for the employee to discuss business problems with the supervisor than to share them with other employees or customers.

OPERATIONS AND THE INVENTORY

The inventory is one of the business's most significant assets. Too much or too little of it can undermine the best sales associates, the best promotional campaign, and the best location. To carry the right amount and type of merchandise, certain information must be available. Data on how much stock is on hand, which vendors are selling or not selling, and which customers are buying or not buying can be accurately accessed if operations and control strategies are put into place.

METHODS OF INVENTORY MANAGEMENT

Careful inventory management is one of the most important contributing factors in a successful fashion business. On the one hand, each piece of merchandise that is simply hanging around, whether on the sales floor or in the stockroom, represents money that has been spent and that is losing value because of the perishability of fashion goods. On the other hand, if there is an inadequate amount of inventory, the entrepreneur cannot expect to reach sales goals. In those cases, often not only are sales lost, but also customers, not finding what they are looking for, do not return. Maintaining the right level of inventory is a balancing act. Information is the key to finding the right balance.

The type and amount of information shared about the customer and the vendors can directly affect the quality of inventory management. If the buyer has access to information about exactly what is and is not selling and relationships with vendors that allow him or her to respond to this information, the inventory will be what customers want when they want it. Just-in-time inventory control is dependent upon the vendor–buyer relationship and adequate communication systems. **Just-in-time** is the system in which inventory is shipped as it is sold. Hanes, for example, provides a just-in-time inventory replenishment system. The retailer provides sales data to Hanes as soon as the merchandise is sold, most often through the computer system. Because the retailer has established a model stock with the vendor, Hanes can automatically ship fill-ins for sold merchandise. As a result, the stock is maintained, customers find what they are looking for, and the buyer does not spend time counting inventory and placing reorders.

A CUSTOMER PROFILE FORM FOR SALES ASSOCIATES

RealWomen, Inc.

CLIENT PROFILE

| NAME | | TITLE or NICKNAME |
| Irene Magnin | | Mrs. |

| DATE ENTERED | ○ CASH | CUSTOMER NUMBER |
| 1/20/12 | ○ CHARGE | 160 01 7872 |

| CHARGE ACCOUNT | | OTHER CHARGE TYPE | VALID/EXP. DATE |
| Visa | | ○ AE   ○ MC | 10/13 |

ADDRESS (Billing Address)
1000 Broadway

| CITY | STATE | ZIP CODE |
| Diva City | State | 555122 |

SECOND ADDRESS
2600 Park Avenue

| CITY | STATE | ZIP CODE |
| Palm Desert | CA | 92260 |

| HOME PHONE | OFFICE PHONE | E-MAIL |
| (114) 555-1212 | (415) 555-0821 | |

OCCUPATION
Owner of Fragrance Company

| CONTACT PREFERENCE | PREFERRED CONTACT TIME |
| ○ PHONE   ○ HOME   ○ WORK   ○ MAIL   ○ EMAIL | No Weekends - 10-12AM (M-F) |

| BIRTHDAY | OTHER SPECIAL DATES |
| 4/14 | 2/22 - anniversary, 10/18 - daughter's birthday |

SIZE INFORMATION
16 - jacket, pants, skirt, dress
14 or 16 - shirt

VENDOR AND STYLE PREFERENCES

Likes updated, Armani-ish styles, lightweight, quality fabrics, subtle, pulled together, combos.
Travels - packable coordinates

PERSONAL INFORMATION

Approximately 5'6"
Age - early 30s
Demanding, sense of humor
ASK ABOUT DAUGHTER

FIGURE 12.8

INVENTORY CONTROL

There are two primary methods for valuing and recording inventory. **LIFO (last in, first out)** places a higher value on the most recently received merchandise. **FIFO (first in, last out)** applies a higher value to goods that were received earlier. Because these methods can have significantly different tax implications, depending on the business, most entrepreneurs consult with an accountant before determining which valuation method to apply.

Shrinkage is the industry term for inventory losses resulting from employee theft, shoplifting, and clerical error. A **physical inventory count** is a formal, item-by-item analysis of the operation's stock on hand. The selling price of each item and, possibly, the vendor and style numbers are recorded, and then all prices are totaled to create a physical price inventory dollar valuation. The physical inventory count is usually conducted at the end of a selling season, when the stock level is at a low point, either annually or biannually. The result of the physical inventory is compared with the **book inventory**, the financial record of the stock. If there is less physical inventory than book inventory, the difference is referred to as a **shortage**. Shortages are caused by theft and bookkeeping errors, such as not recording markdowns or employee discounts. In contrast, if the physical inventory is greater than the book inventory, the difference is called **overage**. An overage indicates that there are clerical errors in one of the accounting functions, such as recording merchandise receipts, posting markdowns, or returning goods to the manufacturer.

MERCHANDISE FULFILLMENT AND CUSTOMER NEEDS

Finding the right product for the customer is the entrepreneur's goal in planning a merchandise assortment. Making certain the customer receives this product, in good condition and in a timely manner, is the critical follow-up step. Training employees, from shipping clerks to sales associates, in customer services can pay dividends in repeat business and referrals. The entrepreneur will want to develop policies and procedures that allow employees to accommodate customers' special orders and special requests. Employees should be empowered to make certain decisions on their own, such as exchanging merchandise, rather than requiring the customer to wait for management assistance.

How does the entrepreneur assess merchandise fulfillment processes as they relate to customer service? **Merchandise fulfillment** is the process of filling customers' requests and orders. This encompasses mail, phone, and Internet purchases as well as on-the-floor sales. Entrepreneurs should develop a process and assign themselves, or a staff member, to hear customer feedback, from complaints to congratulations. In purchasing, the entrepreneur or buyer should assess vendors in terms of who can provide special orders and rush deliveries. In the inventory area, management should evaluate the presentation and accessibility of merchandise. In the sales area, service provided to customers after purchases are made should be examined. Are alternatives, repairs, returns, and warranties adequately provided to the customer? In the receiving area, the level of accuracy and amount of lead time between receipt of new shipments and availability on the selling floor should be examined.

Supply chain management (SCM) is an integrated approach to all the activities of channel members, including the retail business, its vendors, and its shipping companies. With SCM certain activities are performed by the channel member who can do them most efficiently. For example, if a vendor is able to ship merchandise tagged and on hangers more efficiently than the retailer can, the vendor will take over these operations in SCM. In addition, the vendor may ship a special order directly to the customer to save the retailer and the consumer time and money. The vendor may also service products as part of SCM. For example, a customer may purchase a watch with a manufacturer's warranty from a retail operation. If the watch needs repair, rather than returning it to the retailer, the customer may send the watch directly to the vendor for repair or replacement. As the manufacturer has the equipment and knowledge to satisfy the customer most effectively, it takes on the responsibility of repairs. Channel partnerships that benefit all members are the primary objectives of SCM.

RESEARCH AND DEVELOPMENT

Change is at the core of every entrepreneurial operation. Entrepreneurs who view their business from a future perspective have a greater probability of success than those who do not. A business's target market is always changing, as customers relocate, develop new tastes, and seek new products to satisfy new needs. **Research and development (R&D) is** an ongoing analysis of trends and issues that may affect the products, services, operations, promotional efforts, competitors, and customers of the business.

Some companies establish relatively large research and development areas because they deal with constantly evolving technology, rapidly changing fashion trends, or a target market with a great need for new products. Research and development activities may include running a complete department staffed with personnel inventing or experimenting with new products and equipment and devising new promotional techniques. Research and development may also be spearheaded by one person, usually the entrepreneur, who attends conferences and subscribes to publications that focus on the future of the industry or the product classification(s) of the business. Regardless of the scope of the efforts, research and development must be a goal in the operational plan of any type of business.

In research and development the business examines its product types and industry trends from a futuring perspective. Some of the questions that may be asked by the person responsible for managing research and development include the following:

» What new products and services are currently in development?

» What percentage of the staff's time, including the entrepreneur's, is dedicated to research and development?

» What resources, such as publications, seminars, and the Internet, are used by the business to obtain research and development data?

» What equipment and supplies, such as software and merchandise samples, are needed for effective research and development?

» What costs are associated with research and development activities in the business?

» How are research and development findings disseminated within the business?

Research and development may reveal that change provides new opportunities for growth.

OPERATIONS AND THE COMPUTER

Nowhere has change had more impact and speed than in the area of technology. The microcomputer was created by entrepreneurs, and it is as though it was designed for entrepreneurs. The right computer, with the right software, can make all the difference in a business. The computer processes sales transactions, calculates merchandise receipts and returns, cross-checks personnel and merchandise files, figures work schedules and payroll, assesses vendor performance, and analyzes profit potential and cash flow (FIGURE 12.9). It also and keeps the entrepreneur in touch with business information that will help the company survive. An electronic **spreadsheet**, a computer-generated chart, simplifies some of these daunting tasks and increases accuracy. Entrepreneurs have found the computer to be extremely useful in maintaining not only financial records, but also databases on target customers.

Through **cross-filing**, a reference system in which the same information is listed in two or more categories, customer files can be used to generate mailing

FIGURE 12.9

Computer operations are part of each employee's responsibilities, from time cards and work schedules to sales transactions and customer returns.

lists for promotional fliers and newsletters. As an example based on the sample business plan (Appendix D), the owner of RealWomen.Inc., Lucy Rich, can download the names and addresses of all the

customers who have purchased merchandise from a specific vendor, Cool Girl, in order to send these particular clients invitations to a trunk showing for the line. She may also decide to introduce customers to the Cool Girl activewear line by scanning the company database for customers who fit the Cool Girl profile by age (18 to 30 years old) and who have made previous purchases of other activewear lines in the store.

From a different operational perspective retail buyers can gain invaluable information through computerized reports. Using POS software, the buyer can see what customers purchased in terms of item, size, color, cost, retail price, frequency, and vendor. On the flip side, the buyer can see how each vendor has performed in all these variables. The result is a better job of planning purchase orders, placing reorders, and taking timely markdowns.

How does the entrepreneur choose the right computer for the business? The computer selection process consists of three steps. The entrepreneur should identify problems that need solving and tasks that need to be done. The entrepreneur then needs to review the software that can solve the problems and do the tasks, as illustrated in FIGURE 12.10. Finally, the entrepreneur must locate the hardware that will accommodate the software and the company's budget. Computer consultants recommend budgeting at least 50 percent of the total system cost for software. It is important to buy a system that is expandable. The business will grow and so, too, should the computer. Moreover, the entrepreneur should invest time in computer education, either through online training or a computer course, in order to maximize computer's capabilities and, ultimately, its productivity.

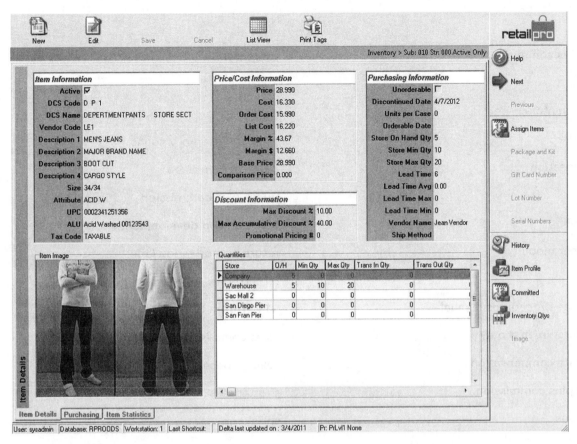

FIGURE 12.10

Retail Pro software.

CONCLUSION

Planning operations and control for a business means determining how the actual day-to-day functions of the company will be run. These are the fundamentals of the business, its foundation. Without a clearly laid out foundation, the business will have difficulty thriving. In operations and control, each internal function is analyzed, and every step is evaluated from facility layout, to merchandise receipts, to product sales. Operational mechanisms are needed to provide staff and customers with consistency, accuracy, and quality.

The first area requiring operational and control standards is the facility. Next, the entrepreneur must develop procedures to make certain the staff is effectively trained. Inventory management and control strategies help ensure that the right products are available to the customer. Research and development strategies are planned as part of operations to ensure business growth. Finally, computer operations are developed to support the facility, employees, inventory, and research and development.

KEY TERMS

base plus commission

bonus

book inventory

client file

compensation

control

cross-filing

customer mobility

dating

employee procedures manual

FIFO (first in, first out)

fixed-rate compensation

hourly plus commission

incentives

invoice

just-in-time

layaway

LIFO (last in, first out)

merchandise discount

merchandise fulfillment

nonselling space

operations

overage

packing slip

physical inventory count

point-of-sale (POS)

quota plus commission

research and development (R&D)

return authorization label

RTM (return to the manufacturer)

RTV (return to the vendor)

sales commission

selling space

shortage

shrinkage

spreadsheet

stockkeeping unit (SKU)

straight commission

supply chain management (SCM)

tracking merchandise

transaction

variable-rate (merit) compensation

DISCUSSION TOPICS

1. Compare and contrast the functions that fall within the classifications of operations and control.

2. Discuss the operations and control policies and procedures that need to be developed for the facility and inventory of a business.

3. Examine the operations and control policies and procedures that must be constructed for the people within a business: vendors, managers, employees, and customers.

4. Identify some of the significant results of research and development that successful entrepreneurs have implemented in the operations of their businesses.

SUGGESTED READINGS

Diamond, J., and S. Litt. *Retailing in the 21st Century*, 2d ed. New York: Fairchild Books, 2009.

Flynn, J. Z., and I. M. Foster. *Research Methods for the Fashion Industry*. New York: Fairchild Books, 2009.

Poloian, L. G. *Retailing Principles: A Global Outlook*, 2d ed. New York: Fairchild Books, 2010.

ONLINE RESOURCES

RETAIL PRO
http://www.retailpro.com/solutions/files/RetailProOverview.pdf
Software programs for retailers.

NATIONAL RETAIL FEDERATION
http://www.nrf.com
The retail industry's largest advocacy organization.

TOPSHOP CODE OF CONDUCT
http://www.topshop.com/files/tscodeofconduct.pdf
Topshop's commitment to international labor and human rights in workplace conditions, wages, and so on.

BUSINESS PLAN CONNECTION
THINKING LIKE AN ENTREPRENEUR

In the business plan the retail operations plan is not thoroughly detailed. Discussion is limited to those operational and control issues essential to running the business efficiently and profitably. The focus is on strategies that will give the business a competitive advantage and the general policies and procedures that will run the business smoothly after it is opened.

The entrepreneur may want to interview noncompetitive business owners about their operations and control plans. In addition, collecting and reviewing employee manuals will provide a jumpstart on this necessary document. Examples are available online and in textbooks on retail management. Topics relating to employees to consider include scheduling, reporting to management, communicating within the organization, and developing the staff. In terms of operations and the facility, security systems and documentation and paper flow are examined. Regarding the vendors used by the business, receiving orders, paying suppliers, handling returns, and monitoring the inventory should be planned.

⊙ ASSIGNMENT 12.1
RETAIL OPERATIONS AND CONTROL

1. Open your saved business plan template.
2. Address the following sections of the retail operations plan. You may also refer to the sample business plan contained in Appendix D.

Topics to address include:

» Reporting Policies
» Employee Development
» Staffing Levels
» Hours/Days of Operation
» Inventory Control
» Security Systems/Shrinkage Control

PROFILE OF AN ENTREPRENEUR
SSEKO: MAKING A GLOBAL DIFFERENCE IN THE FOOTWEAR WORLD

IF you happen to find yourself in Kampala, Uganda, make your way to the Old Taxi Park. From there, grab a taxi van to Matuga. Jump off at the end of the line, and hop on a boda boda to the Cornerstone Leadership Academy. After a (bumpy) ride along a dirt road, you will find yourself in the company of some of the most intelligent and committed young women in Uganda. These women are graduates of the Cornerstone Leadership Academy and employees of Sseko Designs.

Sseko (\say-ko\) Designs was created to help these bright young women continue their education. The Ugandan school system is designed with a nine-month gap between secondary school and university. These nine months are intended to allow time for students to earn money for tuition before continuing on to university. However, in an impoverished and male-dominated society, many of these young women struggle to find fair work during this time.

Sseko Designs hires recent secondary school graduates for this nine-month period to live and work together, and earn money that will go directly towards their university education. These women will not make sandals forever. They will go on to be doctors, lawyers, politicians, writers, and teachers that will bring change and unification to a country divided and ravished by a twenty-two-year-long war.

SSEKO OPERATIONS

Sseko's founder Liz Bohannon describes her company as a "socially proactive, not-just-for profit business." Sseko is not a charity and does not operate on a traditional nonprofit, donor/fundraising model. Instead, its business model was created around Ugandan women and their needs. As in a traditional business, Sseko pays all of the money upfront needed to make the sandals. In contrast to traditional companies, in addition to salaries, Sseko provides funding for its employees' housing and training programs. Because their lodging and basic needs are met by the company, these women are able (and actually required) to put 80 percent of their salary into a fund that goes directly toward their university education. The company's owner gives them 20 percent of their salary each month to do with what they want—send it back to their family, invest it, and so on.

The socially responsible Sseko community of college-bound women and their product line of sandals with interchangeable straps.

Before the sandals are sold to consumers, the women have made their money. The company uses the profits as capital to reinvest into Sseko for buying materials, hiring more women, and developing its training program. The goal of Sseko for the women is that, after working for Sseko for nine months, they are able to fund their entire first year of university (college is typically three years). When the women are accepted by and enrolled in a university, they have a much easier time finding work and still have the option of working for Sseko for the remaining two years on a part-time basis, to earn additional income. Later, the company recruits those women who are in school for more career-specific positions within the company (e.g., fashion design, accounting, management) to continue to build professional skills that will give them a huge advantage once they graduate. The company's founder plans to build a full-time, year-round management team for graduates. They will be the ones running Sseko and will have opportunity to have ownership opportunities.

Liz Bohannon is passionate about using her creative and socially responsible business model to create jobs, build sustainable incomes, and provide educational and professional opportunities. She believes that business and consumerism are the most powerful forces in our world today.

SOURCE: All information obtained from http://www.ssekodesigns.com.

This listing features organizations, publications, and Web sites that support the retail entrepreneur in business planning.

Annual Statement Studies

Robert Morris Associates

A reference book that contains balance sheets, income statements, and sixteen widely used ratios for industries in five categories: manufacturing, wholesaling, retailing, servicing, and contracting. Available through most banks.

Entrepreneurship.org

http://www.entrepreneurship.org

The Ewing Marion Kauffman Foundation and the U.S. Commerce Department's International Trade Administration (ITA) have formed a new public-private partnership focused on leveraging best practices in entrepreneurial leadership to advance economic growth around the world. The goal of this partnership is to assist all nations in developing the environments that allow entrepreneurs to organize and operate a business venture, create wealth, and employ people.

Franchise Handbook Online

http://www.franchisehandbook.com

An online directory of franchise opportunities that can be searched or browsed alphabetically or by category.

FreeDemographics

http://www.freedemographics.com

A new way for novice and expert users of demographic data to view and act upon consumer and market insights, using instant interactive maps, detailed summary and comparison reports, and fast access to U.S. Census data, sorted by geographies and demographic characteristics.

Internal Revenue Service (IRS)

http://www.irs.gov

Provides publications that address the tax issues of concern to the entrepreneur.

Library of Congress

http://lcweb.loc.gov/homepage/lchp.html

National repository of resources.

National Association for the Self-Employed (NASE)

http://www.nase.org

An association that provides members with access to a business consultant. Group health and disability insurance are also available.

National Association of Small Business Investment Companies (NASBIC)

http://www.nasbic.org

A trade association sponsored by the U.S. Small Business Association to provide information about sources of loans for small businesses.

National Retail Federation (NRF)

http://www.nrf.com

NRF's mission is to advance and protect the interests of the retail industry and to help retailers achieve excellence in all areas of their business.

SBA Publications

http://archive.sba.gov/tools/resourcelibrary/publications

The U.S. Small Business Association offers publications and booklets to help establish budgets, personnel policies, and business plans. A list of publications is available.

Service Corps of Retired Executives (SCORE)
http://www.score.org
Provides free individual counseling, courses, conferences, and workshops.

Small Business Development Centers
http://www.asbdc-us.org
Advisory centers, usually university affiliated, located across the United States that provide counseling to small businesses. An Internet search of small business development centers will provide a directory.

Standard & Poors
Industry Surveys
http://www.standardpoors.com
A series covering various segments of industry. Compares growth in sales and earnings of the leading companies in each industry; also tracks profit margins, dividends, price-earnings ratios, and other data for each company over a five-year span.

U.S. Census Bureau
http://www.census.gov
A federal department that provides material on geographic, population, and industry trends.

U.S. Chamber of Commerce
http://www.uschamber.com
Provides data on all types of businesses nationwide. Sources of state information and state industrial directories available. Local chambers of commerce can also supply helpful information.

U.S. Department of Labor
Bureau of Labor Statistics
http://www.bls.gov
A federal agency that reports labor-related information, such as wages, prices, and cost of living.

U.S. Office of Consumer Affairs
Consumer Information Catalog
Publication that identifies and describes major federal agencies and U.S. corporations.

U.S. Small Business Administration (SBA)
http://www.sba.gov
A federal agency that assists with women's businesses, veterans' affairs, disasters, financial management, minority businesses, statistical data, and general business questions.

APPENDIX B
PLANNING TO EXIT THE BUSINESS

In the planning stages it is important for entrepreneurs to consider how they will exit the business. It may feel strange to plan selling or closing a business that is yet to be opened; however, this planning lessens risk and is required by some funding sources in order to secure a loan. At some point the entrepreneur will leave the business.

Many fashion retailers have suffered great financial losses because they did not plan on how the business would eventually be sold or closed. Planning allows the entrepreneur to explore various alternatives to closing the entire business. Alternatives include mergers, acquisitions, initial public offerings, and a joint venture with another company.

Martha Stewart's enterprise is an example of how an entrepreneur can maintain control of a business while making a fortune, by selling shares in the company. In contrast, the Fortunoff chain of jewelry stores was sold by the family to two private companies, only to be repurchased by the family four years later. David Fortunoff said when the family sold the brand, they didn't expect it to dissipate so quickly:

> When the family sold the Fortunoff company in 2005, we fully expected the brand to continue far into the future. No one could envision that it would stumble, be sold, and then close during the height of a stinging recession. Far more painful to us was the loss of jobs for retail professionals we had worked with for decades. We never imagined the Fortunoff brand name going into a free fall when it has served as a retail icon for as long as anyone can remember. It has been a chilling series of events, and we decided to redeem the Fortunoff brand.[1]

By developing and analyzing a clear set of objectives, knowing when to sell all or part of the business, recognizing the strengths and weaknesses of the business, and clarifying the bottom line, the risk of failure diminishes, while the chance of success and financial reward increases dramatically.

The decision to sell all or part of a business is one of the most complex strategic and emotional decisions an entrepreneur can make. Sooner or later, it will happen; it will be time to exit the business. The business is a result of much hard work, sweat equity, and achievement. Various factors can affect the decision to sell—some good, some bad. In many cases, selling may have been the ultimate goal all along. It other cases, selling is a reaction to changes in the market, in personal circumstances, or in company strategy. Retirement, health problems, relocation, or a change in career are common reasons for selling. Some owners will sell when it becomes too difficult to manage the operation or if they lack the necessary capital for expansion. Perhaps the demand for the product has lessened, thereby decreasing sales and profits. Perhaps the lease has expired and will not be renewed or can be renewed only with unfavorable terms. New competitors may be entering the marketplace, taking too great a share of the market.

On the upside, entrepreneurs often relish the excitement and risk of moving on and creating yet another business. Selling an existing business can provide the capital necessary to begin a new venture. The entrepreneur may find that by allowing an acquisition by another company, his or her personal and professional objectives are met faster and at a lower cost. Larger companies will often have the resources, such as capital and people, to move the business forward more efficiently and economically. If the entrepreneur's goal is to build the business and then sell it at a profit, then selling it may accomplish that goal.

Whatever the reason, the decision to sell must be given careful consideration and planning. It is imperative to plan for the exit early, to make it the choice of the entrepreneur and not the choice of another. Selling wisely through careful planning can allow for greater profit and for the flexibility to pursue other opportunities. The maximum selling price will be achieved if the business is sold at some point during its growth stage. Waiting to sell after the company shows declining sales can lead to financial disaster. Trying to sell the business out of desperation or when profits turn downward can be challenging. It reduces the amount the entrepreneur may receive from the sale.

This appendix guides the potential entrepreneur through selecting the best method(s) of exiting the business. The entrepreneur may decide to sell the business, to close it completely, to pass it on to employees or family, or to retain a share of it.

ASSESSMENT

Careful assessment of the objectives, before making the decision to sell, can be accomplished by asking and answering the following questions:

» Is this the right time to sell?

» Where is the business in its industry cycle?

» Where is the company, and what can it reasonably expect to accomplish in the next five to ten years?

» Is the industry in the growth stage, is the industry declining, or has the business reached its maturity?

» Is the business keeping pace with or outpacing the industry as a whole?

To determine the best exit strategy, the entrepreneur must reevaluate the marketing plan, the merchandising/product plan, and the financial position (present and future) of the company. The entrepreneur often begins by analyzing the company's products and its market position. Next, the company's current and potential market share, product strengths and weaknesses, and product development capabilities are examined. Externally, the entrepreneur will investigate competing companies and their products, industry trends, and possible future technological changes. Each of the company's functions should also be analyzed. In marketing and sales the entrepreneur will evaluate the current distribution and pricing strategies. The entrepreneur will assess the company's financial position and needs by estimating how much money will be needed in the future, using cash forecasts, projections of funds needed to maintain and grow the business. Finally, the entrepreneur will calculate the company's current and future profitability.

Prospective buyers will want to know that they can maintain the bulk of the customer base through a change of ownership. They will also want to be assured that the products or services delivered by the company will survive such a change. It may be important to the sale of the business to make sure that certain employees will remain with the company after the business changes hands. Key employees may be part of critical customer relationships; the buyer may want to retain these employees to be sure that the business runs smoothly in the absence of the entrepreneur. The smooth transfer of ownership will directly affect the perception of the company's value.

MANAGEMENT SUCCESSION

If the business is to be sold or passed on, a plan for management succession is critical to its future success. Effective management succession is, in essence, a changing of the guard. It is an evolutionary process, and it is often a time of conflict. In some cases, the business has been such a focal point of the entrepreneur's life that he or she feels a loss of identity when turning it over to others. At the same time, the successor may desire autonomy. The new owner will be, after all, the future operator of the company. Succession planning helps reduce the stress and tension resulting from these issues.

What are the critical stages of a management succession plan? The first phase is a time for the entrepreneur and the successor to communicate. They may want to begin by examining the values they hold about running a business. The ways in which businesses operate reflect their owners' personal values about people, work, money, and power. The entrepreneur should brief the successor about all critical documents. These would include insurance policies, financial statements, bank accounts, key contracts, corporate bylaws, and leases. The entrepreneur should not only provide a list of key suppliers and customers, but also take the time to discuss how these key players should be treated. Employees within the business should also be identified and discussed in terms of their strengths, weaknesses, and contributions to the company.

In the second phase of the management succession plan, the entrepreneur focuses on teaching the successor how to run the business, while promoting an environment of trust and respect among the employees. This process may take months or years, depending upon the preferences of the entrepreneur and the successor. Although most successors will want to implement a management succession plan, some will prefer a straight business sale in which the entrepreneur simply steps away and turns the reins of the company over to the new owner.

SELLING THE BUSINESS TO OUTSIDERS

The techniques for valuing a business are examined in Appendix C. However, it is important to note here that the value of a business can be greatly affected by the economic climate, the time constraints placed on the sale, and the terms under which the sale is negotiated. Some entrepreneurs prefer to maintain a portion of the business, while selling parts of the company. Going public (selling stock in the business) is one way to provide this option. This alternative is available to entrepreneurs who are skillful enough to get the organization to grow to the point at which it can be publicly held, when stock holdings can be sold to the public. Through this option, the privately held business that once had no real market for their stock can be transformed through an initial public offering (IPO), selling publicly traded shares of stock in a corporation to investors. An initial public offering is the company's first sale of stock to the public. Through the initial public offering, the entrepreneur can gradually liquidate personal equity in the business through the sale of publicly traded stock at market price. Venture managers are those who plan to take the business public when its size and profitability allow. Venture managers specialize in starting a business and increasing its size to the point at which it can be sold on the stock market. The fashion retail industry has seen a number of successful entrepreneurial companies take this route, among them Donna Karan, Martha Stewart, Gucci, and dELiA*s.

SELLING THE BUSINESS TO INSIDERS

Selling the business to employees is another route the entrepreneur may take when exiting the company. For the most part, the following options are available to the entrepreneur:

» Sale for cash plus a note

» A leveraged buyout

» An employee stock ownership plan

In the first alternative, sale for cash plus a note, a selling price for the company is established, with one or more employees specified as the buyers. The seller holds a promissory note for a portion of the business. With this option the entrepreneur often takes a seat on a board of directors to help ensure that the business stays on track while the note is being paid. Through a leveraged buyout, employees borrow money from a financial intermediary and pay the owner the selling price at closing. The third option, an employee stock ownership plan, provides the entrepreneur with the opposite result; instead of walking away from the sale with cash, the entrepreneur allows employees to purchase the business gradually. An employee stock ownership plan is a plan regulated under federal law that allows employees to buy stock in the company with funds borrowed from a bank, with the principal repaid from an employee's profit-sharing plan. This is a long-term exit strategy, but it often benefits all involved: employees become owners in the business they are building, while the entrepreneur has the time to transition smoothly out of the company.

LIQUIDATING THE BUSINESS

Finally, the entrepreneur may find it necessary to liquidate the business. Liquidation is the process of closing the business and converting everything to cash. In essence, a company will sell all its assets. Although this may be the only option for an unsuccessful endeavor, there are other reasons for an entrepreneur to choose liquidation. Personal reasons, such as health or financial issues, may create the need for quick cash. Some entrepreneurs choose to close the businesses they have built rather than pass them on to new ownership. Regardless of the reason, liquidating a business is a business in itself.

The entrepreneur liquidating a business will want to minimize financial loses or, in some cases, try to profit from the closing. Closing an operation at the end of the lease prevents the cash loss generated from breaking a lease. Selling off the closing inventory, fixtures, and even the customer mailing list can generate cash. Some entrepreneurs will allocate promotional dollars for a liquidation sale. They will work with vendors and brokers of off-price goods to purchase close-out merchandise. Because these goods were marked down by the manufacturer after being sold at full wholesale price to retailers, they can show the original retail price and be sold as markdowns by the retailer while still carrying a full retail markup. At the end of the liquidation sale, the entrepreneur may elect to donate any remaining goods to charity or to sell the lot off to an off-price broker.

Liquidation value represents the value of the company after all assets have been sold and all liabilities, paid off. Liquidating assets is typically done in an auction format. For fashion retail stores the owner may choose to sell off as much inventory as possible and donate the remaining inventory to charity, which provides a tax deduction. Another option for the fashion retailer is to secure the assistance of a jobber. A jobber is a person or company representative who is paid a flat fee or a percentage of the liquidation sale (sales commission), or both, to sell off inventory and dispose of the unsold stock. In some cases, the jobber may bring in additional inventory to increase the sales commission. Liquidation is an alternative that is not often used, but it is important know what the business may be worth in case a desperate situation arises.

When constructing the business plan, the entrepreneur must consider the worst-case scenario. What options are available if the business is unsuccessful? Will there be assets—property, fixtures, inventory—that can be sold to pay off business loans and other debts? Although planning for failure is not a pleasant task, it is critical to let bankers and other funders know that there is a backup plan if needed.

LOOKING FOR BUYERS

Buyers are interested in purchasing businesses based on what they reasonably believe the company can accomplish down the road. They want a good return on their investment, and they are often very interested in the company's products and technology. Prospective buyers may be found through a number of sources. Advertisements are often placed in the business opportunities sections of local and regional newspapers, in publications specific to the industry in which the business operates, and through business brokers. An existing business has relationships with a banker, accountant, lawyer, suppliers, and manufacturers. They can provide referrals for potential buyers. It is important to remember that it may be to the entrepreneur's advantage to be as discreet as possible in advertising the sale of the business. Employees and customers will begin to look elsewhere for employment and services if they are uncertain about the future of a company.

Often, the reason for selling the business is one of the first things a prospective purchaser will want to know. Earlier in this chapter, various reasons for selling the business are explored. The entrepreneur will need to decide which of these reasons will be presented to prospective buyers. Most buyers are not quick to purchase a business they believe is on its way down. Others see an opportunity to bring on different management teams with new skills and resources to turn the company around. Serious buyers will analyze the business. Withholding vital information may undermine the credibility of the entrepreneur and may be subject to legal penalties.

STRUCTURING THE SALE

When a buyer is found, the structure of the sale becomes critical. The seller may be interested in how involved the current owner wants to remain in the company. The legal structure and whether the entrepreneur is willing to owner finance will be important to the buyer. Owner financing, a situation in which the business owner allows the purchaser to pay off the debt in installments, can be beneficial for two reasons. More often than not, buyers may not have 20 to 30 percent capital available for the down payment required by most lending institutions. Also, if the entrepreneur is willing to owner finance and to take less than 30 percent down, this constitutes a contract of sale and defers taxation obligations until the end of the note. The buyer, on the other hand, will be interested in structuring the sale to reduce the after-tax cost of acquiring the business. Structuring the sale with both parties in mind can lead to a win-win situation for all involved.

NEGOTIATING THE SALE

Successful negotiations are conducted when both parties know and understand the objectives, needs, strengths, and weaknesses of the sale and the business. Ideally, the goal is one of mutual satisfaction that gives both parties what they want from the arrangement.

REFERENCE

1. "Fortunoff Families Re-acquire the Fortunoff Brand." Fortunoff.com. July 15, 2009. http://www.fortunoff.com/AnnouncementRetrieve.aspx?ID=25195

VALUING A BUSINESS

Businesses can be liquidated or sold as an on going concern; they can also be sold in part. Regardless of which option the entrepreneur chooses, when it comes time to sell, the value of the company must be established. Many techniques exist for determining the value. After it is determined, the entrepreneur can begin looking for prospective buyers through advertisements, business brokers, or existing business relationships. When found, the process of selling the business begins.

THE PROCESS OF VALUATION

Why is it important to determine the value of a business? At some point in time, the entrepreneur may want to sell his or her business. The entrepreneur may even want to buy a new business after selling the existing business. To sell or shut down a business, the entrepreneur must ascertain how much it is worth. The entrepreneur should realize that it is not possible to simply use financial ratios. Like many things in life, a business may be one thing to one person and another thing to someone else. Often, personalities and emotions enter the picture.

Although it might not seem of importance at this point, the ability to create value in a business must be evaluated from the onset. What should an effective valuation accomplish? Buyers will want the entrepreneur to be able to justify the asking price. A competent valuation meets two tests—it reaches a supportable fair market value conclusion, and it clearly and convincingly establishes how the conclusion was reached.

The first step in preparing to sell the business and in determining its value is to gather information and to know what is being sold. The following steps provide the necessary data:

1. Determine the assets held by the company. These will vary depending on whether the business is a fashion retail store or an Internet or a service operation. The valuation procedures will vary according to the nature of the assets. It is much easier to place a value on physical assets than on intangible ones, such name recognition or fashion image. Physical assets may be valued by using replacement costs, the amount of money needed to purchase new items rather than resale or used values. The physical assets of a retail business may include store fixtures, leases on the store premises, inventory, customer lists, licenses and franchise arrangements, contractual agreements with key employees, and supplier contracts. Intangible assets may be valued by making comparisons with similar businesses.

2. Collect all financial information for the previous three years and year-to-date financials: existing contracts with employees, customers, or suppliers; any patents, trademarks, or copyrights; and three years of tax returns.

3. Look at adjustments in financial data. Experienced entrepreneurs may legally adjust financial data so as to pay as little in taxes as possible. This approach is done to minimize earnings for tax purposes, but it is also underestimating the true value and earning potential of the business. It does not paint a true picture. The income statement may reflect everything from exaggerated travel expenses, to commissions to employees and owners, to leased vehicles, to shrinkage. The numbers, adjusted for tax purposes, have to be brought back in line. Adjustments must be made in order to compare the performance of the business with the performance

of other businesses in the industry. Just as consumers shop and compare prices on clothing and other items, potential buyers will often compare the sales volume of one business with that of others.

WHAT IS THE BUSINESS WORTH?

If one asks a banker, a business broker, the seller, the buyer, an attorney, or a certified public accountant how to come up with a value for a business, six different answers and methods may be presented. The perception of how much a business is worth depends on which side of the fence one sits on. Sellers typically see the value of the business as being much higher than the buyer will see the value of the same business.

There are numerous valuation methods that can be used to come up with the basis for the asking price or what the seller hopes a prospective buyer is willing to pay for the business. The assets of the company will determine, to some extent, the method for ascertaining its value.

SELECTING THE VALUATION METHOD

The concept of value and the techniques used to determine value can be viewed in the following ways: fair market value, book value, and liquidation value. The Internal Revenue Service defines *fair market value* as the price at which the property would change hands between a willing buyer and a willing seller when the seller is not under any compulsion to sell and when both parties have reasonable knowledge of the relevant facts.[1] The fair market value of a business is a result of internal and external factors. Internal factors include those that are unique to the particular business being sold. For retail fashion businesses these might include things such as the age and desirability of the inventory, name recognition, the quality of employees, and the strength of the existing lease. External factors are typically outside the entrepreneur's immediate control and may include overall economy (including interest rates), competition, taxes and regulations, and interruption

of accessibility to the location. Using the method of fair market value, the business is examined in terms of the amount of money it would bring if it were put on the block, in liquidation rather than book value (determining the value of a company by the value of assets, as reflected in the company's books). Value may be added by using off-balance-sheet valuations, the values within a business that do not appear in the firm's financial reports. These would include assets such as customer lists, special licenses, and agreements for merchandise exclusively from vendors.

One method used to arrive at fair market value applies comparable sales figures. This technique determines a company's value by comparing the company with a similar company or with recently sold businesses. When comparing the company with others, consideration must be given as to whether the company is worth more or less than the comparable companies selected. Price adjustments should be considered on the basis of potential earnings; size, in terms of gross sales; and other criteria. Several databases and organizations compile and maintain data on reliable comparable business sale information for entrepreneurs. Data can be obtained through BIZCOMPS (http://www.bizcomps.com), the Institute of Business Appraisers, and business brokers.

If good financial records have been kept, book value can be the easiest method to apply. In its simplest terms, book value is the difference between a company's total liabilities and its total assets. Book value is a reflection of historical information and can be severely affected by the accounting practices used at the company. For tax purposes a business will accelerate the depreciation of its assets as quickly as possible. By doing so, the book value of the business is lowered.

In this example, depreciation of the retail business is shown as standard versus accelerated. With accelerated, the fixed assets were depreciated over the shortest time period allowed by generally accepted accounting principles. In the standard example the useful life of the fixed assets was extended, resulting in the reduction of accumulated depreciation in the amount of $6,765. The accounting entry has allowed an increase in the value of the business from $21,398 to $28,163 (refer to "Total Net Worth" on the balance sheet).

One of the disadvantages of using book value as a method of arriving at a selling price is that it does not take into account the value of the intangibles. Generally speaking, fashion companies can derive significant value from off-balance-sheet items, such as a

BALANCE SHEET

ASSETS	STANDARD DEPRECIATION	ACCELERATED DEPRECIATION	LIABILITIES & NET WORTH	STANDARD DEPRECIATION	ACCELERATED DEPRECIATION
Cash	$5,726	$5,726	Notes payable—bank	$0	$0
Accounts receivable	0	0	Notes payable—other	0	0
Inventory	50,000	50,000	Accounts payable	397	397
Prepaid expenses	0	0	Accruals	212	212
Total Current Assets	**$55,726**	**$55,726**	Income tax payable	0	0
Fixed assets	22,550	22,550	Current portion of LTD	9,736	9,736
Accumulated depreciation	–4,510	–11,275	Other current liabilities	0	0
Total Fixed Assets	18,040	11,275	**Total Current Liabilities**	**$10,345**	**$10,345**
Notes Receivable	0	0	Long-term debt	39,508	39,508
Intangibles	0	0	Subordinate officer debt	0	0
Deposits	4,250	4,250	Total Liabilities	49,853	49,853
Other Assets	0	0	Common stock	18,000	18,000
Total Net Fixed Assets	22,290	15,525	Retained earnings	10,163	10,163
Total Assets	**$78,016**	**$71,251**	(Less) Treasury Stock	0	0
			Total Net Worth	**$28,163**	**$28,163**
			Total Liabilities & Net Worth	**$28,163**	**$28,163**

loyal customer base, exclusive supplier arrangements, a fashion or price image, and name recognition.

OFFERING MEMORANDUM

When the value of the business has been determined, the entrepreneur can prepare an offering memorandum, also referred to as a selling memorandum. A business broker often prepares this. The offering memorandum contains comprehensive information about the company. It serves as a basis for the buyer's preliminary evaluation of the company. The more information provided, the more comfortable the buyer will be.

For a fashion company, a typical offering memorandum would contain the following components:

» **Executive summary**—An executive summary in the offering memorandum provides an overview of the business (i.e., highlights of the current stage of development of the company, the management team, primary market, the marketing plans, and the financial summary). Similar to the executive summary in the business plan, it is constructed to gain the reader's attention. The executive summary in an offering memorandum explains that the company is being sold and summarizes the key elements contained in the document. The summary is intended to attract the buyer's attention.

» **Management**—The management section should list the key management positions and specify whether the people in those positions will remain with the company. It should describe the experience and skills of each these people; however,

their compensation is not disclosed. The entrepreneur should discuss the number of employees and the manner in which the employees are compensated as well as what benefits they receive.

» **Merchandising/products**—Unique features of the product lines, such as cost, design, and quality, are described in this section. Licensing or royalty agreements associated with the products and plans for future agreements are also discussed. Any distribution rights that have been obtained are presented.

» **Marketing**—The marketing section of the memorandum should be as extensive as it is in the business plan. It should contain an industry profile and a description of competitors, including their strengths, weaknesses, and market share. The entrepreneur should describe existing and future marketing plans as well as related pricing. The target market, market size, market trends, and growth potential, as well as user demographics and psychographics, should be presented.

» **Financial data**—The entrepreneur should include both historical and projected financial information for three to five years, including year-to-date information. Because this document is a reflection of the quality of the company, it should be as comprehensive as possible. After the offering memorandum is in place, the seller can begin looking for buyers.

REFERENCE

1. Internal Revenue Service. Publication 561. http://www.irs.gov/publications/p561/ar02.html#d0e139

SAMPLE BUSINESS PLAN: REALWOMEN, INC.
COVER LETTER (SEE CHAPTER 2)

November 15, 2011

Lucy Smart, Vice President
Best Bank & Trust
983 Main Street
City, State 22222

Dear Ms. Smart:

As we agreed during our meeting on November 6, I am enclosing the business plan to support a loan request in the amount of $60,000 for start-up capital for my company, RealWomen, Inc.

As we discussed, an additional line of credit is requested in the amount of $62,000, required for core stock inventory and start-up costs.

Thank you for your consideration. I look forward to your reply and to the prospect of a long-term relationship with your bank.

Sincerely,

Lucy Rich
RealWomen, Inc.
123 Retail Avenue
Diva City, State 55512
111-555-0101
RealWomen@email.com

Enclosures

REALWOMEN, INC.

Prepared by:

Lucy Rich, Owner and President

RealWomen, Inc.

123 Retail Avenue
Diva City, State 55512
Phone: 111-555-0101
RealWomen@email.com

Date Prepared:

November 15, 2011

CONTENTS

EXECUTIVE SUMMARY (SEE CHAPTER 2)

EXECUTIVE SUMMARY

RealWomen, Inc., was incorporated by Lucy Rich in January, 2010, and has S corporation status. Real-Women, Inc., is a retail store offering contemporary apparel for women sized 11/12 to 19/20 who desire fashion at affordable prices. The product offering will consist of clothing and accessories suitable for business, university, and casual activities. Prices will range from $35 for tops to $129 for dresses and jackets.

The store will be located at 123 Retail Avenue, in downtown Diva City. It will be located on the corner opposite two successful and noncompetitive retailers, Anthony's Store and Town and Country. The location offers shoppers the convenience of a centralized location and a variety of shopping opportunities that cannot be found elsewhere in the area. The location benefits RealWomen, Inc., with its heavy foot traffic and easy parking. It will be located near the university and both Columbia and Sullivan Colleges.

RealWomen, Inc., will be managed by its owner, Lucy Rich, who has employed Larry LaChamp as assistant manager. The management team has more than thirteen years of experience in the industry. RealWomen, Inc., will also employ two part-time sales associates to help with the day-to-day operations of the business. In addition to paid employees, RealWomen, Inc., recognizes its need for outside advisers to lend expertise in various areas. The company has associations with individuals who have agreed to contribute to the success of the company as its advisory board. A list of these experts is located in the management plan.

From a merchandising perspective, providing large-size fashions for contemporary women makes sense. The customer base is increasing. The surgeon general's office reports that more than 17 percent of teenagers are large size, more than three times the rate of a generation ago. The market for contemporary plus sizes (the consumer segment typically aged 18 to 35) has shown strong growth. Research indicates that six of every ten women wear a size 12 or larger and that half of all American women are size 14 or larger, with nearly a third at size 16 or above. Despite these statistics, fashion apparel stores have limited styles and selections for the larger-size woman (ABC 2010 Annual Report).

Price is an important consideration. Decades ago, discount stores surpassed department stores in market share and have been widening their lead since. In 1999 discount stores had a 7 percent revenue gain for the year, making them the fastest growing retail channel for apparel. For the first time in its history, the growth in the discount store market helped bring them above a 20 percent market share in dollar volume. American shoppers are now spending more apparel dollars in discount stores than in any other channel except specialty stores. To offer the service of a specialty store and the prices of mass-merchant chains are keys to the success of RealWomen.

Finding fashionable clothing in this size range, at affordable prices, can be difficult, and this provides a significant market niche. RealWomen, Inc., will fulfill this need in the immediate geographic area. Approximately 25 percent of the population of Diva City falls within the age group of the target market. Other stores in the immediate area are not meeting the current needs of the market with their merchandise offerings. The mission statement of RealWomen, Inc., is to provide affordable fashion for plus-size contemporary women through an excellent merchandise selection and exceptional customer service.

Based on pro formas, RealWomen, Inc., is requesting a loan in the amount of $60,000. A line of credit in the amount of $62,000 is also requested. The funds from the loan will be used to purchase opening inventory and cover start-up costs for opening the business. The owner will have an equity injection of $35,000 cash and will offer all business assets as collateral for the loan.

MANAGEMENT PLAN

BUSINESS STRUCTURE

RealWomen, Inc., was incorporated in 2010 as an S corporation. The Company will be a closely held S corporation owned solely by Lucy Rich. The corporation charter authorizes 100 shares of common stock. These shares have an assigned par value of one dollar. Lucy Rich will be issued 100 shares at the time of filing.

MANAGEMENT TEAM

The key personnel at RealWomen, Inc., are the owner/president, assistant manager, and part-time sales representatives. A summary of the background and qualifications of each position holder follows, and complete résumés are included in the appendices.

Owner/President

Lucy Rich holds a Bachelor of Science in fashion merchandising from the University of State, with a minor in marketing. Her eight years of experience in sales and customer service include positions as a buyer for Saks Fifth Avenue, in New York City; an assistant manager for Lane Bryant; and a public relations assistant for Showroom Seven. While employed at Lane Bryant, Ms. Rich was responsible for supervising employees in the absence of the manager. Her work history and education will provide her with the experience needed to contribute to the success of the company. Ms. Rich will be responsible for purchasing inventory and working with manufacturers. She will be active in customer relations and quality control issues. She will also be responsible for managing visual merchandising efforts and determining markdowns.

Assistant Manager

Larry LaChamp earned a Bachelor of Science in business administration and a Master of Science in business administration, with an emphasis in marketing, from Park City University. He has more than five years of experience in the fields of marketing and advertising for a retail clothing store. Mr. LaChamp was also responsible for many of the daily operations of the store, including receiving, marking, and placing goods for sale and receiving and verifying inventory. As assistant manager he will assume the roles of floor manager and sales associate manager. He will direct the company's marketing strategy. The assistant manager will work thirty hours per week. Larry LaChamp will hold a non-compete agreement with RealWomen, Inc. The agreement will stipulate that upon termination of employment, he cannot open a store within a fifty-mile radius for a period of not less than three years from the date of termination.

Sales Associates

RealWomen, Inc., will employ two part-time sales associates. Sales associates must have two to three years of experience in fashion retail sales. Their responsibilities will include folding and steaming new merchandise and displaying merchandise on the floor. They will be responsible for assisting customers and following up on sales. They must demonstrate excellent skills in customer relations. Each sales associate will work twenty-five hours per week. Advertisements will be placed in local newspapers to locate candidates for these positions.

MANAGEMENT COMPENSATION

RealWomen, Inc., will employ an assistant manager at a salary of $25,000 per year as well as the employee benefits of health insurance and two weeks of paid vacation. Health insurance is reflected in the financial statement at $250 per month.

COMPENSATION AND OWNERSHIP

The owner will receive a draw of $1,000 a month for the first six months, with an increase to $2,000 per month beginning in month seven.

PERSONNEL COMPENSATION

Part-time sales associates will earn $10.00 per hour for twenty-five hours per week. Wages for part-time employees are based on fifty working weeks per year, with rotation for time off.

KEY ADVISORS/DIRECTORS

At this time, RealWomen, Inc., has no outside members on the board of directors; however, management recognizes the need for outside advisers to provide expertise in various areas. Each advisory council member, as well as employees, will receive a discount on merchandise each year, up to $1,200 per year in total compensation. The company is pleased to have associations with the following persons:

Legal
Tom Lawyon
Lawyon and Stemmons
3456 Almond Street
Some City, State 22222

Accounting
Carrie Winston
Hitt and Hitt
48987 BKD Blvd., Suite 100
Some City, State 22222

Insurance (general business and professional liability)
John Munch
Always There Insurance Company
456587 Pine Street
Some City, State 22222

Retailing
Kathie Cryderman
Store Owner
The Harem
4879 Any Street
Some City, State 22222

Insurance (medical)
Cindy Cure
Cure & Associates
5858 Walnut
Some City, State 22222

Marketing
Molly May
GoGettem, LLC
487 Cherry Street
Some City, State 22222

COMMUNICATION

Open and consistent communication is critical to the success of all businesses. Written policies and procedures, as well as updates on marketing activities and new receipts of merchandise, will be posted for all employees to review when they arrive for work. Weekly staff meetings will be scheduled prior to Saturday openings. Special meetings will be scheduled for high-sales-volume holidays, security training, and sales education workshops.

GOVERNMENT APPROVALS

The Federal Trade Commission (FTC) regulations require retailers and manufacturers to sell clothing that is accurately and completely labeled with information on where a product is made and the proportions of fibers present in the product. The rules apply to storefront operations, mail-order companies, and Internet businesses. Although this company is not a manufacturer, it is aware that such regulations exist within the industry and will sell merchandise with such labeling.

LOCAL LICENSES AND PERMITS

Diva City requires a city business license and occupancy permit in order to conduct business in that city. All local licenses and permits will be obtained as required by local and state laws and regulations.

MERCHANDISING/PRODUCT PLAN

MERCHANDISE/PRODUCT DESCRIPTION

RealWomen, Inc., will carry contemporary apparel for women sized 11/12 to 19/20 who desire fashion at affordable prices. The merchandise assortment will consist of clothing and accessories suitable for business, university, and casual activities. The size range, current fashion styling from new vendors, and moderate prices are keys to differentiating the product lines from those of competitors.

UNIQUE CHARACTERISTICS

The size range of 11/12 to 19/20, the contemporary fashion looks, the exclusive vendors in the city, and the moderate price points provide a high level of unique characteristics to the merchandise assortment.

PROPOSED LINES

RealWomen, Inc., will carry six primary product lines, five secondary product lines, and an assortment of accessories. The specific vendors are listed in the merchandise assortment section, to follow. These vendors have three characteristics in common: availability of sizes 11/12 to 19/20, forward designs representing current fashion trends, and moderate price points. Each vendor, however, provides a different look or type of apparel and accessories, such as casual sportswear, daytime dresses, related business wear separates, and denim bottoms. The range of vendors provides a breadth of selection for the target market, while focusing on the age range, price acceptance, and fashion sense of the designated consumer.

PROPRIETARY ASPECTS

Initially, RealWomen, Inc., will carry lines designed and produced by national vendors. With the growth of the business, the owner plans to develop private label lines that will provide complete exclusivity for the customers of RealWomen, Inc. The private label lines will be manufactured by an apparel producer, yet carry the RealWomen, Inc., label, which will be copyrighted and registered.

MERCHANDISE ASSORTMENT

The merchandise classification breakdown will be as follows:

CLOTHING

Careerwear	30%	Tops, bottoms, skirts, pants, and jackets
Sportswear	20%	Tops, pants, and skirts
Dresses	20%	Career and casual
Activewear	15%	Tops and bottoms
Denim	10%	Jeans and skirts

ACCESSORIES

Accessories	5%	Jewelry, sunglasses, handbags, wallets, and gifts

Primary vendors will include:

XCVI

Girly Girl

Bechamel

Kenneth Cole

Trendsetter

Onyx

Secondary vendors will include:

Fossil

Tommy Hilfiger

Nine West

Cool Girl

Luxury

Company descriptions and photographs of primary and secondary lines that will be carried by Real-Women, Inc., are included in the appendices.

In addition to clothing, RealWomen, Inc., will carry 5 percent of its stock in related stock—accessories. Accessories will include jewelry, sunglasses, handbags, wallets, and gift items. The store will carry product lines by Kenneth Cole, Fossil, and Nine West in these merchandise classifications.

MARKET TRIPS

Merchandise will be ordered at apparel markets located in Dallas and Los Angeles five times annually. Travel expenses (e.g., hotel, meals, transportation) for buying trips to market five times per year are included in the financial plan. Open-to-buy, the monthly amount of dollars (calculated at retail) to be spent on new merchandise, will be calculated based on the current six-month plan to determine the amount of funds

to be spent at each market. To follow is an annual schedule for market trips:

Where	When	Objective
Dallas	September	Purchase stock for holiday
Los Angeles	January	Purchase stock for spring
Los Angeles	March	Purchase stock for summer
Dallas	June	Purchase stock for fall

MARKUP/MARKDOWN POLICIES

The women's apparel industry introduces new fashion trends each season. This causes the inventory to be dated, so unsold goods must be discounted toward the end of the season in order to sell and move outmoded stock out of the store. Markdowns on merchandise will be taken monthly on poor-performing merchandise at a rate of 30 percent off retail for the first markdown, followed by 50 percent off original retail if unsold after thirty days following the first markdown. Merchandise will be gradually discounted until sold. Markdowns will be designated by the owner and tabulated by the assistant manager. The subtotals will be input into the computer system by vendor number to enable vendor performance analysis and to maintain an accurate book inventory. The majority of markdowns will be taken on fall/winter merchandise during the month of January and on spring/summer merchandise during the month of July for two major annual clearance sales.

In terms of markup policies, RealWomen, Inc., will use the keystone method of retail pricing. With this method, retail prices are set at double the cost of the merchandise at wholesale to obtain the original selling price. The store will mark up merchandise 122 percent based on cost, 45 percent based on retail.

BRICK-AND-MORTAR LOCATION PLAN (SEE CHAPTERS 2 AND 6)

BRICK-AND-MORTAR LOCATION PLAN

The store will be located at 123 Retail Avenue, in downtown Diva City. It will be located on the corner opposite Anthony's Store and Town and Country. This centralized location, along with the unique downtown area shopping experience, offers shoppers convenience, variety, and shopping opportunities that cannot be found elsewhere in the area. The 123 Retail Avenue location allows the store to capture the marketing benefits of heavy foot traffic throughout the year, easy parking, and customer access to a variety of other retail establishments and restaurants in the area. The retail customer mix already attracted to this location by the existing stores includes residents of approximately six adjoining counties, the university, and two colleges. RealWomen, Inc., is located within two blocks of a free municipal parking complex, very near the university and college area. Parking spaces are typically available in this garage.

Inner cities have room for more apparel retailers. Inner-city markets can account for $85 billion in annual retail spending, according to estimates found in a recent study by the Initiative for a Competitive Inner City (ICIC), a national nonprofit organization. In most locations, however, retailers are only taking $64 billion because of the perception that inner cities are difficult and unprofitable markets. Many retailers believe that a low-income area means low sales potential. This is a myth. In an inner-city square mile the number of retail dollars is two to six times higher than in an affluent, suburban square mile, according to ApparelNews.net (2010). Other findings indicate that "inner-city shoppers are more fashion conscious, buy at the beginning of the season at full price, have an orientation to brand and service, have a greater interest in credit, are attracted to specialty stores, and will

seek out discount department stores" (Small Business Research and Information Center, 2010).

LOCATION FEATURES

RealWomen, Inc., will be visible from all directions of a major downtown intersection. Retail Avenue runs directly to both colleges and is the street most used to reach these destinations. Because RealWomen Inc., will rely to a large extent on foot traffic, this location provides the best possible scenario.

Location within the inner city is not conducive to attracting a majority of shoppers from the suburbs. Stores located within this area indicate that most customers are shopping on lunch hours and as they go to and from school. This excellent visibility will contribute to the success of RealWomen, Inc.

The 3,000-square-foot facility will host 2,500 square feet of sales floor space and 500 square feet of additional space for fitting rooms, storage, office, and receiving use. Receiving facilities are accessible at the rear of the store, next to the office space. The lessor requires a deposit of $2,500, with rent at $2,500 per month. Utilities are not included in the lease payments. Utilities, based on historical information, are $250 per month (see cash flow statement in the appendices).

This lease is a triple net (N-N-N) lease. The lessee is responsible for taxes, insurance, and maintenance of the leased space of the building. The financial plan reflects the cost of the taxes, insurance, and maintenance fee.

The initial lease is for a three-year period, with an option to renew for two additional three-year periods. A rent increase of 10 percent will be reviewed at the end of three years. RealWomen, Inc., will have a first right of refusal should the property be placed on the market for sale. An adjoining 1,500 feet of retail space could be available to lease within two years should RealWomen, Inc., decide to expand its facility.

TARGET MARKET CONSIDERATIONS

The mission of RealWomen, Inc., is to be the premier specialty store for contemporary women sized 11/12 to 19/20 by providing affordable fashion through an outstanding merchandise selection, excellent customer service, and to be the fashion leader for our target customers. The long-term objective is not only to achieve profit goals, but also to be the number one fashion specialty store for the specified target market in Diva City.

The abbreviated mission statement of Real-Women, Inc., is to provide affordable fashion for plus-size contemporary women through an outstanding merchandise selection and excellent customer service.

FACILITY DESCRIPTION

The facility currently features a brick façade with large display windows flanking a double-door entry. Parking spaces are available directly in front of the store and in the adjacent parking lot. New Berber carpeting will be installed throughout. Large stone tiles will be added to the entryway and around the cash desk. The décor will be "feminine eclectic," in neutral colors. Fixtures will be primarily distressed, whitewashed pine. Mannequins will consist of fabric-covered dress forms. A crystal chandelier will be the focal point in the center of the store. The lighting will be custom designed to highlight merchandise offerings, provide a true reflection of color, and facilitate work areas, such as the cash desk. The cash desk, located at the front of the store, will be constructed to hold the POS system, telephone, wrap equipment and supplies, credit card materials and machine, and a telephone/fax machine. Fitting rooms will be located toward the back of the store, comfortable yet minimally furnished and well lit. A three-way mirror and pedestal outside the fitting room will allow the customer to view the back and front of a garment, while facilitating alteration needs. The layout plan is included in the appendices.

LEASEHOLD IMPROVEMENTS

Leasehold improvements will include painting, lighting, new floor covering, construction of two dressing rooms, and remodeling of the bathroom. The total for these improvements will be $10,000. An additional $8,900 will be spent on furniture, display racks, tables, and office equipment.

OTHER LOCATION COSTS, INCLUDING SIGNAGE

A large sign featuring the store name will hang over the entry, and additional signing will hang below the canopy. Signage will cost approximately $2,500.

WEB PLAN SUMMARY (SEE CHAPTERS 2 AND 7)

WEB PLAN SUMMARY

OVERVIEW

In a recent survey conducted by Zona Research, data indicate that people shopped online to save time (36 percent); save money (15 percent); avoid crowds, rude clerks, and angry drivers (11 percent); find a better selection (10 percent); and have fun (10 percent). Online apparel retailing is growing; an expanding list of fashion firms and retailers are online. Apparel has risen from one of the least-purchased categories to the sixth spot in 13 kinds of merchandise sold on the Web (*Women's Wear Daily*, 2010). The on-line shopping population is roughly divided into thirds, among buyers, nonshoppers, and browsers. Women's apparel accounts for the majority of Web shopping purchases (*Women's Wear Daily*, 2010), and women now account for the majority of Web shoppers.

RealWomen, Inc., will begin its Web presence through a Web site introduction scheduled for one month before the opening of the store. The Web site will be used to introduce the business, the management team, and the sales staff; to promote new vendors; and to inform Web site viewers about the development of the store and, later, its activities and events. In the future, management will determine whether selling inventory online is a channel of distribution that would increase the profits of RealWomen, Inc.

INTERNET STRATEGIES

Participating in social media will be a strategic part of the company's marketing plan. Facebook, LinkedIn, and Twitter will be updated daily to communicate with current and potential customers about store events and new merchandise arrivals as well as to share customer profiles. Customers will be featured as models in apparel and accessories from Real-Women, Inc., and their profiles (e.g., name, occupation, interests and hobbies, favorite fashions) will be presented.

ONLINE MARKETING STRATEGIES

E-mail blasts will be used to inform customers who register for these communications about sales, trunk showings, new products, and events. In addition, print advertisements will be copied and sent via e-mail to the customer listserv.

WEB DEVELOPMENT AND HOSTING

Shane McCoy and Associates will be responsible for the company's Web development and maintenance. If the management of RealWomen, Inc., determines that Web sales will grow the business further, additional staff will be required, as discussed in the following section.

COSTS

It is anticipated that Web sales would necessitate two additional employees to take orders and ship merchandise to the customer. Additional Web development and maintenance services would also be required.

MARKETING PLAN (SEE CHAPTERS 2, 3, AND 8)

MARKETING PLAN

INDUSTRY PROFILE

A younger plus-size market segment has emerged: It is estimated that 22 percent of the teenage population now fits into this category. Many catalogers and retailers see the plus-size segment as no different from mainstream women's clothing. The problem is that the plus-size woman has a difficult time finding the fashion items she wants in retail stores. The chain store Lane Bryant and the catalog Silhouettes, as well as many other plus-size retailers, have gone to the Web to reach more consumers.

The NPD Group is a leading global provider of consumer and retail market research information for a wide range of industries. According to the NPD Group, the following facts describe the women's plus-size market in 2010:

» Within the women's market in 2010, large/plus-size apparel continues to outperform all other segments.

» Sales of plus sizes grew 10 percent for the year at a time when most apparel classifications declined.

» Apparel sized 16 and over now comprises a $26 million market, which accounts for 27 percent of all dollars spent on women's apparel.

» Last year, sales of plus sizes to girls and young women ages 13 to 34 reached $5.8 billion. (NPD, 2010)

According to Ruth LaFerla, of the *New York Times* (June 18, 2009), "It is fashion first, whatever the size." Jeff Van Sinderen, a retail analyst at B. Riley, a research and investment firm, agrees: "Up to now it's been difficult to provide adequate fashion content to a large-size customer. The woman of size, as she is euphemistically known, still wants to wear the same clothes as her slimmer counterparts."

MARKET ECONOMIC FACTORS

Currently, in the United States, 168,025 firms are apparel retailers with annual sales of approximately $162.4 billion. In addition to the 168,025 firms that are primarily apparel retailers, 21,948 firms sell apparel, but not as their primary business; however, these stores post significant annual apparel sales of approximately $90.2 billion (Marketplace, 2010).

Most apparel retailers in the United States have four or fewer employees, and Diva City also reports this statistic. Apparel retailers having annual sales of less than $200,000 make up a significant portion of the industry. Those with annual sales of more than $500,000 represent 5 percent of the market or less (Small Business Research & Information Center; Bureau of Labor Statistics, Industries at a Glance; Apparel Retailing NAICS code 448120). Diva City's specialty store retailers average $200,000 in annual sales.

MARKET ANALYSIS SUMMARY

The customer profile for RealWomen, Inc., is a contemporary woman aged 18 to 35 who wears a size between 11/12 and 19/20 and purchases fashion apparel and accessories in a moderate price range. She believes in "fashion first," regardless of her size. She embraces her curves and seeks apparel and accessories for the many activities in her day, including casual and work wear. She may be a college student or a working woman, as both of these demographics are supported by the location of RealWomen, Inc., in Diva City's inner city. This woman spends approximately $750 annually on her wardrobe, largely outside of the city of Diva. Twenty-five percent of Diva City's population fits this consumer description, and no retailer is focusing on her apparel preferences in this location.

MARKET NEEDS

The marketplace of Diva City does not include a retailer specializing in contemporary plus-size apparel and accessories. Instead, there are two stores carrying plus-size clothing for more mature women. Direct competitors are examined more closely in the competitive analysis section that follows.

CUSTOMER PROFILE

Within Diva City's population, 25 percent are women between the ages of 18 and 35. This age group makes up one-fourth of the large-size market population in this geographic area. Demographics also show a median income level of $40,500, with the vast majority being college students or working professionals. Their primary motivations for purchase are the

» desire to buy in their geographic area;

» need for quality clothing in sizes 11/12 to 19/20;

» ability to purchase fashion apparel and accessories at reasonable prices.

In a survey conducted by the local chamber of commerce and the university, 300 female consumers (ages 18 to 35) who indicated they were a plus size reported that they would purchase clothing in the area if the selection existed. They also indicated that they spend approximately $750 on their clothing each year.

The intention to market RealWomen, Inc., in the mid-income-level, mid-price, plus-size niche will put the store in competition with some established stores in the area. The business will be located in the downtown district, thus providing visibility and easy access. Because this is a start-up company, management conservatively estimates that the company will capture 10 percent of its target market for the first year, and from 15 to 20 percent of this market by the end of Year 3.

It is anticipated that competition will increase as the success of the store becomes evident. The window for establishing the customer base prior to seeing an increase in competition is approximately 3 years. This assumption is based on the time frame in which new competition typically enters this market.

FUTURE MARKETS

RealWomen, Inc., understands the importance of focusing on what the customer wants and staying on top of the latest fashion trends. It is anticipated that merchandise will remain relatively constant in terms of the amount of inventory and the size of the store. It is the intent of the owner to keep the store at 2,500 square feet for at least three years. Future related merchandise lines, such as hosiery, lingerie, and shoes, may be added as the customer base grows.

RealWomen, Inc., recognizes the opportunity to create awareness of the store and expand sales with the strong customer base of Internet consumers. Apparel goods are typically the first level of items purchased on the Web and are among the leaders in online purchases. The business will continue to monitor sales and weigh options with regard to Web sales distribution; however, a Web site and social media outreach will be available upon opening of RealWomen, Inc.

COMPETITIVE ANALYSIS

The city of Diva has six businesses that carry women's apparel, with combined sales of approximately $3 million. Competition in the area is based primarily on selection and quality of merchandise. RealWomen, Inc., will compete on this basis. The six businesses located in Diva City do not offer a large selection of clothing for plus-size women. Two of the stores, Midvale and Only Yours, offer higher-end clothing at higher prices and do not carry sizes above size 12. The other three businesses offer these sizes but are limited in selection and are not fashion forward (a competitive matrix to follow). Women in Diva City spend approximately $750 on clothing each year (Diva City Chamber of Commerce, 2010). Many are traveling to other cities or ordering online to meet their needs. Ordering online, however, can be a problem for the plus-size customer who does not know how a garment will fit or look on her.

COMPETITIVE ADVANTAGE

The primary competitive advantage is fulfilling a market niche that is not being met in the area. The city of Diva has no plus-size women's clothing store. The large-size women's apparel market continues to grow nationally, yet this customer segment is not accommodated in this geographic area. The target market of women ages 18 to 35 is one that provides a tremendous opportunity for sales in itself. By specializing in the plus-size niche as a sole provider in Diva City, the competitive advantage becomes even greater. Another competitive advantage lies in understanding this consumer and catering to her needs. Other competitive advantages include fashion-forward goods, moderate price points, and new vendors not carried by other retailers in the city.

PRICING

Price List
Retail prices will range from $35 for tops to $129 for dresses and jackets.

Pricing Strategies
Prices will be set based on keystone, which refers to doubling the wholesale price of goods. Slow-selling merchandise will be marked down toward the end of the season—30 percent off initially, followed by 50 percent, and so on, monthly—to make room for new inventory.

MARKET PENETRATION

Brand Strategy
Through a concentrated, consistent, and exciting advertising campaign using a variety of media channels (e.g., radio, newspaper, television, Internet), the RealWomen name and logo will be marketed as a brand, one that represents the shopping destination for the plus-size woman of fashion. The messages the brand will communicate include confidence in and respect for the plus-size consumer, an understating of fashion trends and styles that meet this customer's needs, and a commitment to exceptional customer service. It is the goal of RealWomen, Inc., to be "branded" in Diva City as the premiere specialty store in the area in fashion, value, and customer service.

Advertising and Promotion
Four of the Diva City stores have been in the market for more than six years. They advertise through radio, television, and newspaper. As RealWomen, Inc., must establish an image in the retail consumer market, the company's entry into the market will be accompanied by an intense twelve-month promotional campaign consisting of a grand opening and radio, Internet, and newspaper advertising. The total promotional budget for the first year of the business is $13,000. The company will create a circular to run in the local newspaper every Sunday for the first four months of operation. Two weeks prior to the opening of the store, a circular will be placed in the local newspaper, and radio spots will announce the opening. Radio spots will be run on stations KFOX 226 and KGAL 822. Advertising spots will run for thirty seconds and will be focused on prime drive home time, from 3:00 PM to 8:00 PM. These stations and time slots have been selected based on statistics indicating that most female listeners between the ages of 18 and 35 listen to these stations at these times (Media Market, 2010).

Both the manager and assistant manager will be responsible for developing advertisements and placing them with the media. Initial ads have been developed and are included in the appendices. In addition, radio advertising will be conducted in conjunction with special events, such as fashion shows and the introduction of new seasonal product lines. Social media outreach will be initiated online, as will a company Web site.

Sales Strategy
To track sales, customers' names and contact information will be inputted into the POS system when customers are making their purchases. This information (i.e., who is buying and how often) will be compiled for customer mailings. Sales associates will also be required to maintain personal customer logs with the names, contact information, purchase details, and merchandise preferences of the customers with

whom they work. When RealWomen, Inc., has sales events, new merchandise arrivals, and so on, it will be the sales associates' responsibility to touch base with their personal customers by phone or e-mail to let them know about these activities. Regarding sales events, outdated merchandise will be marked down according to the markdown plan, and customers will be contacted when items they are interested in are reduced. This is a prime example of the level of customer service that will be provided by the staff of RealWomen, Inc.

Publicity

The owner and assistant manager will collaborate on publicity opportunities, such as the introduction of a new line, a trunk show, a philanthropic fashion show, or a customer profile. Press releases will be written and the media contacted to access local publicity. Fashion trend reports for the local lifestyle magazine and wardrobing of the top news broadcaster, in exchange for a promotion of RealWomen, Inc., will be offered.

Fashion Trade Shows

RealWomen will participate in local fashion trade shows open to the public. The Women's Expo, Breast Cancer Awareness Bazaar, and College Days are examples of some of the local events that attract thousands of women who fit the target market of Real-Women, Inc. The cost for participating in these events, including advertising, ranges between $250 and $500 per event.

EVALUATING MARKETING EFFORTS

Marketing efforts will be continually assessed. Actual sales of advertised merchandise and weekly sales volume totals will be tabulated by the assistant manager during radio and television advertising periods to assess the productivity of all advertising efforts. Coupons will be offered in the newspaper and on the Web site to help track the outcomes of these media options. The effectiveness of radio advertising will be evaluated by providing a "secret" password or phrase in radio spots for customers to give to the sales associate when checking out.

FINANCIAL PLAN (SEE CHAPTERS 2 AND 11)

FINANCIAL PLAN

SALES FORECAST

Sales figures are presented in the sales forecast worksheet of the financial plan.

CASH REQUIREMENTS

Based on pro forma financials, RealWomen, Inc., is requesting a loan in the amount of $60,000. A line of credit in the amount of $62,000 has also been requested. The funds from the loans and the owner's cash investment will be used to purchase opening inventory and cover start-up costs for opening the business.

Inventory

RealWomen, Inc., will have a stock inventory of $50,000 and will maintain an average inventory level of $50,000 (at cost), with the exception of holiday periods. Vendors for the inventory will be paid cash on delivery at the start-up of the business and until RealWomen, Inc., establishes a business credit rating. After a credit rating is established, suppliers will provide payment terms of 8/10 EOM (i.e., 8 percent discount if paid within ten days past the end of the month in which the goods were shipped) or net thirty days from the date of invoice. It is anticipated this business will have an established credit rating after Year 3. Merchandise is typically shipped thirty to ninety days from the date the orders are placed.

Taxes/Licenses

These include the business license of $125 (start-up) and a $425 property tax on business assets. Real estate taxes will run $1,200 per year.

Cash on Hand

Principal will inject savings in the amount of $35,000. This amount will cover building improvements, overhead, and payroll in the start-up phase.

Loan

A loan for start-up expenses is requested in the amount of $60,000. For projection purposes, the loan had been calculated at an interest rate of 10 percent for a period of sixty months. The loan and equity injection will be used as follows:

Security Deposits

    Rent—$2,500

    Utilities—$450

    Other—$100

Start-Up Expenses

    Insurance—$3,300

    Legal and consulting fees—$600

    Office supplies—$250

    Preopening advertising—$3,000

    Printing—$500

    Sales tax permit—$4,000

    Other—$1,500

Opening Stock Inventory

    Stock inventory—$50,000

Capital Expenditures

    Computer equipment—$3,500

    Equipment—$6,000

    Furniture and fixtures—$8,900

    Leasehold improvements—$10,000

Revolving Line of Credit

A working capital line of credit in the amount of $62,000 has been requested to purchase inventory. For projection purposes, interest accrues at the rate of 10 percent and will be paid monthly.

Advertising

Management will advertise regularly through the local newspaper and radio stations. Advertising will increase in the months of November and December to promote the holiday season. Newspaper ads will run two times per month, at a cost of $3,900 per year. Radio ads will run two times per week for twenty-eight weeks, for a cost of $9,100.

Accounting and Legal

Professional fees of $250 per month have been allocated for accounting services. Legal services will be engaged on an as needed basis. An allocation of $600 has been made for start-up and first-month legal expenses.

Insurance

Insurance includes casualty, hazard, and liability and will cost $300 per month. Liability, theft, and fire insurance, as well as normal business coverage, are provided by Always There Insurance Company. Health insurance will be provided through Cure & Associates. RealWomen, Inc., was issued a written quote of $250 per month.

Bank Charges

Bank charges are based on a 2 percent service charge for credit/debit card transactions and standard account service fees of $60 per month.

BREAK-EVEN ANALYSIS

Year 1 of the projected income statement, of the financial statements, includes some start-up costs that are incurred prior to opening. The break-even point based on sales for Year 1, including these expensed start-up expenses, is $315,249. Break-even for Year 2 is $302,555.

PROJECTED FINANCIAL STATEMENTS

This section includes a set of assumptions and pro forma financial statements for one year.

COMPANY BUDGETS

Budget meetings will be held with the advisory board every six months. The owner will monitor cash flow on a monthly basis. Budgetary issues will be addressed with the advisory board at each quarterly meeting.

FINANCIAL ASSUMPTIONS FOR REALWOMEN, INC., BUSINESS PLAN

START-UP FUNDING AND EXPENDITURES ASSUMPTIONS

The owner's equity injection is $35,000. Funds have been transferred from a savings account to the business checking account.

In addition to the equity injection of $35,000, a small business loan in the amount of $60,000 amortized over 60 months with a maximum interest rate of 10 percent is being requested to fund the start-up expenditures.

Security deposit includes rent, $2,500; utilities, $450; and Web site hosting, $100.

Other start-up expenditures that will be expensed are insurance, $3,300; legal/accounting fees, $600; initial office supplies, $250; preopening advertising, $3,000; printing, $500; sales tax bond, $4,000; and grand opening celebration, $1,500.

The business will purchase stock of $50,000 to open the store and will maintain an average stock level of approximately $50,000. Inventory will be higher during delivery of stock purchased in the months of February, April, July, and October.

Capital expenditures include a computer/point-of-purchase system, $3,500; signage and security system for the building, $6,000; racks/shelving/displace cases, $8,900; and leasehold improvements, $10,000.

(CONTINUED)

FINANCIAL ASSUMPTIONS FOR REALWOMEN, INC., BUSINESS PLAN

(CONTINUED)

SALES AND OPERATING EXPENSE ASSUMPTIONS

The business will track four profit centers, as follows:

Clothing sales: 60 percent of total sales

Accessories: 20 percent of total sales

Innerwear: 10 percent of total sales

Outerwear: 10 percent of total sales

Slow-moving merchandise will be discounted as needed. This is reflected as discounts on the sales worksheet and will be applied to approximately 40 percent of stock. The discount will average 33 percent of retail on the discounted stock.

The merchandise calendar will run from February through July and August through January on a 4-5-4 week-per-month schedule. This is standard in the fashion industry.

A $62,000 working capital line of credit will be needed to fund the operating cycle of the business. Inventory will be ordered at market in the months of January, March, June, and September for delivery on a COD basis in February, April, July, and October. Sales lag inventory delivery will be approximately 8 weeks. This is standard in the industry.

Operating expense assumptions are as follows:

The business will spend $1,000 per month on newspaper and radio advertising. In December an additional $1,000 will be spent to promote holiday sales.

Bank services charges consist of a $60 checking account fee and a 2 percent fee for using credit/debit card transactions. It is estimated 70 percent of sales will be paid by credit/debit cards.

Insurance includes casualty and liability on the business, as required by the landlord and the bank to protect all business assets and the building against fire, wind, water, and vandalism.

Outside services include hosting of the Web site and monthly fee for security system monitoring.

Wages are based on the owner's draw of $2,000 per month after month 7, a store manager $25,000 annual salary, and three part-time sales clerks at $10 per hour for 25 hours per week.

Benefits include health insurance for the owner and store manager.

Professional fees include an accountant on a monthly basis and an attorney as needed.

Rent of $2,500 per month. This is a triple-net, fixed-rate lease for 3 years, with an option to renew for two additional 3-year fixed-rate terms with a 10 percent renewal rate increase. The business is responsible for all maintenance to the leased space, insurance on the leased space, and property taxes on the leased space.

Telephone includes one land line with a phone system that rolls calls over to the owner's cell phone if the land line is busy.

Travel expenses includes the owner's trips to market in January, March, June, and September, totaling $4,800 and $300 for employee training.

Utilities include gas, electric, water, and trash.

Employee and advisory discounts reflect the discounts allowed on merchandise purchased by employees and the advisory council.

SAMPLE PRO FORMA CASH FLOW STATEMENT

RealWomen, Inc.
Cash Flow Statement (projected)
Year 1

2010	Pre-Start-Up	1	2	3	4	5	6	7	8	9	10	11	12	TOTAL
Cash In														
Cash Sales		17,400	17,400	21,750	20,010	21,750	26,100	21,750	21,750	26,100	27,188	40,542	43,500	305,240
Collections from Accounts Receivables														
Equity Received	35,000													35,000
Loans Received	60,000		27,000				6,000			4,000				97,000
Other Cash In (receipts from other assets)														
Other Cash In (interest, royalties, and so on)														
Total Cash In	95,000	17,400	44,400	21,750	20,010	21,750	32,100	21,750	21,750	30,100	27,188	40,542	43,500	437,240
Total Cash Available	95,000	17,800	48,388	35,181	41,655	23,674	43,387	51,550	31,973	48,386	60,887	43,388	73,339	437,640
Cash Out														
Inventory Expenditures														
Inventory/Raw Material (cash)	50,000		22,620		27,144			27,840			44,492			172,096
Inventory/Raw Material (paid on account)														
Production Expenses														
Operating Expenses														
Advertising	3,000	1,000	1,000	1,000	1,000	1,000	1,000	1,000	1,000	1,000	1,000	1,000	2,000	16,000
Bank Charges		260	260	260	310	310	310	310	310	310	372	372	372	3,756
Dues and Subscriptions		150												150
Insurance	3,300	300	300	300	300	300	300	300	300	300	300	300	300	6,900
Licenses and Fees	4,000	125												4,125
Marketing and Promotion	500													500
Meals and Entertainment														
Miscellaneous		50	50	50	50	50	50	50	50	50	50	50	50	600
Office Expense		50	50	50	50	50	50	50	50	50	50	50	50	600
Office Supplies	250	25	25	25	25	25	25	25	25	25	25	25	25	550
Web and Security Services		120	120	120	120	120	120	120	120	120	120	120	120	1,440
Payroll Expenses														
Salaries and Wages		5,233	5,233	5,233	5,233	5,233	5,233	6,233	6,233	6,233	6,233	6,233	7,233	69,796
Payroll Taxes		524	524	524	524	524	524	624	624	624	624	624	724	6,988
Benefits		250	250	250	250	250	250	250	250	250	250	250	250	3,000
Property Taxes	600	250	250	250	250	250	250	250	250	250	250	250	250	3,600
Professional Fees													1,625	1,625
Rent		2,500	2,500	2,500	2,500	2,500	2,500	2,500	2,500	2,500	2,500	2,500	2,500	30,000
Repairs and Maintenance		50	50	50	50	50	50	50	50	50	50	50	50	600
Shipping and Delivery														
Telephone		100	100	100	100	100	100	100	100	100	100	100	100	1,200
Training and Development					100				100				100	300
Travel		1,200		1,200	100		1,200		100	1,200			100	5,100
Utilities		250	250	250	250	250	250	250	250	250	250	250	250	3,000
Vehicle														
Merchandise Discounts														
Employee and Advisory Discounts		100	100	100	100	100	100	100	100	100	100	100	100	1,200
Other	1,500													1,500
Paid on Account														
Nonoperating Costs														
Capital Purchases	28,400													28,400
Estimated Income Tax Payments														
Interest Payments		500	494	487	480	474	467	460	454	447	440	433	426	5,562
Loan Principal Payments		775	781	788	794	801	808	814	821	828	835	842	849	9,736
Owner's Draw	3,050													3,050
Other Cash Out														
Total Cash Out	94,600	13,812	34,957	13,537	39,731	12,387	13,587	41,327	13,687	14,687	58,041	13,549	17,474	381,374
Monthly Cash Flow (cash in - cash out)	400	3,588	9,443	8,213	(19,721)	9,363	18,513	(19,577)	8,063	15,413	(30,853)	26,993	26,026	55,866
Beginning Cash Balance		400	3,988	13,431	21,645	1,924	11,287	29,800	10,223	18,286	33,700	2,846	29,839	
Ending Cash Balance	400	3,988	13,431	21,645	1,924	11,287	29,800	10,223	18,286	33,700	2,846	29,839	55,866	55,866

SAMPLE YEAR-END INCOME STATEMENT

RealWomen, Inc.
Year-End Income Statement (projected)

	2010
Net Sales (less returns and allowances)	305,240
Cost of Goods Sold	137,358
Gross Income	**$ 167,882**
Operating Expenses	
Advertising	16,000
Bad Debt Expense	-
Bank Charges	3,756
Depreciation and Amortization	5,295
Dues and Subscriptions	150
Insurance	6,900
Licenses and Fees	4,125
Marketing and Promotion	500
Meals and Entertainment	-
Miscellaneous	600
Office Expense	600
Office Supplies	550
Web and Security Services	1,440
Payroll Expenses	
Salaries and Wages	69,796
Payroll Taxes	6,988
Benefits	3,000
Professional Fees	3,600
Property Taxes	1,625
Rent	30,000
Repairs and Maintenance	600
Shipping and Delivery	-
Telephone	1,200
Training and Development	300
Travel	5,100
Utilities	3,000
Vehicle	-
Merchandise Discounts	-
Employee and Advisory Discounts	1,200
Other	1,500
Total Operating Expenses	**$ 167,825**
Operating Income	**$ 56**
Interest Expense	5,562
Other Income (interest, royalties, and so on)	-
Income before Taxes	**$ (5,505)**
Income Taxes (if C Corporation)	-
Net Income	**$ (5,505)**

RealWomen, Inc.

Year-End Balance Sheet (projected)

			2010
Assets			
Current Assets			
	Cash and Equivalents		55,866
	Accounts Receivable		-
	Inventory		34,738
	Security Deposits		3,050
	Other Current Assets		-
Total Current Assets		$	**93,654**
Fixed Assets			
	Property, Plant, and Equipment		28,400
	Less: Accumulated Depreciation		(5,295)
	Other Noncurrent Assets		-
Total Noncurrent Assets		$	**23,105**
Total Assets		$	**116,759**
Liabilities			
Current Liabilities			
	Accounts Payable		-
	Line of Credit		37,000
	Other Current Liabilities		-
Total Current Liabilities		$	**37,000**
Long-Term Liabilities			
	Loans		50,264
	Mortgages		-
	Other Noncurrent Liabilities		-
Total Noncurrent Liabilities		$	**50,264**
Total Liabilities		$	**87,264**
Equity			
	Equity Investments		35,000
	Retained Earnings		(5,505)
	Less: Owner's and Investor's Draws		-
Total Equity		$	**29,495**
Total Liabilities and Equity		$	**116,759**

RETAIL OPERATIONS PLAN

REPORTING POLICIES

All sales associates will report to the assistant manager. The assistant manager will report to the owner/manager. All incidents occurring within the store will be reported to the assistant manager, who will in turn return report to the manager. An incident form is included in the appendices. It is required that the form be completed and given to management within twenty-four hours of the incident.

EMPLOYEE DEVELOPMENT

To stay informed about customer expectations and the degree of customer satisfaction achieved, RealWomen, Inc., has established policies that include conducting surveys of existing customers and adopting a "customer is always right" attitude in responding to complaints about merchandise or service. Sales training meetings will be attended three times per year at the expense of RealWomen, Inc. The cost of training seminars is approximately $100 per person for a two-day session and is reflected in the financials.

EMPLOYEE PHILOSOPHY

RealWomen, Inc., will adhere to the philosophy that three groups are responsible for the company's success: its customers, the people in the company, and the management team that leads the organizational personnel. The owner, Lucy Rich, believes that it is management's responsibility to create an atmosphere that emphasizes the importance of each member of the company and to give appreciation for the contribution made by each to the company's success. She further believes that:

RealWomen, Inc., customers are its lifeblood. Customers must be treated by all RealWomen, Inc., representatives as if they are the company's best customers. At RealWomen, Inc., the adage "the customer is always right" means the customer has the right to a quality product, quality service, and a quality shopping experience.

The employees of RealWomen, Inc., are the company's most important assets. Employees are vital members of the organizational team, and what the company accomplishes is accomplished through them. The management team will treat subordinates with the utmost respect. As leaders, the management team is responsibility for creating an atmosphere and work environment that allow the staff to perform to the best of their ability. Employee performance will be fairly evaluated. Employees have the right to expect that their job performance will be measured and evaluated by standards that are free from personal bias and that reflect the valuing of positive effort, results, and attitude toward customers and the degree to which the employee is a cooperative team player.

STAFFING LEVELS

The owner/president, assistant manager, and two part-time sales associates will staff the store during holidays and other peak traffic periods. During times of normal traffic, the store will have two staff members on the sales floor at all times.

HOURS/DAYS OF OPERATION

RealWomen, Inc., will be open for business seven days a week, from 10:00 AM to 7:00 PM. These hours are consistent with those of neighboring retail businesses.

INVENTORY CONTROL

A complete physical inventory will be taken two times per year, at the beginning of the month in January and

July. The owner or store manager will verify actual shipments against invoices and will note the date received and retail pricing of all goods.

SECURITY SYSTEMS

All packages brought into RealWomen by employees must be checked into an authorized location during the day. Purchases made by employees during the day will be processed by management and held in the authorized location. All employee packages will be subject to inspection. Merchandise will be tagged with security devices to reduce the risk of shoplifting. Regular meetings with security and police personnel on how to identify, handle safely, and report shoplifting will be held.

DOCUMENTATION

Documentation used to purchase merchandise (purchase orders) and receive or ship merchandise is included in the appendices. All orders must be verified by the manager or assistant manager.

PLANNING CHART/PRODUCT AVAILABILITY

It will be the responsibility of management to ensure that all merchandise is received in time for opening. A market trip three months before the store opening will help guarantee that merchandise will be on the sales floor for the grand opening. Four additional market trips during the year will provide a consistent flow of new inventory during peak-selling periods.

APPENDICES (SEE CHAPTER 2)

APPENDICES

Résumé for Lucy Rich

Résumé for Larry LaChamp

Company Organizational Chart

Store Layout Diagram

Purchase Order Form

BLANK BUSINESS PLAN TEMPLATE

Following is a blank template for completing your business plan. This template is also available electronically in the Templates folder on the accompanying CD-ROM. Before you begin, please refer to the the business plan template instructions in the Templates folder on the accompanying CD-ROM as a guide for creating your plan. You may also refer to the sample business plan in Appendix D of this book for further assistance.

COVER LETTER

PREPARED BY:

DATE PREPARED:

CONTENTS

EXECUTIVE SUMMARY

Business Overview

Critical Success Factors

The Management Team

The Market

Financial Plan

MANAGEMENT PLAN

Business Structure

Management Team

Management Compensation

Personnel Compensation

Key Advisors/Directors

Communication

Governmental Approvals

MERCHANDISING/PRODUCT PLAN

Merchandise/Product Description

Unique Characteristics

Proposed Lines

Proprietary Aspects

Six-Month Merchandise Plan

Merchandise Assortment

Market Trips

Markup/Markdown Policies

BRICK-AND-MORTAR LOCATION PLAN

Physical Location

Location Features

Target Market Considerations

Leasehold Improvements

Other Location Costs

Signage

WEB PLAN SUMMARY

Overview

Internet Strategies

Online Marketing Strategy

Web Development and Hosting

Costs

Buying and Shipping Methods

Future Features

MARKETING PLAN

Industry Profile

Market Economic Factors

Market Analysis Summary

Market Needs

Customer Profile

Future Markets

Competitive Analysis

Competitive Advantage

Pricing

    Pricing Strategy

    Price List

    Pricing Policies

Market Penetration

    Brand Strategy

    Advertising and Promotion

    Sales Strategy

    Publicity

    Promotional Events

Evaluating Marketing Efforts

FINANCIAL PLAN

Sales Forecast

Cash Requirements

Break-Even Analysis

Projected Financial Statements

    Monthly Cash Flow Statement

    Year-End Income Statement

    Year-End Balance Sheet

    Ratio Analysis

RETAIL OPERATIONS

Reporting Policies

Employee Development

Staffing Levels

Hours/Days of Operation

Inventory Control

Security Systems/Shrinkage Control

APPENDIX

BUSINESS OVERVIEW

CRITICAL SUCCESS FACTORS

THE MANAGEMENT TEAM

THE MARKET

FINANCIAL PLAN

BUSINESS STRUCTURE

MANAGEMENT TEAM

MANAGEMENT COMPENSATION

PERSONNEL COMPENSATION

KEY ADVISORS/DIRECTORS

COMMUNICATION

GOVERNMENTAL APPROVALS

MERCHANDISE/PRODUCT DESCRIPTION

UNIQUE CHARACTERISTICS

PROPOSED LINES

PROPRIETARY ASPECTS

6-MONTH MERCHANDISE PLAN

MERCHANDISE ASSORTMENT

MARKET TRIPS

MARKUP/MARKDOWN POLICIES

PHYSICAL LOCATION

LOCATION FEATURES

TARGET MARKET CONSIDERATIONS

LEASEHOLD IMPROVEMENTS

OTHER LOCATION COSTS

SIGNAGE

OVERVIEW

INTERNET STRATEGIES

ONLINE MARKETING STRATEGY

WEB DEVELOPMENT AND HOSTING

COSTS

FUTURE FEATURES

MARKETING PLAN

INDUSTRY PROFILE

MARKET ECONOMIC FACTORS

MARKET ANALYSIS SUMMARY

MARKET NEEDS

CUSTOMER PROFILE

COMPETITIVE ANALYSIS

COMPETITIVE ADVANTAGE

PRICING

PRICING STRATEGY

PRICE LIST

PRICING POLICIES

MARKET PENETRATION

BRAND STRATEGY

ADVERTISING AND PROMOTION

SALES STRATEGY

PUBLICITY

PROMOTIONAL EVENTS

EVALUATING MARKETING EFFORTS

FINANCIAL PLAN

SALES FORECAST

CASH REQUIREMENTS

BREAK-EVEN ANALYSIS

PROJECTED FINANCIAL STATEMENTS

Monthly cash flow statement (for at least one year and until the business shows a profit)

Year-End income statement

Year-End balance sheet

Ratio analysis

REPORTING POLICIES

EMPLOYEE DEVELOPMENT

STAFFING LEVELS

HOURS/DAYS OF OPERATION

INVENTORY CONTROL

SECURITY SYSTEMS/SHRINKAGE CONTROL

APPENDIX

GLOSSARY

A

advertising Paid nonpersonal communication delivered through mass media. (Chapter 8)

advertising allowances Funding provided to retailers by manufacturers for advertisements featuring their products. (Chapter 10)

advisory team A team of people identified by the entrepreneur to offer advice in starting and growing the business. (Chapter 9)

angel investors Sometimes referred to as private investors; people of wealth who decide to invest in a business in return for a higher rate of return than can be obtained through other investments, a financial interest in the business, or the desire to be part of a new concept. (Chapter 11)

apparel mart A building or group of buildings that house showrooms in which sales representatives present apparel lines to retail buyers. (Chapter 10)

asset Any item of economic value that is owned by the business. (Chapter 11)

assumptions A written document accompanying the financial statements that provides an explanation of the source and thought processes behind the numbers, especially in the cash flow statement. (Chapter 11)

augmented product The final product level that includes the product extras, such as advertising and promotion, warranty, and after-sale service. (Chapter 4)

B

backstock Merchandise held off the sales floor until needed. (Chapter 10)

backup order Shipments planned for later deliveries, with the vendor's agreement that a specific percent of the merchandise may be cancelled if necessary. This is not a common option, however, and is not offered to buyers placing small orders. (Chapter 10)

balance sheet An accounting statement that shows the financial condition of a company at a point in time. It includes assets, liabilities, and net worth. (Chapter 11)

banner advertisements Similar to the traditional advertisements found in print venues, online rectangular advertisements that display basic information about an e-business or its product line. They differ from print advertisements in that they are interactive and take an interested viewer to the Web site when they are clicked. (Chapter 7)

base plus commission An employee payment method in which sales associates earn a set amount for each week or month worked, as well as a percent of their individual sales volume. (Chapter 12)

blog An online digital diary or forum where text, photos, videos, and other material can be posted and made available to the public. (Chapter 7)

blue sky The dollar amount determined as a fee for the business's image or personality; it may include the business's existing customer base and intangible assets such as its reputation, and possibly, its name. (Chapter 5)

board of directors A group of people elected by the stockholders of a corporation who will be responsible for overseeing the overall direction and policy of the corporation. (Chapter 9)

bonus A lump-sum payment for an employee that is based on performance over an extended period of time; used to motivate and reward successful work.

book inventory The financial record of the stock or inventory. (Chapter 12)

book value A company's worth on paper. (Chapter 11)

boutique layout A floor plan that divides the store into a series of individual shopping areas, each with its own theme, much like building a series of specialty shops in a single store. (Chapter 6)

brand A name, term, sign, design, or combination of these that is intended to identify the goods or services of one seller or group of sellers and to differentiate them from those of competitors. (Chapter 4)

branding The process of attaching a name, an image, and a reputation to a thing, person, service, or idea; the sum of all the associations, feelings, beliefs, attitudes and perceptions customers have with a company. (Chapter 4)

brand mark The visual part of the brand that can be recognized but cannot be spoken. (Chapter 4)

brand name The part of the brand that can be vocalized. (Chapter 4)

brand sponsorship The selection between three primary brand alternatives available to the fashion retailer: manufacturer's or national brand, private brand, or private label. (Chapter 4)

brand value The worth of the brand in terms of customer recognition, image, and potential sales volume. (Chapter 4)

break-even point The point at which the company shows neither a profit nor a loss but simply covers all its costs. (Chapter 11)

brick-and-mortar location plan The section of the business plan that describes the business in terms of its physical location. (Chapter 2)

business location Traditionally, the site and facility where the business is physically situated; however, today it can be the destinations to which catalogs are mailed, the company's Web site, or Internet links. (Chapter 6)

business plan An evolving document that outlines the focus and direction for the business. (Chapter 1)

buyers Individuals who determine the merchandise needs of departments or entire stores and, ultimately, make the purchases. (Chapter 10)

C

cancellation (completion) date Agreed upon by the buyer and the vendor at the time the order is placed, the last day that the vendor is authorized to ship merchandise specified on a particular purchase order. (Chapter 10)

capital expenditures Assets purchased by the business that create a future benefit. (Chapter 11)

cash flow statement A document that shows the difference between the cash a company expects to receive and its expected cash expenditures on a monthly basis; a historic cash flow statement identifies the changes in account balances that have affected the cash balance during the prior year. (Chapter 11)

central business district Often the historical center of a city or town, the area where downtown businesses were established early in the development of a city. (Chapter 6)

channel of distribution The avenue selected for moving goods from producer to consumer. (Chapter 8)

classified advertisement A text-formatted promotion used in print or Internet media. (Chapter 7)

click-through rate (CTR) A method of analysis used to track how advertisements and keywords are working for an e-business by calculating when the Web site viewer actually clicks on the advertisement. (Chapter 7)

client file A customer profile form that contains contact information, size, brand preferences, past purchases, and personal information; used by sales associates to provide personal service to clients. (Chapter 12)

closeout merchandise Merchandise available at reduced wholesale prices that has been overproduced or returned by retailers due to a lack of sales or shipment past the cancellation dates specified on orders. (Chapter 10)

communication The process of transferring information and ideas from one person to another, with consistent understanding of the meaning. (Chapter 9)

compensation The employee's payment for services rendered. (Chapter 12)

compensation package The monetary or other value an employee receives in exchange for services. (Chapter 9)

competitive pricing A strategy in which a retailer bases its prices on those of the competitors. (Chapter 8)

concept statement A document used to present an idea for a business. (Chapter 1)

control The process through which results are compared to the goals and objectives; what can be done to do things better and what obstacles to quality performance should be removed. (Chapter 12)

convenience goods Products that the customer purchases frequently and easily, usually with minimal comparison shopping and evaluating. Pantyhose and some beauty products are examples of convenience goods. (Chapter 4)

cooperative advertising A program in which the vendor shares the cost of advertising with the retail operations that carry the vendor's line. (Chapter 10)

copyright The exclusive rights to reproduce, publish, or sell a trademark in the form of a literary, musical, or artistic work. (Chapter 4)

core product The primary level of a product; the true product; its main benefit or service. (Chapter 4)

cost of goods sold The purchase price of the merchandise to be resold. In other industries, it can mean the direct costs attributable to the production of the goods sold by the company. (Chapter 11)

cost per click (CPC) A method of payment in which the advertiser, or e-retailer, pays a fee each time a viewer clicks on the advertisement that takes him or her to the retailer's Web site. (Chapter 7)

cost per thousand (CPM) A method of payment for banner advertisements. The charge for cost per thousand is dependent on the number of people who visit the Web site. (Chapter 7)

cross-filing A reference system in which the same information is listed in two or more categories. This information can be used to generate mailing lists for promotional fliers and newsletters, among other tasks. (Chapter 12)

current ratio Measures whether or not there is enough cash available to pay the bills. (Chapter 11)

customer mobility The ability of customers to enter the establishment, move about the business, and find the merchandise they are seeking. (Chapter 12)

customer traffic patterns The routes customers take as they make their way through the store. (Chapter 6)

cyclical patterns Those recurring swings that move the business activity—its sales, cash flow, and profits—from a downslide to an upswing or vice versa. (Chapter 3)

D

dating An additional amount of time the vendor allows the retailer for payment due on orders shipped, usually an additional thirty days before payment is due. This is noted on the purchase order as "30X." (Chapter 12)

debt Money loaned to a company that is expected to be repaid. (Chapter 11)

debt financing Involves securing funds by borrowing money that must be repaid. (Chapter 11)

debt ratio The portion of total assets that are financed through debt. (Chapter 11)

debt-to-equity ratio Measures the proportion of assets that are financed by creditors with assets that are contributed by the owners. (Chapter 11)

decline stage The final stage of the product life cycle. At this point, the product is often found in discount stores and on markdown racks. (Chapter 4)

demographics The segmentation of markets based on age, gender, education, occupation, geographic location, race, nationality, income, religion, and other commonly used census classifications. (Chapter 3)

depreciated value A noncash expense that reduces the value of an asset as a result of wear and tear, age, or obsolescence. (Chapter 11)

depreciation The allocation of the cost of an asset over the term of the asset's useful life. (Chapter 11)

diffusion labels Secondary lines offered by designers. (Chapter 8)

direct competitors Businesses that offer essentially the same product or service. (Chapter 3)

distribution channels The routes taken to move the product to the consumer. (Chapter 3)

distribution practices A manufacturer's policies concerning where a line is to be shipped. (Chapter 10)

domain name The part of the URL that specifically identifies the name of the Web site. (Chapter 7)

durable goods Products that normally survive many uses, such as apparel, accessories, and fabrics. (Chapter 4)

E

e-commerce The buying and selling of merchandise via the Internet; term used by some interchangeably with e-retailing. (Chapter 7)

efficiency ratios Measure how effectively a company utilizes its resources. (Chapter 11)

employee procedures manual A guide that specifies business policies and procedures for employee tasks, such as assisting a customer with a return, processing shipments, arranging merchandise, and operating the computer. (Chapter 12)

entertailing An industry trend in which retailers add entertainment facilities, such as music venues, coffee shops, or cafes, to their stores to build customer traffic. (Chapter 6)

entrepreneur A person who starts or grows a business venture and assumes the risk. (Chapter 1)

entry strategy The method the fashion entrepreneur chooses to begin ownership of a business. (Chapter 5)

equity Money invested in a company that is not intended to be repaid, but represents an ownership interest. (Chapter 11)

equity financing The personal investment of the owner or other source of capital in the business; money invested in a company that is not paid to investors in the normal course of business. (Chapter 11)

e-retailing Used concurrently with the terms, virtual storefront and virtual mall, e-retailing is the activity of direct retail shopping online. (Chapter 7)

exclusive goods Merchandise that is limited in distribution to specific retail operations; aid in providing prestige and patronage motives for the consumer. (Chapter 4)

exclusivity The limited availability of merchandise; critical to specialty operations. (Chapter 10)

executive summary The section of the business plan that provides a sketch or overview of the business. (Chapter 2)

exit strategy A plan for closing a business. (Chapter 5)

expenses The costs incurred in operating the business and providing the product or service. (Chapter 11)

external sources Buying information the retailer can access outside of the business such as resident buying offices, fashion forecasters, trade publications, and reporting services on the Web and in print. (Chapter 10)

F

fashion goods Products that are popular among consumers for a given period of time. (Chapter 4)

fashion items Products that are frequently available in a wide range of styles and have a life expectancy that is relatively brief due to seasonal changes. (Chapter 10)

fashion seasons Most manufacturers of fashion merchandise develop five seasonal lines: fall I, fall II, holiday, spring, and summer. Some manufacturers, particularly those catering to designer customers, have an additional season—cruise or resort—which is delivered between holiday and spring seasons. (Chapter 10)

FIFO (first in, first out) A method for valuing inventory, it applies higher value to first receipt goods by recording to the order in which they were received. (Chapter 12)

financial patterns The financial standards and norms used to determine pricing, to evaluate merchandise performance, and to specify billing terms within the fashion industry (Chapter 3)

financial plan The section of the business plan that provides sound financial statements that reflect the potential profitability of the business. (Chapter 2)

first-ring suburbs Early-stage communities that develop through suburban sprawl. (Chapter 6)

fixed costs Those costs that will be incurred whether a sale is made or not. (Chapter 11)

fixed rate compensation Employee payment that is not tied exclusively to performance, but is set at a specific level for a specified time period, such as an hourly wage or a monthly salary. (Chapter 12)

flexible markup policy A technique allowing the entrepreneur to apply different levels of markup to varying merchandise classifications. (Chapter 10)

focus group A form of research in which a group of people are gathered and asked their opinions, perceptions, beliefs, and attitudes towards a product or service, advertisement, idea or packaging. (Chapter 3)

forecasting The science of estimating what is likely to happen given an assumed set of conditions. (Chapter 10)

formal product The product level includes the packaging, the brand name, the quality of the product, its styling, and any other tangible features, such as a product identification tag. (Chapter 4)

four-five-four calendar Its purpose is to compare the same days of the week against one another from year to year in order to forecast sales accurately. Four weeks are indicated for one month, five weeks allocated to the next month, then back to four weeks, and so on. (Chapter 10)

franchise The right or license an individual or a group is granted to sell products or services in a specified manner within a given territory. (Chapter 5)

franchisee The person, or group of persons, paying a franchise fee to operate a business under the guidelines designated by the franchisor. (Chapter 5)

franchise fee The money paid by an the entrepreneur to receive a format or system developed by the company (franchisor), the right to use the franchisor's name for a limited time, and assistance in business operations. (Chapter 5)

franchisor The provider of the right or license that an individual or a group may purchase to sell products or services in a specified manner within a given territory. (Chapter 5)

free-form layout Utilizes displays of varying shapes and sizes to create a relaxed and friendly shopping atmosphere that encourages customers to take their time. (Chapter 6)

funders A person or organization that provides funds for a business. (Chapter 1)

G

general line Describes a wide variety of merchandise, one of great breadth. A department store that features women's, men's, and children's apparel, as well as home furnishings and home accessories, carries a general line of merchandise. (Chapter 4)

grid layout Displays are arranged in a rectangular fashion so that aisles are parallel to one another. This formal layout that controls traffic in the store as it uses space efficiently, creates an organized environment, and facilitates shopping by standardizing the location of items. (Chapter 6)

gross income Net sales minus cost of goods sold. (Chapter 11)

gross margin Net sales minus cost of goods sold. (Chapter 11)

gross margin ratio Measures overall profit. (Chapter 11)

gross profit Net sales minus cost of goods sold. (Chapter 11)

growth capital Money needed to help a business grow and expand. (Chapter 11)

growth stage The product life cycle stage when a larger number of consumers begin to accept and purchase the item or service. The product typically generates its peak sales volume as it moves through the growth stage. (Chapter 4)

H

hard goods Products in the classifications of appliances, electronics, and home furnishings. (Chapter 4)

high-end goods Products that are at the top of the pricing scale. (Chapter 4)

hourly plus commission An employee payment method in which sales associates earn a set amount for each hour worked, as well as a percent of their individual sales volume. (Chapter 12)

I

incentives Methods developed to generate high performances by employees. (Chapter 12)

incidental costs Those costs which may occur sporadically, such as shipping charges and ticketing expenses. (Chapter 10)

income statement Also referred to as a profit and loss (P&L) statement. The income statement reflects how much

money the business made or lost during a given time period. (Chapter 11)

Index of Retail Saturation (IRS) A measure that calculates the number of customers in a specified area, customers' purchasing power, and the level of competition. It combines the average retail expenditures with the average dollar amount that each person spends for a certain type of merchandise in a given trading area. (Chapter 6)

indirect competitors Businesses that offer different types of products or services that may meet the same need or want of the buyer. (Chapter 3)

industry All companies supplying similar or related products (which can include services). (Chapter 3)

initial markup The first markup calculation on the wholesale price of an item, it determines the item's original selling price. (Chapter 10)

intangible product Those products that cannot be touched or held, such as a service or an idea. (Chapter 4)

intellectual property Any product, service, or retail operation that is the result of a creative process and that has commercial value. Intellectual property can be protected through the use of trademarks, patents, and copyright. (Chapter 4)

internal sources Records that show merchandise performance by vendor, including markdowns, returns, delivery, sales, and profit margin performance. (Chapter 10)

intrapreneurship Working within a company in an entrepreneurial capacity, using creativity and skills. (Chapter 9)

introductory pricing Internal resources also include employees and customers. (Chapter 10)

introductory stage The first stage of the product life cycle when innovative goods that appeal to fashion leaders, or trendsetters, are first offered. During this stage, the focus is on marketing the new product to potential consumers. (Chapter 4)

inventory The merchandise selection carried by a retailer, including fashion or basic goods and hard or soft goods, or a combination of these. (Chapter 4)

inventory management Planning a merchandise assortment that is heavy in the styles, colors, and sizes customers will order and light in those that are ordered less frequently. (Chapter 7)

inventory turnover ratio Measures how many times the company's inventory is sold and replaced over a period of time. (Chapter 11)

investment turnover ratio Tells how efficiently a company uses its assets. The measurement shows how quickly and how often an asset (piece of machinery or investment) pays for itself. (Chapter 11)

invoice The vendor's detailed shipment listing with prices. (Chapter 12)

J

job analysis Outlines information about the duties, tasks, or activities necessary to perform a job. (Chapter 9)

job description Outlines the tasks, duties, and responsibilities of the position based on the job analysis. (Chapter 9)

just-in-time An inventory replenishment system set up between a vendor and retailer in which inventory is shipped as it is sold. (Chapter 12)

K

key vendors Lines carried in depth in a retail organization's inventory. (Chapter 10)

L

layaway A customer service in which the customer can hold merchandise by making a deposit and then making weekly or monthly payments on it until the merchandise is paid off. (Chapter 12)

layout The arrangement of the physical facilities in a business. (Chapter 6)

leadership Deals with guiding and motivating people. (Chapter 9)

lead time The amount of time needed between placing an order and receiving the goods at the retail operation. (Chapter 10)

letter of intent A memo from a prospective buyer addressed to a company owner stating the desire to conduct business; usually indicates that the prospective buyer is serious and sets a timeline for negotiations. (Chapter 5)

liability An obligation or amount owed to others. (Chapter 11)

licensing The practice of buying or selling the use of a brand name from one company to another. The brand name can be that of a celebrity, a designer, a manufacturer, or a company. (Chapter 4)

LIFO (last in, first out) A method for valuing and recording inventory; it places a higher value on most recently received merchandise. (Chapter 12)

limited line A particular product category with depth of selection. Limited line retail operations, for example, may feature ladies' accessories including handbags, belts, jewelry, and watches. (Chapter 4)

line of credit A short-term loan that provides cash flow for the day-to-day operations of the business. (Chapter 11)

liquid open-to-buy Unspent funds that the buyer can use to purchase new merchandise to update inventories and to replenish items that have sold out. (Chapter 10)

liquidity ratio Measures the ability of the business to pay its current obligations as they come due. (Chapter 11)

loan amortization The repayment of a loan over a period of time. (Chapter 11)

loss leader A pricing and promotional strategy in which one or a few items are sold at or just above cost price in order to attract customers. (Chapter 10)

low-end goods Products that are at the lower or budget end of the pricing range. (Chapter 4)

M

magalog A hybrid fashion magazine and catalog, one that combines fashion articles, photographs, and advertising with products that can be purchased. (Chapter 5)

maintained markup The dollar amount added to the cost price at the time the merchandise was sold at retail. (Chapter 10)

management The organization and coordination of activities of a business in accordance with certain policies and in achievement of certain objectives. (Chapter 9)

management plan The section of the business plan that defines the management team. (Chapter 2)

manufacturer's brand Often referred to as a national brand, it's the most traditional type of brand sponsorship. Manufacturer's brands are those brand names promoted by the producers, often advertised nationally and sold through a broad range of retailers. (Chapter 4)

markdown The amount deducted from the cost of the product to establish the sale price. (Chapter 10)

market analysis The process of determining factors, conditions, and characteristics of a market. (Chapter 3)

marketing mix The planned mix of the controllable element's of product, place, price, and promotion. (Chapter 8)

marketing plan The section of the business plan that describes the entrepreneur's specific actions intended to bring their product or service to market and persuade consumers to buy. (Chapter 2)

market research An organized effort to find out information about an industry, the market, and its customers. (Chapter 3)

market value The amount of money someone will pay for an asset at any given time. (Chapter 11)

market weeks Traditional purchase periods when buyers begin to make selections for the next season; predetermined times when buyers go to regional apparel markets to review new lines. (Chapter 10)

markup The amount added to the cost of the product to establish the selling price of the product. (Chapter 8)

maturity stage The product life cycle stage when the product is either at a peak or plateau in sales, and it is mass-produced and mass-marketed. During this stage, sales generally continue to increase, but typically at a slower rate than during the growth stage. (Chapter 4)

merchandise assortment The selection of stock or inventory a retailer carries or a manufacturer produces—the amount, type, size, color, and style representation in the inventory. (Chapter 4)

merchandise classification (category) The related group of items found in an area or department of the retail operation. For example, menswear is a merchandise classification. (Chapter 10)

merchandise discount An incentive that many fashion retailers use to recruit and reward employees; the employee is provided a specified percent off the retail price store merchandise. (Chapter 12)

merchandise fulfillment The process of filling customers' requests or orders. (Chapter 12)

merchandise plan Incorporates a number of quantitative categories for the business, designated in retail dollars for each month, as follows: planned sales, beginning of the month and end of the month inventory levels, markdowns, average inventory, stock turn, and so on. (Chapter 10)

merchandise subclassification Items that are part of a specific merchandise classification. In men's tailored apparel, for example, suits, sports coats, and dress trousers are subclassifications. (Chapter 10)

merchandising The buying and selling of goods. (Chapter 10)

merchandising/product plan The section of the business plan that describes the products and services being offered to the customer. (Chapter 2)

minimum order The dollar or unit amount that a vendor requires before accepting an order. (Chapter 10)

mission statement A statement addressing the purpose of the company. (Chapter 1)

motivation The internal and external factors that stimulate desire and energy in people to be continually interested in and committed to a job, role, or subject, and to exert persistent effort in attaining a goal. (Chapter 9)

mystery shopper A person hired to visit retail stores posing as a casual shopper to obtain information about the store's display, pricing, and customer service. (Chapter 3)

N

national brand *See manufacturer's brand.*

National Retail Traffic Index (NRTI) An organization that provides information about shopper traffic and conversion trends (i.e., sales volume) for retail executives, mall developers, industry analysts, real estate consultants, and advertisers. NRTI evaluates department store traffic from two perspectives—the mall in which the department store is located and the department store itself. (Chapter 6)

net income The remaining income or revenue after all expenses have been paid. (Chapter 11)

net margin ratio Shows how many cents on each dollar of sales are profit. (Chapter 11)

networking The ability to connect with a broad range of contacts for the purpose of sharing useful information and resources. (Chapter 8)

newsgroups Online communities of people composed of individuals who are interested in a certain topic, rather than general news. Because newsgroups are similar to a public bulletin board, an e-company can post new and exciting information or offer promotions on products to a group of potential customers who fit in the e-business's target market. (Chapter 7)

newsletter A communication tool distributed by e-mail and containing articles, specials, discounts, and other information promoting an e-business and its products. (Chapter 7)

niche A small, specialized part of a market that is not served or may not be cost effective for the major, well-established companies to serve. (Chapter 7)

niche market A subset of a market on which the particular product is focused; a narrowly defined group of potential customers. (Chapter 3)

nondurable goods Products that are normally consumed in one or a few uses, such as shampoo. (Chapter 4)

nonselling space The amount of square footage allocated to offices, storage, employee lounges, and so on; space not used for selling merchandise. (Chapter 12)

nonstore retail operations Retail businesses that do not have a physical environment through which the customer can see, touch, and try on the merchandise, such as Web sites, mail-order catalogs, and television shopping channels. (Chapter 10)

nonverbal communication Relates to how one acts. (Chapter 9)

North American Industry Classification System (NAICS) A set of industry categories standardized between the United States, Canada, and Mexico. (Chapter 11)

O

off-price merchandise Goods that the buyer has been able to purchase from the manufacturer at below the wholesale price. (Chapter 10)

on-hand stock Merchandise, or inventory, that is currently available. (Chapter 10)

on-order Orders that the buyer has placed with the vendors but that have not yet been shipped or received. (Chapter 10)

online auction An e-business model that allows persons to buy or sell items, mostly through a bidding process, such as is found at e-Bay. (Chapter 7)

online storefront E-business model that most closely resembles a traditional brick-and-mortar store. It is the most common type of e-commerce site in that it displays information about the product or service for sale, and then accepts orders for those services, usually through a shopping cart. (Chapter 7)

open-to-buy (OTB) The buyer's budget, calculated in retail dollars, that dictates how much money the buyer will spend in each merchandise classification for each month of business; the difference between how much the buyer needs in inventory at retail to reach sales goals less the merchandise that is currently available. (Chapter 10)

operating costs The day to day expenses incurred in running a business, such as rent, utilities, and telephone. (Chapter 10)

operating expenses The ongoing cost of running a business including overhead costs such as rent, utilities, payroll, and marketing. (Chapter 11)

operating margin ratio Indicates how well a business is managing its overhead costs. (Chapter 11)

operations The procedures put in place to actually run the business; the procedures and policies that an organization must develop and implement for its merchandising and management functions. (Chapter 12)

organizational chart Defines how the business is organized and illustrates the relationships among the job positions. (Chapter 9)

organizational culture Sometimes referred to as company culture, it's the personality of the business—its attitudes, values, and communication style. (Chapter 9)

organizational structure The way in which the organization defines job tasks, how these tasks are divided and grouped, and how they are coordinated. (Chapter 9)

overage If the physical inventory is greater than the book inventory, the difference is called overage. This indicates that there are clerical errors in one of the accounting functions, such as recording merchandise receipts, posting markdowns, or returning goods to the manufacturer. (Chapter 12)

owner's equity Total assets minus total liability of a company. The actual dollar value of an owner's total investment in a business, plus any net profits that have been retained in the business from year to year. (Chapter 11)

P

packing slip The vendor's listing of merchandise packed in a particular carton or container. (Chapter 12)

participative management style Style that encourages employees at all levels of the organization to be trusted and empowered to make decisions and to take the actions necessary to get the job done. (Chapter 9)

penetration pricing Pricing a product at a low price point to introduce the product to a market, and promoting that product heavily with the hope that consumers will buy the product, try it, then purchase more of the same. (Chapter 8)

percentage of sales method A method of pricing in which costs are budgeted as a percentage of sales. (Chapter 8)

performance appraisal Measures an employee's actual performance against the performance desired. (Chapter 9)

perpetual markdown policy A plan for the buyer to reduce prices on slow-selling merchandise every month to generate the quick disposal of less desirable goods and provide funds to purchase new items that may have a greater profitability. (Chapter 10)

physical inventory count A formal, item-by-item analysis of the operation's stock on hand. The selling price of each item and, possibly, the vendor and style numbers are recorded, and then all prices are totaled to create a physical price inventory dollar valuation. (Chapter 12)

planned obsolescence The concept that a fashion item does not usually become unwanted because it is no longer functional; instead, it is no longer fashionable. (Chapter 10)

podcasting Online audio programming that can be produced with a computer, microphone, software, and a Web site for posting programming, and can be listened to on any computer connected to the Internet that can play standard MP3 audio files. (Chapter 7)

point-of-sale (POS) A system using a computerized cash register that generates a customer receipt while adjusting the retail dollar inventory level, maintains a record of merchandise that is sold, tracks items that are returned or exchanged, and provides an analysis of sales and stock by unit and by vendor. (Chapter 12)

pop-up advertisement A window that automatically opens on a user's computer whenever the viewer visits an advertised Web site or one from which an ad has been purchased. (Chapter 7)

population density The number of people per square mile residing in a given area. (Chapter 6)

portal A Web site that offers a variety of Internet services from a single convenient location, aggregating information on a broad range of topics and linking online merchants with online shopping malls and auction sites. Portals assist users in collecting information and browsing multiple independent storefronts from one convenient location, as illustrated by BizOffice. (Chapter 7)

position The place a product occupies in the marketplace. (Chapter 8)

power center Combines the drawing potential of a large regional mall with the convenience of a neighborhood shopping center. Anchored by large specialty or department stores, these centers frequently target affluent baby boomers. (Chapter 6)

premium pricing Pricing merchandise at the top of the relevant price range. (Chapter 8)

press release Editorial copy that can be used by media representatives to promote an event or newsworthy item. (Chapter 8)

price ceiling The highest price a business can ask for its product or service; it is often set by customers. (Chapter 8)

price floor The lowest price a business can charge for its products or services; it is determined by costs. (Chapter 8)

price range The price between the floor price and the ceiling price. (Chapter 8)

price lining (all-in-one pricing) A process though which the buyer groups inventory into categories and then sets the same price for all items in each category, resulting in some items at below-average markup, whereas others may be at above-average markup. (Chapter 10).

price skimming A pricing strategy in which entrepreneurs set a relatively higher price for a product or service initially, then lower the prices over time. (Chapter 8)

primary data Data collected from first-hand experience. Collection of this data may be obtained through focus groups, observation, or interviews. (Chapter 3)

prime selling space The location with the highest level of customer traffic. (Chapter 6)

private brand May be referred to as the agent (intermediary) distributor or dealer brand; a brand name that is developed by the distributor to create consistency among the distributor's product offerings. A distributor sells and ships merchandise purchased from a variety of manufacturers under the one brand name. (Chapter 4)

private label Merchandise that carries a brand name created for or by the retail operation. (Chapter 4)

product Anything offered to a market for attention, acquisition, use, or consumption. Primarily developed to satisfy a customer's want or need, it may be an object, a service, a place, an organization, or an idea. (Chapter 4)

product life cycle A model designed to identify the maturation stage of a particular product by approximating its level of customer acceptance. (Chapter 4)

profit Determined by subtracting the expenses of the business from revenues generated. (Chapter 11)

profitability ratio Measures how efficiently a business is being managed. Entrepreneurs use these ratios to help identify inefficient operations, expenses that are too high, and profitable margins. (Chapter 11)

pro forma financial statements Accounting reports, including income statements, balance sheets, and cash flow statements, which represent the estimated future plans of a business. (Chapter 11)

promotion Involves the activities used to inform the potential consumer about the product. (Chapter 8)

proprietary brand May also be referred to as private label; lines that are often represented by celebrity partners who add prestige and familiarity to the brand image. Miley Cirus and Max Azria for Walmart and Isaac Mizrahi for Target are examples of proprietary brands. (Chapter 4)

Ps of marketing (marketing mix) The four Ps of marketing include product, price, place, and promotion. (Chapter 8)

psychographics Segmenting markets based on their lifestyle or personality characteristics. (Chapter 3)

publicity Free advertising in which the media publishes stories about the business at no cost. (Chapter 8)

purchase agreement A binding document that outlines the terms of sale for a business, such as the selling price, payments, and items involved such as fixtures, equipment, and inventory. (Chapter 5)

purchase journal A spreadsheet used to keep track of all orders that the buyer has placed. (Chapter 10)

Q
qualitative data Information that is based on attitudes, beliefs, behaviors, views, or emotion; informed estimates used for forecasting. (Chapters 3, 10)

quantitative data Information that is based on numbers (e.g., sales figures, number of retailers in a geographic area, and an individual's size); mathematical analyses of historical or estimated data. (Chapters 3, 10)

quick ratio Shows whether the business has enough cash to cover its short-term obligations. (Chapter 11)

quota plus commission A method of employee payment in which the sales person is assigned a sales goal (i.e., hourly, weekly, or monthly sales volume performance) by management and receives a specified percent of commission on sales generated above the set goal. (Chapter 12)

R
racetrack layout Aisles, fixtures, and signing are located to guide the customer around the store in a large loop to give customers an outside-in view of most departments and conveniently directs them around the entire store. (Chapter 6)

ratio analysis Allows the entrepreneur to examine the relationship between one financial value and another. Ratio analysis enables the entrepreneur to spot trends in the business and compare its performance and condition with the average performance of similar businesses in the same industry. (Chapter 11)

research and development (R&D) An ongoing analysis of trends and issues that may affect the products, services, operations, promotional efforts, competitors, and customers of the business. (Chapter 12)

resident buying office Also referred to as a consulting service; a company that offers suggestions for merchandise suppliers and assists the entrepreneur or buyer by providing services in trend forecasting, merchandise selection, promotions, and so on. (Chapter 10)

retail layout The arrangement and method of display of merchandise in a store. (Chapter 6)

retail operations plan The section of the business plan that illustrates that the entrepreneur understands the importance of administrative policies, procedures, and controls. (Chapter 2)

return authorization label A sticker that is attached to the carton containing the return to ensure that the shipment will be accepted at the receiving dock of the manufacturer. (Chapter 12)

return on assets (ROA) ratio Measures a company's ability to produce net profits by effectively utilizing its assets. The higher the ratio, the more effective the company is at using its assets to produce profits. (Chapter 11)

return on equity (ROE) ratio Measures the return on the owner's investment in the company and is perhaps the most important measure of a business' financial viability. The higher the ratio, the higher the rate of return on the owner's investment. (Chapter 11)

revenues Money earned or received from providing a good or service. (Chapter 11)

risk ratios Show the extent to which the entrepreneur relies on debt, as opposed to equity capital, to finance the operations of the business. (Chapter 11)

royalty Payment to a licensor that can vary in terms of amount based on a percent of wholesale sales, often with a required minimum amount of sales. (Chapter 4)

RTM (return to the manufacturer)/RTV (return to the vendor) Merchandise to return to the manufacturer due to defects, substitutions, not as ordered, or shipment past the cancellation date; requires an approval label (return authorization label) from the vendor before shipping. (Chapter 12)

S

sales commission Payment to a sales associate based on a percent of merchandise he or she sells to customers. (Chapter 12)

sales forecast An informed estimate, based on a given set of assumptions about the future of sales volume for a specific target market and specific merchandise classification. (Chapter 10)

sales tax bond A sales tax bond is essentially a deposit held by the state to offset any unpaid sales tax incurred in the business. (Chapter 1)

salvage investment *See turnaround.*

search engine advertisements With these advertisements, products or Web sites are tied to specific keywords. When a computer user types those keywords in the search box, a related advertisement is displayed. (Chapter 7)

seasonal patterns Distinct changes in activity within a calendar year. (Chapter 3)

secondary data Information that is already there for the taking such as government census reports, information from news organizations, the Internet, commercial online services, and trade associations. (Chapter 3)

seed capital Money used by the entrepreneur in the beginning stages of an enterprise. (Chapter 11)

selling space The amount of square footage allocated for displaying and housing merchandise to be sold. (Chapter 12)

service products These are activities, benefits, or satisfactions that are offered for sale, such as custom design work, alterations, and personal shopping. (Chapter 4)

shopping cart An e-business model application with an order form used to process orders with payments through credit cards or services like PayPal. Products are then shipped to the customer or delivered by an immediate download, such as music and software. (Chapter 7)

shopping goods Products that the customer shops around for and often compares on the basis of price, quality, style, and other related factors. Special occasion apparel, outerwear, and career wear are examples. (Chapter 4)

shortage When there is less physical inventory than book inventory, the difference is referred to as a shortage. (Chapter 12)

shrinkage An industry term for inventory losses resulting from employee theft, shoplifting, and clerical errors. (Chapter 12)

six-month plan A plan that incorporates a number of quantitative categories for the business, designated in retail dollars, as follows: planned sales, beginning of the month and end of the month inventory levels, markdowns, average inventory, and stock turn. (Chapter 10)

soft goods Textile and apparel products, including accessories. (Chapter 4)

space value The value of each square foot of space in the store with respect to its ability to generate sales revenue. (Chapter 6)

spam An inexpensive promotional tool used by the multitude of companies that purchase large, mass mailing lists to send promotional emails out by the thousands. (Chapter 7)

specialty goods Products for which a significant group of buyers is habitually willing to make a special purchase effort as this merchandise has unique characteristics or specific brand identification, or both, for example, Polo Ralph Lauren sportswear and Arche shoes. Merchants work to move their products into the specialty goods arena, as this is where the devoted, repeat customer resides. (Chapter 4)

spreadsheet A computer-generated chart that allows for inputting formulas, changing variables, and creating reports for the entrepreneur to assess the business. (Chapter 12)

staple (basic) goods Products that are steadily in demand and rarely influenced by fashion changes. (Chapter 4)

staple (basic) items Merchandise that is in demand for extended periods of time and that is not subject to rapid style changes. (Chapter 10)

start-up costs Expenses that are incurred by the entrepreneur to begin the operation of a business; the costs involved in starting a venture. These costs include expenses such as initial marketing efforts or one time deposits, and capital expenditures. (Chapter 11)

stockkeeping unit (SKU) The identification numbers used to identify and tag each item in the inventory. (Chapter 12)

stock-to-sales ratio A calculation in which the inventory for a given period of time is divided by the sales volume for the same period. (Chapter 10)

stock turn (turnover) A statistical measurement representing sales for a period and the average size of stock during that same period, it is a measurement of inventory performance that guides the entrepreneur in assessing the productivity of inventory. (Chapter 10)

straight commission Through this plan, sales associates are paid a percent of their sales volume. (Chapter 12)

styles The specific looks within a merchandise subclassification. (Chapter 10)

supply chain management (SCM) An integrated approach to cost and time efficiencies in all the activities of channel members, such as the retail business, its vendors, and its shipping companies. (Chapter 12)

supply channels The companies that provide materials and equipment needed to manufacture the product, as well as the companies that actually produce the goods. (Chapter 3)

SWOT analysis Provides a way to identifying the strengths, weaknesses, opportunities, and threats of the proposed business against the competition. (Chapter 3)

T

tangible product Products that are physical and touchable. Tangible products are divided into two primary classifications, nondurable goods and durable goods. (Chapter 4)

target market The specific group of customers with similar characteristics that a business intends to capture. (Chapter 3)

tracking merchandise Monitoring the performance of items in inventory by vendor. (Chapter 12)

tracking plan A plotted pattern that is created from observing the movements of random samples of shoppers in the store. (Chapter 6)

trade dress The combined visual components of a trademark, to include the word, design, symbol, logo, shape, and color. (Chapter 4)

trademark A word, design, symbol, logo, shape, color (or a combination of these) that a company uses to identify and distinguish itself from others. (Chapter 4)

transaction A customer's cash or credit sale, exchange, or return. (Chapter 12)

turnaround A business that is failing, but for which there are obvious changes that, when implemented, would make the business successful. (Chapter 5)

turnkey operation A business that, when purchased, is ready to go; inventory, fixtures, equipment, and procedures are in place. (Chapter 5)

U

unsought goods Customers do not seek out this type of product; they did not even know they needed or wanted it until it found them through promotional activities. An example is the Snuggie. (Chapter 4)

V

value-based pricing A pricing method based on the perceived worth of the good or service to the intended customer. (Chapter 8)

variable costs Expenses that vary in proportion to changes in the level of activity or in proportion to sales such as stock or merchandise. (Chapter 11)

variable-rate (merit) compensation A method of employee payment that ties pay directly to the performance of the individual or group. (Chapter 12)

vendor analysis A report that summarizes sales, markdowns, and returns for each manufacturer, or vendor, carried in the retail operation. (Chapter 10)

venture capitalists Individuals or organizations that purchase an equity position in the company in exchange for a return of their investment. (Chapter 11)

verbal communication Relates to what is said or written. (Chapter 9)

virtual companies A company offering goods and services on the Internet. (Chapter 1)

vision statement Addresses what the owner stands for and what he or she believes about the business. (Chapter 1)

W

Web plan summary The section of the business plan that describes how the products or services will be sold or introduced through the Web. (Chapter 2)

wheel of retailing A retail marketing process whereby original low-price discounters upgrade their services and gradually increase prices. (Chapter 8)

wholesale Products are purchased at a discounted price and then resold at a marked-up price. (Chapter 7)

working capital The money needed to operate the business. Working capital is typically the difference between current assets and current liabilities. (Chapter 11)

REFERENCES

FRONTMATTER

1. Victor Kiam Quotes. BrainyQuote. http://www.brainyquote .com/quotes/quotes/v/victorkiam176215.html
2. Richard Branson Quotes. BrainyQuote. http://thinkexist.com/quotes/richard_branson

CHAPTER 1

1. InvestorWords. http://www.investorwords.com/1715/ entrepreneur.html
2. Timmons, Jeffry. *New Venture Creation: Entrepreneurship for the 21st Century*, 5th ed. Boston: Irwin McGraw-Hill, 1999, p. 27.
3. Miller, Claire Cain. Site Wins Fashion Friends by Letting Them Down. *New York Times*, July 26, 2009. http://www.nytimes.com/2009/07/27/technology/ companies/27polyvore.html?_r=1&page
4. *Entrepreneur*. (n.d.) 10 [1/2] Trends to Watch. (n.d.) http://www.entrepreneur.com/trends/index.html
5. Saunders, Kay. Interpersonal Skills Development Tools and Resources, Human Asset Imaging Institute. Bellewether, 2009.
6. http://www.dawn-wells.com/Wishing_Wells/wishing_ wells.html
7. Wyatt, Edward. Ripples of September 11 Widen in Retailing. *The New York Times*, December 10, 2001.
8. *Fortune* Magazine, March 16, 2010, http://money.cnn .com/2010/03/16/smallbusiness/toms_shoes_blake_ mycoskie.fortune/index.htm
9. Fast Company. http://www.fastcompany.com/mic/2010/ industry/most-innovative-retail-companies

CHAPTER 2

1. Bruce, Margaret, and Tony Hines. *Fashion Marketing: Contemporary Issues*. Woburn, Massachusetts: Butterworth-Heinemann, 2002.

2. Easey, Mike. *Fashion Marketing*. UK: Blackwell Publishing, 2009.
3. Harder, Frances. *Fashion for Profit*. Harder Publications, 2009.
4. Gerber, Michael. *The E-Myth Revisited: Why Most Business Don't Work and What to Do about It*. New York: HarperCollins, 1995, 2001.
5. Belbin, Meredith. *Management Teams: Why They Succeed or Fail*, 3d edition. Oxford, UK: Butterworth-Heinemann, 2010.

CHAPTER 4

1. Bluefly, Inc. http://www.fundinguniverse.com/ company-histories/Bluefly-Inc-Company-History.html
2. 40 under Forty. *Crains*, 2004. http://mycrains .crainsnewyork.com/40under40/profiles/2004/2
3. Slattala, Michelle. Bargain Hunters Stalk the Bluefly. *New York Times*, May 26, 2005. http://www.nytimes .com/2005/05/26/ fashion/thursdaystyles/26online.html?_r=1
4. Young Millionaires. *Entrepreneur*, November 2000. http://www.entrepreneur.com/article/33606-10

CHAPTER 5

1. Reference for Business: Encyclopedia of Small Business. dELiA*s. http://www.referenceforbusiness.com/ history2/41/dELiA-s-Inc.html#ixzz0iOZs6uuy
2. Alloy Buys Retailer dEliA*s. Promo. September 1, 2003. http://promomagazine.com/retail/marketing_alloy_ buys_retailer_2/
3. Franchise Gator. Pigtails & Crewcuts. http://www .franchisegator.com/Pigtails-Crewcuts-franchise

CHAPTER 6

1. U.S. Census Bureau. http://www.census.gov, 2011

CHAPTER 7

1. ebay. http://www.ebay.com
2. Rich, Jason R. *The Unofficial Guide to Starting a Business.* Hoboken, NJ: John Wiley & Sons, 2006.

CHAPTER 8

1. Wolfe, Lahle. "8 Tips for Naming Your Business." About. com Guide. http://womeninbusiness.about.com/od/businessnames/a/8nametips.htm
2. The Marketing Mix and 4 Ps. MindTools. http://www.mindtools.com/pages/article/newSTR_94.htm
3. Ostrow, Rona. *The Fairchild Dictionary of Retailing,* 2nd Ed. New York: Fairchild Publications, 2008.
4. Schewe, Charles D., and Alexander Hiam. *The Portable MBA in Marketing.* John Wiley and Sons, 1998.
5. The Marketing Mix and 4 Ps. MindTools. http://www.mindtools.com/pages/article/newSTR_94.htm
6. *Ibid.*
7. Wilson, Sara. "Right of Fashion." *Entrepreneur,* February 1, 2006. http://www.entrepreneur.com/article/printthis/82964.html
8. The Marketing Mix and 4 Ps. MindTools. http://www.mindtools.com/pages/article/newSTR_94.htm

9. *Ibid.*
10. http://www.esp-conference.de/handouts.pdf
11. Walmart U.S. Refreshes Stores' Logo. Walmart.com http://walmartstores.com/pressroom/news/8411.aspx
12. Burke, Sandra. *Fashion Entrepreneur.* Burke Publishing, 2008.

CHAPTER 9

1. Scarborough, Norman and Thomas Zimmerer. *Effective Small Business Management: An Entrepreneurial Approach.* 6th ed. Upper Saddle River, NJ: Prentice-Hall, 2000.
2. Hesselbein, Frances, Goldsmith, Marshall, and Richard Beckhard (eds.). *The Leader of the Future: New Visions, Strategies and Practices for the Next Era.* San Francisco, CA: Jossey-Bass, 1996.
3. Timmons, Jeffry A. *New Venture Creation Entrepreneurship for the 21st Century.* 7th ed. Boston: Irwin/McGraw-Hill, 2007.
4. *Ibid.*
5. http://www. Businessdictionary.com

CHAPTER 10

1. Cash, Patricia. *The Buyer's Manual.* New York: National Retail Merchants Association, 1979.

CREDITS

Illustrations rendered by Mike Miranda unless otherwise noted

1.1 Courtesy of Polyvore

1.2 Courtesy of Hautelook

1.3 Simon Winnall/Getty Images

1.4 ©Ariel Skelley/Blend Images LLC

1.5 © Sonja Pacho/Corbis

1.6 © Steve Hix/Somos Images/Corbis

1.8a/b AP Photo/Ali Burafi

Box Figure 1.1 Robert Holmgren/Getty Images

2.3 Dann Tardif/Getty Images

2.4 Sandra Burke, Fashion Entrepreneur, (Burke Publishing, 2008)

2.5 © Juice Images/Corbis

2.6 Photo by Sarah Silberg

3.2 © Monalyn Gracia/Corbis

3.5 Eric Piermont/AFP/Getty Images

3.6 © Holger Winkler/Corbis

Box Figure 3.3a © HBSS/Corbis

Box Figure 3.3b Courtesy of Footwear News

Box Figure 3.3c Courtesy of WWD

4.1 Hill Street Studios/Getty Images

4.3 Courtesy of WWD/Coach

4.4 Courtesy of Bluefly.com

4.7 Courtesy of Nike, Inc.

4.8 © WWD/Condé Nast/Corbis

4.9 Image © The Andy Warhol Foundation/Corbis

4.10a AP Photo/ John Stillwell

4.10b AP Photo/ Matt Dunham

4.11a © Walter McBride ./Retna Ltd./Corbis

4.11b Theo Wargo/WireImage/Getty Images

4.12 Courtesy of WWD/Diesel

Profile Figure 4.1 Courtesy of Spanx®

5.1 © Siri Stafford/Getty Images

5.2 © Steve Ryan/Getty Images

5.3a Courtesy of Delia's

5.3b Julia Ewan/The Washington Post/Getty Images

5.4 Junko Kimura/Getty Images

5.5 © Peter M. Fisher/Corbis

5.6 © Richard Baker/In Pictures/Corbis

Profile Figure 5.1 Courtesy of Plato's Closet/ Winmark Business Solutions

Case Study 5.1 Courtesy of Apricot Lane Boutique

Case Study 5.2 Courtesy of Pigtails and Crewcuts

6.1 Paul Simcock/Getty Images

6.2 Courtesy of WWD/ Yukie Kasuga

6.4 © Bob Krist/Corbis

6.5 © Steven Vidler/Eurasia Press/Corbis

6.6 Photo by Sarah Silberg

6.7 Courtesy of Andrea Coulter

6.8 © Morgan David de Lossy/Corbis

6.10a/b Jason Kempin/Getty Images

6.11 © Stuart O'Sullivan/Corbis

6.12 © Thomas Northcut/Getty Images

6.13 © Peter Inselmann/Corbis

Box Figure 6.1 © Miguel Navarro/Getty Images

Profile Figure 6.1a/b/c Images courtesy of Littlearth Productions, Inc.

7.1 Mike Kemp/Getty Images

7.2 Courtesy of shopbop.com

7.3 Courtesy of WWD/ George Chinsee

7.4a/b Courtesy of Etsy.com

7.5 Courtesy of CupcakesandCashmere.com

7.6 Courtesy of Madewell.com

7.7 Courtesy of FreePeople.com

7.8 Courtesy of UrbanOutfitters.com

7.9 Courtesy of Lee.com

7.10 LandsEnd.com